Rebels in Bohemia

The Radicals of *The Masses*,

1911–1917

by Leslie Fishbein

The University of North Carolina Press   Chapel Hill

© 1982 The University of North Carolina Press

Manufactured in the United States of America

Library of Congress Cataloging in Publication Data

Fishbein, Leslie, 1947–
　Rebels in Bohemia.

　Bibliography: p.
　Includes index.
　1. Socialism—United States—History—20th century.
2. Masses (New York, N.Y.)　I. Title.
HX86.F527　320.5′3　81-24105
ISBN 0-8078-1519-5　AACR2

Frontispiece:
John Sloan, cover of *The Masses*, June 1914
Courtesy Tamiment Library, New York University

To my husband

ZOLTAN KEMENY

and our son

ALEXANDER JOSEPH KEMENY

Contents

Foreword by Frank Freidel *xi*

Acknowledgments *xiii*

Chapter 1 The Cradle of Radical Culture *3*

Chapter 2 *The Masses*: A Socialist Magazine of "Free Expression" *15*

Chapter 3 Cracks in the New American Culture *30*

Chapter 4 Greenwich Village—Home as Bohemia *59*

Chapter 5 The Sexual Revolution *74*

Chapter 6 The Road to Religion *113*

Chapter 7 The New Feminism *127*

Chapter 8 The Exotic Other *160*

Chapter 9 Art in the Class Struggle *182*

Chapter 10 Life-style and Radicalism *193*

Chapter 11 The End of Radical Innocence *205*

Notes *209*

Bibliography *237*

Index *259*

Illustrations

John Sloan, cover of *The Masses*, June 1914 *iii*

Max Eastman addressing an Ettor and Giovannitti
protest meeting on Union Square *19*

John Sloan *23*

Art Young *27*

Robert Minor, "O Wicked Flesh!," *The Masses*,
October–November 1915 *33*

Sketch by Floyd Dell labeled "Floyd Dell, 7 a.m.,
Sunday, July 27, 1911" *43*

George Cram Cook in Greece *46*

John Sloan, "Isadora Duncan in the 'Marche Militaire,'"
The Masses, May 1915 *47*

Mabel Dodge *49*

Randolph Bourne *56*

John Reed and Louise Bryant at Croton *80*

K. R. Chamberlain, "Family Limitation—Old Style,"
The Masses, May 1915 *105*

Maurice Becker, "Their Last Supper," *The Masses*, December 1913 *115*

Hutchins Hapgood *169*

Photograph of Floyd Dell from lecture poster *200*

Foreword

The radical renaissance in Greenwich Village just before World War I was fascinating in its kaleidoscopic vitality and inconsistencies. Chief among the anomalies was that between the title and the content of *The Masses*, the celebrated organ of left-wing bohemians between 1911 and 1917. Its thrust was not toward a readership among the underprivileged but rather the artists and intelligentsia who sought to lead the exploited toward a new utopia. Nor were the editors disposed to set policy otherwise. When one of them proposed tailoring the contents of a successor magazine to working-class reading levels, his colleagues emphatically squelched him. In any event, most working people, like Nixon's hard-hat supporters during the Vietnam years, on social issues at least were far to the right of the reformers. The revolt the editors and writers were proclaiming so energetically was as much against the bonds of an outmoded Victorianism as against the social injustices heaped upon the underprivileged.

The intellectual universe of the bohemian left who wrote for *The Masses* was one of chaotic incongruity, not the clockwork balance of orthodox Marxism, as Leslie Fishbein points out in this rich and significant study. These gentle rebels bearing more kinship to Bloomsbury than to Petrograd were as concerned with obtaining their own libertarian release from the genteel tradition as with bringing about a socialist economic and political order. Inevitably that led to a confused eclecticism; as Fishbein writes, it was "the true source of the era's creativity, its attempts to resolve tensions among conflicting ideals."

With few exceptions, the radicals were more concerned with individualism than with collectivism. Most of them considered themselves Marxists, but few had thoroughly studied Marx and Engels, and even fewer were willing to accept the ideological restraints or personal discipline of Marxian revolutionaries. There were far more among them like Walter Lippmann, who in the 1920s abandoned socialism completely, than like John Reed, who came to be buried within the walls of the Kremlin. Nietzsche had a pervasive influence upon them, but they read him selectively as a justification for their rejection of puritanism rather than in acceptance of his authoritarianism. Their "new paganism" led them with enthusiasm toward the blacks of Harlem, less in search of brotherhood than of the joys that came with a supposed release of civilized restraints. Mabel Dodge was their doyenne. One evening in her salon she presented some black musicians, and on another occasion she passed out peyote to her guests. Both times she recoiled afterwards with distaste. Similarly, "free love" became more a topic of discussion than a fixed mode of life. Among most Greenwich Villagers it was only a way station toward monogamous marriage. As Fishbein suggests, the puritan they tried to exorcise still lurked behind the pagan facade. Theirs was the revolt of the elite, not the masses.

There is much instructive about these anomalies; they should be more than a source of amusement. This generation trying so hard to rid itself of a lingering Victorianism, and yet still so much of it, seems quaint and naive to its grandchildren and their descendants. Yet there was a good bit of the universal in their inability entirely to discard their background. There was a greater irony in the "jazz age" of the 1920s when bohemianism became the escape of the newly affluent, and the effort to improve the lot of the poor became anathematized as "red." And there were the further ironies in the ideology of the freshly radical generation of the 1960s. The conflicts in the ideology of *The Masses'* generation is illustrative of much of the normal inconsistency of modern America, inevitably substituting trade-offs for an unattainable ideological purity.

Substantively, the left-wing bohemians made a considerable contribution. As Fishbein demonstrates, "Many of the ideas they popularized—Freudianism, birth control, the kindergarten movement, women's suffrage, simplified clothing, industrial unionization . . .—did achieve widespread popular acceptance in the two decades following the war."

In this comprehensive, luminous, and thought-provoking study, Leslie Fishbein re-creates the conflicts and consensus of this bygone movement, and she gives them a significance that transcends the boundaries of both class and time.

Frank Freidel

Acknowledgments

To those not fortunate enough to have lived "before the revolution" writing about such a period can provide both consolation and hope. Despite the naïveté and neuroses of *The Masses'* group, their utter sincerity of purpose disarmed me, and I decided to become the chronicler of their madcap escapades and serious missions. This work originated from a paper on the impact of Freud and Marx on Floyd Dell, presented to Gordon Taylor in his graduate American literature survey, and another on the federal suppression of left-wing antiwar agitation, presented to the late Arthur Sutherland in a seminar on civil law and the judicial process, both at Harvard University during 1967–68.

For complete freedom to develop my ideas and a firm but sensitive hand in shaping the material once it was submitted, I would like to thank my adviser Frank Freidel, whose patience (infinite) and support (profuse) eased my labor pains considerably. Daniel Aaron questioned my premises, improved my style, and guided me to sources familiar to him from his vast reading in the field. Andrew Rolle, my colleague at Occidental College, kindly made his psychohistorical and editorial skills available to me through his detailed and insightful criticism of my chapter on the sexual revolution. Subsequently Gary Nash of the University of California at Los Angeles and Allen Matusow of Rice University read sections on Greenwich Village feminism and the popularization of Freudianism respectively and offered critical guidance in strengthening my thematic organization.

I am indebted to the staffs of the Widener, Houghton, Lamont, and Law School libraries at Harvard, the Butler Library at Columbia, the Newberry Library in Chicago, the New York Public Library, and the Tamiment Institute Library in New York City. Those dedicated workers were always courteous and helpful, and the crew in the microfilm room at Lamont also provided comic relief in that Dark Hole of Calcutta.

Maurice Becker and Helen Farr Sloan graciously answered my letters of inquiry about the period, and I also carried on fruitful correspondence with other scholars in the field—Marta Dennis, Richard Fitzgerald, Steve Fox, and Frank Stricker—all of whom were exceedingly generous and helpful. Morton White made some early research suggestions, and the late Alfred H. Kelly read a preliminary draft. The thesis from which this book is derived, after many metamorphoses, probably would have been stillborn without "a little help from my friends," who buoyed me up or calmed me down, whichever seemed appropriate at the time. But I would like to acknowledge personally the aid given me by Mary Jo Henry, who thoroughly read most of the first version to provide me with the critical distance I lacked at the time (and still do); Mark Gould, who demystified sociology so that I could apply it to the problems at hand; and Zoltan Kemeny, who guided me to the appropriate literary critics and spared me the rest. And if ever a Purple Cross for typing is established, Mary Arnold will be its deserving first recipient.

Throughout its various incarnations, this manuscript has benefited from the continued support of Frank Freidel, whose faith in it was unwavering. As a dissertation this book won the 1976 New York State Historical Association Manuscript Award; Wendell Trip, editor of *New York History*, and the other folks at the N.Y.S.H.A. have continued to be helpful and supportive in the intervening years. Certainly it has been a pleasure to have this work published by the University of North Carolina Press. The commitment of its editors, particularly Lewis Bateman and Sandra Eisdorfer, has been to maintaining the integrity of my work while strengthening its style and clarity of presentation. All the errors in this book are my own. I hope only that they are as exciting as the ones the people on *The Masses* made. This book is dedicated to my husband Zoltan Kemeny because he has been an unfailing source of both support and criticism and to our infant son Alex, who could teach the Wobblies a thing or two about sabotage.

Permission to quote has been kindly granted by the following archives: Randolph Bourne Papers, Rare Book and Manuscript Library, Columbia University; Floyd Dell Papers, The Newberry Library, Chicago; the Robert Minor Papers, Rare Book and Manuscript Library, Columbia University; Robert Charles Post's "The Absence of Radical Novels, 1910–1918: The Case of the Anomalous Hiatus; Suggestions on the Moral Implications of Literary Form," Harvard University Archives. Material from "The Reminiscences of Carl Van Vechten" is used by permission of Donald Gallup, Literary Trustee for Carl Van Vechten. "The Reminiscences of Walter Lippmann" is copyright by The Trustees of Columbia University in the City of New York, 1975, and is used with their permission. "The Reminiscences of Upton Sinclair" is copyright by The Trustees of Columbia University in the City of New York, 1972, and is used with their permission.

The excerpt from *Greek Coins* by George Cram Cook, copyright 1925 by

George H. Doran, is reprinted here by permission of Doubleday & Doran, Inc.

I am grateful for permission to reprint material that has appeared previously, in somewhat different form, in the following publications: "Greenwich Village—Home as Bohemia, 1899–1920," *National Forum* 59 (Summer 1979): 28–31; "Radicals and Religion before the Great War," *The Journal of Religious Thought* 37 (Fall–Winter 1980–81): 45–58; "Harlot or Heroine?: Changing Views of Prostitution," *The Historian* 43 (November 1980): 23–35; "Freud and the Radicals: The Sexual Revolution Comes to Greenwich Village," *The Canadian Review of American Studies* 12 (Fall 1981): 173–89; "Dress Rehearsal in Race Relations: Pre-World War I American Radicals and the Black Question," *Afro-Americans in New York Life and History* 6 (January 1982): 7–15; and "The Failure of Feminism in Greenwich Village before World War I," *Women's Studies* 9 (1982). In addition, "Floyd Dell: The Impact of Freud and Marx on a Radical Mind" is reprinted from *The Psychoanalytic Review*, vol. 63, no. 2, 1976, through the courtesy of the Editors and the Publisher, National Psychological Association for Psychoanalysis, New York, New York, and my review of *The New York Little Renaissance: Iconoclasm, Modernism, and Nationalism in American Culture, 1908–1917*, by Arthur Frank Wertheim, in *New York History* 58 (January 1977): 93–94, is reprinted courtesy of the New York State Historical Association, Cooperstown, New York.

Rebels in Bohemia

They draw nude women for *The Masses*
Thick, fat, ungainly lasses
How does that help the working classes?
                                    —Anonymous

Chapter 1 The Cradle of Radical Culture

Intellectuals in Conflict

To live before the revolution is in many ways to be alive in the best of times. Radicals who lived and worked in America's Gilded Age, before the Great War in Europe disrupted our society and before the Bolshevik Revolution became a reality and then a disappointment, were alive in a time of great possibility. They were the beneficiaries of America's abundance: industrialization and urbanization had proceeded to the point where artists, intellectuals, and organizers could find full-time support for their activities. They lived at a time of significant unionization and labor agitation and in a period when the Socialist party recorded impressive and encouraging electoral gains. Moreover, they even benefited from the imperialism they opposed: America's rise to a world power brought with it an increasing cosmopolitanism and receptivity to European ideas, including those of Karl Marx and Sigmund Freud.

The difficulty for radicals in this period lay in the fact that they were not committed to a narrow political ideal. Christopher Lasch has demonstrated in his study of this generation that they attached much greater importance to a cultural transformation of America than they did to political reform per se.[1] Their concern was for the quality of American life and of their own. As a result, they erected an elusive, perhaps even impossible, standard for their own achievement. They would have to succeed in all of their many roles despite the contradictory demands imposed by each: as artist, political propagandist, educator, intellectual, feminist, Freudian, bohemian. Success demanded tremendous energy and even greater powers of resolution and synthesis.

The radicals associated with *The Masses*, a socialist literary and political magazine published in New York between 1911 and 1917, were chosen as the basis of this study because their lives represent a variety of attempts to resolve the fundamental conflict confronting left-wing artists and intellectuals in the first two decades of the twentieth century. The premise behind this study is

3

that somewhere along the continuum from normality to neurosis can be found a creative resolution of the conflict; at that juncture imagination and self-control combine to allow a successful fusion of the demands of art, politics, and life-style.

The rebels who congregated in Greenwich Village before World War I were pioneers in bohemia. To a far greater degree than any of their nineteenth-century predecessors, the prewar Villagers attempted a fusion of the personal and the political: theirs was to be a cultural rebellion in which no aspect of life was to be exempt from revolutionary change. Lacking the kind of ideological tradition that shaped the thought of European radicals, these Villagers selected the elements of their creed with reference neither to intellectual coherence nor to political purity. Rather their concerns were personal and pragmatic: how could each new idea aid them in resolving their role conflicts?

They operated without precedent. The doctrinal debates of nineteenth-century American socialists had little relevance to those who refused to be constrained by a narrowly political ideal. Nor was the experience of the utopian socialists any more useful to those who hoped to influence directly the world outside their personal haven, Greenwich Village, since many of the prewar rebels held regular jobs in that world and had definite programs in mind for its reformation. The risks they faced were far greater than those of their nineteenth-century counterparts. The cultural nature of the prewar rebellion meant that ideas became a measure of identity, yet those ideas would not be valorized merely by their ability to effect political change nor by their usefulness in creating a viable alternative to established society. Instead they would be measured by the far stricter standard of their ability to transform culture and personality alike.

Fortunately for their psychic well-being, few of the prewar rebels had the intellectual maturity and sophistication necessary to comprehend the schizophrenic nature of the competing beliefs they had embraced. *The Masses'* group most clearly exemplifies this problem, since its open editorial meetings, which anyone of any political persuasion might attend, and its commitment to publishing a magazine of "free expression," which opened its pages to arguments by socialists, anarchists, and syndicalists alike, meant not merely an absence of dogmatic rigidity but also a dearth of ideological coherence as well. The prewar rebellion was more a matter of temperament than of theory, and it fostered more conviviality than commitment among its exponents.

Part of the difficulty lay in the bizarre amalgam of belief that characterized most of *The Masses'* group. They defined themselves as artist-rebels without fully realizing that the desire for free expression in art might conflict with a demand that art be used as a weapon in the class struggle. They chose to be both socialists and bohemians without acknowledging that revolutionary discipline might demand that they sacrifice the pleasures of an interlude in bohemia. They claimed to be feminists yet often failed to comprehend that liberated women might not view birth control and free-love arrangements merely as a means of freeing male rebels from the constraints of the bourgeois family. *The Masses'* radicals could define themselves simultaneously as Marxists and Freudians without adumbrating any conflict between Marx's materialism and Freud's mentalism or between a disposition to change the world itself rather than one's view of it. They might equally well define themselves as both Freudians and feminists yet fail to note Freud's belief in innate feminine passivity or his support for the traditional family.

Since ideas often were judged in terms of personal efficacy, they might readily be extracted from entire systems of belief and thus selectively adopted. For example, *The Masses'* writers were among the earliest exponents of Freudianism in the United States, but in popularizing Freudian doctrine, they distorted its meaning for their own ends. Although Freud claimed that the curse of the artist, his own neurosis, might be the basis of his achievement and, in fact, essential to creativity, James Oppenheim, Floyd Dell, and Max Eastman used psychoanalysis to free themselves from psychosomatic illness and depression, to overcome their writer's blocks, and to release their creativity; psychotherapy represented personal salvation for them as artists.[2] Although Freudian therapy preached adjustment to reality, i.e., conformity, the early Village proponents of Freudianism preferred to view it as a harmless panacea that promised fulfillment in love, art, and rebellion. They also viewed it as yet another weapon in their campaign against American Puritanism and embraced its intellectual rationalization for endless discussions of sex and repression shocking to the bourgeoisie. These rebels conveniently ignored the fact that Freud was no exponent of sexual or social experimentation, that he undermined certain cultural illusions only in order to reestablish the individual and society on a more stable base.

Despite this tendency to distort Freudian doctrine to make it amenable to radical ends, some intellectuals began to perceive that psychoanalysis might pose a threat to their values as radicals.[3] The debate took place on the pages of *The Seven Arts*. Alfred Booth Kuttner, a former patient of the Freudian analyst A. A. Brill, argued that the artist fails at the essential human task of adaptation but is saved from neurosis by his technical ability to create an ideal reality.[4] Kuttner viewed the artist as living in a greater degree of intimacy with his unconscious than does the normal individual; he is fixated at an infantile stage of psychic development, but his artistry affords him personal relief and socially valuable expression of his inner conflicts.[5] However, Kuttner contended that the artist is not and never could be normal; if he were to sublimate his unconscious impulses as the normal person does, "he would undoubtedly cease to be an artist."[6] James Oppenheim, the editor of the *The Seven Arts* and a contributor to *The Masses*, saw the necessity of rescuing the artist from the limbo to which Kuttner had consigned him. In an editorial appearing in February 1917, Oppenheim stated that the artist should not seek to be normal, for normality implied repression with its corollary of conventionality. Instead the artist should seek to be supernormal. Rather than repress his desires, he should express them through sublimation:

> Instead of wasting much of his energy in fighting himself, in being misunderstood, in becoming the victim of childish habits, he is to understand himself, to be able to see and analyze the causes of his maladjustments, to overcome his childishness, and so to be free to devote his total energy to his work and to the world. He may then render unto Caesar that which belongs to Caesar, and render unto God that which belongs to God: he may be at the same time, both a citizen and an artist.[7]

Oppenheim realized that for radicals of his generation the crucial problem was to discover how to change themselves so that they could change the world.

Family as Haven

In his recent study of prewar bohemianism, *Children of Fantasy: The First Rebels of Greenwich Village* (1978), Robert E. Humphrey has attributed the failure of the prewar rebellion to the fact that its leaders, suffering scars of loneliness and alienation in childhood and adolescence, tried unnaturally to preserve adolescent fantasies in the confines of a community of like-minded rebels.[8] Examining the lives of Hutchins Hapgood, George Cram Cook, John Reed, Max Eastman, and Floyd Dell, Humphrey argues that Village rebels in general perpetuated childhood fantasies that had protected them against rejection in their youth, thereby undermining the kind of objective self-assessment and discipline necessary to effect social change. Although *Children of Fantasy* provides richly detailed biographies of these five men, it fails to present a cogent argument for its choice of focus on so few male writers. Apart from its extended treatment of Mabel Dodge, the book deals only peripherally with the other figures active in the Village renaissance, although many of these, including John Sloan, Randolph Bourne, Art Young, Isadora Duncan, Margaret Sanger, and Emma Goldman did leave a wealth of autobiographical material, and it never treats them in the psychohistorical terms applied to the five male writers.

Humphrey's attack is essentially an ad hominem one, attributing the failure of the Village rebellion to the immaturity and lack of self-discipline of its leading participants. Such a treatment avoids dealing with the Villagers' ideas on their own merit. Although it is true that the bohemian community they had established did not survive in spirit beyond World War I, many of the ideas they popularized—Freudianism, birth control, the kindergarten movement, women's suffrage, simplified clothing, industrial unionization, among others —did achieve widespread popular acceptance in the two decades following the war. Nor is it clear why embracing any or all of these ideas should be proof of immaturity when subsequently many people lacking the neurotic childhood experiences of these five writers should have no difficulty accepting the same set of ideas.

Although Village rebels may have been more sensitive and introspective than most adolescents, to explain their adult experiences merely in terms of escape from the pains of youth hardly seems adequate. Their rebellion against conventional mores did not imply a revolt against the family. In fact, they often cherished fond memories of their families and sought to win for their parents' standards a respect that a mercenary world failed to offer. Their homes cushioned the pains of maturation and sheltered them from succumbing to the dominant cultural ideal.

The Masses' radicals did not tend to view their own families as repositories of outmoded and oppressive social ideals. The fragmentary evidence available through memoirs and biographical accounts does not suffice for psychoanalytic generalization, but certain family patterns do emerge. There is a recurrent pattern of a close family in which the mother is a strong figure and the father is economically unsuccessful. Since such a family could provide emotional support despite adversity, adolescent rebellion tended to be directed against forces external to the family—the church, village mores, the political status quo.

The personal experience of declining fortune or poverty meant that the socialism of *The Masses'* radicals often was rooted in intimate individual circumstances rather than being the product of intellectual abstraction. In an era when Americans were avid readers of success literature, paternal failure to meet the tests of the Gospel of Wealth needed explanation. In few cases was the explanation a simple one. Upton Sinclair was born into a genteel but decaying border-state family; his father was a liquor salesman who became an alcoholic.[9] Sinclair's subsequent extreme asceticism may well have been a result of this childhood experience. But Sinclair's case was exceptional; in most instances it was impossible to pin the blame for failure on the father's moral weakness.

In some cases the fathers were victims of their own idealism in an age of enterprise. John Sloan's father was a natural craftsman whose sense of vocation had been rendered obsolete by the machinery of mass production; melancholy in defeat, he copied pictures in oil at night, decorated china, and worked as a handyman.[10] Sloan himself had to deal with the exigencies of the market as the demand for engraving decreased with the increased journalistic use of photography.[11] He chose to contribute his work to the socialist press, thereby reaffirming its value apart from market demand and dedicating it to the struggle for a world in which art would not be hampered by the restrictions of capitalism.

Margaret Sanger's father was expected to be the "guardian of his home," but he never fulfilled his wife's expectation in that regard. By occupation he was a chiseler of saints and angels of marble or granite for tombstones, but his professional interests did not keep him from joining the Knights of Labor or espousing anti-Catholic ideas in a largely Irish community. The final blow to his wage-earning ability came when he protected the agnostic orator Robert Ingersoll against mob vengeance; from that day the local Catholic priest led a boycott of her father's wares.[12] Margaret Sanger respected her father's firm convictions, and she herself was willing to face financial ruin, police harassment, and even exile in her own fight for birth control.

Charles Edward Russell, the socialist muckraker, was also the child of a man with "advanced" ideas. His father was a newspaper editor who had been one of the founders of the Republican party, an exponent of free trade, Populism, Henry George, and assorted reforms. However, "sturdy Republicanism practiced in the Lincoln tradition reduced the fortunes of the Russell family," and the younger Russell was forced to work for his support. Hurt by the political and financial failures of Republicanism, he secured his own freedom from want through his journalistic success and then went on to a personal triumph by publishing his first book of poems.[13] He continued his muckraking but tried to use his journalistic talents in the interest of hastening the socialist commonwealth.

Failure came in many forms. Robert Minor's father was "a dreamy improvident man who proved to be a most trying breadwinner in a time when many grew rich—as others grew poor, or poorer." The family often had little or nothing to eat. Minor recalled surprising his mother in a field near their home, munching the prickly pears that no respectable Texan would eat unless on the verge of starvation.[14] Joseph Freeman's father was a failure because he had shattered the Jewish family tradition of learning in order to become a merchant. Economic failure came in the wake of this more important fall from grace. On his tenth birthday Joseph Freeman learned that there would be no party for him, that the grocer had refused credit so that there was no food in the house. Several days later the family was evicted, victims of economic panic. Unwilling to confront the cause of their humiliation, the father preferred to attribute their fate to bad luck. The younger Freeman found a more cogent explanation in the doctrines of the Socialist party.[15] Occasionally failure meant only a relative loss of status. Hutchins Hapgood's father, upon graduating from Brown University and qualifying for the bar, had gone to Chicago to make his fortune. His failure to succeed in that booming metropolis meant that the Hapgoods could no longer move in the society to which they had been accustomed. This descent from social respectability led him to refer to himself, a prosperous manufacturer, as merely "a link between generations of merit."[16] Hutchins Hapgood responded by ignoring the claims of society and finding genuine pleasure in the company of the denizens of the underworld.

Whether the deprivation was relative or absolute, it impinged heavily on a child's consciousness. Elizabeth Gurley Flynn recalled that she was serious for her age because she was the oldest child of a poor family and privy to the anxieties of her parents. Her family's plight led her to search for a solution to poverty. At her mother's suggestion, she read Edward Bellamy's *Looking Backward* and embarked on a campaign of self-education in radical literature that in turn led to her career as a teenage socialist agitator for the labor movement.[17]

The experience of paternal failure might be transmuted into social criticism as it was in the case of Randolph Bourne. Bourne's father was the first rebel in the family, a handsome, dashing man who neglected his business ventures. He consented to leave home when his brothers-in-law made such a departure their precondition for supporting his wife and their four children. The father did not actually disappear. Instead he moved to a neighboring town and surreptitiously visited his family after dark. This unusual situation permits the possibility of "a critique of a bourgeois family's precepts about the duties of a breadwinner, without an estrangement from that same family." His father's banishment left its mark on Bourne's development. He spoke of his father rarely but always fondly and with compassion. Carl Resek contends that "it is probable that the father's experience was the source of many of Bourne's sharp barbs against the older generation and at least some of his fury against the Protestant ethic."[18]

The inability of his father to function as a breadwinner allowed Max Eastman's mother to transcend the prevailing stereotypes of a woman's role. After the death of her seven-year-old son Morgan, an angelic child viewed as "the spiritual prop of the family," Eastman's mother was stricken by an unexplained illness that lasted for more than a year. She recovered only to minister to her husband's neurasthenia, which lasted through all the years of his prime. There came a time when the father, a minister, could preach no more. Faced with three children and neither money nor health to sustain her, Annis Ford Eastman took on the burden of preaching to the meager congregation of a debt-ridden church near Ithaca in addition to performing all the household chores of her own family. She kept her first parish for three years, inspired her parishioners to repair the church, and won ordination at the hands of men who once had been skeptical about a female minister.[19] Her resiliency proved an inspiration to her son Max, who became a warm advocate of women's suffrage and a firm believer in women's abilities to perform the same tasks as men.

Floyd Dell's desire to understand his family's economic failure led to an odd blending of the ideas of Marx and Freud. Dell viewed authority in Marxist economic terms and freedom in Freudian ones. It is noteworthy that Dell began *Homecoming*, his autobiography, with recollections of childhood incidents that took place between the ages of three and seven, the early years that, according to Freudian theory, figure decisively in molding the adult. In Pike County, Illinois, where the Dells lived during this period, "respectability" provided a sense of identity for the middle class, for all those "who lived by their superior brains, preferably upon profits, interest or rent, rather than unambitiously and stupidly by manual labor." In Marxist terms, it was only the exploiting classes who could experience bourgeois identity, and it was their economic power that vested them with the authority to establish psychic norms for the community. A series of economic failures had divested Dell's father of his claim to the "needed status of middle-class 'respectability.' " The elder Dell lost his butcher shop and then his job as foreman for a woolen mill. Aging and unable to compete on the job market, he was forced to the poverty of manual labor. And it was this poverty that deprived him of the full faith and respect of his sensitive son. He lost his heroic, godlike proportions in his son's mind and was reduced to "this jobless workingman who sits around the house trying to maintain authority over growing children who are supporting the family."

Dell projected upon his father all his childish disillusionments. One Christmas Eve he came to realize that his parents could not afford to celebrate the holiday. His world view suddenly collapsed. He could no longer identify with the respectable people who gave charity to others. This realization crystallized lurking suspicions of poverty that he successfully had repressed earlier. He knew with the pain of full consciousness why he had taken only a small bag of potatoes to Sunday School as a donation for the poor, why his mother had enclosed pennies instead of dimes in his charity envelope, why he had lacked the new shoes necessary to attend school, why his family had been living on potato soup all winter. His immediate reaction was the defensive one of vowing that he never would allow himself to be hurt again. He felt ashamed of ambitious dreams of political success and marriage. His shocking confrontation with his poverty led him to deny himself basic pleasures. As long as Dell allowed economic circumstances to define him, he was plagued by doubts that he would ever find fulfillment. It became desperately important that he reestablish his father's image so that he might have an acceptable pattern to emulate in seeking his own manhood: "This is not especially the story of my political opinions or of my intellectual development, but rather of my quest for life, liberty and happiness. It seems to me that I was engaged at this time in a desperate search for grounds of emotional reconciliation with my father."

The reconciliation proved to be a romantic one. When their home caught on fire, father and son worked side by side to extinguish the flames, and the father's heroism rekindled the respect of the young boy. Dell came to believe that it did not matter that his father was a poor businessman; his heroism had redeemed him. He merited respect for supporting his family, for providing compassion and understanding to a son questioning the authority for which he yearned. It was Marxism that applauded the everyday heroism of the workman and that, therefore, was crucial in the reconciliation process: "American respectability had taken my father away from me. Socialism was giving me a chance to get him back."[20]

Thus paternal failure led *The Masses'* radicals to an implicit critique of the American myth of success, to a reexamination of sexual stereotypes within the family, and often to socialism. Similarly the influence of strong mothers led many of them to feminism. It is astonishing to realize what impact these women had on their children. Eugene Debs, the ofttime presidential standard-bearer of the Socialist party, stated without hesitation, "The dominant influence in my life has been my 'mother.' Whatever of good there is in me I owe to her. Do you know," he said, "I care absolutely nothing for the praise or condemnation of the world so long as my wife and my mother think I am in the right." Debs was an advocate of women's suffrage and of full sexual equality from his earliest days in politics.[21] Carl Van Vechten's mother had attended Kalamazoo College, where she had become a close friend of Lucy Stone and, as a result, an advocate of women's suffrage.[22] Boardman Robinson's mother was less politically minded and did not actively participate in any movement, but she gave her sympathies to those who advanced the right of women to do more than confine themselves to housework.[23] Elizabeth Gurley Flynn's mother also rebelled against the monotony of household chores and after her marriage continued to work at a tailoring establishment as long as she could find caretakers for her children. She was an early advocate of equal rights for women and shocked her relatives and neighbors by having women doctors officiate at the birth of her four children in the 1890s.[24]

Ernest Poole's mother was a heroic figure who symbolized for him "all the old safe settled little world" he had known as a boy and that would always be a part of him. At a businessmen's dinner to celebrate the rebuilding of Chicago, the principal speaker told the moving tale of a woman who had saved her baby from the Chicago fire of 1871 by wrapping it in a wet blanket and carrying it to a tugboat. The pathos of the story stirred Poole's father so deeply that he wiped his eyes and said to the speaker, "Judge, I think we should be told the name of this heroic young woman." The disgusted judge replied, "Why, Poole, you damned fool, she's your own wife!" As a child Ernest Poole was amazed at the tale of his mother's heroism. When he married, his wife proved to be a suffragist. She marched up Fifth Avenue in one of the first of the colorful women's suffrage parades while Poole "humbly walked behind in a rear guard of husbands, fathers, and friends, to the tune of hoots and jeers from our fellow males along the curbs."[25] Thus the feminism of many of *The Masses*' radicals was based on a belief in women's capacities bolstered by the example of their own mothers who were extraordinarily literate, outspoken, and courageous.

However, maternal influence pervaded other spheres of the child's life. If Floyd Dell's father helped to formulate his son's sense of ego, Dell's mother provided him with a conscience, or superego, to regulate his behavior. He viewed her as the "Lawgiver"; her sorrowful eyes would shame him into compliance with her standards. Failing initially to find paternal authority, Dell idealized its alternate source. His mother enshrined gentleness, love, devotion; she patiently initiated her son into the mysteries of the universe over which she reigned as queen. His idealization of his mother inhibited him from forming mature sexual *and* emotional relationships with women; it stifled him as a poet and lover. And even when Dell sought escape from the parochialism of the Midwest by moving to the bohemia of his day, Greenwich Village, he imported the moralism with which his mother had imbued him. For example, when he defended William and Margaret Sanger's violation of the Comstock Act forbidding the dissemination of birth control information, it was in the moral tones of a man convinced of a religious duty to break unrighteous laws. Dell championed freedom but could not condone license. He was ashamed of his behavior when intoxicated and claimed that he preferred to "get drunk on ideas, on talk, in argument, or in any kind of play." He abjured the release and rest promised by alcoholic stupor since it dulled men's revolutionary drives.[26] Sublimation became an inherent part of his radical regime and tempered his adjustment to life in a bohemian community.

Max Eastman's mother also did more than provide him with a model of a strong and capable woman. Her public career as a minister left her family richer in spirit; they never lacked for mother love or good housekeeping. Moreover, as the clerical burdens on his mother increased, their household came to be run on feminist principles: "In West Bloomfield my sister took her turn at hoeing the garden and cleaning out the stable for Merrilegs, a superannuated racing mare that took my mother on pastoral calls. And my brother and I took turns at making beds and washing dishes." Thus Eastman came to learn from firsthand experience the domestic implications of women's liberation. His mother also provided him with the kind of relaxed friendship that he longed for in a romantic relationship with a woman. The image of his mother as an intelligent, dynamic woman allowed him to transcend the notion that women were useful largely for decoration and/or sexual release; Eastman, like many of the other *Masses*' radicals, demanded the companionship of equals in love. His upbringing also enabled him to transcend prevailing stereotypes of male behavior: "There was nothing harder for a man with my mamma's-boy complex to do than stand up and be counted as a 'male suffragette.' It meant not only that I had asserted my manhood, but that I had passed beyond the need of asserting it." It was his mother's vital force that sustained Max Eastman in his years of blind wandering in search of love and in his evolution as a socialist.[27]

It is important to realize how much *The Masses'* radicals derived sustenance from their family background. Economic adversity did not weaken family ties. In general, there was close communication and understanding in the relationships between parents and children. Robert Minor recalled a father and mother who never lost their regard for each other despite years of intense hardship; love lasted until death.[28] Ernest Poole found that the security of his family sustained him when he went to Europe to pursue his writing career: "It was good to have such a father still—to cross the Atlantic and work and explore and adventure into strange new fields, with always a sense of that father behind us, that strong safe father, that strong safe home in that strong safe America!"[29] Margaret Sanger spoke affectionately of the devotion of her parents and of the loving atmosphere in which she was raised:

> The relationship existing between our parents was unusual for its day; they had the idea of comradeship and not merely loved but liked and respected each other. There was no quarreling or bickering; none of us had to take sides, saying, "Father is right," or, "Mother is right." We knew that if we pleased one we pleased the other and such an atmosphere leaves its mark; we felt secure from emotional uncertainty, and were ourselves guided towards certainty in our future.[30]

We have already seen evidence of the cohesiveness of the families of Max Eastman, Floyd Dell, and Randolph Bourne despite years of financial adversity; John Sloan and Art Young have similar fond recollections of their childhood. The radicalism of *The Masses'* artists and writers did not derive from any failure of their home life as children; instead it often found nurture in homes where the parents were willing to explore new ideas and to listen to their children.

In fact, there is some evidence to indicate that a number of the parents fostered free thinking in religious matters. Although Max Eastman's mother was one of the first women ordained in the Congregational church, she struggled all her life with doubt. She communicated her doctrinal uncertainties to her children while trying to imbue them with the ideal of being truly good.[31] Claude McKay, the black poet born in Jamaica, grew up without any religious instruction at home and in his youth joined a free-thinking band of ten boys in his mountaintop village.[32] Elizabeth Gurley Flynn had been baptized as a Catholic, but her parents themselves never attended church and never forced their children to do so. A Catholic in his youth, her father became a skeptic, but a tolerant one, resenting prejudiced and unprincipled attacks upon Catholics.[33] Robert Minor's mother mounted a quiet but firm campaign against her husband's religiosity. Whenever her husband would broach the subject of spiritual instruction in the Episcopal church for their children, she would feign preoccupation. Finally she stated her position: "If the children want to go to church, I shall wash and iron their clothes and let them go. But I shall not send them."[34] In such an atmosphere of religious latitude as was found in these homes, critical thinking on religious matters was a genuine possibility for the children.

For many of *The Masses'* radicals their homes had been a haven from a world that failed to share their fantasies and dreams. Their families nurtured their rebellion, proving to them that there was dignity in work apart from its market demand, providing them with maternal examples of feminine strength, fostering iconoclastic belief, and sustaining them with the love that would provide security in their struggles. The world of their youth may have failed to cherish their familial ideals and may have scorned noneconomic measures of success, female achievement, and religious doubt. But from their new haven of Greenwich Village these prewar rebels would try to transform that world to make it conform to the aspirations of their youth.

Chapter 2 *The Masses*: A Socialist Magazine of "Free Expression"

The Literary Context: The Little Magazines and Socialist Literature

The Masses was the product of a revolt against the genteel tradition and against commercial control of publishing. It benefited from a flurry of new interest in socialism and from a proliferation of alternatives to the established press; by the early twentieth century a small, increasingly sophisticated audience existed for experimental socialist publications. The first two decades of this century witnessed in America the rise of many little magazines that accepted contributions from socialists and the production of several explicitly socialist novels a year.[1] It was this quickening of literary activity that provided a context for the rise and fall of *The Masses*.

In the Progressive era socialism no longer seemed as distinctive and as threatening as it once had been. The Socialist party attracted to its ranks such urban reformers as Joseph Medill Patterson, Upton Sinclair, J. G. Phelps Stokes, William English Walling, Robert Hunter, and Charles Edward Russell, and it grew increasingly respectable. The capitalist press opened its pages to news about socialism. The *New York Times* and the *New York Evening Post* interviewed Morris Hillquit during his 1906 congressional campaign, and William Randolph Hearst's *New York Journal* invited the Milwaukee socialist Victor Berger to write a series of articles.[2] This leftward drift resulted in the unexpected conversion of the *Metropolitan Magazine*, a popular monthly, that announced early in 1912 that it would "give socialism a hearing." Suddenly it began printing contributions from Morris Hillquit, Algernon Lee, W. J. Ghent, Professor George D. Herron, and Helen Keller.[3] This receptivity on the part of the capitalist press was helpful for the purpose of socialist propaganda, but it was crucial as a means of economic support for radical artists and writers. Since *The Masses* could not afford to pay for contributions, its writers and illustrators often tried to sell their work to the

Metropolitan in order to support themselves while working gratis for *The Masses*.[4] John Reed reported the Mexican Revolution for the *Metropolitan* and later, with the artist Boardman Robinson, sent back dispatches on the war in Europe. Art Young supplied regular monthly cartoons from Washington. Even *Life* became a haven for radical cartoonists and humorists whose work would later appear in *The Masses*.[5]

Since the older generation controlled all the vantage points—the editorships, professional chairs, and executive offices—the younger generation had to develop its own means of political and literary expression to avoid relying on the benevolent indulgence of its elders: hence the disproportionate interest in and support for the little magazines.[6] Although many of these literary magazines were intended primarily as organs for the avant-garde in prose and poetry, they gladly printed contributions of a political nature, at times even at their own risk. The first issue of Margaret Anderson's *The Little Review* contained articles on feminism by Floyd Dell; his wife, Margery Currey; and Cornelia Anderson, Sherwood Anderson's first wife.[7] The pre-World War I period was an era in which many intellectuals believed that America could be regenerated through art, and *The Seven Arts* immodestly set out to be *"the* magazine which should evoke and mobilize all our native talent, both creative and critical, give it freedom of expression and so scatter broadcast the new Americanism which would naturally have the response of America."[8] The editors viewed their period as the first days of an American renaissance, a time in which the arts would cease to be a private endeavor and would become instead an expression of the national life. Thus *The Seven Arts* was not intended as a magazine for artists but as "an expression of artists for the community."[9] It printed two of the most incisive and devastating antiwar articles after America's entry into World War I—Randolph Bourne's "The War and the Intellectuals" in June 1917, followed by John Reed's "This Unpopular War" in August—lost its financial backing as a result, and was forced to stop publication.[10]

On the other hand, the socialist magazines for the most part paid only perfunctory attention to literature. The only magazine to devote itself expressly to socialist art and literature was *The Comrade*, founded in 1901.[11] *The Comrade* was proof of the catholicity of turn-of-the-century socialism. It printed utopian fantasies as well as revolutionary propaganda; anyone critical of the social order might appear on its pages: Walt Whitman, Heinrich Heine, Thomas Nast, Ella Wheeler Wilcox, Edward Markham, Jack London, Maxim Gorky, Clarence Darrow, Upton Sinclair, Eugene Debs, and Mother Jones.[12] Doctrinal purity was sacrificed in the interest of placing socialism within a broad humanitarian tradition. Like *The Seven Arts*, *The Comrade* proclaimed, "We are in the early days of a great renaissance." It greeted its readers with a more modest but nonetheless original statement of purpose: *"The Comrade* will endeavor to mirror Socialist thought as it finds expression in Art and Literature. Its function will be to develop the aesthetic impulse in the Socialist movement, to utilize the talent we already have, and to quicken into being aspirations that are latent."[13] The magazine lasted for only four years and attained a circulation of only a few thousand, but it did succeed in creating a meeting place for artists and radicals.[14] In 1905 *The Comrade* merged with Charles H. Kerr's *International Socialist Review*.[15] Not until 1912, when Max Eastman took over the editorship of *The Masses*, was there another magazine devoted principally to art and the class struggle.[16]

A Brief History of *The Masses*

The Masses was the unappointed successor of *The Comrade*.[17] It was founded by Piet Vlag, a Dutchman who ran a restaurant in the basement of New York's Rand School of Social Science. The magazine began publication in January of 1911 as an organ of the cooperative-store movement. Vlag, a dreamer by temperament, somehow managed to interest Rufus Weeks, a vice-president of the New York Life Insurance Company in this latest scheme, and Weeks paid the expenses of printing and engraving *The Masses* during its first year of publication.[18] Since *The Masses* never set out in earnest to make a profit, Weeks was only the first in a series of rich patrons. Muckraking proved profitable since it brought subsidies from wealthy liberals who were willing to finance the presentation of news ignored by the regular press. Yet, according to a reminiscence by Floyd Dell, the coeditor, *The Masses'* staff felt uncomfortable about that solution to their financial woes: "our getting money from the rich was a sort of skeleton in our proletarian revolutionary closet."[19]

In contrast, the financial and editorial structure of *The Masses* was meant to reflect the ideals of cooperation. Piet Vlag was proud to announce in the July 1911 issue that *The Masses* was cooperatively owned by its producers. The artists, writers, and office workers were in full control of The Masses Publishing Company; all profits from their management would be devoted to socialist propaganda.[20] The editors each owned shares in the corporation, but only two editors, Max Eastman and Floyd Dell, received pay for their work, which consisted of attending to the prosaic details of publication that the other contributors preferred to ignore.[21]

At the monthly meetings of *The Masses'* staff, the writers and artists decided policy. When after a year of experimentation Vlag grew discouraged with both the cooperative stores and the magazine that championed them, he conceived the brilliant scheme of combining *The Masses* with a socialistic women's magazine published in Chicago. *The Masses'* staff had no desire of losing their journalistic identity and called a meeting in September 1912 to save *The Masses* from merger. They decided to continue publishing the magazine without funds—"something nobody but artists would think of doing." The cartoonist Art Young suggested that Max Eastman, a philosophy professor recently discharged from Columbia University, be asked to accept the editorship.[22] John Sloan and Louis Untermeyer spent hours in arriving at the ultimate phraseology of the offer: "You are elected Editor of *The Masses*. No pay."[23] Eastman accepted the offer, and under his guidance *The Masses* was transformed from a drab peddler of a single nostrum to a buoyant, colorful, bohemian champion of socialism and the arts.

The Masses aimed its appeal at those who were not yet socialists.[24] Its monthly circulation averaged 14,000, and its readership extended well beyond the bounds of doctrinaire socialists, as is evidenced by the wide variety of letters it received.[25] When Max Eastman took over the editorship for the December 1912 issue, he announced a decision to "make THE MASSES a *popular* Socialist magazine—a magazine of pictures and lively writing." He promised that *The Masses* would take no further part in the factional disputes of the Socialist party, that it was opposed to dogmatism on principle.[26] Flushed with the success of the December issue, *The Masses'* editors published their credo in the January number. *The Masses* would be:

> A revolutionary and not a reform magazine; a magazine with no dividends to pay; a free magazine, frank, arrogant, impertinent, searching for true causes; a magazine directed against rigidity and dogma wherever it is found; printing what is too naked or true for a money-making press; a magazine whose final policy is to do as it pleases and conciliate nobody, not even its readers—there is room for this publication in America.[27]

It was this catholicity of *The Masses*, its freedom from rabid devotion to a single cause, that Eastman viewed as his chief contribution to the magazine. In retrospect both he and Floyd Dell chose to emphasize the libertarian nature of *The Masses* and to neglect its support for the doctrinaire socialist cause. In his autobiography *Enjoyment of Living* Eastman claimed that, insofar as he shaped policy, the guiding ideal of *The Masses* was that "every individual should be made free to live and grow in his own chosen way," an essentially bourgeois ideal.[28] Dell actually signed an affidavit attesting to the fact that *The Masses* "was not a socialistic magazine but a magazine of free expression."[29] It is true that the magazine never became an organ of the Socialist party, that it championed the cause of anarchists, Industrial Workers of the World, advocates of birth control, and exponents of free love. But it was clearly in the forefront of the struggle to achieve a socialism broadly conceived, one in which changes in the economic and political realm would have to be accompanied by a transformation of culture and life-style.

Max Eastman addressing an Ettor and Giovannitti protest meeting on Union Square

From Max Eastman, *Enjoyment of Living* (New York: Harper & Brothers, 1948). Copyright 1976 by Yvette Székely Eastman. All rights reserved.

In any event, the opposition took *The Masses* seriously enough to attempt repression. By May 1916 *The Masses* had been indicted for criminal libel by the Associated Press (*Associated Press* vs. *Max Eastman and Art Young, 1913–1914*), ejected from the reading rooms of many libraries and the subway stands of New York, boycotted by the large magazine distributing companies of Boston and Philadelphia, and excluded from the mails by the Canadian government.[30]

The Associated Press suit was the result of *The Masses'* interest in the great labor war of 1913, which was taking place in the coal fields of West Virginia. When Max Eastman introduced Mother Jones to a Carnegie Hall audience of strike supporters, he learned from her that a local representative of the Associated Press was an officer of the military tribunal, the first in the history of American labor struggles, that had been set up to mete out punishment.[31] So Eastman and the cartoonist Art Young set out in turn to punish the Associated Press. Young drew a picture of the Associated Press pouring lies out of a bottle marked POISON into a reservoir supplying news to an American city while Eastman wrote an editorial entitled "The Worst Trust" in which he accused the Associated Press of suppressing news of the West Virginia military despotism for fourteen months.[32] Their attack occurred in July 1913. The Associated Press sally came in December, when at its instigation the government initiated a suit for criminal libel against Eastman and Young.[33] They engaged Gilbert Roe to defend them gratis and then learned that they also had been indicted for libeling the president of the Associated Press personally. For a while it appeared likely that Eastman and Young would go to jail for a year.[34] But their defense dealt some telling blows against the Associated Press. Roe was able to subpoena the records of the Associated Press's Pittsburgh office to determine the actual handling of news from West Virginia.[35] A mass meeting was held at Cooper Union on behalf of the beleaguered editors. A number of left-wing luminaries addressed the gathering: Inez Milholland, Lincoln Steffens, Charlotte Perkins Gilman, John Haynes Holmes, William English Walling, among others.[36] The climax of the meeting occurred when the noted progressive Amos Pinchot declared his willingness to stand behind the charge made by Eastman and Young that the Associated Press was a monopoly "in constraint of truth." The Associated Press's Washington attorney demanded a retraction under threat of a libel suit for $150,000, but Pinchot persuaded him that a trial would do much greater damage to the Associated Press than to him, and the case against Pinchot was dropped. On the advice of Arthur Brisbane, editor of the *New York Evening Journal*, Eastman consulted another lawyer, Sam Untermeyer, who promised to "subpoena the whole gang from J. P. Morgan down" and indicated that he had been present when the news was altered. After two years the government suit was dropped without explanation, and Roe turned over the defense material to Upton Sinclair, who used it in writing *The Brass Check*.[37] Art Young took his comic revenge when he drew two cartoons that later appeared in *The Masses*:

> I pictured the Associated Press as a grand high-bred madam strolling along carrying several neat packages: one was Probity; she also carried a nice poodle dog called Aristocracy; and out of this armful a legal scroll had fallen to the ground—The Masses Case. The title was "You Dropped Something, Madam." This was followed by another—a double-page cartoon—showing the Associated Press as an angel hovering over the reservoir of news delicately pouring perfume from a pretty bottle labeled "Truth."[38]

The Masses had less success in responding to the other forms of suppression. It could do nothing about the boycott by the Magazine Distributing Company in Boston and by the United News Company of Philadelphia, the ejection from college libraries and bookstores, and its exclusion from the Canadian mails.[39] The January 1916 issue of *The Masses* failed to appear on the New York subway stands because the distributors, Ward and Gow, disapproved of an "unpatriotic" cartoon and a "blasphemous" poem.[40] *The New Republic* printed an editorial in support of the magazine and against the censorship of news by a private monopoly, but *The Masses* never brought suit.[41] Instead it urged its readership to purchase the magazine at other newsstands, and it was gratified by the increase in sales at these other outlets.[42]

However, *The Masses* remained sufficiently vigorous to rescue another socialist journal that was foundering, the *New Review*. This publication had been founded in January 1913 to provide an analysis of international socialism. Its editorial board included such *Masses'* personnel and contributors as Max Eastman, Floyd Dell, Walter Lippmann, Arturo Giovannitti, William English Walling, and W. E. B. DuBois. When reorganization failed to rescue it from financial disaster, the editors decided to combine it with *The Masses* by providing a section at the back of the magazine called the *Masses Review*.[43] Readers soon objected to the pedantry of the supplement, and the experiment lasted only from July to December 1916.

The external threat of repression did not create a united front within the magazine; the staff was too rambunctious to conform. The revolt of the artists, which took place in March 1916, may at first glance seem like consummate ingratitude on their part. Max Eastman was opposed to the treatment that artists received at the hands of popular magazines. In *Journalism versus Art*, a book that he dedicated to "the artists of *The Masses* staff, including those who have withdrawn and those who are to come," Eastman criticized the way in which magazine drawings were mutilated and belittled. In fact, *The Masses* was the first magazine to give adequate space to the drawings and cartoons of its artists. But Eastman also endorsed a *"standard of amateurism"* for contemporary magazine writing.[44] The accompanying lack of professional discipline proved an annoyance to Eastman. The monthly editorial meetings turned into squabbles between the literary editors and the artists over the question of intelligibility and propaganda versus artistic freedom.[45] The difficulty of voting on art and the practical impossibility of not voting on it were highlighted by a visit from Hippolyte Havel, "the gentlest anarchist who ever threw an expostulation." Havel objected to the notion of putting art to a vote, especially to a vote determined by the bourgeois majority. "But," Floyd Dell argued, "even anarchists must decide things by some sort of democratic method." "Sure—sure," replied Havel. "We anarchists make decisions. But we don't abide by them."[46]

In retrospect Max Eastman viewed the artists' revolt as "a war of the Bohemian art-rebels against the socialists who loved art."[47] The artists wanted a place to express themselves without any policy restrictions whatsoever while he assumed the editorial right to publish their work in a "class-conscious, social revolutionary organ" whose policy he controlled.[48] The rebellion was led by Stuart Davis, Glenn Coleman, and Robert Carlton Brown, and it had John Sloan, an older, more established artist who was also a Socialist party member, for its spokesman. They wanted to divide the editorial responsibility between the artists and the writers with each judging contributions in their own field and to abolish the positions of "Editor" and "Managing Editor." All letters that could not be handled by the business office would be read and discussed at the monthly meetings; there would be committees formed to raise the subsidy. The proposal was wildly impractical.

Eastman responded by tendering his resignation with a statement that cooperative editing had proved a sham, that the preparation of a magazine was a task too complex and continuous to be carried on by a large group meeting occasionally. The vote on the proposal came to a tie, but there was no quorum present so the editors decided to postpone the decision until a subsequent meeting. Eastman, Dell, and Young electioneered furiously for votes and proxies, and at the meeting held on 6 April John Sloan's proposal was voted down 11 to 6, and Eastman was reelected editor by the same vote.[49]

Without warning Floyd Dell moved that Sloan, Stuart Davis, Glenn Coleman, Robert Carlton Brown, and Henry J. Glintenkamp be dropped from the magazine. Maurice Becker angrily demanded that his name be appended to the list. Dell accepted the amendment as did the normally genial Art Young, who announced: "To me this magazine exists for socialism. That's why I give my drawings to it, and anybody who doesn't believe in a socialist policy, so far as I go, can get out!" The motion was lost by a vote of 11 to 5, and in a mood of contrition the staff elected the offenders to office: Sloan, vice-president of the corporation; Coleman, treasurer; Becker to the Board of Directors. John Sloan resigned in a letter composed that night, and his depar-

John Sloan

ture was followed by that of Stuart Davis, Glenn Coleman, Maurice Becker, and the writer Robert Carlton Brown. To replace the missing artists, *The Masses'* editors elected Boardman Robinson, Robert Minor, the humorist G. S. Sparks, and the painter John Barber, and the magazine continued steadily along its assigned course.[50]

It was World War I that proved to be the ultimate disruption of *The Masses'* activities. The need to protest the war and American involvement diverted a good deal of proletarian-revolutionary energy to antimilitary ends.[51] *The Masses'* editors composed antiwar articles and drew antiwar cartoons; they attended demonstrations and addressed protest meetings. They risked the fate of the magazine to protest a popular war because they deemed it imperialistic, a bankers' war inimical to the well-being of the working class.

The country was in a state of paranoia in which thousands of radicals were persecuted for opposing the war, often with little proof that they had done any damage to the war effort.[52] Gripped by the same fear, Congress passed the Espionage Act of 1917, which violated the protections of the First Amendment and rendered nugatory the constitutional definition of treason.[53] The act read in part:

> Sec. 3. Whoever, when the United States is at war, shall willfully make or convey false reports or false statements with intent to interfere with the operation or success of the military or naval forces of the United States or to promote the success of its enemies and whoever, when the United States is at war, shall willfully cause or attempt to cause insubordination, disloyalty, mutiny, or refusal of duty, in the military or naval forces of the United States, or shall willfully obstruct the recruiting or enlistment service of the United States, to the injury of the service or of the United States, shall be punished by a fine of not more than $10,000 or imprisonment for not more than twenty years, or both.

Moreover, the act included a section on conspiracies to perform the above acts, making them liable to the same punishment.[54]

Somehow the warning failed to take full effect on *The Masses*. Hearing rumors of censorship, Merrill Rogers, the business manager, took an issue of the magazine to George Creel, presumably the national censor, and was assured that it did not violate the law. Yet shortly thereafter the United States Post Office refused the use of the mails to the August 1917 issue, and when the courts ruled temporarily in favor of *The Masses*, the Post Office retaliated by having the government launch charges that the editors had "conspired to effect insubordination or mutiny in the armed and naval forces of the United States" and that they had "conspired to obstruct enlistment and recruitment."[55]

Still *The Masses'* radicals were not impressed. They sent postcards to each other: "We expect you for the—ssh!—weekly sedition. Object: Overthrow of the Government. Don't tell a soul." Art Young devised a form letter that circulated freely among them: "Dear Bill: Come to the conspiracy Tuesday night. Yours, The Conspirators."[56] The full seriousness of their situation did not dawn on them until the cases reached trial, and even then they were a good-humored lot of defendants. By 15 April 1918, the start of the court proceedings, *The Masses*, suppressed by the Post Office, had resurrected itself in the form of *The Liberator*, a magazine that stood for the prewar Wilsonian program and called for a negotiated peace; hence the trial seemed anachronistic at best.[57]

It took place in the Federal Building in City Hall Park at the height of the war fever and literally to the tune of patriotic songs echoing from the park below. The codefendants were Max Eastman, Merrill Rogers, Floyd Dell, Art Young, and Josephine Bell, a young poet who had never met her coconspirators.[58] Judge Augustus Hand presided while Morris Hillquit, a recent Socialist candidate for mayor of New York, and Dudley Field Malone, who had resigned as collector of the Port of New York to protest Woodrow Wilson's refusal to fulfill the Democratic party pledge to grant women's suffrage, served as counsels for the defense.

The Masses' trial took place under several auspicious circumstances. It was held in New York City, where there were some remnants of cosmopolitan tolerance. "American-born and bred, obviously well-educated, belonging by prescriptive right among those who give rather than among those who take orders," the editors received more courteous treatment at the hands of the court than did foreigners, the poor, and the ignorant indicted for the same offense.[59] They also benefited from the ineptness of the prosecution and from the stubbornness of one juror.

The government was able to prove that *The Masses* existed and that it circulated but no more. Judge Hand quashed the first count of the indictment, the charge of conspiring to get the army and navy to mutiny, but he ruled that the editors would have to stand trial on the second count, that of conspiring to obstruct enlistment and recruitment.[60]

The trial moved from extremes of impassioned rhetoric to outright farce. Max Eastman spoke for nearly three days on the nature of patriotism while Floyd Dell lectured the jurors on war, militarism, conscientious objection, and an assortment of other topics.[61] Eastman's speech, however, was viewed by many socialists as a betrayal of their cause. He claimed that the editorials for which he had been indicted could not really be unpatriotic because they espoused positions later adopted by President Wilson. He further claimed that he had undergone a change of heart with regard to the war after American entry and urged the prosecution to dismiss *The Masses'* case so that it could better employ itself hunting enemy spies, war profiteers, and friends of Prussianism.[62] No one could accuse Max Eastman of doctrinal purity.

And it seemed ridiculous to accuse Josephine Bell of conspiracy. She had written a poem honoring Emma Goldman and Alexander Berkman, anarchists imprisoned for their antiwar activities, which had appeared in *The Masses*, but she was unknown to her codefendants. The defense attorney Morris Hillquit offered the poem to the judge to prove that it contained no violation of the law. Judge Hand perused it slowly, then handed it back to Hillquit, saying: "Do you call that a poem?" The counsel replied, "Your Honor, it is so called in the indictment." "Indictment quashed" was the response.[63]

Willing though he was to face jail, Art Young found it difficult to pay attention in court. At one point he fell asleep, was prodded awake by his attorney, and promptly did a pencil sketch of himself snoring soundly, which he entitled "Art Young on Trial for His Life." Young took no egoistic pleasure in being on the stand; he prided himself more on his good nature than on his intelligence. The prosecuting attorney, Earl Barnes, seemed convinced that Young's ingenuousness masked some dark conspiratorial intent. He questioned him closely about Exhibit F, Young's cartoon "Having Their Fling," which represented the war-madness of the press, pulpit, politics, and business. As if to reveal some seditious subtlety, Barnes asked Young why there was an orchestra playing on war instruments in the background and why the Devil was the leader of the orchestra. The cartoonist simply cited General Sherman's definition of war as Hell, so the Devil seemed an appropriate conductor.[64] These humorous aspects to the trial were no accident of circumstance; they reflected the bohemian nature of *The Masses'* radicals.

The jury deliberated for several days and then reported that it could not reach a decision.[65] Only one juror, Mr. H. C. Fredericks, voted for acquittal. He had announced to his fellow jurors that he would hold out for *The Masses'* staff "till hell froze over" so he was never recalled to jury duty in New York City despite years of regular service.[66] The court had to dismiss the jury and declare a mistrial; *The Masses'* crowd celebrated the event as a victory until their second trial in October.[67]

The second *Masses* trial took place under even more favorable circumstances. All the defendants—Max Eastman, Floyd Dell, Art Young, and John Reed—were of old American stock and were given great latitude by the presiding judge, Martin J. Manton. New York City was once again the site of the trial. And the time was propitious: the war was over, Germany had been defeated, and the Allies were victorious.[68] John Reed, moved by his sense of honor and ties of fellowship, had journeyed underground back from Soviet

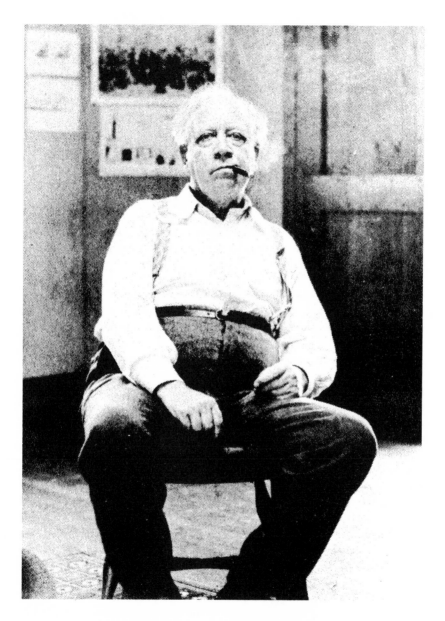

Art Young
From Max Eastman, *Enjoyment of Living* (New York: Harper & Brothers, 1948). Copyright
1976 by Yvette Székely Eastman.

Russia to stand trial with the other editors, much to the dismay of Leon Trotsky, who could not comprehend Reed's un-Marxian behavior.[69]

The second trial proved a better forum than the first for the expression of socialist ideas. In the spring Germany had invaded Russia; the fall was marked by an American incursion. The persecution of radicals had intensified, and the trial reflected this fact by the emphasis the defendants gave in their testimony to the class struggle. Max Eastman defended the antiwar St. Louis declaration of the Socialist party, Floyd Dell praised conscientious objection, John Reed justified the class war and recounted his experiences under Bolshevism, while Art Young expressed his disapproval of all wars.[70]

Given a second chance at conviction, Prosecutor Barnes wrapped himself in the flag and offered the jury some of his best theatrics. He ended his address with a melodramatic appeal. "Somewhere in France," concluded Barnes, "a man lies dead. He is but one of a thousand whose voices are not silent. He died for you and he died for me. He died for Max Eastman. He died for John Reed. He died for Merrill Rogers. He demands that these men be punished." At this very instant Art Young, roused by the ascending pitch, woke from his customary doze. "What!" exclaimed Young. "Didn't he die for me, too?" The peroration was ruined, and Louis Untermeyer contended that Art Young's interruption may have done as much as the brilliant speeches to divide the jury. In any case, the jury disagreed, this time eight for acquittal and four opposed; the second *Masses* trial proved to be the last.[71]

These trials consumed time, energy, and money at a rapid rate, but they failed to deliver a fatal blow. That had come earlier in the form of persecution by the United States Post Office. Under the terms of the Espionage Act, Postmaster General Albert Burleson had ordered the postmaster in New York City not to accept the August 1917 issue of *The Masses* for mailing. He specifically objected to three articles, four cartoons, and a poem that either opposed the war as imperialistic, denounced conscription, or upheld conscientious objection. Although opposed to *The Masses'* views, Judge Learned Hand issued a temporary restraining order against the Post Office on the ground that the magazine's criticism of existing law and war policies stopped short of counseling resistance to the law.[72]

When notified of its exclusion from the mails, the publisher of *The Masses* indicated a willingness to delete the offending passages, but the postmaster refused such information. Despite the court order, Burleson continued to deny *The Masses* access to the mails. He decided to deny the September issue second-class mailing privileges even if absolutely free from objectionable passages on the ground that since the magazine had skipped an issue, it had ceased to be a periodical because it was no longer regularly issued.[73] Burleson soon received judicial support for his decision. In August Circuit Judge Hough stayed the injunction and gave notice that the courts should not normally interfere with decisions by the executive branch of government.[74] In November a three-member Circuit Court of Appeals reversed the injunction. It held that any decision by the postmaster general to exclude a publication from the mails must be regarded as conclusive unless clearly wrong; the burden of proof rested with the publishers of the periodical. Furthermore, the court held that it was not necessary to demonstrate overt counsel to perform illegal acts: "If the natural and reasonable effect of what is said is to encourage resistance to a law, and the words are used in an endeavor to persuade to resistance, it is immaterial that the duty to resist is not mentioned, or the interest of the persons addressed in resistance is not suggested."[75]

The decision wreaked its damage in many places. It dealt a death blow to *The Masses*, for the magazine could not survive economically if denied access to the mails. It established a precedent for the revival of the doctrine of remote bad tendency as an excuse for repression in the minds of district court judges throughout the country, and it enabled the officials of the Department of Justice and the Post Office to turn the Espionage Act of 1917 into a "drag-net for pacifists." It was a final irony that the "poetry in the *Masses* was excluded from the mails only to be given a far wider circulation in two issues of the *Federal Reporter*."[76]

In order to placate the Post Office, *The Masses* was reorganized and called *The Liberator*.[77] Max Eastman suddenly began to detect in Woodrow Wilson a steady drift to the left, and *The Liberator* concluded that the best revolutionary policy was to support Wilson's pronouncements.[78] Expediency also dictated the same course. *The Liberator* retained much of *The Masses'* staff (though Reed resigned as editor in disgust at the new policy) and championed many of the same causes, but with greater caution.[79]

There have been quarrels as to the true holder of *The Masses'* legacy. It is ironical that in the realm of the cartoon the staid and respectable *New Yorker* is in the definite line of succession. The illustrated single remark, a stylistic innovation that was for the artists on *The Masses* part of the revolt against commercial journalism, when adopted by *The New Yorker* "succeeded in greatly improving the technique of the tyrant."[80] In the political and literary realm, Max Eastman held that the *Modern Monthly* was the duly appointed heir while Mike Gold, the Communist herald of proletarian literature, contended that *The New Masses* was the true successor.[81] The quarrel is not so much important for the merit of the contending views as it is as proof that the revolutionary impulse of *The Masses* did not die out in succeeding generations.

Chapter 3 Cracks in the New American Culture

New York City's Cultural Renaissance

The pre-World War I years in New York City marked a revolt against the genteel tradition and in favor of decidedly modern values. In fact, they produced a miniature renaissance marked by greater realism in arts and letters, the emergence of modern drama and dance, and increased cultural nationalism in all realms of expression. The exponents of this modern culture abandoned the Victorian precept that art should serve the ends of moral uplift, that it should inculcate the mass with the ideals of an unquestioned elite. Instead new radicals stressed the liberating functions of art: it should be spontaneous, cosmopolitan, tolerant, democratic. In short, art should assist in the cultural transformation necessary to effect meaningful social change.

The early twentieth century saw a spate of innovations in theater, education, poetry, painting, psychology, and politics, which Arthur Frank Wertheim has chronicled admirably in *The New York Little Renaissance: Iconoclasm, Modernism, and Nationalism in American Culture, 1908–1917* (1976), a work in which he seeks to provide a comprehensive view of the era's transformation of art and ideology.[1] Examining groups as distinctive as the anarchists, Wobblies, Freudians, feminists, the *Others* Group in poetry, the Stieglitz Group in photography and art, the Independent movement in painting, the little theater movement, the cultural nationalists, and the writers affiliated with H. L. Mencken, Theodore Dreiser, and *The Smart Set*, Wertheim concludes that all of these disparate Little Renaissance participants were bound by a common commitment to demolish the genteel tradition in order to create a new American culture in its place.[2]

However, in seeking uniformity in the Little Renaissance, claiming that its participants shared a common spirit of "iconoclasm, modernism, and cultural nationalism," Wertheim belies the era's true diversity. Much of the iconoclasm he cites was a matter more of style than of substance. Hutchins Hapgood was not alone in being "a Victorian in the modern world." As William L. O'Neill has demonstrated, even free-love arrangements might mask the old slavery in a new form, demanding as much fidelity as the marital bond they had been intended to replace.[3] Little of the era's radicalism involved commitments that transcended the demands of personal life: Jack Reed and Mabel Dodge fled from the Paterson Pageant and the failing strike by the Industrial Workers of the World (IWW) that they had sought to energize to find refuge in Europe; Max Eastman retired from antiwar activities to contemplate his failing marriage.

The modernism of the period had its limits as well. American artists of the Ash Can School never achieved the experimental vitality of their European counterparts whose works were displayed in the Armory Show of 1913. Although avant-garde poets like Ezra Pound, T. S. Eliot, and William Carlos Williams might promote modern verse, they hardly could be accused of modernism in politics, and the most radical poets like Max Eastman, Floyd Dell, and Louis Untermeyer clung to Victorian forms. Despite nearly universal pretensions to cultural nationalism, its most avid exponents might invoke Freud, Marx, Nietzsche, and other European intellectuals in evoking that vision.

Wertheim captures the enthusiasm of the age without its confusion, its ardor without its ambiguity. He tends to uncritical acceptance of the self-assessments of the New York rebels. Yet can free lovers reasonably be dubbed Freudians even if they claim to be? Was Floyd Dell a feminist when in *Women as World Builders* he argued that the modern women's movement was but another example of feminine willingness to adapt to masculine demand?[4] Could Max Eastman, a self-proclaimed scientific socialist, be a committed Freudian as well? In imposing historical coherence on the Little Renaissance, Wertheim has neglected the true source of the era's creativity, its attempts to resolve tensions among conflicting ideals.

For *The Masses'* radicals in particular, the era was marked by a confusion of idea and desire. Their eclecticism enabled them to embrace mutually contradictory ideas to achieve short-term affectional resolutions of the tensions that plagued them as radicals. By refusing to discriminate among pleasing ideas, by eschewing any attempt to assess their relative worth and mutual compatibility, new radicals avoided an immediate crisis of role definition by postponing the day of final reckoning. But that postponement meant that they generally lacked the intellectual rigor and discipline to weather that crisis when it finally came.

Critique of Puritanism

As rebels against the genteel tradition, *The Masses'* radicals led the crusade against America's neo-puritanism. Their struggle was essentially an ahistorical one, since they lacked genuine knowledge of Puritan wit or warmth or sexual behavior, and it demonstrated an inability to recognize the potency of a common desire to build a utopian community as both refuge from and example to a world that had failed to see the light.

Ignoring the historical roots of puritanism, new radicals viewed its modern manifestation as proof of the decayed nature of genteel culture. To Randolph Bourne puritanism represented Anglo-Saxonism, New England exclusiveness, and a moribund literary tradition.[5] To Sherwood Anderson, who viewed its impact on his homeland in the Western Reserve of Ohio, puritanism was associated with the capitalist ethic of saving for investment: "God and property are so closely bound together in the American notion of goodness and respectability."[6] Socialists, too, held capitalism and puritanism to be bulwarks of middle-class rule. A number of them responded by advocating a "new paganism"—revolutionary new attitudes toward marriage and sexuality.[7] But these devotees of the "new paganism" failed to acknowledge that there was little working-class support for undermining traditional morality and that the primary beneficiaries of any attacks on censorship and repression would be new radicals themselves.

The early twentieth century witnessed a simultaneous discovery of poverty and vice by urban reformers, followed by a series of vice crusades that swept the nation. This spasmodic reform attacked only the symptoms of poverty rather than its roots in capitalism. It diverted popular energy from attacks upon corporate wealth, but it is noteworthy that new radicals stressed the hypocrisy of such reform rather than its diversionary effect.[8]

The most eminent and powerful of the vice crusaders was Anthony Comstock, a man who almost singlehandedly changed the laws of the United States to conform with the most conservative position in morals. It is significant that his crusading energy was directed mainly against sins of thought rather than against sins of action: "He pursued the pornographer and not the prostitute." He worked to hamper the rise of realism in the arts, but his objections were not merely stylistic.[9] In a Comstock pamphlet entitled, "MORALS, Not Art or Literature" (1914), cited by H. L. Mencken in his own work, *A Book of Prefaces*, "there is no hypocritical pretension to a desire to purify or safeguard the arts; they are dismissed at once as trivial and degrading."[10]

The arts were left practically defenseless against Comstock's attacks. The defendant in a Comstock case could not allege in his defense that the work was decent in intention, that the passage in question came from a standard work in general circulation, that the work failed to deprave its audience or the jurymen, that the language in question was unobjectionable, that the circulation of similar material had set up a presumption of toleration, that the general character of the work in which an objectionable passage was included was decent, or that the literature had been obtained by an *agent provocateur* under

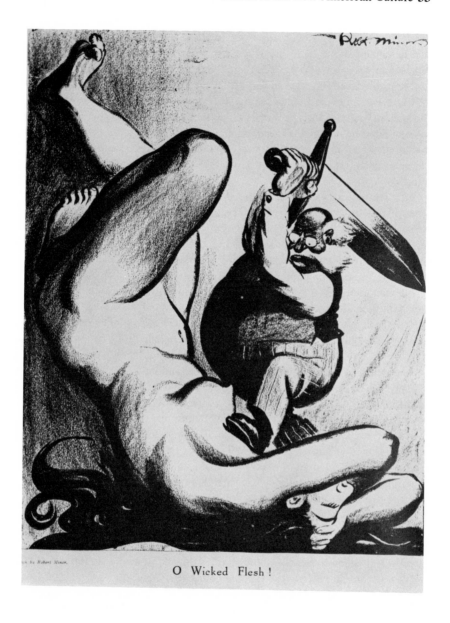

O Wicked Flesh!

Robert Minor, "O Wicked Flesh!," *The Masses*, October–November 1915. The rotund little man pictured is Anthony Comstock.

Courtesy Tamiment Library, New York University

false representation. Moreover, all the judicial decisions in such cases denied the defendant the right to introduce any testimony that a work had artistic value and was not pornographic, that it had no pernicious effect upon a normal audience.[11] Comstock also felt special wrath against birth control advocates and devoted much energy to the suppression of contraceptive information.[12] Comstock's personal convictions were writ large for a generation of Americans in national law and judicial decision. They circumscribed access to the arts and abrogated personal freedom to control sexuality and reproduction, concerns that impinged most heavily on the consciousness of new radicals.

Neo-puritanism was based on the idea that human passions were finite and controllable by simple repression. The rising generation had a more complex view of psychology. The youthful Floyd Dell in 1906 wrote for *The Tri-City Workers Magazine*, "Amusement is a law of life. We must accept it or ignore it. If we ignore it, we must suffer the consequences."[13] Under the influence of Freud, Walter Lippmann argued in *A Preface to Politics* that repression of the demand for pleasure could unleash havoc. Human desires could be channeled into socially acceptable ends, but they could not be abolished altogether, hence his simplistic and ahistorical critique of Puritanism: "The Puritans tried to choke the craving for pleasure in early New England. They had no theaters, no dances, no festivals. They burned witches instead."[14]

The effect of neo-puritanism was to stifle individual expression. Mabel Dodge Luhan described its impact on the people who lived in her girlhood home of Buffalo, New York. Although there was no privacy—everybody knew one another through personal acquaintance and through gossip—neither was there any intimacy. As if by mutual agreement, people "pretended to ignore each other's inward lives."[15] Theodore Dreiser complained that in his youth he had been taught to sham piety and to shun most human experience.[16] The reticence with regard to sexual matters could be devastating to a child coming to a preliminary recognition of his own sexual impulses. For years the young Hutchins Hapgood suffered from the secret misery of a constricted foreskin, a plight "which might have been alleviated by a society not held in the grip of a destructive Puritanism." Convinced of his own sinfulness, Hapgood was plagued by years of intense suffering and ill health. In retrospect he wrote: "I am convinced that the shamefacedness of adults is the cause of immense unnatural misery to children, and that the application of the conceptions of Right and Wrong to the subject of sex has done more to bring about the evils of intemperance than full knowledge and thorough experience could ever do."[17]

The cult of purity by repressing sexual energy distorted its final expression: "If ever a people has refined eroticism to a greater degree than the American, I am not aware of it," commented Theodore Dreiser. Women became the victims of a mythology that portrayed them as pure, saintly creatures with no sexual needs or desires of their own. American men, in turn, fell victims to the same myth as the women they knew were rendered mysterious and inaccessible to them:

> The purity, the sanctity, the self-abnegation, the delicacy of women— how these qualities have been exaggerated and dinned into our ears, until at last the average scrubby non-reasoning male, quite capable of visiting the gardens of Venus, or taking a girl off the street, is no more able to clearly visualize the creature before him than he is the central wilds of Africa which he had never seen. A princess, a goddess, a divine mother or creative principle, all the virtues, all the perfections, no vices, no weaknesses, no errors—some such hodgepodge as this has come to be the average Anglo-Saxon, or at least, American conception of the average woman.[18]

In short, on the personal level the cult of purity thwarted intimacy, repressed sexuality, and stifled communication between the sexes. And we have seen that its wider social implications were an attack on artistic freedom and a major blow against the forces championing birth control.

The pre-World War I era in America saw the "repeal of reticence." The greater willingness of the rising generation to recognize sexuality and to discuss its implications met a mixed reaction. Although liberals admitted that the social climate was much healthier as a result, they worried that a lack of balance and restraint would lead to an obsession with sex.[19] In fact, it was not so easy to exorcise the puritan demon. We have already seen how Floyd Dell felt compelled to adopt a tone of righteousness in supporting birth control. And a popular social critic of the day, William E. Carson, described in *The Marriage Revolt* the moralism that pervaded the works of the most influential European critics of sexual relations: "There is, indeed, something almost puritanical in Ibsen's fierce denunciation of vice, in Bernard Shaw's arraignment of social hypocrisies and in Tolstoy's eloquent demands for sexual purity."[20]

Most social radicals sought a release from the rigors of puritanism in the "new paganism." Randolph Bourne was almost alone among them in being willing to understand and explain the persistence of puritanism. He acknowledged that even the most emancipated age would have to deal with the remnants of puritanism and expressed concern that the belief in sexual freedom in the new age might be accompanied by a cult of efficiency that would reward acquisitiveness and support eugenics. Bourne viewed puritanism as a stage on the road to paganism: "Perhaps no one can be really a good appreciating pagan who has not once been a bad puritan." However, to remain in the thrall of puritanism was to fail to reach adulthood: "The puritan is a case of arrested development. Most of us do grow beyond him and find subtler ways of satisfying our desire for power. And we do it because we never can quite take that step from self-abasement to self-regard. We never can quite become proud of our humility."[21] Although others thought that they could evade repression by repressing all vestiges of puritanism they encountered, Bourne knew that there would be no freedom without confrontation of the puritan within each of us.

The Impact of Nietzsche and European Thought

When American intellectuals of the early twentieth century wanted to attack the failings of the older generation, they turned first to Europe for inspiration. It is probable that they would have preferred to rely on a domestic intellectual tradition—many of them hoped for the creation of a new American culture—but there were too few native thinkers who had dealt with the subtleties of psychology and sexuality as had their European counterparts.

It is important to realize that Americans were not disinterested borrowers of foreign culture. Certain European ideas seemed interesting or useful, and these were adapted, or some might say distorted, to fit the needs of their American adherents. In the pre-World War I era the antirationalist ideas of Friedrich Nietzsche and Henri Bergson found great favor in America.[22] Even men like Max Eastman with pretensions to scientific socialism embraced such foreign thought. The interest in these ideas demonstrated that Americans were dissatisfied with the state of psychology in this country; except for certain thinkers like William James, most American psychologists operated in a Newtonian universe of simple cause and effect.

The reading of Nietzsche in particular proved to be a kind of intellectual Rorschach test. As early as the 1890s artists invoked Nietzsche in defense of their right to take a stand against the evils of their civilization; *Thus Spake Zarathustra* and *The Birth of Tragedy* were quoted liberally to buttress this position.[23] By the early twentieth century the meanings of Nietzsche's philosophy were as infinite and as various as the needs of the intellectuals who came to espouse them. Mounting contending claims to launching the "Nietzsche cult in America," Upton Sinclair found a "curious resemblance" between Nietzsche's vision in *Zarathustra* and the Beatitudes while H. L. Mencken "used the German prophet to belabor religion, women, and, most roughly of all, democracy in his already familiar manner."[24]

A most unlikely conglomeration of people, including those who considered themselves socialists and democrats, declared themselves apostles of Nietzsche. To Randolph Bourne Nietzsche was a pagan, liberating influence who could be used to attack the old puritan ideals.[25] Sherwood Anderson had a passing flirtation with Nietzschean ideas. He especially liked the notion of both truth and its opposite being true, an idea that fit admirably his own theory of the relation of truth and romance.[26] When Mabel Dodge, the patroness of radicalism and the arts, could no longer abide her husband Edwin, she accused him of being unable to understand her inner struggles: "I was a Nietzschean, I thought, beyond good and evil, indomitable, unbreakable."[27] Walter Lippmann's writings echoed the Nietzschean concern with man's control of his destiny.[28] Alienated from traditional religion, during her London exile Margaret Sanger turned to Nietzsche for inspiration and strength. She repudiated as unhealthy the priestly rejection of physical joys, while approving the Nietzschean "Overman" who, with trained intellect and passions in control, could experience life fully. She confided to her journal that it was better to develop the God within oneself than to worship "at the shrine of other egos"; and she closed her autobiography, written a quarter of a century later, with the Nietzschean injunction, "Build thou beyond thyself."[29] Even Isadora Duncan could find inspiration for her art, modern dance, in Nietzsche; she dubbed him "the first dancing philosopher."[30]

Nietzsche also had a profound influence on two of the men who helped to found the modern little theater movement in the United States. George Cram Cook, the founder of the Provincetown Players, claimed that the reading of Nietzsche in 1896 saved his soul from "Christ, Tolstoi, and Mr. and Mrs. Browning":

> In order to understand what I'm saying you should know
> That
> I was the third man in America to read him
> With my blood.[31]

During his personal crises with regard to World War I, Cook was haunted by the words of Nietzsche: "All nations claim to be armed for self-defense. Then let Germany, the strongest, disarm." His wife later claimed that Cook "coveted for his own country that gesture Germany had not made."[32] And Eugene O'Neill's wife, Agnes Boulton, stated unequivocally that *Thus Spake Zarathustra* had had more influence on her husband than any other single book: "It was a sort of Bible to him, and he kept it by his bedside in later years as others might that sacred book."[33] O'Neill's reading of Nietzsche was reflected in his art; his plays argue consistently that the worst failure of the capitalist state is its spiritual sterility.[34]

Even the most avowedly left-wing intellectuals could find a use for the Nietzschean philosophy. Emma Goldman invoked Nietzsche in her attacks against Christianity as a slave morality that held men in bondage to capitalism.[35] William English Walling saw as Nietzsche's central idea the notion that for an individual to develop his capacity he must use others and in turn be used by them, that it was in accord strictly with morality to view other people as means. Once this notion could be spread from the superior few for whom Nietzsche had intended it to the masses, there would be no power that could prevent a popular revolution.[36] There were other radicals, Jack London among them, who found themselves torn between Nietzsche and socialism. And Van Wyck Brooks points out that two semiautobiographical novels written by *Masses'* radicals to express their feelings about the fight for social justice in an era of rapid, brutal industrial growth show the same conflict: "In Max Eastman's *Venture*, Jo Hancock, who finally goes over to syndicalism, is fascinated for a while by the captain of industry Forbes whose gospel is Nietzsche's *Anti-Christ*. The hero of Ernest Poole's *The Harbor* is also captivated by the great engineer Dellon, his Nietzschean father-in-law."[37] Eastman used to advise young radicals to read Nietzsche to purge themselves of any softness so that they could develop a tough, scientific approach to social problems.[38] Yet he cautioned that because Nietzsche had had no contact with the world of affairs, he failed to see that the principle of survival of the strong had been destroyed by the existence of hereditary wealth and opportunity.[39]

It is clear from the foregoing account that the radicals associated with *The Masses* did not read Nietzsche simply for their own enlightenment. His work became a many-faceted mirror that could refract at will those of their ideas that they wished legitimized by reference to an avant-garde European source. They selectively ignored Nietzsche's elitism, his virulent hatred of Christianity, and his disdain for women. They were unable to read Nietzsche openly and critically, to deal with his ideas on their own terms. In this sense *The Masses'* radicals failed as intellectuals.

The fascination with Nietzsche was only a part of the intellectual ferment of a period that welcomed artistic and critical stimulation from abroad. A perusal of the books offered for sale to its readers through *The Masses* Book Shop indicates a great breadth of interest in European ideas. There were books by George Bernard Shaw, August Strindberg, Havelock Ellis, Henri Bergson, Nikolai Gogol, Emile Zola, August Bebel, Feodor Dostoevski, Sigmund Freud, and various minor novelists, playwrights, and psychologists whose names have since faded into obscurity.

One of the most fashionable of the European thinkers was Henri Bergson. His antirationalism may have provided an indirect justification for the uncritical subjectivity with which *The Masses'* radicals approached the works of Nietzsche or other theorists from abroad. Bergson held that reality was in constant flux and change; hence thinking about it would only distort it. The only possible means of apprehending reality was through intuition. His ideas expressed the dominant trend in American philosophy before World War I, and they won great appeal in this country.[40] Bergson gained favor among a restless younger generation who wanted a world filled with new ideas, new hopes, and new opportunities. He appealed to feminists because of his emphasis on instinct, feeling, and intuition, and to democrats because of his concern with human solidarity and his belief that the instinctive and intuitive perceptions of the common man had more value than the abstract thought of philosophers.[41]

Pre-World War I radicals were in search of means of attacking oppressive social institutions and the tyranny of convention. Therefore, George Bernard Shaw found favor for his attacks on marriage and organized religion.[42] The repeal of reticence in the early twentieth century meant that it was possible to discuss sexuality in an open and scientific manner. The prolific pen of Havelock Ellis had much to do with this change. His multivolume study *The Psychology of Sex* made sex the object of scientific inquiry. His writings served to dignify sex and to preserve it from prudishness. Ellis himself was a champion of unlimited sexual freedom for both men and women in the belief that love could purify all relations; hence his ideas, like those of Shaw, could be used to attack the institutions of marriage and the family.[43] In fact, Margaret Sanger acknowledged Ellis to be the "guiding spirit" of the study that led to her launching of the birth control movement.[44]

Despite a nearly universal commitment to creating a "new American culture," new radicals borrowed extensively and uncritically from European thought. They failed to question whether the antirationalism of Nietzsche or Bergson could ever be compatible with the scientific socialism of Marx. In their eclecticism they were unable to postulate any coherent theory of social change; opting for a series of unrelated ideas from European avant-garde thought, new radicals failed to articulate a social dynamic that would explain the relationship between institutional changes and the transformation of consciousness.

The Impact of Walt Whitman

When radicals turned to an American cultural tradition to find weapons for social change, they alighted most frequently on the works of the great American bard of the "barbaric yawp," Walt Whitman. It was a natural choice; Whitman in *Democratic Vistas* had seen that only through a dramatic transformation of political life would a dynamic new American culture be possible.

Moreover, Whitman had repudiated the culture and conventions of the middle class. George Santayana dubbed him perhaps the "one American writer who has left the genteel tradition entirely behind."[45] So when hopes for an American renaissance were ripe, many intellectuals turned to Whitman. In his book written to herald the new order, *America's Coming-of-Age*, Van Wyck Brooks wrote: "The real significance of Walt Whitman is that he, for the first time, gave us the sense of something organic in American life."[46]

In following Brooks's injunction to invent a usable past, Randolph Bourne thought that the new American classicist would have to rescue Thoreau, Whitman, and Mark Twain to arrive at a tradition that would unite vitality and moral freedom.[47]

In cultural terms Whitman was the apostle of liberation. The hobo poet, Harry Kemp, called *Leaves of Grass* his bible and through it hoped to reform the world.[48] Similarly, the poet and editor Horace Traubel declared *Leaves* the "Bible of the Cosmos" and his friend Whitman the most significant figure in literature, and he gladly devoted most of his life to popularizing Whitman's works.[49] To Floyd Dell Whitman had renovated the modern soul by enabling his readers to overcome their puritanism and see the goodness of the whole body. Dell viewed Whitman as a pagan and a feminist, a poet who found vigor and sensuality in both men and women. And when Isadora Duncan sought to restore women's original strength and natural movements through modern dance, she found inspiration in Whitman.[50] Like Traubel she was willing to dedicate her life to a Whitmanesque vision. Duncan was deeply moved by Whitman's language in "I Hear America Singing": "When I read this poem of Whitman's I, too, had a Vision—the Vision of America dancing a dance that would be the worthy expression of the song Walt heard when he heard America singing."[51] And she spent her life in creating a dance that would be athletic, sensual, and democratic, one that would reach audiences left unmoved by the exquisite formalism of the ballet.

Whitman also proved to be an apostle of sexual liberation. He reveled in the joys of the flesh and took great pleasure in nakedness. He uncovered intimacy and found it pure in daylight. He went to the frontiers of sexuality with the openness of exploration. After years of lecturing on Whitman, Emma Goldman came to discover that Whitman's bisexuality was essential to his knowledge of human complexity, his sensitivity to the nature of women through his own femininity, and his greatness as a poet and rebel.[52] Sherwood Anderson saw Whitman as expressing the importance of restoring male love to the modern world: "It must be proclaimed. Walt Whitman proclaimed it. It must be understood. Upon the understanding of it, the acceptance of it with pride, may hang the chance we males have of again getting, a little again, on top of our lives."[53] Bisexuality, the full and free expression of all loving sexual impulses, posed the most striking alternative to puritanism conceivable to America's social radicals.

In addition, Whitman proved attractive to those who sought political change. By expressing democracy in poetic form, he endowed it with dignity and elevated the working class to heroic stature. Hutchins Hapgood complained that his own initial encounters with labor left him with an impression of workers as "suffering, hard, sullen, ugly." But as time passed he discovered Whitmanesque qualities of passion, poetry, and warmth in the working class, and he came to find workers more intelligent about economic and social questions than university professors.[54] Whitman's comprehensive view of the nature of democracy also found appeal. One of the leading theorists of left-wing socialism, William English Walling, proclaimed:

> The American who has come nearest, perhaps, to an adequate expression of the larger socialism is Walt Whitman. For Whitman realized that his ideals were not to be reached by a struggle against nature alone, or against social inertia and disorganization, ignorance and poverty, but declared war also against social forces and classes hostile to democratic progress. He says, almost in so many words, that political democracy can become social democracy and build up a new society only through an actual conflict of the new civilization with the old.[55]

Whitman could speak eloquently to a generation that found the cultural transformation of America far more significant than political reform alone; he echoed its concern for the quality of American life.

The New Paganism

In seeking to establish a new nonrepressive culture in America, radicals searched through history to discover an epoch in which arts and letters had flourished in a society that still paid tribute to physical beauty and expression, hence the new paganism. Radicals turned to pre-Christian cultures, especially to ancient Greece, to find the athleticism and sensuality that puritanism had extinguished in their own country. In celebrating ancient Greek culture, new radicals consistently ignored the fact that pagan achievement was the product of a slaveholding society that subordinated women and, in short, that its cultural contribution necessitated elitism and repression.

Many socialists complained that orthodox Protestantism and modern capitalism had combined to buttress the morality of the middle class and to impose it on the entire society. Sigmund Freud in *Leonardo da Vinci* provided a historical description of the process. Freud claimed that in primitive times pagans had worshiped the genitals and revered fertility, but in the course of cultural development "so much godliness and holiness had been extracted from sexuality that the exhausted remnant fell into contempt."[56] Freud thus pinned much of the blame for centuries of repression on the Christian religion. When some radicals came to desire the renovation of Christianity to imbue the religion with the personal ideals of Jesus, whom they viewed as a revolutionary figure, they, too, called for a new paganism. Bouck White, the head resident of Trinity House in New York, was a contributor to *The Masses*. In his book on Jesus, *The Call of the Carpenter*, White called for a return to pagan ideals:

> Perhaps the best term by which to describe an artistic renaissance dominated by the ideals of The Carpenter is, a new paganism. In getting away from pagan morals, the world did wisely. But in getting away from the pagan view of nature, the world did unwisely. To the theistic mind— the theologically orthodox mind to-day—the powers and agencies of nature have no spirituality of their own, but are thought of as dead, unsensing implements. To the early Greeks, however, nature had a life of its own; so that man and nature were in a sort of comradeship.[57]

Hence Greek ideals could serve the dual purpose of attacking the rigidities of puritanism while providing a model for the new American culture radicals intended to build on its ruins.

Radicals like Floyd Dell also linked the Greek revival to socialism. Dell cited an address by the classicist Gilbert Murray in London in which Murray had said that socialism and the rising consciousness of labor were bringing about a situation comparable only to that of the ancient Greek world. Dell applauded the intellectual flexibility, courage, and curiosity of the Greeks; he felt a kinship with their "propaganda spirit."[58] In his novels Dell described the pagan spirit that had reached small-town intellectuals in their lonely struggles at home or after they had become residents of the bohemias of New York or Chicago. In *Runaway* Dirk Tillinghast, the married reporter who has wooed Michael Shenstone's daughter Amber, talks about love affairs in Beaumont to her surprised father: "We defy the Puritans—discreetly, of course. Strictly on the q.t.—the Puritans mustn't get wind of it because they happen to be our fathers and mothers and aunts and uncles, and we need them to foot the bills. But it's understood among ourselves that we're young pagans. Vine leaves in our hair!"[59] Similarly, in *The Briary-Bush* Rose-Ann Prentiss tells her husband Felix Fay how she became a settlement-house worker in Chicago: "It seemed to me a good pagan life, to try to bring about a better world for everybody—a world in which beauty would count for something. . . . It was the Greekliest thing I knew to do."[60] Dell only dimly realized the intrinsically privileged nature of the new pagan rebellion, and he utterly failed to realize that pagan culture never could reach the masses unless society was transformed to permit them the health, leisure, and education necessary for the full enjoyment of art and athleticism.

Yet Dell himself retained too much of the puritan demon within his own soul to feel at ease being a pagan. In "A Psycho-Analytic Confession," written for *The Liberator* of April 1920, Dell describes a dialogue between his socialist Consciousness and his Utopian Unconscious. As long as communism seemed a remote possibility, his Unconscious gave it complete alle-

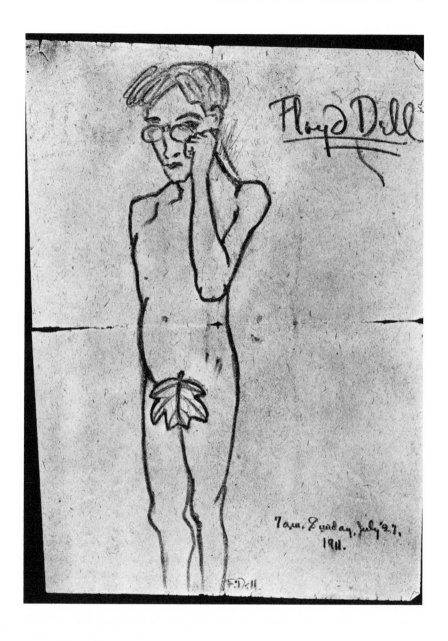

Sketch by Floyd Dell labeled "Floyd Dell, 7 a.m., Sunday, July 27, 1911."
Courtesy Floyd Dell Papers, The Newberry Library

giance, but once it approached reality, the Unconscious decided that communism looked too much like work. Dell was torn between his puritanical and pagan impulses, between his belief in socialism and his desire for bourgeois comforts. Finally his Unconscious levels a telling accusation:

> I think you are a Socialist simply because you want a different kind
> of world, one you can be happy in. And you work for the social revolution just as other people work to make a fortune. You want to see your
> dream come true. But the dream which you want to see come true is my
> dream—not Lenin's seven hundred million electric bulbs, but a houseboat and a happy family living in a state of moderately advanced
> and semi-nude savagery![61]

Dell found some amelioration of the conflict through psychoanalysis and through his happy second marriage to B. Marie Gage, but he never managed a full integration of his socialism and his paganism.

The Greek revival had a more literal meaning for insurgents in theater and the dance. George Cram Cook, the founder of the Provincetown Players, and Isadora Duncan, the originator of modern dance, both were devotees of ancient Greek culture and actually lived in Greece and practiced their art in a Hellenic setting. A socialist and a mystic, Cook hoped to revive on the American stage the Dionysian "madness" of the ancient Greeks.[62] Isadora Duncan became for many radicals of her day the embodiment of the pagan spirit. She had studied Greek vases to ascertain the steps of the dancers, dressed her dancers in simple tunics, and had them perform on an uncluttered stage akin to the Greek proscenium. Her life, too, was led in the pagan spirit. She entitled one chapter of her autobiography "An Apology for Pagan Love." Once Isadora discovered that "Love might be a pastime as well as a tragedy," she abandoned herself to it "with pagan innocence." With unthinking narcissism she wrote of *herself*: "The divine pagan body, the passionate lips, the clinging arms, the sweet refreshing sleep on the shoulder of some loved one—these were joys which seemed to me both innocent and delightful."[63]

In her life and her art Isadora Duncan was the quintessential symbol of paganism. Years after her tragic life came to an end, Max Eastman paid her a final tribute: "She rode the wave of the revolt against puritanism; she rode it, and with her fame and Dionysian raptures drove it on. She *was*—perhaps it is simplest to say—the crest of the wave, an event not only in art, but in the history of life."[64] In her own time Isadora won adulation for her youth, her vitality, her beauty, her revelation of "the full glory of the human body"; Van Wyck Brooks, Louis Untermeyer, and Floyd Dell were among those who paid tribute to her in prose and verse.[65] Claude McKay, the Jamaican poet, was one of the few who recognized that Isadora's sensibility, nevertheless, was so refined in its paganism that she failed to appreciate more primitive forms of culture. In her formula for a new dance worthy of Walt Whitman, she specifically ruled out any reference to the sensual rhythms of jazz.[66] McKay pointed out that Isadora lacked any feeling or regard for black dancing and its imitations and derivations: "She had no real appreciation of primitive folk dancing, either from an aesthetic or an ethnic point of view. For her every movement of the dance should soar upward."[67]

Only a select few ventured to explore other more threatening aspects of the primitive. Carl Van Vechten was always in the vanguard of the exploration. He used to visit Harlem regularly, one of the few whites to do so, in order to hear the jazz and be part of the night life. In the 1920s he used these experiences as the basis of his novel about Harlem, *Nigger Heaven*. Ostensibly the novel is only a description of black society, but implicitly it provides a critique of the white society it seems to ignore. At one point in the novel the heroine Mary Love states that Christianity was the religion of slavery because it promised eternal joy and a reunion with family members sold to new owners in the hereafter; but once that oppression was removed, blacks reverted quite simply to their natural paganism.[68] Greenwich Village radicals unable to liberate themselves from their own Victorian heritage envied what they viewed as the true paganism of the blacks. Later in the novel the white editor Russell Durwood suggests to the black hero, Byron Kasson, that he write about blacks in Harlem. Durwood noted that the Harlem fast set had the same pastimes and vices as its white counterpart on Long Island, "but it is vastly more amusing than the Long Island set for the simple reason that it is *amused*."[69] The assumption here is that whites cannot deny the genteel tradition long enough to enjoy decadence; lacking such a tradition, blacks are free to enjoy dissipation. Carl Van Vechten once managed to engineer an encounter between Harlem and Greenwich Village. He persuaded Mabel Dodge to invite two black entertainers to her salon for her first "Evening." The hostess left posterity a horrified account of the occasion:

> . . . an appalling Negress danced before us in white stockings and black buttoned boots. The man strummed a banjo and sang an embarrassing song while she cavorted. They both leered and rolled their suggestive eyes and made me feel first hot and then cold, for I never had been so near this kind of thing before, but Carl rocked with laughter and little shrieks escaped him as he clapped his pretty hands. His big teeth became wickedly prominent and his eyes rolled in his darkening face, until he grew to somewhat resemble the clattering Negroes before him.[70]

Needless to say, the invitation never was repeated.

Van Vechten also took the lead in experimentation with drugs. In his reminiscences for the Columbia University oral history collection, he claimed to have taken "heroin or cocaine or something like that a couple of times" as

George Cram Cook in Greece
Courtesy Floyd Dell Papers, The Newberry Library

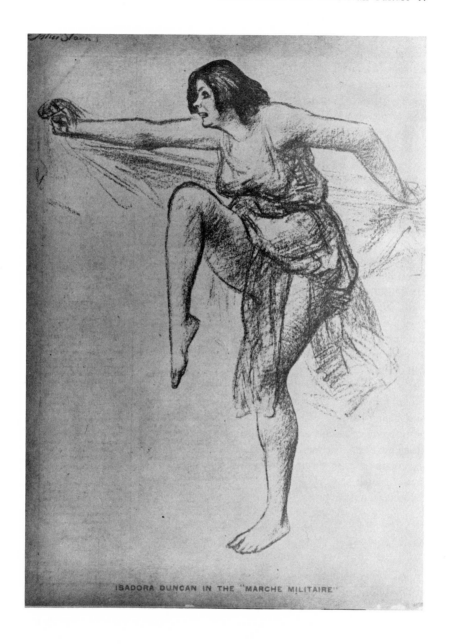

ISADORA DUNCAN IN THE "MARCHE MILITAIRE"

John Sloan, "Isadora Duncan in the 'Marche Militaire,' " *The Masses*, May 1915
Courtesy Tamiment Library, New York University

early as 1912.[71] In his 1929 semiautobiographical novel of pre-World War I life in Greenwich Village, *Peter Whiffle*, the hero had experimented with hashish, marijuana, peyote, and cocaine: "I have dabbled in drugs, for you know that the old Greek priests, the modern seers, and the mediaeval pythonesses, all have resorted to drugs to assist them to see visions."[72] Here the affinity between paganism and experimentation with drugs is rendered explicit. It was hoped that the use of drugs might release primitive impulses and creativity stifled by too much civilization.

History also records an infamous peyote party held at the Fifth Avenue salon of Mabel Dodge. In the spring of 1914, Raymond Harrington, a cousin of the Hapgoods, who had been living among the Indians of Oklahoma doing ethnological research, told Mabel Dodge and the Hapgoods about the ceremonies of the Peyote Cult. The result was that Mabel Dodge decided to hold a peyote evening in which to experiment with consciousness. By hiding some of the drug behind her on the floor, she managed to take less of it than the others and thus became the annoyed observer of the singing and madness that filled her house. One of her guests, Genevieve Onslow, disappeared into the night, and it was learned later that she had been the victim of a nervous breakdown resulting from the traumas caused by the drug. As with her encounter with the blacks, Mabel Dodge's reaction to this latest experiment with drugs was one of selfish horror. She expected the titillations of voyeurism without any attendant personal responsibility: "What bothered me most was that I should be personally implicated in the eyes of my acquaintances with a situation that was ambiguous enough to deserve, even at any angle, the name of a 'Dope Party.' Horrors!"[73] Yet another exploration of the frontiers of the primitive ended in grotesque failure. But new radicals who experimented with drugs never considered the possibility that such dabbling with drugs might be incompatible with disciplined radical political activity, that it might expose them to legal prosecution or divert their energy from the tasks of social and cultural reconstruction.

New American Culture

It may seem baffling to realize that many of the pre-World War I writers and critics who turned to Nietzsche and other European thinkers for inspiration and who engaged in the movement for a new paganism were the very same people who championed the call for a new American culture. In striking an Emersonian note in demanding the creation of a distinctly native renaissance of arts and letters, these American intellectuals echoed as well Emerson's belief that a "foolish consistency is the hobgoblin of little minds."[74] For example, Randolph Bourne, a man willing to employ Nietzsche in tilting

Mabel Dodge
Courtesy Beinecke Rare Book and Manuscript Library, Yale University

against puritans, claimed in his essay "Our Cultural Humility" that Americans strangled native genius by relying on European art and taste: "The only remedy for this deplorable situation is the cultivation of a new American nationalism. We need that keen introspection into the beauties and vitalities and sincerities of our own life and ideals that characterizes the French."[75]

The attack on foreign domination and the call for a new American culture pervaded the avant-garde little magazines and the bohemias of the period. Waldo Frank complained of the debilitating effect of American cultural reliance on England. Frank noted that English authors had surrendered to the chaos of the new industrial order, so that to employ them as literary models was to forego self-examination and improvement.[76] Yet in writing his literary history, *On Native Grounds*, Alfred Kazin claimed of the authors and journalists of the Chicago Renaissance: "There was a hunger for culture, a culture of America's own, and every new current from Europe seemed to help it along."[77]

In fact, there was little outright repudiation of European culture: jealousy proved to be the dominant motif. Americans wanted to emulate Europe in arrogating to themselves a cultural tradition that could provide a sense of national unity and purpose. Even John Dewey, perched on a philosophical height above the literary battles of his day, argued that the America of May 1917 could no longer be spoken to in the language of the Old World; it must be addressed on its own terms.[78] But we find the same underlying ambivalence in Dewey that we found in Bourne and in the writers of the Chicago Renaissance. In his essay "In a Time of National Hesitation" written for *The Seven Arts*, Dewey informed his readers that the battle for democracy and civilization then being fought on French soil did not involve Americans because they were committed to fight for another democracy and another civilization; months later Dewey became one of the most ardent champions of American participation in support of the Allies in World War I.

The Seven Arts sought to become the self-conscious organ of an American literary renaissance. It aimed to become *the* magazine that would evoke all native talent, both creative and critical, and mobilize it on behalf of proselytizing the new Americanism.[79] The most immediate and obvious problem was the lack of a cultural heritage. Editorially *The Seven Arts* argued, "We have no tradition to continue; we have no school of style to build up. What we ask of the writer is simply self-expression without regard to current magazine standards," a plea that would be echoed by *The Masses*.[80] In lieu of a tradition, *The Seven Arts* offered the notion that change was the essence of Americanism, that the country lived with the fullness of possibility that characterized adolescence.[81] The writer could invent a native tradition if need be. James Oppenheim, the editor, ends his poetic paean "America" with the following affirmation:

This is my city, this is my land . . .
What care I if it have no Past?
I have a Past. . . . I bequeath it to America. . .
Is it dreamless? I bring it a dream!
Lacks it vision? It shall have mine![82]

Here the note that Oppenheim strikes is Whitmanesque: poet and prophet shall be one. Only a special vision could preserve for America the role of a messiah-nation that distinguished her from all others. We are faced with a sublimated puritanism, a transmuted form of the belief in a city on a hill that would serve as a religious beacon, when Oppenheim states, "But the time has come. A new poet must appear among us."[83]

One of the leaders of the American literary renaissance, Van Wyck Brooks, in the 1920s claimed that Randolph Bourne had been endowed with the necessary vision. Detached from the genteel tradition but gifted with exposure to the intellectual ferment that brewed among the second-generation immigrants who attended Columbia, Bourne was peculiarly able to tap sources of vitality for American culture: "Here was Emerson's American Scholar at last, but radiating an infinitely warmer, profaner, more companionable influence than Emerson had ever dreamed of, an influence that savored rather of Whitman and William James."[84] Bourne was able to articulate an American tradition distinguishable from Old World culture; in it he included Emerson, Thoreau, Whitman, William James, Henry James, Josiah Royce, and George Santayana.[85] Moreover, he was able to offer a renewed sense of mission. He claimed that America was uniquely able to embody the cosmopolitan ideal of unity through diversity. As a transnationality, America would weave peoples of many different origins into a single national fabric that would gain strength from the very nature of its construction.[86] The American ideal could pose a potent alternative to the German cultural threat in World War I. By the deliberate application of intelligence and taste to the use of our human and cultural resources in the interests of democracy, America would have the power to unite the world in its image.[87]

The intellectual would play a crucial role in this process: an aristocracy of thought would provide the analysis needed to guide the labor movement on the path of radical social and economic change.[88] It was, therefore, natural that Walter Lippmann's *Drift and Mastery* should exert tremendous appeal for Bourne. Of it he said, "There is a book one would have given one's soul to have written." Lippmann was committed to the notion that intellectuals could best analyze and control the course of political events. The two men met in England, and months later Bourne joined Lippmann on the staff of *The New Republic*, the most vocal organ of liberal reform.[89] But Bourne had altered the role of the intellectual. Not only was there a commitment to activism, even if only in an advisory capacity, but the intellectual would employ new tools borrowed from both the natural and the social sciences.[90] The faith in science and in expertise may be naive at times, but at least it demands intellectual rigor, a quality noted for its absence in much of pre-World War I radicalism.

Bourne also believed that America would have to revise the artistic ideals that it had borrowed from Europe. He particularly objected to Matthew Arnold's notion of the tyranny of the "best," whereby the cultural ideals of an elite could be imposed for purposes of uplift on the undifferentiated mass of mankind. It was futile to emphasize the acquisition of art at the expense of its enjoyment. Art appreciation should be devoted to "clarifying and integrating natural taste" rather than to imposing foreign standards; only such an approach would develop a distinctive native art spirit and style.[91]

Bourne's plea for new, indigenous standards of art was echoed by American artists engaged in a revolt against European standards of taste imposed by the country's art galleries. Some of the more experimental artists resorted to independent exhibitions for their work to stimulate new tastes in the American art public. One of these artists, the painter Robert Henri, wrote an article for *The Craftsman* of May 1910 to elucidate the purpose of the New York Exhibition of Independent Artists, a landmark in the development of native art. Henri stated that the purpose of art was to express the spirit of the American people. Thus Henri rejected any notion of art for art's sake and aligned himself with the writers of *The Seven Arts* who viewed their magazine not as a magazine for artists but as "an expression of artists for the community."[92] The passivity of the idea of art as expression was mitigated by Henri's belief that true art must affect and shape every aspect of life: "It is not learning how to do something which people will call art, but rather inventing something that is absolutely necessary for the progress of our existence."[93] Here Henri, like Bourne, shared the pragmatic conviction that education and culture must be intimately related to life experience. On *The Masses*, in his painting and graphic work, John Sloan tried to be guided by the principles enunciated by Henri, his teacher and friend. Sloan's work was literally a reflection of the life around; his consuming passion was the American scene, which he painted with a buoyancy and optimism characteristic of his time and place.[94]

On the literary front the battle for a new American culture was part of the revolt against the genteel tradition. James Oppenheim, editor of *The Seven Arts*, championed the need for vulgarity in art: "The truth of the matter is that great art was never *pure*. It was the expression of the whole man, and not merely his sublimated upper layer." He argued that it was impossible to substitute "the art of subtlety and intellect" for "the art of vitality and sensation" that characterized popular culture. In fact, for Oppenheim vulgarity had its merits: "If one must choose, there is much to be said for the street and the mill and the saloon, and all places where life is a hot flame, and not the curling wisp of incense."[95] Sherwood Anderson agreed with Oppenheim in viewing subtlety as somehow un-American. Artists should accept the limitations of American character and seek to emulate it by producing an art that would be at once both more simple and real: "We shall have to begin to write out of the people and not for the people." Again we hear the plea for vulgarity in art: "For a long time I have believed that crudity is an inevitable quality in the production of a really significant present-day American literature."[96] Oppenheim and Anderson paved the way for the consideration of popular culture as art, but their theories robbed the artist of the right to educate and inform public taste. Although their own novels—Oppenheim's *The Nine-Tenths* and Anderson's *Windy McPherson's Son* and *Marching Men*—recognized the oppression and alienation experienced by masses of Americans, their literary theories would have the artist seek to reflect tastes spawned under those conditions.

Harold Stearns struck the same note with regard to the theater. Although he did not actually defend vulgarity, he argued that drama sprang from the inarticulate aspirations of the American people. Regardless of the validity of these aspirations, they would have to be accepted as real and compelling for a genuine dramatic art to exist. Stearns held that of all the arts drama was the most popular. If such an art were to become too specialized, esoteric, or subtle, it would lose its vitality. Hence for Stearns widespread appeal, popularity, the ability to mirror the felt life of the audience were all indexes of dramatic success. Stearns, too, included a plea to end didacticism in art: "In America there is a distinct tendency to look upon the drama as a cultural agent rather than what it is, a cultural expression. The true function of the drama does not lie in guiding and controlling and setting the pace for our emotional life, but in revealing and expressing that life."[97]

There is an obvious irony in the fact that men like Oppenheim, Anderson, and Stearns, all engaged in writing for little magazines that abjured the standards imposed by the popular commercial magazines, should view literature and drama as reflections of popular taste. Moreover, a secondary irony was that an American audience, raised on Victorian romance and melodrama, had to be educated to accept its own vulgarity as expressed by new American authors. Nor did these authors see that a mimetic art could merely reflect reality, not serve to change it. Their populism lacked intellectual content; certainly Oppenheim's and Anderson's novels of the era failed to articulate responses to oppression and alienation that went beyond a demand for human solidarity. In casting off the genteel tradition, in discarding the Victorian belief in didactic art, they failed to salvage the notion shared by Victorians and Marxists alike, that art need not merely reflect reality but should shape the world as well.

In this period the drama was undergoing a transformation that only years later would result in the popularity of Eugene O'Neill. The Provincetown Players provided short, simple plays that could be produced on a low budget by either amateur or professional actors. Although at times the subjects had greater appeal for bohemians than for a general audience, the style was inherently democratic. With few props or costumes, the separation between actors and audience practically vanished. The Players refused to be constrained by the dictates of professionalism and used amateur playwrights and actors for their productions.

The inspiration for the Provincetown Players came from George Cram Cook, a mystic who hoped to "revive the Hellenic ideal in modern America." Cook wanted to restore the unity between the workaday and artistic worlds that had been provided by ancient Greek culture. He felt that America's pioneer spirit had crushed artistic creativity. In a mood of whimsy and nostalgia, he once said to his longtime friend Floyd Dell, who had been a fellow member of the small literary set in Davenport, Iowa, "Floyd, let's gather the old Davenport crowd together, and go back there, and make it a new Athens!" But in his saner moments Cook avoided the utopian solution. He worked with Floyd Dell as his editorial partner on the Friday Review of the *Chicago Evening Post*, a critical pioneer and champion of the new American literature, and founded and directed the Provincetown Players, a group whose contribution to the new American culture was the renovation of the drama.[98]

In the dance Isadora Duncan, the heroine of the new paganism, mounted the attack on foreign cultural domination. She argued that the ballet expressed the artificial culture of the epoch of Louis XIII and, therefore, could have no more than antiquarian value for the American people. In its place she hoped to offer a new form of dance that would evoke an equally great new form of music. Together these media would express the Whitmanesque diversity of America.[99]

The pre-World War I period was one of ferment in all the arts. America proved to be quite culturally ambitious yet without the introspection and self-awareness necessary to produce a true renaissance. Her critics failed to grapple with the causes underlying America's lack of a sustained cultural heritage; they preferred inventing a tradition to dealing with its absence. They often refused to acknowledge their own cultural indebtedness to Europe. And they failed to articulate a role for the artist that would enable him to shape American tastes and aspirations.

Cult of Youth

New radicals celebrated the crudity, the plasticity, in short, the youthfulness of American culture; in fact, Randolph Bourne believed that it was the young who would redeem America and usher in a cultural renaissance. Although Bourne may be the figure most prominently associated with the cult of youth, he was only part of a generation that had grown up in an era when children were ignored in favor of adults only to reach maturity in a child-centered age. In his social history of the American family, Arthur W. Calhoun pointed to the decline of paternal supremacy during the first two decades of the twentieth century. The new regime of abundance permitted the lengthening of infancy and the elevation of childhood, thereby increasing the concern for child care and education. Since twentieth-century fathers tended to work away from home, they were unable to keep pace with advances in education and lost the prestige and power needed to guide their offspring.[100]

The celebration of youth took many forms. James Oppenheim described America as naturally adolescent, a nation characterized by the flux and possibility that precede maturity.[101] It was this openness to experience that appealed to intellectuals engaged in the effort to create a new American culture. Even if the older generation were to reject their art, the younger generation might be open enough to accept it, thereby providing ultimate vindication of their efforts. The painter Robert Henri went so far as to suggest that the only people of worth in life were the babies, for they alone had the conviction of their own opinions. Young art students might begin their careers with the same bravery, but they soon succumbed to the lure of money and the dictates of public opinion. Henri's personal solution was to try to remain forever young.[102] In order to further the modern dance movement, Isadora Duncan decided to found her own school of dance for children of talent whom she would adopt. She felt that the young would be peculiarly able to respond to nature, "to feel in their souls a secret attachment, unknowable to others, to initiate them into Nature's secrets."[103] To such artists childhood represented a time of receptivity to new artistic stimuli. Moreover, childhood was a time of experimentalism and play. There was a childlike quality to the kind of amateur theatricals originally produced by the group of friends who dubbed themselves the Provincetown Players. By rejecting professionalism they turned the work of the theater into play and allowed their performances to be judged by fluid standards conducive to a young art.

Randolph Bourne was the apostle of the cult of youth: "*Place aux Jeunes* might have been his motto; he seemed indeed the flying wedge of the younger generation itself."[104] Bourne opposed the tyranny of the aged who used guilt to manipulate the young to support them and minister to their needs at the expense of youthful creativity.[105] He would have preferred a situation in

Randolph Bourne
Courtesy Randolph Bourne Papers, Rare Book and Manuscript Library, Columbia University

which progressive generations were independent and self-reliant; he wanted parents to lead stimulating lives of their own apart from the raising of their children.[106] In a very real sense, the cult of youth was intended to liberate the older generation as well. Yet it placed a tremendous burden on the young, the responsibility for revitalizing their culture:

> The ideas of the young are the living, the potential ideas; those of the old, the dying, or the already dead. This is why it behooves youth to be not less radical, but even more radical, than it would naturally be. It must be not simply contemporaneous, but a generation ahead of the times, so that when it comes into control of the world, it will be precisely right and coincident with the conditions of the world as it finds them. If the youth of to-day could really achieve this miracle, they would have found the secret of "perpetual youth."[107]

Bourne was merely the most articulate intellectual of his generation to celebrate the inherent radicalism of youth.

Although openness to change is certainly a virtue in the modern world, the notion of youth as inherently radical has hardly stood the test of time. Neither the "flaming youth" of the 1920s nor the apathetic adolescents of the 1950s were noted for their political radicalism or even activism. These latter-day beneficiaries of the cult of youth might flaunt the social mores of their elders, but their challenge was an ephemeral one because their rebellion did nothing to undermine the institutions that shaped society. At its height just before and during World War I the cult of youth virtually treated the young as a class without recognizing that in a Marxist sense its members shared no common class interest. It failed to deal with the economic and social differences that kept youth apart and with the invidious effect of dividing the young from their elders in terms of the class struggle. Instead of rooting their rebellion in an enduring history of oppression, the champions of the cult of youth chose to root it in the fleeting modernity of adolescence, thereby imperiling the very survival of that rebellion into maturity. If the cult of youth served to foster change in its own time, it had no ready applicability to the problems of the future.

Culture in Conflict

Instead of creating a genuine renaissance founded on common values of iconoclasm, modernism, and nationalism, prewar radicals championing a new American culture embraced competing ideals. They preferred an immediate affective resolution of the tensions that were thus generated to the disciplined task of evolving a coherent ideology. The moral earnestness of

Victorianism coexisted with the flaunting of bourgeois proprieties, the irrationalism of Bergson and Nietzsche with the scientific socialism of Marx, cultural nationalism with an intellectual indebtedness to European thought. The revolt against puritanism and the celebration of paganism shared a common indifference to historical accuracy and a common desire to shape one's life in the context of a mythologized past. In celebrating crudity, youth, and vulgarity as most characteristic of American culture and in demanding an art that would mirror those attributes, new radicals were denying a critical or didactic function for art. It was this intellectual failure—an unwillingness to discriminate between competing ideas, an inability to achieve coherence of thought—that provided new radicals with immediate gratification at the expense of the discipline necessary for long-term commitment to radical ideals.

Chapter 4 Greenwich Village—Home as Bohemia

The Sense of Bohemian Community

The pre-World War I revolt of artists and intellectuals found its home in Greenwich Village, New York's haven for wayward spirits since the days of Edgar Allan Poe and Walt Whitman. Although bohemia has come to symbolize rebellion, it has a rich and colorful tradition that sustains those who seek refuge within its bounds. Balzac introduced the term to the literary world in his *Un Prince de Bohème*, and the general public took note of the phenomenon with the publication of Henry Murger's immensely popular *Scènes de la vie de Bohème* in the 1850s. Thackeray through his novel *Vanity Fair* helped to bring bohemia to the attention of the English-speaking public, and in the 1890s du Maurier's semiautobiographical novel *Trilby* precipitated a second bohemian craze.[1] The notion of bohemia when imported to America was redolent of European exoticism. It bore with it a charm that had general appeal; it smacked more of the quaint and the curious than of outright revolt against social mores.

The writers who described America's bohemia emphasized its homage to social proprieties and its sense of civic responsibility. For example, William Dean Howells in *The Coast of Bohemia* (1899) presents us with a bohemian artist-heroine named Charmian who lives with her mother and does nothing more risqué than puff at a cigar. The members of New York's art colony whom Howells depicts are either married or court under chaperonage; all the niceties are observed.[2] Howells thus refuses to examine seriously the roots of social rebellion and reduces the bohemian desire for freedom to a silly wish to smoke. For his characters an interlude in bohemia is merely a way station on the journey to respectability.

The historians of Greenwich Village also emphasized the high moral tone of the area. Anna Alice Chapin dismissed the sexual notions of the Villagers as mere talk and stressed instead their unquestionable idealism: "But in the Village there is very little scandal, and practically no slander. They are very slow to think evil."[3] Floyd Dell even claimed later that the *"real* Villagers" disdained the term bohemian and formed a solid group of respectable citizens who "paid their bills and bathed regularly":

> Those Greenwich Villagers were schoolteachers, college professors, social workers, doctors, lawyers, engineers and other professional people. As for artists and writers who then lived in the Village—such as John Sloan and Art Young, Mary Heaton Vorse, Inez Haynes Gillmore, Susan Glaspell, Theodore Dreiser—they already had positions of importance in the realm of art and letters. None of these Villagers were what I called poor; some of them owned houses in the country, in Westchester County, in Connecticut, New Jersey, or on the Massachusetts coast. They had most of the familiar middle-class virtues, and in addition, some of their own; they were an obviously superior lot of people.[4]

In the early years of the twentieth century Greenwich Village was pervaded by a zeal for social reform that accounted for its earnest, optimistic commitment to a series of humanitarian crusades.[5] Van Wyck Brooks recounts that when Max Eastman arrived in New York in 1907, Greenwich Village already had been captured from the artists by a swarm of reformers and social workers whose concerns were more explicitly ethical and political than those of their predecessors.[6] Eastman's friend Arthur Bullard noted that whereas Paris had an aesthetic bohemia, New York appeared to be creating an ethical one: "for the moment the world of the arts seemed secondary."[7]

Yet for many the convergence of politics and life-style was not complete. Even those Villagers who offered their support to social settlements, union activities, or the fight for birth control might neglect the political and social implications of their presence in Greenwich Village as a neighborhood. There was no dialogue between the newcomers to the Village and its older inhabitants, who were mostly Italians and Irish, traditionally Catholic and conservative in family matters. In fact, the older Villagers viewed the newcomers as a threat to the moral decency of the neighborhood, and the new Villagers made no special effort to correct that impression.[8] In addition, the influx of newcomers caused a rise in rents that resulted in the eviction of many of the Village's earlier inhabitants.[9] Mary Simkhovitch of Greenwich House pointed to the social irony of the situation: "It was certainly amusing and astounding to us who had fought against cellar lodgings as unhealthful, damp and unfit for human habitation, as they were, to see them revived as 'one room studios' and let often at six times the price of former rentals."[10] John Reed's poem *The Day in Bohemia* highlights the irresponsibility and childishness of Village artists who were only dimly aware of the appalling conditions in nearby tenements.[11]

The problem in part was one of definition. Greenwich Village had come to have different meanings for the various people who sought it as a refuge. For some it permitted a nonconformist life-style free from the surveillance of parents or the village elders. For others it represented a chance at adolescent experimentation in sex and work before settling down to responsibility elsewhere. The Village could be a haven for like-minded souls in politics or the arts; it could free them from the constraints of the outside world or alternately provide them with the emotional sustenance that could support their rebellion and efforts at social change. Greenwich Village and the smaller worlds it encompassed—the clubs, salons, theater groups, art and literary cooperatives —all served to fill the void left by the breakdown of communal institutions in American society at large. The men and women who came to Greenwich Village dedicated themselves to rebuilding the lost sense of community. Mary Heaton Vorse lamented that Western civilization no longer was able to satisfy the elemental need for community: "This is our weakness. Our strength does not multiply in our daily lives. There is a creative force in people doing things together. The great creative power of the multiple spirit is almost cut away from us."[12]

Although the Villagers were motivated by this sense of loss, in many ways their situation rendered them unequal to the task of building a lasting community. The Village as a community was too diffuse and social networks too intricate and variable to depend on affectional ties for stability. There was little concrete personal investment in Village institutions beyond small contributions to some of the cooperative enterprises. And in an era of free thought there was no pervasive philosophy that could unify the diverse elements of America's bohemia. For many residence in Greenwich Village represented a transitional phase on the road to maturity, fame, and respectability; therefore, the Village failed to offer an aura of permanence to even those who longed for a stable sense of community within its bounds.[13]

If Greenwich Village failed to provide its inhabitants with an enduring sense of community, it did satisfy many of their more immediate needs. In many instances it freed them from the cash nexus of society, from the workings of an economic order that had victimized many of their families in their youth. The Village was a community in which it was acceptable to live on a marginal income, to ignore saving in favor of present gratification. There was a vacation atmosphere provided by fancy dress balls, all-night poetic orgies, the evenings at Mabel Dodge's salon, or summers with the theatrical crowd at Provincetown. Floyd Dell wrote enthusiastically of his summer at Provincetown with George Cram Cook and Susan Glaspell: "the life at P—— is the life for me. Would that I didn't have to get a job!"[14] For *The Masses'* radicals work often represented merely whatever gainful employment would enable them to work on their own art and writing in their spare time while free from market demands. In Dell's novel *This Mad Ideal* (1925), the young hero, Roy Sopwith, wants to be an artist and tells his sweetheart Judy: "You see, I'm not interested in anything but drawing pictures, and I'll never make any money at that."[15] Roy and Judy at first acquiesce to the small-town mores of Pompton and plan to be married, but they both rebel against the constraints on their creativity, and Roy goes to Boston to study art while Judy foregoes romance to seek a career in New York. They both reject considerations of practicality and prefer to dream impossible dreams in places in which they might come true. One model of the Village hero was the hobo poet Harry Kemp who in his autobiographical novel *More Miles* presents us with the figure of John Gregory, a penniless poet who spends his time in versification and assorted hedonistic pursuits. Gregory finally decides to walk aboard an ocean liner bound for England as a first-class passenger without funds to seek adventure abroad; the reader is left both thrilled and dismayed at his bravado.[16]

To be free of economic responsibility is to have a second chance at child-hood. We have seen the importance that *The Masses'* radicals attached to childhood through an examination of the pervasive cult of youth. Moreover, Freudianism viewed childhood as a time of special creativity and, therefore, provided a rationale for playful or immature behavior in the interests of art. Joseph Freeman states that the worship that Villagers paid to childlike inno-cence may have itself been infantile, but it was a necessary myth for those breaking from unsatisfying conventions of behavior: "To say that the Villagers were children is not to condemn them; it is rather to condemn the civilization which dooms childhood to sterility and pain, and compels so many sensitive spirits to fight grotesquely for a second chance to live."[17]

It was never clear, either in the pre-World War I era or in retrospect, what constituted the rebellious impulse that attracted radicals to Greenwich Village. To some degree radicals could find an escape from social conflict within the Village. Before the Soviet Revolution there was no sense of authoritative ideology, and socialism in this period was a blend of social realism and poetic romanticism: "This accounts for the lyricism of much of *The Masses* verse, for the serious and lengthy discussions on the sexual problem by Floyd Dell. *The Masses* was, after all, a Village magazine. And, somehow, in art conflicts can be resolved in the imagination; or they may be clarified by a visit to a psychoanalyst."[18]

What in other eras might be viewed as a highly personalistic concern with psychological well-being, an individual attack on the constraints of bourgeois morality, at this time was regarded by *The Masses'* radicals as an organic part of their socialist outlook.[19] Max Eastman responded to communist charges of mere bohemianism leveled against him during the height of proletarian real-ism in the mid-1930s by stating that the bohemian desire to live free of bourgeois convention and respectability was akin to the aim of nineteenth-century utopian socialists, that of creating an egalitarian society on a small scale within a capitalist regime. He claimed that even revolutionaries would tend to live such bohemian lives while working to make such a life-style available to all humanity through an attack on capitalism, which restricted it to a few.[20] Eastman informed his critics: "The wish to live a free and real life, and to cherish and communicate its qualities in works of art, deserves the respect of every revolutionist. It is the substitution of this personal revolt, and this impractical communication of qualities, for the practical scientific work of mind or hand that the revolution demands of every free man in its desperate hour—it is that which is to be condemned."[21]

But a number of his former colleagues, most notably Mike Gold (known in the days of *The Masses* as Irwin Granich) and Joseph Freeman, took issue with Eastman's portrayal of the boom years of bohemianism. Freeman argued that the rebellion had been an individualistic attack on bourgeois mores rather than an outright attack on capitalism. He accused bohemians of being too immature and too irresponsible to accept the imposition of social order, whether that order be capitalism or communism. Thus in Freeman's view it was necessary for bohemians to mature politically before they could become committed radicals.[22] It is true that with few exceptions such as John Reed, Mary Heaton Vorse, Mike Gold, and Robert Minor almost none of *The Masses'* radicals entered the post-World War I era in the ranks of a disciplined political organization and that those who did had to sacrifice their bohemian life-styles. Yet by virtue of its example Greenwich Village had impinged deeply upon the public consciousness. By promoting the spread of birth control and popularizing Freudian ideas, Villagers had helped to change the nature of sexual politics in the country at large.

In fact, one might argue that some of the lack of discipline was useful in promoting experimentation and the free flow of ideas. It was possible for reformers and radicals of various political persuasions to meet as friends and acquaintances and to test their beliefs in a number of public forums. The members of *The Masses'* staff and Emma Goldman and her anarchist associates used to frequent the Liberal Club to participate in discussions and to plan joint demonstrations.[23] Mabel Dodge's salon at 23 Fifth Avenue provided a variety of political entertainment that would have done credit on any vaudeville bill:

> "One was sure of an interesting evening at No. 23 Fifth Avenue; but one wondered sometimes what was being aimed at. You might find, for instance, one evening, a learned and eminent professor from Columbia University holding forth enthusiastically on Freud's theory of psychoanalysis to a roomful of absorbed 'high-brows.' Or it might

be that Mr. Haywood of the I. W. W. would be expounding to the unini-
tiated what the I. W. W. really stood for. Or Lincoln Steffens, or Walter
Lippmann, would be talking about 'Good Government'; or a corre-
spondent, just back from Mexico, would be telling about the war, or a
scientist from England would make eugenics a topic; or it might be feminism, or primitive life, or perhaps anarchism would bring a queer
but harmless-looking crowd."[24]

This kind of exchange would have been impossible in a period of ideological
rigidity and strict political discipline such as the Communist party experienced
in the 1920s; free thought was a luxury shared by those who lived before the
revolution.

Nevertheless, despite this aura of freedom, the Village was not devoid of
self-criticism and mechanisms to police itself. Rosabeth Moss Kanter in her
book *Commitment and Community* points out that groups that leave the established order to escape its restrictions often duplicate that very order in their
own internal structures.[25] The Village, too, had its code of behavior, one that
might evade the notice of outsiders while serving to punish social deviance
within the community. Floyd Dell discovered the existence of this code when
he tried to dissolve a free-love alliance with one of the early Villagers to begin
a love affair with a more recent immigrant to bohemia; his friends ostracized
him for his lack of sufficient snobbishness and sexual restraint. Dell later
complained in his autobiography, "The breaking-up of a settled though illegal
domesticity in Greenwich Village appeared to be as great a shock to the
community as the breaking-up of a home in any other part of the United
States."[26]

This high seriousness was intermingled with a sense of humor that allowed
Villagers to poke fun at their most earnest preoccupations. The Provincetown
Players satirized the stormy love adventures of bohemia. Neith Boyce wrote a
play called *Constancy*, which was a witty portrait of the tempestuous romance
of Jack Reed and Mabel Dodge. George Cram Cook and Susan Glaspell wrote
Suppressed Desires to satirize the Freudian fad of the moment.[27] John Reed
composed a long poem entitled *The Day in Bohemia, or Life Among the
Artists* to mock the pretensions of those Villagers who "Talk about talking
and think about thinking, / And swallow each other without even blinking."[28]
The criticism even reached the popular press when Sinclair Lewis wrote
"Hobohemia," which appeared in the *Saturday Evening Post* of 7 April 1917.
"Hobohemia" is a heavy-handed satire of Mabel Dodge's salon, Freudianism,
feminism, literary fads, birth control, eugenics, and various other avant-garde
concerns.[29] To the extent that this rambling article has a point of view, it
seems to uphold the plodding virtues of rural respectability with the merest
leaven of romance. But insofar as it unmasks the puritan lurking behind the

pagan facade—Mrs. Saffron (Mabel Dodge) has a secret back parlor à la Northernapolis—it serves to sharpen the self-analysis of Greenwich Village as much as the more lucid writing of Randolph Bourne.

The Greenwich Village known by *The Masses'* crowd was an ephemeral thing that flourished for several years and then succumbed to the changes wrought by time, its own weaknesses, and the pressures of World War I. As rents began to rise, poor artists and writers could no longer afford to live in the Village. The new people who flocked to the Village were less naive and idealistic than their predecessors, more accustomed to a world devoid of ultimate meaning.[30] The Village lost its isolation from the uptown world of business and respectability, and friendships began to develop between erstwhile Villagers and the uptown folk. Floyd Dell speculated about the death of the old Village as follows:

> Could this be because oneself was becoming bourgeois? Perhaps! For one could hardly possess a talent and exercise it in the Village for several years without attracting some notice from the outside world and beginning to reap some worldly rewards from it. And gradually one discovered in oneself certain bourgeois traits—the desire for, say a house in the country, and children, and a settled life—for one becomes tired even of freedom! Then let the bourgeoisie take Greenwich Village, by all means! We would move to the country, and be respectable![31]

Yet the destruction of the old Village was no accidental product of changes in the market for real estate or art. By 1920 Greenwich Village had developed an ideology that was at least in part inimical to the survival of a radical community. Villagers had come to believe in the necessity of psychological adjustment. They held that if individual repressions could be removed, by resorting to any of a variety of faddish cures—confession to a Freudian analyst, an operation on one's glands, or the practice of some psychophysical discipline as that taught by Gurdjieff—people then could adjust to any situation. Malcolm Cowley in *Exile's Return* complained of the escapist nature of these solutions: "The implication of all these methods is the same—that the environment itself need not be altered. That explains why most radicals who became converted to psychoanalysis or glands or Gurdjieff gradually abandoned their political radicalism."[32] The artistic and the psychological rather than the radical political aspects of Greenwich Village survived. Freudianism degenerated into a mere mechanism of adjustment instead of being used as a means of critiquing social myths. Even though the Village had failed to sustain its promise, those who had migrated to it held fast to their belief in the efficacy of changing place, hence the escape in the 1920s from the Village to the country or to Europe.[33]

The death blow to the old Village was struck by the coming of World War I.

In the days before the war the strains of revolt—the individual and the social, the aesthetic and the political—were hard to distinguish. There was no need for rigid self-definition, and the Villagers enjoyed the freedom offered by flux. The war put an end to such freedom. Rebels against puritanism could continue their existence in safety, but those who chose the course of political radicalism and opposed the war became victims of persecution, jail, and self-imposed exile: "Whatever course they followed, almost all the radicals of 1917 were defeated by events. The bohemian tendency triumphed in the Village, and talk about revolution gave way to talk about psychoanalysis."[34]

Alienation

Life in Greenwich Village provided a context in which radicals could examine some of the problems of urbanization and industrialization. The Village was an oasis in an industrial desert, a place in which remnants of a craft tradition could survive, a community with the closely knit social relations reminiscent of small-town life. Many of the Villagers had come under the influence of John Ruskin and William Morris, English advocates of a return to craftsmanship. Ruskin powerfully affected Carl Sandburg, Van Wyck Brooks, George Cram Cook, and Susan Glaspell.[35] The Villagers tried to lead simple lives free of bourgeois trappings; they donned smocks and sandals in the summer, and took to the production of handicrafts. Anna Alice Chapin, a historian of the Village, noted that the burgeoning interest in craftsmanship had spared the country at large the production of much inferior art. Those who appreciated fine art but could not produce it now could immigrate to the Village and find a sense of vocation: "I know of nothing which is so typical or so significant in all the Village as this new urge toward good craftsmanship, elementary poetic design,—the fundamentals of a utilitarian, beautiful and pervading art life apart from clay or canvas."[36] However, Ruskin's influence by implication could lead in either of two directions, "into more radical socialism or toward the dangerous doctrine of art for its own sake."[37]

The concern with craftsmanship was a response to the alienation generated by the new industrial order. Marx and Engels had explicated the nature of alienation under capitalist production, most notably in Engels's *Anti-Dühring* and Marx's 1844 Manuscripts. They condemned the separation between the city and the country that consigned rural life to stagnation, the mechanization of labor that robbed work of its creative purpose and reduced it to a means of sustaining life, whatever the personal expense.[38] Under industrial capitalism men and women could no longer live in an organic relationship with nature and as a result became estranged from themselves and from mankind.[39] Marx and Engels assumed that alienation could not be eradicated under capitalism, that only under communism could all work be meaningful and fulfilling.[40]

American liberals approached the discussion of alienation as freshly as if Marx and Engels never had broached the subject. Herbert Croly, one of the leading ideologues of progressivism, so detested the profit motive that he advocated a society close to pure communism while repudiating contemporary Marxism.[41] Like the Marxists, Croly was dismayed by the fragmentation of industrial life, but his solution was that of a reformer: "The only way in which work can be made entirely disinterested is to adjust its compensation to the needs of a normal and wholesome life."[42] By ignoring the complexity of the Marxist critique, Croly's solution evaded the problems posed by the alienating nature of the industrial process per se and failed to raise the issue of whether capitalism could afford to offer such generous compensation to its workers.

Alienation also posed a challenge to educators faced with the problems of preparing workers for life in an industrial world. John Dewey supplied a critique of alienation in *Democracy and Education* (1916). He argued that mass production fragmented the nature of work so that each worker came to view his own input solely in terms of the pay derived rather than in being able to understand the collective and social aspects of labor.[43] Dewey assumed that most workers lacked insight into the social aims of their work and took no direct personal interest in them because their employers determined such goals and enforced them by the payment of wages. Therefore, he held that it would be illiberal and immoral to educate workers for participation in such an unfree activity.[44] Yet Dewey weakened his argument by implying that if workers could be taught to comprehend the collective purpose behind industrial production, the atomization of work could be ended.[45] He also realized that specialization tended to create a regimen adapted to the dynamic of machinery rather than to human needs.[46] To the extent that this situation could not be modified in a competitive world, education would be reduced to an instrument of adjustment, a means of providing an intellectual rationale for unsatisfying and alienating work.

Radicals, too, were concerned with alienation, but they were less hopeful regarding a general solution for the problem under capitalism. Their theories often derived from firsthand factory experience, as in the case of Emma Goldman and Floyd Dell, or at least from the observation of workers' lives, as in the case of Hutchins Hapgood. Emma Goldman complained that mass society, with its emphasis on sheer quantity, was destroying pride in craftsmanship and creating a class of "brainless, incompetent automatons, who turn out enormous quantities of things, valueless to themselves, and generally injurious to the rest of mankind."[47] Work needed to be endowed with a transcendent purpose to be rendered meaningful. For Hutchins Hapgood the plight of modern workers was that they were robbed not only of the material result of their labor but also of the very ideal of work.[48] Hapgood had a sanative view of labor. In his view work could provide a buffer between sensitive nerves and intense life experience, so that when work became fragmentary or intermittent, workers would be forced into strenuous personal relations and would find life overbearing.[49]

In his youth Floyd Dell worked in a candy factory in Davenport, Iowa. Unlike Hapgood, Dell found no escape from reality in work. His destiny as a factory hand would thwart his true vocation, for if he thought about poetry on the job, he would be fired.[50] Dell did write an exposé of factory work for the socialistic *Tri-City Workers Magazine*. Under the pseudonym of "Sally Thompson," Dell described the boredom, difficulties, and danger of the industrial process. Like Emma Goldman and Upton Sinclair in *The Jungle* (1906), Dell believed that the products of such factories often were manufactured under unsanitary conditions and were dangerous to an unsuspecting public.[51] There could be no pride in such a shoddy product. Dell's critique of alienation was Freudian rather than Marxian in nature; he emphasized the psychological deprivation felt by the individual rather than the collective dislocation. Dell's focus on personal psychology becomes most apparent in his later attempts to analyze modern love and family life. In *Love in the Machine Age: A Psychological Study of the Transition from Patriarchal Society* (1930) Dell wrote that "our civilization will have to realize that work is not the instinctive center of our human lives and that love is; that work gains its chief emotional and practical importance as a means, not of *self*-support, but of *mutual* support of those who are joined together in mate-love and family-love."[52]

The solutions offered by radicals to the problems of alienation tended to be short-range and personalistic or long-range and collective. But it is important to realize that radicals were not disinterested observers of the situation. They, too, were victims of alienation and sought refuge in the collective life offered by the Village community. Moreover, economic conditions were creating a new class of disadvantaged, the "college proletarians." As educational institutions flooded the country with doctors, lawyers, professors, teachers, and scientists who competed against one another in the fight for the few available places, college graduates found themselves bereft of any assurance of employment or economic security. As a result, colleges filled with protest against social wrongs, and college-trained workers began to discover an identity of interest with manual laborers. Radicals hoped that both classes of workers would join in the battle for "the elimination of industrial tyranny."[53]

A personal solution to the problems of alienation was readily available to those who immigrated to Greenwich Village. Those who were dissatisfied with the conditions of work imposed by the demands of the art market or of professional journalism could opt for work with art collectives or join in the cooperative production of *The Masses*. Many worked on a free-lance basis according to their own rhythms of production. The craft tradition continued to flourish on Village soil while the problems of industry were consigned to the uptown world; Villagers intervened only when on a crusade. Occasionally Villagers would attempt to take refuge from the complexities of modern life by creating a community that would value older virtues, one in which a simpler, more integrated life would be possible. Susan Glaspell, cofounder with George Cram Cook of the Provincetown Players, wrote of Provincetown: "Life was all of a piece, work not separated from play."[54] The solution proved initially satisfying, but Provincetown was buffeted by the war and did not outlast the temptations of commercial theatrical success. Most of the institutions created by Villagers to deal with the problems of alienation lay in ruins after World War I; those who believed in personal solutions tended to continue their quest in the suburbs or in Europe. The Village was left to the cynics.

Political radicals posed more comprehensive solutions. Hutchins Hapgood believed that alienation compelled workers to seek an ideal outside their own labor; hence many of them became anarchists, trade unionists, free lovers, and socialists.[55] The critique of alienation posed a much more fundamental threat to capitalism than the wage-and-hours demands of ordinary trade unionism. Walter Lippmann warned the public that syndicalism, with its protest against the destruction of pride in work, evoked some of the deepest and most explosive human emotions. In *A Preface to Politics* Lippmann wrote:

> I believe too that the fighting qualities of syndicalism are kept at the boiling point by a greater sense of outraged human dignity than can be found among mere socialists or unionists. The imagination is more vivid: the horror of capitalism is not alone in the poverty and suffering it entails, but in its ruthless denial of life to millions of men. The most cruel of all denials is to deprive a human being of joyous activity. Syndicalism is shot through with the assertion that an imposed drudgery is intolerable—that labor at a subsistence wage as a cog in a meaningless machine is no condition upon which to found civilization. That is a new kind of revolt—more dangerous to capitalism than the demand for higher wages.[56]

Although many of the Villagers displayed a general sympathy with these new demands of labor, few of them made any theoretical contributions to the subject. The Industrial Workers of the World did commit themselves to training workers under capitalism for their future responsibilities as members of a cooperative commonwealth, but the complicated structures devised for such training disintegrated in the organizational chaos and persecution experienced by the IWW.[57] John Reed was one of the few Villagers to deal explicitly with the problems of worker control. After the Bolshevik Revolution he wrote an article in *Revolutionary Age* in which he pointed out that it would be difficult to achieve worker control in America as a result of the specialization of labor. He recommended the formation of shop committees to study the problems of factory production in the belief that workers thus would discover the inefficiency and exploitative nature of capitalism. In this process of discovery they would come to learn the techniques of control. "It is not only necessary," Reed wrote, "to plan the political downfall of the capitalist class, but also to get into the minds of the workers some conception of the industrial framework which will underlie the new socialist political commonwealth."[58] Reed's solution had the twin advantage of combating worker anomie while providing a positive structure within which social change could be produced. The liberal approach to alienation involved changes in worker compensation or education that would leave the industrial process virtually untouched; the personal approach was little more than a temporary escape. Only the radical solution faced the problem in its full complexity, and its failure does not detract from the valor of the attempt.

The Anti-Urban Tone

In many ways Greenwich Village was an attempt to correct one of the alienating aspects of industrial life, the separation between the country and the city. New York's bohemian community tried to re-create the American village with its intimate, closely knit social relations. The Village was filled with men and women born and raised in the country who disdained the impersonal nature of the life led by uptowners, who lived in the heart of the metropolis. They preferred the informality and isolation of the Village in the prewar days.

Although many of the Village radicals enjoyed the diversity and cultural opportunities offered by urban life, they continued to cherish the bucolic ideal. Max Eastman, Floyd Dell, and Malcolm Cowley all shared the belief that no poet born in the country could endure city life.[59] Eastman in his semiautobiographical novel *Venture* presents us with a hero, the poet Jo Hancock (John Reed), who needs to escape from the tyrannies of life in the metropolis. Jo takes a railroad trip away from New York City to the farmlands: "He felt as though he had solved the chief problem of his future life in the metropolis, the problem of getting away quickly into the real country where men and animals walk on the ground and live."[60] Throughout his life Floyd Dell, too, found peace and fulfillment in communion with nature. He resented the encroachments of industrialism on the rural landscape; "theoretically approving the machine age as the blessed means through which the co-operative commonwealth should be brought into being," the youthful Dell mourned the loss of his "breathing space" to a factory "in stanzas of grief and indignation."[61] Eventually his needs as an artist impelled him to detach himself from the immediacies of politics by taking up residence in the country to renew his contacts with "the ageless and timeless aspects of nature, which afford refreshment to the restless mind."[62] Another of the poets of *The Masses*, Clement Wood, wrote dreadful poetry imbued with rural nostalgia, most notably "The Return," a poem based on the back-to-the-earth theme with such eminently forgettable lines as "Shall I refuse to look at the moon, / Until it adopts an 8-hour day?"[63] Some of the attention paid to nature may be attributable to the conventions of romantic verse, for Eastman, Dell, and Wood were all traditionalists in style, but their love of country life was quite genuine.

The country was seen as a repository of ancient virtues. Under the influence of Tolstoi and Kropotkin, George Cram Cook decided to take up farming and write during the winter months when the land lay fallow. Dissatisfied with the life of an academic at Stanford, Cook sought an "escape from overintellectuality": "The farmer-writer would be a healthier person, a more rounded personality, than the professor-writer."[64] In practice the country did not provide Cook with adequate stimulus for creative thought and writing, yet he could not bring himself to abandon the rural ideal. On 4 October 1904 he confided to his journal, "The chief drawback of the rural life as it opens before me is its isolation. No stimulating people. Will it be possible to draw around us a community—a less visionary Brook Farm?"[65] The theatrical community at Provincetown a decade later was the fulfillment of that dream.

The reverence for country life at times approached religious awe. For Sherwood Anderson the urban environment destroyed his ability to pray; he had to take to the fields to find his way back to God.[66] He felt ashamed of the way in which he had allowed the luxuries of the city to corrupt him and make him neglect the lessons of nature and his own "gods forgotten in the fields."[67] Anderson believed that the country supplied a natural order for human life, that it regulated conduct according to higher law while the city, impersonal and avaricious, spawned disorder and chaos. This notion underlies Anderson's novel *Marching Men* (1917), which assumes that the city is such a center of vice and anomie that any means of unifying urban workers, no matter how mindless or crude, has ultimate value. The agrarian myth appears full-blown in Anderson's description of Chicago:

> Chicago is one vast gulf of disorder. Here is the passion for gain,
> the very spirit of the bourgeoise [*sic*] gone drunk with desire. The result
> is something terrible. Chicago is leaderless, purposeless, slovenly, down
> at the heels.

And back of Chicago lie the long corn fields that are not disorderly. There is hope in the corn. Spring comes and the corn is green. It shoots up out of the black land and stands up in orderly rows. The corn grows and thinks of nothing but growth. Fruition comes to the corn and it is cut down and disappears. Barns are filled to bursting with the yellow fruit of the corn.

And Chicago has forgotten the lesson of the corn. All men have forgotten. It has never been told to the young men who come out of the corn fields to live in the city.[68]

Anderson was not alone in his distrust of city life. At this time the existence of widespread and thriving commercialized prostitution in American cities reached public attention and provided "the basis for a blanket indictment of urban living."[69] One of the prewar radicals to feel most keenly the existence of urban vice was Upton Sinclair, who supplied posterity with a portrait of New York City in *The Metropolis* (1908) that would have done credit as a description of the latter days of the Roman Empire. Sinclair was preoccupied with the unnatural vices of the urban leisure classes and feared that these would spread like a pestilence to the rest of the country.[70] It is interesting to note that Sinclair echoes Anderson's belief in a natural order, which is rural and productive, as opposed to manmade chaos, which is urban and sterile. Sinclair's portrait of New York confronts us with a city in which beauty fails in the struggle with ugliness and disorder:

It was a city which had grown up by accident, with nobody to care about it or to help it; it was huge and ungainly, crude, uncomfortable, and grotesque. . . . Nowhere was any order or system—everything was struggling for itself, and jarring and clashing with everything else; and this broke the spell of power which the Titan city would otherwise have produced. It seemed like a monstrous heap of wasted energies; a mountain in perpetual labour, and producing an endless series of abortions. The men and women in it were wearing themselves out with toil; but there was a spell laid upon them, so that, struggle as they might, they accomplished nothing.[71]

The obvious question to answer is why people so deeply attracted to country life remained in the city for so many years. For someone like George Cram Cook the answer lies in his inability to cope with the isolation imposed by rural living. On the positive side Greenwich Village offered a small, friendly community in which like-minded souls might congregate free from the prejudices they would encounter scattered across the countryside. In the city one could find the stimulus for artistic labor and political involvement available nowhere else.

Some Villagers tried to escape from their problems via a return to nature, but the experiments failed. When Max Eastman's marriage to Ida Rauh began to disintegrate, he decided to focus his "defeated forces of rebellion" against something he associated with his surrender to his wife, namely city life. In his autobiography he confessed, "If I couldn't be free, I would at least be rural." Eastman then imposed eight months of rural housekeeping in Tenafly, New Jersey, upon his family, discovered that his muse did not frequent Tenafly, and found his marriage in no way improved by a country idyll graced by a bout with poison ivy.[72] Art Young, too, tried to renew his marriage by moving his wife and family to a farm south of Bethel, Connecticut. But the return to nature failed of its purpose. Young deplored the "excess of conventional sameness" in his life, could not concentrate on his art, and admitted that he "was simply no longer equal to the duties and courtesies of married life."[73] As a result, he abandoned his bucolic existence, returned to New York, and began to use his art in the service of his anticapitalist ideology.[74]

No matter how ugly or disordered the city might be, its problems lay heavily upon the consciences of prewar radicals and reformers. Those problems had such immediacy that they undermined any easy hopes of rural escapism. Arthur Bullard in *A Man's World* presents us with a vignette of social work in the slums. A hard-working nurse, who works against overwhelming odds to combat dirt and disease, inspires a cynical young social worker to similar commitment:

> I had seen so much I could never forget. It was something from which there was no escape. No matter how glorious the open fields, there would always be the remembered stink of the tenements in my nostrils. The vision of a sunken-cheeked, tuberculosis-ridden pauper would always rise between me and the beauty of the sunset. A crowd of hurrying ghosts—the ghosts of the slaughtered babies—would follow me everywhere, crying "Edward," if I ran away. The slums had taken me captive.[75]

As long as there was a sense that the battle for social justice could be fought and won on urban soil, radicals remained in the city and lived in hope.

Chapter 5 The Sexual Revolution

Sex O'Clock in America

With the rise of industrialization in the nineteenth century and the accompanying problems of alienation, there was a growing separation between work and personal life among the proletariat. Those who could no longer rely on their ownership of property to define their right to community esteem turned to the subjectivity of the family in order to establish a sense of identity and self-worth: "The proletariat itself came to share the bourgeois ideal of the family as a 'utopian retreat.' "[1] At the same time that personal life grew more crucial to individual self-esteem there was a dissolution of the moral authority of the family as a result of urban conditions.[2] The freedom from moral scrutiny that cities provided weakened methods of social control so drastically that a "revolution in manners and morals" occurred during the Progressive era well before the first rumbles of the Roaring Twenties.[3]

The most intimate aspect of personal life—sexual behavior—became a focus of public discussion. If the "repeal of reticence" meant that the "conspiracy of silence" on the subject of sex had been broken, many worried that the new concern with sexuality verged on obsession.[4] The tone of popular magazines reflected the general dismay: "A wave of sex hysteria and sex discussion seems to have invaded this country. Our former reticence in matters of sex is giving way to a frankness that could even startle Paris. Prostitution, as *Life* remarks, is the chief topic of polite conversation. It has struck 'sex o'clock' in America, to use William Marion Reedy's memorable phrase."[5] For bohemians, talk about sex helped to clarify the ambiguities of their nonconformist life-style, and for artists it provided a means of breaking free from the narrow confines of romantic tradition to discuss the whole of life, to recognize lust as well as love. In his Chicago period Sherwood Anderson wrote approvingly of the "healthy new frankness . . . in the talk between men and women, at least an admission that we were all at times torn and harried by the same lusts."[6] Aside from improving personal relations, the new

74

frankness injected a note of realism into art. Anderson said of his literary cohorts: "I do not think that any of us, at that time, wanted to over play [*sic*] sex. We wanted in our stories and novels to bring it back into its real relation to the life we lived and saw others living."[7]

The demand for honesty in relationships surfaces through some of the worst romantic claptrap. In *The Heart's Country* Mary Heaton Vorse presents us with a heroine, Ellen Payne, who acknowledges that love does not abide forever and prefers that the man she loves, Roger Byington, deal honestly with his emotions rather than pursue a course of "cowardly drifting" in order to preserve social amenities.[8] Although the rest of the novel never deviates from its pursuit of the romantic cliché, here we have a note of real freedom from the myth that love is true and eternal. Emma Goldman held similar views to those of Vorse about the inability to coerce love through duty or institutional restraints. The demand that these two women raise is for personal honesty to stand in lieu of the false pieties of Victorianism.

Among the earliest critics of sexual mores were the purity crusaders of the late nineteenth century, a diverse group of women, doctors, prohibitionists, and progressives who championed a single standard of sexual morality "not only for both sexes, but for all classes as well."[9] Feminists were especially interested in the right of married women to control access to their bodies in order to safeguard wives from sexual abuse by their husbands. They demanded feminine control of the male child's moral education and an end to sexual segregation in childhood as the only means of achieving a uniform moral code among adults.[10]

Twentieth-century feminists, even when unconcerned with the problem of social purity, joined their predecessors in attacks on the double standard. Susan Glaspell in *The Visioning* (1911) condemns the hypocrisy of treating a woman's "past" as more damning and self-destructive than the sexual meanderings of the male.[11] Glaspell believed that the double standard victimized both those women who observed the code and those who defied it. Conventional morality encouraged "good" women to flirt, trifle, and skim the surface of life while other women were forced into desperately serious lives of sin. As a result, both categories of women were denied healthy, open, committed sexual experience.[12] The anarchist Emma Goldman carried her crusade for sexual equality to the lecture platform. She would climax her lectures on the subject by daring any man present who had no premarital sexual experience to stand up. Few ever did, and those few merely substantiated her main point, that men lived by a different standard of morality than that expected of women.[13]

Demands for greater honesty in sexual relations and for an end to the double standard were presented both by socially conservative reformers and by bohemians. The reforms proposed could serve equally well to foster social control or to encourage greater sexual freedom. Similarly the growing support for sex education for the young reflected the concerns of moral reformers regardless of the conservatism or liberalism with which they approached other social issues. As divorce increased, there was growing public recognition of the need to begin training for marriage at an early age. Most advanced writers included not only moral training but instruction in sex hygiene and physiology in their prescriptions.[14] Even such an eminent conservative as Charles W. Eliot, about the time he retired from the presidency of Harvard University in 1911, argued that public schools should teach physiology more frankly: "We have got to get rid of the idea which has been taught us for thousands of years, that man is born in sin. The transmission of life is the sacredest and holiest thing in life. We must get rid of those monstrous things brought down to us from Leviticus."[15]

In an industrialized urban society community vigilance was inadequate to protect the young against sexual perils. Unwanted pregnancy and venereal disease among children could not be prevented by relying on the supervision of family and neighbors; social controls had to be internalized to be effective. Lincoln Steffens in *Upbuilders* (1909) presents us with a portrait of Judge Ben Lindsey of the County Court of Denver, a reformer dedicated to spreading sexual knowledge among the young. From his personal experience with juvenile offenders and their friends, Lindsey knew that "parental ignorance and Anglo-Saxon prudery" never helped to maintain childhood innocence. Instead children obtained their knowledge of sex from the vilest sources and seldom failed to put that knowledge into practice.[16] The judge was especially concerned with the resulting promiscuity among little girls, the future mothers of the race.[17]

This concern was echoed by James Oppenheim in his novel *Wild Oats* (1910), a tragedy of sexual ignorance. An innocent seventeen-year-old Jewish typist, Edith Kroll, whom the author dubs the "wild-rose," falls in love with a salesman, Frank Lasser, a man who has led the life of a rogue but who succumbs to her beauty and purity and decides to wed her. He believes himself cured of venereal disease and resists the warning of Edith's hero, the physician of the slums, Dr. Rast, that he should postpone their marriage until a complete cure is effected. Denied the knowledge that would save her, Edith weds him, and a year later their marital happiness is blighted by the birth of a girl baby blinded by gonorrhea and by Edith's own weakness resulting from the disease.[18] For the author sex education was dedicated to the service of the cult of motherhood; it would not free women to seek new forms of sexual self-expression but rather would safeguard their ability to find fulfillment within their traditional sphere.[19]

Socialists and anarchists tended to view the treatment of sex simply as an integral part of a normal education. William English Walling, the left-wing socialist, wanted sex education to be integrated into the study of biology, physiology, history, and literature. Walling, like the Freudians, recognized the existence of childhood sexuality and saw the need to channel healthy sexual impulses for educational ends: "But to attempt to repress all reference to sex matters is not only to misrepresent life generally, to leave young people unprotected against mistaken impressions, and to drive them to strange courses; it is also to deprive education of the keenest impulse that urges human beings to learning and all activity, especially at this age."[20] Emma Goldman in her lectures on modern drama struck the same note. In discussing Frank Wedekind's *The Awakening of Spring*, she argued that knowledge of their own sexuality was vital to children:

> The play deals with a group of school children just entering the
> age of puberty,—imaginative beings speculating about the mysteries of
> life. *Wendla*, sent to her grave by her loving but prudish mother, is
> an exquisite, lovable child; *Melchior*, the innocent father of *Wendla*'s
> unborn baby, is a gifted boy whose thirst for knowledge leads him to
> inquire into the riddle of life, and to share his observations with his
> school chums,—a youth who, in a free and intelligent atmosphere,
> might have developed into an original thinker. That such a boy should
> be punished as a moral pervert, only goes to prove the utter unfitness
> of our parents and educators.[21]

Whether sex education for the young was seen as a means of preventing unwanted pregnancy and disease or as a means of enriching education and channeling childhood sexual awareness, such instruction could serve the social imperatives of conservatives as well as radicals. It was almost inevitable that the conditions of urban life would prompt moral reformers to take up the issue of sex education.

The real sexual revolution involved an attack upon marriage and the family, for the challenge to these institutions would divide radicals from conservatives. In her influential book *Woman and Labour* the British feminist Olive Schreiner argued that humanity had progressed beyond a concern with mere physical replication to the recognition "that sex and the sexual relation between man and woman have distinct aesthetic, intellectual, and spiritual functions and ends apart entirely from physical reproduction."[22] Such a notion represented a forthright attack on the Victorian belief that the only legitimate form of sexual expression was intercourse within context of marriage, strictly for the purpose of reproduction. A more extreme version of the emphasis on sexual fulfillment came from Havelock Ellis, whose prolific work on human sexuality found an eager audience among contemporary radicals in the United States. Ellis argued that intercourse was an entirely private matter that became the concern of the state only when children were born. He advocated trial unions to insure sexual compatibility in marriage but admitted that there was no way to guarantee lifelong fidelity so that it was best to avoid extracting such promises: "The new ideal of sexual hygiene, then, was an experienced couple, who filled each other's sexual needs, and for whom, it is probably fair to say, children were a secondary consideration."[23]

Margaret Sanger met Havelock Ellis while in exile in England and invoked him as the "guiding spirit" in her study of birth control.[24] She ascribed to him a peculiar insight into the nature and needs of women: "To women he may indeed seem a god-sent liberator."[25] Under Ellis's influence Sanger returned to America, in the words of Mabel Dodge, "an ardent propagandist for the joys of the flesh."[26] In turn, Mabel Dodge fought her own bourgeois tendencies in order to have a flaming affair with the journalist John Reed, and she made her salon a forum for such previously taboo topics as sex, psychoanalysis, and birth control.[27]

Free love, divorce, and communal housekeeping arrangements all seemed to pose threats to the nuclear family. Certainly many Villagers refused to subscribe to the bourgeois notion that the best way to deal with gratification was to postpone it. This carpe diem attitude is particularly clear in Louise Bryant's play *The Game*, a stock allegory in which Life and Death contend for the lives of a poet and a dancer bent on suicide; predictably enough, love triumphs and death is averted. Life appeals to the girl to live for the moment, implicitly suggesting that the future is even more uncertain than the present, hence undermining the basis for middle-class caution:

> Life: (*To Girl.*) Why ask too much of me? I can only give happiness
> for a moment—but it is real happiness—Love, Creation, Unity
> with the tremendous rhythm of the universe. I can't promise it
> will endure. I won't say you will not some day be forgotten.
> What if it is himself he loves in you? That, too, is Love.
> Girl: To be supremely happy for a moment—an hour—that is worth
> living for![28]

But the pursuit of pleasure did not come easily to *The Masses'* radicals. One has only to read the autobiographies of Max Eastman, Floyd Dell, Mabel Dodge, or Hutchins Hapgood, or the letters of Randolph Bourne, to see the puritan lurking behind each pagan gesture. Sex is seldom truly spontaneous; it is fraught with responsibility. Casual sex is seen as a moral lapse and is sufficient cause for the dissolution of marriage, as in the cases of Eastman and Dell.[29] Hutchins Hapgood, in concluding his autobiography, evokes the spirit of high seriousness with which those raised in the Victorian era viewed sexuality:

I think that my book shows clearly that my Victorianism is in the background of all my political and social interests. Also, though less obviously, it is there when I am dealing with sex. In the simple and casual way in which many of these experiences are told, I am miles away from the modern youth of today, who would leave such things out as too obvious. The reason we Victorians put such things in as important in our lives is because in our imagination some of the mystic inheres in the simplest act; something of the symbolic marriage, in at least an insignificant degree, is always there. This is incomprehensible to the modern imagination, so that to make the casual relationship interesting, it has to be told in sophisticated manner, otherwise it is omitted.[30]

At times the New Freedom seemed more apparent than real. William L. O'Neill in *Divorce in the Progressive Era* argues that "the Village had freed itself from wedlock only to replace the old slavery with a way of life that was sometimes hardly distinguishable from marriage itself, except for being a good deal more exacting."[31] We have seen the stream of reproach that greeted Floyd Dell's dissolution of his three-year affair with an old Villager. When this apostle of the "free union" not only married in practice but also printed a defense of marriage and babies in theory, according to Joseph Freeman, "it meant practically the sexual counterrevolution."[32] Many other Village radicals—Max Eastman and Ida Rauh, John Reed and Louise Bryant, Hutchins Hapgood and Neith Boyce, Susan Glaspell and George Cram Cook—also married in practice but sought to maintain their separate identities, at least in name. However, these marriages were characterized by the same expectations of conjugal fidelity as the most bourgeois unions; although Villagers often claimed that marriage was merely a concession to social pressure, they did view it as a serious commitment.[33]

If the sexual revolution failed in its attack on marriage and the family, if the concessions to convention were often all too obvious, nevertheless, it did manage to illuminate new areas of sexual experience and to popularize Freudianism in America. Not only did sex become a topic of public discussion, but it was discovered to exist where no Victorian would have considered looking for it, namely among women and children. With the growing interest in Freud came the first recognition among American intellectuals of the universality of sex. It was no longer possible to view sexuality as a monopoly of the marital state. A fragment of a fictional conversation reported by Elsie Clews Parsons for *The Masses* of July 1915 in an article entitled "Privacy in Love Affairs" highlighted the implications of the new awareness. A Respectable Married Woman argues that mating should be a strictly private matter. She rejects both the proprietary theory which held that marriage was merely the public announcement of the sexual monopoly of the male and the feminist contention

John Reed and Louise Bryant at Croton
Courtesy Houghton Library, Harvard University

that marriage was advantageous because it automatically limited the sexual advances made to a woman. To the Married Woman it was the very universality of sex that rendered it a perfect instrument of individual expression; she replies: "Why keep sex so tagged and docketed? So shunted off from human relations? Sex is a part of every personality, and into any personal relations between a man and a woman it naturally enters—more or less. Whether more or less is to be decided for itself in each case, otherwise a relationship isn't personal at all, it's impersonal, a status relationship, a relationship of the old order."[34]

The initial demand for the recognition of female sexuality in particular came from free-love proponents and women's rights advocates in the nineteenth century.[35] The free-love defenders assumed that celibacy was unnatural and dangerous for men and women alike.[36] Their twentieth-century counterparts in Greenwich Village were equally loathe to deny the demands of the flesh. They assumed the right of women to find sexual gratification, whether in free-love unions or in marriage. There is some evidence in the early twentieth century to indicate that men began to feel a greater sense of personal responsibility for the sexual satisfaction of their mates. One index of the new concern with female sexuality is the proliferation of books dealing with the subject. For example, a single page of advertisements for *The Masses* Book Shop in the May 1917 issue of *The Masses* offers five books dealing with the physiological, social, and psychological aspects of the sexual life of women.[37]

This sensitivity to female sexuality is particularly apparent in an early poem by Floyd Dell, "I Doubted Not" (1906), in which the author attempts to describe a young girl's initiation into sexual love, including the experience of orgasm from the female perspective. Dell later commented on the task that this literary experiment set for the young poet both as artist and lover:

> The experience he gives the girl in his poem is no paltry experience.
> It approaches the violence of a volcanic eruption. And it sets for himself
> a high standard in respect to the capacity to evoke in his partner this
> magnificent response. This is a matter to be taken seriously. Unselfish-
> ness is required, patience, and self-control. In this realm, according
> to his views, reckless masculine self-indulgence is contemptible. Phy-
> sically as well as spiritually, love is a responsible and egalitarian
> relationship.[38]

Recognition of the legitimacy of the female sexual drive, coupled with the male willingness to gratify it, spelled a dramatic change in sexual politics. If sexual equality were to exist at this level of utmost intimacy, it was only natural that it be extended throughout the spheres of social, economic, and political life.[39] A feminism that extended to the bedroom could not reduce the demand for female equality to the question of suffrage; it recognized that changes in the economic sphere as well as in marriage and family life would have to accompany the transformation of relations between the sexes.

Another, though less prominent, aspect of the sexual revolution was the growing recognition and acceptance of homosexuality. The poetry of Walt Whitman with its celebration of the love of man for man served to legitimize the expression of homosexual emotion. Sherwood Anderson invoked Whitman in his memoirs when he insisted on the need to proclaim male love if men were ever to regain emotional control of their lives.[40] Against the advice of her fellow anarchists, Emma Goldman took to the lecture platform to inveigh against the persecution directed against homosexuals. She sympathized with those who confided to her that they had struggled for years to avoid accepting society's image of them as victims of a shameful affliction, and she offered them a refuge within anarchism. Goldman later wrote of her response to the plight of homosexuals: "To me anarchism was not a mere theory for a distant future; it was a living influence to free us from inhibitions, internal no less than external, and from the destructive barriers that separate man from man."[41]

As women began to gain economic independence and public recognition of their sexual needs, it became possible for at least some of them to admit their own homosexual feelings. The growing support for free motherhood as championed by Max Eastman, Isadora Duncan, and Rose Pastor Stokes among others contained the underlying assumption that if freed from economic dependency upon men, women might sever sexual and affectional ties with men as well.[42] There was a gradual realization that women might find fulfillment apart from the reflected glory of the men with whom they were associated by marriage and family ties. For example, in his review of a production of *Getting Married* by George Bernard Shaw *The Masses'* drama critic Charles W. Wood claimed that there were thousands of women like Shaw's Lesbia who wanted children without the subsequent encumbrance of a husband. Wood believed that if romantic heterosexual love could not be preserved within marriage, it was better to avoid marriage than to kill romance.[43] This notion falls far short of an endorsement of lesbianism, but it does undermine the primacy of heterosexual love for women.

Although all of the women associated with *The Masses* were heterosexual by preference and many were married or had male lovers, two of them, Margaret Sanger and Mabel Dodge, aware of homosexual tendencies in their past, appreciated the validity of the love adolescent girls felt for one another. Sanger stressed the purity of these adolescent relations, which, she held, rarely involved physical sex expression, and she claimed that such love was as vital as sunshine and air for growth into womanhood.[44] On the other hand, Mabel Dodge's sexuality was a crazy-quilt pattern of tenderness and pure venom. As a girl she disdained men like her Uncle Carlos who desired her and was repelled by the brutality of Frank Wiley, a childhood sweetheart, when he moved from tenderness to passion. Both left her cold. She preferred the innocence and tranquillity of girlhood and feminine affection. In her *Intimate Memories* she supplies the reader with several portraits of homosexual encounters in her youth ranging from morbid curiosity (her pummeling of the naked breast of a sleeping maid) through various stages of alienated affection (loving the breasts of her friend Margaret Strane while indifferent to the girl herself) to the exquisite sensuality of her love for Violet Shillito: "It was a more delicious life I felt in me than I had ever felt before. I thought it was a superior kind of living too."[45] In fact, when dissatisfied in her marriage with Edwin Dodge, she sought revenge and refuge in love relations with women.[46]

Although such awareness of homosexuality is largely personal in implication, it does serve to undermine a rigid Victorian definition of sex and to create in the individual a sense of sexual ambiguity. To acknowledge in oneself socially unacceptable sexual tendencies is to reject the most intimate expression of social control. Whereas the sexual revolution was potentially radical, it never was adequately integrated into a socialist perspective that could explain the nature of authority and control in American society. The revolution in manners and morals that did occur in pre-World War I America left unchanged the economic and political balance of power.

The Coming of Sigmund Freud

The stage was set for the introduction of psychoanalysis to America long before the main actor in the drama, Sigmund Freud, made his initial appearance at the now historic Clark University conference of 1909. America in the early twentieth century had arrived at a stage of wealth and leisure that made possible a concern with personal life and the mental well-being of disaffected individuals. At this time a segment of the medical profession rebelled against the pessimistic attitude of current psychiatry and neurology and began to experiment with means of adapting patients to their environment. As a logical corollary of this process, the more forward-looking psychiatrists acknowledged a need to change that environment and found themselves committed to programs of social meliorism and part of the wave of Progressive reform.[47] Progressive psychiatry and psychology were imbued with optimistic social reformism absent from the corresponding European professional literature.[48] Psychoanalysis met with initial success in America because it coincided in time with the first stage of the moral revolution—the repeal of reticence—and because it seemed to coincide in tone with the optimism and ethical realism of the Progressives.[49] American psychoanalysts hoped to use sublimation to harness the errant sexual drives of their patients; though their rhetoric may have appeared revolutionary, they themselves remained committed to a faith in "civilized" morality and ethical progress.[50]

The artists and radicals who lived in Greenwich Village were equally ready to respond to the appeal of Freudianism. The Village had a traditional interest in the various sciences and pseudosciences of the mind. Old Village figures Edgar Allan Poe and Walt Whitman in a previous generation had been serious advocates of phrenology.[51] As we have seen, the Villagers of the early twentieth century had conducted various experiments with mind-altering drugs. Products of the Victorian world, they hoped to use Freudianism to free themselves from artistic and sexual inhibitions to rebel more effectively against the "civilized" morality and political liberalism of the Progressives.

Freud came to America with a flourish. In September 1909 he and his colleague, Carl Jung, came to Clark University in Worcester, Massachusetts, at the invitation of its president, G. Stanley Hall, to present German-language addresses in celebration of the university's twentieth anniversary. Freud was amazed at the scholarly attention that his work had received and at the respect American audiences accorded his ideas: "In prudish America it was possible, at least in academic circles, to discuss freely and scientifically everything that in ordinary life is regarded as objectionable."[52] In the view of G. Stanley Hall, the spread of Freudianism in the United States owed "most of its initial momentum" to Freud's lectures at Clark.[53]

Although the debut of Freudianism was a scholarly one, popularization soon followed. The earliest mention of Freudian theory in America came in an article entitled "The Psychopathology of Everyday Life" by Boris Sidis in the *Journal of Abnormal Psychology* in 1906.[54] In the next few years medical periodicals were full of references to Freudianism, and by 1910 there were allusions to the new psychology, most of them disapproving, in the popular press.[55] Meanwhile an American psychologist, Abraham A. Brill, arranged to translate some of the works of Freud and Jung for presentation to an American audience.[56] The impact of the academies on the popular acceptance of Freudianism was marginal. In the words of the historian Mark Sullivan: "The medium through which Freud's ideas were impressed upon the country, and altered its standards, consisted mainly of the novelists, dramatists, poets, critics, college teachers, and a type of intellectual called, somewhat condescendingly, 'high-brows.' "[57]

In 1912 Freudianism won over the young intellectuals in Chicago and New York, who joined its ranks as patients and enthusiasts. Floyd Dell sought treatment with Samuel Tannenbaum while his friend Max Eastman consulted Smith Ely Jelliffe and A. A. Brill in addition to reading every book by or about Freud written in English. Mabel Dodge, who serialized her treatment for the Hearst papers, had in turn consulted both Jelliffe and Brill.[58] The Freudian "contagion," which Bobby Edwards, editor of *The Quill* maintained had originated at the Bonis's Washington Square Bookshop, soon infected the entire Village.[59] Disregarding the immense cost of treatment, which by implication at least should have troubled the socialists among them, Villagers welcomed the new brand of psychoanalysts "with arms and purses that are both wide open."[60] The central event in the introduction of Freudianism to the Village was an "evening" at Mabel Dodge's salon in the winter of 1913. At the request of the young journalist Walter Lippmann, A. A. Brill engaged in such a provocative exposition of Freudian ideas that some of the guests, "incensed at his assertions about unconscious behavior and its give-aways," departed in haste.[61] However, for those who remained the evening was a memorable occasion and a significant date in the cultural history of the decade.[62]

The rapid conversion to Freudianism created apostles of the new doctrine. In June and July of 1915 *Everybody's Magazine* published two articles by Max Eastman, which were the first extended popular treatment of Freudian psychology.[63] Although these articles simplified Freudianism for transmission to the lay public, they also distorted it in much the same way Progressive psychiatry had done. Eastman presented the Freudian notion of sublimation as a panacea that would lift all unacceptable animal impulses out of the unconscious, where they were wont to "make trouble," and channel them neatly into a "socially, or professionally, or artistically, creative sphere," where they would make "*no* trouble" at all.[64] In Eastman's account all the pessimism and ambiguity that troubled Freud and led eventually to his concept of the death-wish were bathed in the light of the American faith in progress. There is evidence to indicate that Eastman was the victim of his own will to believe. In a polemic against the Harvard psychologist Hugo Munsterberg in *The Masses* of October 1913, Eastman had characterized psychology as "a shapeless and immature science" that "has reached hardly any final conclusions of general acceptance."[65] Yet six months later Eastman hailed the appearance of the *Psycho-Analytic Review* as the herald both of "a new science" and "a new method of healing." By April 1915 he assumed that the major tenets of Freud's doctrine had been proven conclusively for use by posterity: "But it is long past time to say that his working-hypothesis of the Unconscious Mind, and the effects of repressed impulses that linger there, forms the ground plan, not only of the psycho-pathology, but of a great part of the Wisdom of Life for future men."[66]

Floyd Dell echoed Eastman's optimism in his own popular account in *Vanity Fair* of December 1915. He, too, believed that an awareness of repression would enable patients to remain "law-abiding and peaceable" citizens and commended sublimation as a "simple business proposition" by which his audience could be assured of praise and payment in life and an eloquent obituary upon death.[67] Dell was in search of a theory that would explain, and perhaps even vindicate, his own romantic tendencies to evade reality. As a result, he welcomed the publication of *Psychology of the Unconscious* by Carl Jung, a book whose mythopoeic analysis reduced all dreams to "the dream of escape from the realities and difficulties and dangers of life" and all sex to "an infantile sexuality whose desire is to return to the rest and comfort of the mother's womb."[68] For Dell the *Psychology* was autobiography writ large; *Homecoming* is the story of a young man's flights from reality to seek maternal comfort. Only after his analysis did Dell take on the responsibility of commitments to write novels, sustain a marriage, and raise a family.[69]

For those like Dell and Eastman who were trying to escape from puritanism, Freudianism was a convenient tool in that escape. Yet they failed adequately to consider its implications for their socialism. The contradictions implicit in an acceptance of both Freudianism and Marxism are many and obvious. Many Marxists condemned Freudian therapy as calculated to produce the patient's readjustment to society without any desire to remedy its ills. Moreover, Freud's notion of the unconscious seemed a superstitious contradiction of the materialism of Karl Marx.[70] It was not fully amenable to the scientific approach of Marxist analysis and involved a belief in hidden, antisocial drives that would deny the Marxist claim that man was essentially good and, therefore, could live in harmony with his fellows after the "withering away of the state" described by Friedrich Engels in his *Anti-Dühring*. Psychoanalysis aimed at curing these antisocial drives on an individual basis while Marxism, viewing the class struggle as a product of material conditions, hoped to revolutionize social and political institutions to remove the environmental stimuli to human evil. Freudianism posed additional difficulties for radical artists: "Their position was especially difficult since the Freudian system put the rebel from social norms at a disadvantage—by the act of refusing conformity he incurred psychic scars which made him less than equal in a morality of mental health."[71]

Nevertheless, on a nontheoretical level there were possibilities available for reconciling Freudianism and Marxism, more in style than in spirit, more in impulse than in object. Both doctrines "actually amount to elaborate systems of hermeneutics," which assume that the manifest nature of phenomena must be probed to reveal the true latent meaning hidden from casual observation.[72] Thus both Freudianism and Marxism posit the need for an aggressive attitude toward the universe. Moreover, both doctrines assume that theory should provide people with the weapons needed to transform reality, that understanding enhances freedom.[73] Both uphold an ethic of complete honesty. In examining the psychological history of a patient or the historical record of a class, one must eschew conventional bourgeois stereotypes of behavior to understand the true nature of the processes at work. Using such an analysis, Marxism exposed the illegitimacy of prevailing social authority by revealing its basis in class exploitation. Freudianism shared this antiauthoritarian impulse: "Authoritarian doctrines generally sanctify the social process; Freud questions it. His social psychology is also a critique of authority, partly because he saw politics in such an ineluctably authoritarian guise. The exposure of authoritarian prototypes, in all their power, becomes the aim of psychoanalysis."[74]

Since Marxism examined economic relationships within society in depth but tended to neglect personal life, an area of growing concern to early twentieth-century American intellectuals, Freudianism, in fact, provided a theoretical supplement to Marxism.[75] Victorians had hoped to use the family as a refuge from the competitive world of business, but an examination of those who appealed for psychoanalytic help indicated that the bourgeois family had failed at that task. Freud's own early cases came from the Viennese bourgeoisie, and in America it was the middle class and the wealthy who turned to psychoanalysis for help. Few American Marxists have made any significant contributions regarding the usefulness of Freudianism in a socialist critique of everyday life. Most of the body of Freudo-Marxist theory has been developed in Europe, but before the Bolshevik Revolution and the subsequent imposition of doctrinal rigidity upon American Marxists by the Communist party, American intellectuals were free to speculate about the interrelationships between Freud and Marx.[76] Many of the radicals associated with *The Masses* were especially well equipped to articulate a socialist critique of everyday life for, as we have seen, many came from family backgrounds supportive of their own radicalism.

Some of the insights later formulated by the European theorists Erich Fromm, Wilhelm Reich, Max Horkheimer, Antonio Gramsci, and Herbert Marcuse had found expression in the work of *The Masses'* radicals without ever being located within a general theory of behavior. There is a belief that sexual satisfaction will merely intensify the demand for happiness through material changes in the political, economic, and social spheres. This belief is expressed equally well by the notion that the spread of birth control information will free the energy of the masses for the revolutionary task at hand or in the notion that psychoanalysis will free a repressed radical to take his or her place in the class struggle.

The revolt against puritanism and the sexual revolution were both attacks against symbols of repressive authority, particularly against the patriarchal family, the church, and the business interests who used piety and the Protestant ethic to cloak their own machinations. The only refuge from the authoritarian relations of the economic order lay in the family and in personal life. The autobiographies of such *Masses'* radicals as Max Eastman, Floyd Dell, Ernest Poole, and Louis Untermeyer, and the diaries and letters of John Reed, Randolph Bourne, and John Sloan all bear witness to the sustenance that their family, friends, and lovers gave to their radical activities. Yet each of them viewed the support derived from personal life in purely individual terms and posited no implications for a more general socialist critique.[77] Their failure at theory construction lies not merely in the fact that few of *The Masses'* radicals were knowledgeable and disciplined students of both Freud and Marx; the intellectual superficiality of the age did not prevent a rash of other unsubstantiated theories regarding love, war, and the rest of the human condition. However, in the realm of personal life the most pressing desire was not for intellectual understanding but for emotional reconciliation.

Few approached psychoanalysis with any degree of detachment; most desired a rationale for past behavior or a panacea for present ills. According to Nathan Hale, Jr.: "For some journalists psychotherapy represented personal salvation. James Oppenheim, Floyd Dell, Lucian Cary, and Max Eastman all suffered from neurotic symptoms, mysterious backaches, depression, writer's block. They wrote about psychotherapy and psychoanalysis after experiencing its benefits."[78] Some of the adherents of the new psychology, most notably Mabel Dodge and Floyd Dell, were uncritical enthusiasts. The former "veered from one analyst to another" while dabbling in assorted brands of healing.[79] Analysis proved vastly entertaining, whether the fun involved the speculation and "tattletaling" of her encounters with the Jungian analyst Smith Ely Jelliffe or her arguments over the nature of normality with the more orthodoxly Freudian A. A. Brill.[80]

Dell's approach to Freudianism was more serious but nonetheless eager. In 1914 Dell became acquainted with the new psychology through discussions at the Liberal Club and began reading on the subject until he became convinced of the applicability of free association to his own dream work.[81] Although he had written two or three novels that had been "discreetly destroyed," Dell found himself suddenly suffering from a writer's block regarding his current novel, and he decided to consult Dr. Samuel Tannenbaum, an orthodox Freudian analyst, to obtain aid in his "love life and literary work."[82] Dell supplied Tannenbaum with a "never-ending torrent" of memories, dreams, and associations and claimed that the analysis, which occurred intermittently through 1917 and 1918, gave "a new emotional center" to his life.[83] Both Dell and Eastman were so eager to cooperate with their analysts that they presented none of the resistances traditionally associated with therapy.[84] In fact, Floyd Dell gleefully confessed to the prescribed litany of Freudian sins: "My psychoanalyst gave me no interpretation of my dreams, but let me interpret them myself; nor did he tell me I had a terrific mother-complex, and was narcissistic, had a great deal of unconscious homosexuality, and a variety of other frightful-sounding traits; I found all that out myself, and told him."[85] Although his analysis never was completed, Dell emerged from the experience thoroughly pleased. Psychoanalysis had supplied him with "a basis for a new view of history, not supplanting the Marxian one but supplementing it."[86] It had imbued him with a new sense of happiness and self-confidence, which left him free to love deeply and to begin work on his novel.[87] Little wonder that Dell became the Village apostle of Freudianism. When in the early 1920s the young journalist Joseph Freeman turned respectfully to Dell for advice about how he should resolve those conflicts he shared with the rest of the American "intelligentsia," Dell replied:

> Have yourself psychoanalyzed. It's the only thing to do. Everybody is being psyched these days. You will unravel your complexes and thus overcome them. You will relive your life, discover its secret pattern, and learn to direct it consciously. Confession has always been good for the soul; now we have a scientific confessional whose catharsis liberates us from the tyranny of our unconscious fears and taboos.[88]

Dell's proclivity for Freudianism, regardless of the cost to his professed socialism, becomes fully obvious by the 1930s. In a letter written in 1937, Dell confesses, in effect, that the Freudian impulse had always been stronger than the Marxian one: ". . . it is not politics, ever, which has set my pen flowing across paper—it is and always has been a different motive, the pursuit of some kind of psychological rather than political truth."[89] Dell failed to realize the possibility that the therapeutic situation, in which the expertise of the analyst is used to free the patient through a process of reeducation, might serve as a model for radical political activity. In the guise of an amateur sociologist, Dell in his book *Love in the Machine Age* dismissed the notion that political leaders might be capable of the kind of dissolution of transference that analysts practiced at the end of therapy to free their patients. For him politics remained an infantile stage of development and deserved "no place in the affairs of a socially adult and self-determining humanity."[90] Dell had been exposed to the IWW belief that workers could be trained to build the new world within the shell of the old, in short, that a political leadership could equip its followers with the tools of self-determination and independence. However, Dell's most basic concern was with his own maturity and development, and that concern mitigated any willingness on his part to be distracted by the demands of politics.[91]

Even for those who never had experienced psychoanalysis and who obtained their ideas about Freudianism secondhand, the new psychology could be tapped to provide metaphors to shape their life experience. Isadora Duncan, who spent much of her youth in pursuit of a man sufficiently unawed by her presence to deflower her, rationalized her series of misadventures by claiming that they served the purpose of sublimation, turning all the force of her emotional nature toward her art, which gave her the joys that love withheld.[92] A little theory masks with obfuscation all absurdity. And what could be more absurd than America's master of asceticism, Upton Sinclair, who spent much of his youth in premarital and postmarital celibacy with a dash of fasting cure thrown in for good measure? Sinclair preserved his chastity at such great expense that he had to abandon the study of Renaissance art because his senses were overwhelmed by the "mass of nakedness." His reward also came in the form of sublimation; he gained the "intensity and power of concentration . . . to work fourteen hours a day at study and creative effort" in order to put the demon of lust behind him.[93]

Even for Max Eastman, who found his own analysis unsatisfactory and who deemed Marxism the more compelling scientific theory, Freudianism provided a rationale for conduct.[94] Troubled by marital difficulties with his wife Ida Rauh, Eastman turned for help to the Freudian analyst, Dr. Beatrice Hinkle, who, in turn, referred him to the morally conservative Smith Ely Jelliffe and to A. A. Brill, the leading exponent of Freudianism in America. Although Eastman admired the "breadth and sweetness of character" of both Jelliffe and Brill, he remained unconvinced of the theoretical soundness of Freudianism and felt that he emerged from analysis knowing more about Freud's psychology than he did about his own neurotic constitution. He took particular offense at Jelliffe's assertion that Eastman's Oedipal impulses were working themselves out in "prejudiced radicalism."[95] The failure of formal therapy did not weaken the appeal of the analytical mode. On 27 July 1914 Ida Rauh left to visit some friends in New York, and Eastman retired to his boat-house loft to undertake a self-analysis. This interlude, by his own later admission, was a luxury for a radical at that time: "Thus during the approach and outbreak of the First World War, this international revolutionist, 'cultural leader of socialism in the United States,' was engaged in a search within the tiny corridors of his own brain for his own wish."[96] Only by implicitly accepting the primacy of personal life, as Dell had done, could Eastman justify his own priorities.

In the one area in which Max Eastman tried to make an original contribution regarding the application of Freudian psychology, namely in understanding the nature of war, he was clearly guilty of misunderstanding Freud's intent. In his book *Understanding Germany* (1916) and in an article for *The Masses*, "War Psychology and International Socialism" (1916), Eastman presented a Freudian model of the roots of war which assumed that war originated in and was sustained by patriotic drives that were instinctual and hereditary. Thus he discounted the Marxist economic interpretation of war.[97] By virtually reducing war to a compulsion that only those whose instincts were abnormally weak, i.e., extreme pacifists, or those whose ideation was abnormally strong, i.e., intellectual heroes, could combat, Eastman posited a situation in which opponents of war would be rendered impotent to check its course.[98] Freud, as early as 1915, had published his own antiwar essay, "Thought for the Times on War and Death," in which he argued that the state in war arrogated to itself every act of violence and wrongdoing that it forbade to the individual citizen in time of peace.[99] Freud assumed that individuals were foolish to sacrifice themselves and to allow incursions into their privacy and rights of free expression in order to support the warring state. Such a state had no intention of abolishing violence, only a desire to monopolize it for its own ends.[100] When Eastman met Freud in Europe in the mid-1920s, Freud kept returning to the point in the conversation at which Eastman had termed the war a "watershed" in America. Eastman later reported the dialogue in his book *Great Companions*:

> For instance, I said that the war was a watershed in America, dividing radicals from liberals, but not in Europe because in Europe everybody was in it whether he wanted to be or not.
> "Officially," he put in with a sly inflection. And then he exclaimed: "You should not have gone into the war at all. Your liberal Woodrow Wilson was the silliest fool of the century, if not of all centuries."[101]

The ultimate irony was that Eastman, who preached Freudianism as a highly developed science, arrived at a "Freudian" interpretation of World War I that evoked only skepticism from Freud himself.

For those who did not seek a resolution of their personal problems through Freudianism, it was possible to maintain enough detachment to use the new psychology as a tool. In the spring and summer of 1912 Walter Lippmann shared a cabin in the Maine woods with his friend Alfred Booth Kuttner, who was at work on a translation into English of *The Interpretation of Dreams*. Lippmann read the translation, discussed it with Kuttner, and grew increasingly aware of the significance of Freud's contributions to the psychology that Lippmann had learned at college.[102] His approach was pragmatic. Lippmann found in Freudianism a hypothesis, derived from actual clinical experience, that could be applied to anthropology, education, sociology, literary criticism, and to the study of philosophy and religion.[103] Lippmann's own book, *A Preface to Politics*, which appeared in 1914, bore the effects of its author's interest in Freudianism, and the merit of his interpretation was confirmed when the book was reviewed by Ernest Jones in Freud's German-language journal *Imago*.[104] Another young intellectual, Randolph Bourne, actually submitted to analysis by a consulting psychologist but viewed the experiences as a fascinating intellectual puzzle. He was delighted by the complexities of the new science but managed to preserve his political self against the Freudian attack:

> The diagram of my personality, when finished, will be a most interesting document,—to me, at any rate, and just the little way we have gone has thrown a flood of light on the contrast between the fabric of his

[referring to the consulting psychologist, S. M. Bligh] ideas and mine. The effect of economic security on personality has come out repeatedly in the strongest way. I feel that I can size him up and put him into my philosophy much better than he can me, and so am confirmed in my Socialism, which is practically that of Kropotkin.[105]

Bourne simply used the therapeutic situation to satisfy his own boundless curiosity about human nature.[106]

Although many pre-World War I radicals viewed Freudianism as a panacea in their personal lives, they were able to spoof it on the stage. One of the worst offenders, Floyd Dell, produced a play entitled *The Angel Intrudes*, which poked fun at the power of sex to produce self-deception, and *King Arthur's Socks*, a drawing-room comedy that set out to prove that "civilized morality" rendered its victims too cowardly for concupiscence.[107] The Provincetown Players, for whom Dell wrote these plays, managed to resist the vogue of Freudianism enough to satirize its excesses. According to Helen Deutsch and Stella Hanau, who wrote a history of Provincetown: "It speaks well for the group that, at a time when psychoanalysis was being taken up seriously by every housewife and professor, they should have been able to poke good fun at it."[108] The guiding spirit of the Players, George Cram Cook, viewed the theater as "a laboratory of human emotions" in which actors could develop personally through the roles in which they performed. Hence he was willing to produce a play such as *Enemies*, written by Neith Boyce and Hutchins Hapgood, in Cook's view "to get it off their chests," the story of a couple whose petty arguments really represented a quarrel about themselves.[109] In fact, Cook collaborated with his wife, Susan Glaspell, to produce one of the most popular plays spoofing Freudianism, namely *Suppressed Desires*, the tale of a wife who pries open a Pandora's box of repressed wishes when she persuades her husband and her married sister to seek analysis.[110] The play avoided one common American misinterpretation of Freud cited by Frederick Hoffman—the notion that all repression is bad—in affirming that some repression was socially necessary only to err as dangerously in assuming that raising suppressed desires to full consciousness would result in automatic cure.[111] Although the Provincetown plays mock the faddishness of Freudianism, they reserve their strongest barbs for the kind of middle-class conventionality that confines its awareness of sex to polite conversation. The plays all acknowledge the personally explosive implications of the new psychology.

Few young radicals made original contributions to Freudian theory or found social applications for Freudianism. Most of their energy was devoted either to soul-searching or to propagandizing an end to repression. It was ironic that as socialists they were unwilling to deal with the problems generated by the high cost of psychoanalysis, its sexist assumptions, and its emphasis on preserving social order. However, Randolph Bourne in random speculations and Walter Lippmann in a more orderly fashion both tried to use Freudianism in their critiques of American society. Bourne was able to appreciate the value of repression in molding character. He believed that repression could serve to make its victims more interesting and purposeful.[112] And he believed that the failure of the younger generation to find direction and meaning among its multiple opportunities was attributable to "that absence of repression in our bringing-up, . . . that rigid moulding which made our grandfathers what they were."[113] Bourne hoped to borrow the tools of Freudianism and to use them in creating a richer and more noble national life. He explicitly used the Freudian notion of sublimation in his argument for a national educational service that would provide a moral equivalent of war while improving American culture.[114]

Walter Lippmann was even more eager than Bourne to view social problems in the light of the new psychology. He credited Freudianism with unleashing great possibilities for the study of mental life ("The impetus of Freud is perhaps the greatest advance ever made towards the understanding and control of human character"), and he hoped to adapt it to a more sophisticated analysis of the complexities of politics.[115] Like Bourne Lippmann used the Freudian notion of sublimation to substantiate a theory of moral equivalents in which lust if ignored or tabooed would "break forth in some barbaric or morbid form," but, if acknowledged and channeled, could be used to enhance civilization.[116] Lippmann realized that political beliefs originated not in logic but in desire.[117] Hence the work of the political theorist resembled that of the Freudian analyst; both would use their special skills to pierce the symbolic masks that cloaked unconscious desires, to interpret the true, irrational nature of human behavior in order to channel it toward socially acceptable goals.[118]

Apart from this limited use of Freudianism by Bourne and Lippmann, there were few attempts by pre-World War I radicals to adapt insights from the new psychology for use in a comprehensive socialist analysis of American culture and society. Instead these radicals turned to Freudianism to find a weapon in the attack against puritanism and a tool in their personal liberation. Since there was no genuine attempt to fuse Marxism and Freudianism, the strands of political and psychological radicalism disentangled in the postwar era. The left found itself without an ideology that could explain the relationship between radicalism and personal life. Cultural and political radicals parted ways, and the left entered a period of temporary decline.

Free Love and the Pangs of Jealousy

Sigmund Freud never intended that psychoanalysis be used in the service of the more extreme forms of sexual liberation; certainly he was no advocate of free love. However, his radical following in the United States generated a variety of misinterpretations of Freudianism to sustain them in their search for alternative life-styles. Villagers who wanted to explore sexual possibilities, most often as a prelude to marriage, developed a cult of free love to legitimize their explorations.

The free-love ideal had been expounded in the late nineteenth century by two notorious feminists, Victoria Woodhull and Tennessee Claflin, the editors of *Woodhull and Claflin's Weekly*. The two sisters took to the lecture platform to defend and proselytize their views. On 20 November 1871, in a speech at Steinway Hall in New York, Victoria Woodhull responded affirmatively to audience accusations that she was a "Free Lover." Woodhull upheld her right to love whomever she pleased for as long as was her wont without public interference; moreover, she demanded that the community protect her in the unrestricted exercise of that right.[119] The sisters optimistically hoped that the Steinway Hall speech would "ultimately bring on the Social Revolution, and eventuate in woman's complete freedom."[120] They believed that the resolution of the sexual question in support of the "inherent natural right" to freedom of choice would have revolutionary implications for the rearing and education of children and for the relations between men and women.[121] They also held that the spread of the doctrines of scientific socialism had educated the public to realize that the institution of marriage had been outmoded and should be replaced by a combination of free love and stirpiculture.[122] Although Woodhull and Claflin were repudiated by most of the reformers and suffragists of their day, their ideas are significant because they did try to forge links between sexual freedom, feminism, and political radicalism.

In the twentieth century much of the ideological support for free love originated abroad. Citing Bachofen's *Mutterrecht* (1861) and Lewis H. Morgan's *Ancient Society* (1877), Friedrich Engels in *The Origin of the Family, Private Property, and the State* (1884) theorized that the family had originated in a state of group marriage that sanctioned various sexual partners for members of both sexes.[123] He assumed that both jealousy and the taboos against incest were relatively late developments in the evolution of the family.[124] If Engels supplied prewar American radicals with the anthropological underpinnings for their ideas of sexual freedom, Ellen Key from Sweden and Edward Carpenter from England provided them with a romantic sociology that projected a future of complete sexual freedom nurtured by the free-love ideal. Although a feminist, Key was more concerned with the freedom to love than with the freedom to labor. Her ideas provoked controversy on both sides of the Atlantic, and all segments of the American press devoted substantial attention to her works in translation.[125] However, few recognized the underlying conservatism of her paeans to free love. Ellen Key was an exponent of the cult of motherhood; she held that the noblest career open to woman lay in maternity. Moreover, the mother must subordinate her own aspirations to the larger and more important task at hand: "The child must be an end in itself."[126] Although Key was willing to dispense with the legal formality of marriage as a preliminary to childbearing, she demanded that the woman be bound to the father of her child by ties of affection and by a mutual desire to live together to raise the child: "But to receive her child from a man with whom she knows in advance that she never intends to live, this is having an illegitimate child in the deepest sense of the word."[127] Thus she foreclosed the possibility of single motherhood or communal child-raising. The woman in a free-love union would remain as dependent upon a man as her married predecessor.

Although Edward Carpenter disagreed with Ellen Key's contention that motherhood was central to the feminine role and suggested other productive outlets for womanly self-expression, he shared her belief that a solution to the problems of feminism would have to "include the redemption of the terms 'free woman' and 'free love' to their *true* and rightful significance."[128] He argued that the new woman would have to be granted complete freedom with regard to the disposal of her sex in the belief that, in general, freedom would be used rationally and well.[129] Carpenter's feminism led him to advocate a radical transformation of society that would obviate the need for women to rely upon male support: "The freedom of Woman must ultimately rest on the communism of society—which alone can give her support during the period of motherhood, without forcing her into dependence on the arbitrary will of one man."[130] Despite his romantic effusions, Edward Carpenter was able to comprehend the practical difficulties that free-love unions foisted upon their female participants, difficulties that often eluded the understanding of free-love advocates in the United States.

The advocacy of free love can form part of a radical critique of society, but alternatives to monogamy can and do exist under capitalism. Support for sexual freedom may imply an attack on anticommunal attitudes that reduce sexuality to a matter of private consumption; an attack on the marriage *contract* can imply an attack on other contracts that reduce human relationships to a cash nexus. But the radicals associated with *The Masses* simply assumed that free love fit into a more comprehensive socialist perspective; they failed to transcend their own romanticism to deal with the practical and theoretical difficulties entailed by free love.

There was a fatal tendency to assume that all mothers who bore children out of wedlock were modern madonnas and that their offspring were of superior stock to those more traditionally conceived.[131] In viewing such children as products of free nature and hence superior to the offspring of marriages of economic necessity, radicals often neglected the fact that nonmarital relationships among the working class might equally be products of economic coercion, and they failed to deal with the economic and social burdens that free motherhood placed upon women. A perfect case in point involves some observations made by a European representative of *The Masses*, who was entranced by the healthy, happy baby produced by an unwed Hungarian peasant woman. The observer commented, "This was Beauty and Power; a beauty which most women aspire to produce in their children, but cannot achieve because men will not let them; which men have deprived them from achieving because they have subjected race function to their individual feelings, a power which they cannot achieve either because they do not live truly. Power can come only from following natural laws."[132] There is something immediately suspect about an appeal to natural law in a socialist periodical, and further suspicion is raised when the blame for reproductive failure is pinned solely upon men rather than on an economic system that constrains men and women alike.

A much more balanced account of the virtues of free motherhood occurs in a stilted example of proletarian art produced by a woman who was once herself a worker. Rose Pastor Stokes's play *The Woman Who Wouldn't* is the story of Mary Lacey, a poor flower maker unable to obtain an abortion, who suffers innumerable difficulties and deprivations to raise a child out of wedlock in support of the principle that no marriage should occur except on the basis of mutual love.[133] Middle-class radicals, for whom free love might mean little more than sexual experimentation en route to marriage, often failed to weigh the cost of freedom to the working class.

The Masses' radicals were exponents of an optimistic philosophy, quasi-Freudian in nature, which denigrated chastity and celebrated free love. Sexual experience became as much of an imperative for the practitioners of the new paganism as abstinence had been for the puritans who had preceded them. The poet Clement Wood in "The Withholder" argued that to dam the flood of sex would result in corruption and disease; free love thus became a measure of health.[134] In his review of *The Sexual Crisis* by Grete Meisel-Hess, Floyd Dell invoked "Freud and his school" to buttress his claim that prolonged celibacy, in either men or women, was hardly the best training for a happy marriage.[135] Condemning both the "cold-storage" of celibacy and the undemocratic, irresponsible nature of prostitution, Dell argued for the public acceptance and support of free unions to provide a healthy outlet for sexual desires and to permit these unions to become "fruitful with children of love" even if they bore no pledge of permanency.[136] Both Wood and Dell here fell victim to the common American misinterpretation of Freudianism that all repression was harmful and free love the cure.

The problem with the cure was that it assumed that people were able to withstand a good deal of flux and ambiguity in their personal relationships, that they could overcome all feelings of jealousy and insecurity in order to practice the free-love ideal. Such psychic heroism generally resulted in failure, at times even tragedy. For some a series of erotic adventures merely cloaked a more fundamental, but temporarily unacceptable, desire for monogamy. In his autobiographical novel *More Miles* (1926), the poet Harry Kemp wrote, "But each flitting experience, instead of bringing me any deep satisfaction, sent me further a-field, seeking for the dream I was victim of; I continually was possessed of the obsession that some day, somehow, I would come across the golden-headed, beautiful girl who would prove to be my true and ultimate mate."[137] Similarly Floyd Dell viewed all his romantic experimentation merely as a prelude to his second marriage to his dream-girl incarnate, B. Marie Gage; this struggle to overcome immaturity and indecision in order to achieve happiness and stability in marriage provided the material for Dell's 1921 novel, *The Briary-Bush*.[138]

The failure of the free-love ideal proved less devastating to those like Floyd Dell and Max Eastman who could derive satisfaction in monogamy; it was tragic for those who clung to their former faith once it ceased to work in practice. Neith Boyce and Hutchins Hapgood tried to preserve the free-love ideal within the confines of marriage. Neith Boyce once wrote to her friend Mabel Dodge, "Both Hutch and I feel that we are free to love other people— but that nothing can break or even touch the deep vital passionate bond between *us* that exists now as it always has."[139] Yet her friend subsequently revealed that their love had been marred by a failure to achieve the free-love ideal: "Hutch never loved any woman but Neith. He tried to, but he couldn't. He felt that he ought to. He believed that if he could become successfully the lover of a woman, enjoying her body and giving her pleasure, that it would be the gesture of purest comradeship. But it was a gesture he could not make completely."[140] Unfulfilled by his attempts at sexual friendship, Hapgood also deemed himself an utter failure at marriage because he could not achieve total intimacy with the woman he had chosen to be his wife.[141]

The radical community was not strong enough to sustain those who fell victim to its sexual ideology; as a result, many radicals such as Dell, Eastman, Reed, Bourne, and others sought refuge in introspection and analysis. For someone as emotional as Isadora Duncan such isolation was disastrous. Forced to bear a child out of wedlock as a result of her liaison with Gordon Craig and denied patronage from prominent Berlin women who disapproved of the affair, she hired the Philharmonic Saal to champion the twin rights of free love and free motherhood.[142] However, her biographer Victor Seroff revealed that in her need for self-justification, Isadora Duncan obscured the fact that she could confide her plight to no one, not even her mother or sister, that she had been driven to such desperation that she even contemplated suicide.[143]

The rock on which the free-love ideal foundered most often was simply jealousy. Admitting to jealousy was considered bad form among social radicals, yet repressing the emotion conflicted with the ethic of personal honesty and resulted in bizarre and unnatural behavior. Jealousy revealed the dilemma posed by the failure of radicals to resolve what were the proper claims of the ego. One could grant primacy either to the sexual freedom of all members of the community (in which case individual selfishness or petty jealousy could not be permitted to interfere with the exercise of that right) or to the right of individuals to personal health and happiness (in which case jealousy would be merely a means of defending that right).

The lives and literature of *The Masses'* radicals were both filled with quixotic attempts to suppress jealousy. We have seen how the inability to cope with sexual infidelity caused the dissolution of the first marriages of both Floyd Dell and Max Eastman. Dell dated the deterioration of his marriage to Margery Currey from the time that he attempted to live according to the radical ideal that all sexual repression was evil. With the knowledge and consent of both their respective spouses, Dell and a married woman in Chicago decided to carry on an affair, which he and her husband dissected in conversation. When the husband finally pleaded jealousy, the affair was terminated, but the damage had been done. Dell began to drift into other liaisons, and he and his wife separated. Only later did Dell realize the danger of his course. He confided to the social historian Emily Hahn, "But my friend and his wife, the one who started it all, they're still married to each other, still together. I found out after our adventure that it wasn't their first experience of that sort, nor the last either. That girl was always falling in love. Why, she busted up marriages right and left."[144] Dell went on to a series of free-love liaisons in New York, but it seems likely that his final disappointment at the failure of his affair with Edna St. Vincent Millay left him dissatisfied with the temporary nature of most free-love involvements and willing to abandon his bohemian ways for the permanency of marriage.[145]

As the years passed, Dell grew more willing to admit to jealousy. Dell wrote two plays on the folly of suppressing sexual jealousy, the fragment "Babes in the Wood" and "The Perfect Husband." Nearly identical in character and plot, both plays criticize a loving husband for catapulting his wife into an affair with a mutual friend; they share an awareness of the difficulty of overcoming both jealousy and public censure in sustaining an extramarital free-love union.[146] In the 1920s the erstwhile Villager summarized his disillusionment with free love. In response to an unfavorable review by Upton Sinclair of his novel *Janet March*, Dell wrote: "Free-love, that beautiful ideal of the utopian mind, is indeed a delusion and a snare; I thought my book brought that point home. Jealousy is a human reality, and so is the deep craving of both men and women for permanence and security in love: I thought my story showed as much."[147]

Dell was not alone in being forced to realize the power of jealousy to thwart the operation of the free-love ideal. Both Max Eastman and Harry Kemp produced autobiographical novels depicting their experiences in the Village that viewed jealousy as an inescapable instinct, the psychological equivalent of original sin.[148] Hutchins Hapgood engaged in a bit of amateur sociology in assessing the practice of varietism among the anarchists in Chicago. These radicals disdained marriage and felt that it was obligatory, for reasons of hygiene and imaginative stimulation, to encourage their mates to act upon even the briefest sexual impulse toward another person. Yet Hapgood noted that human nature could not bear the strain of such libertarian ideas, and the final result was always "separation, sorrow, and disappointment."[149] His observations led him to conclude that it was impossible to control fundamental human instincts such as jealousy: "Revolutionary criticism plays a fruitful and creative role in the world of economics and politics, and perhaps even in literature and art, though that is more doubtful. But to have it change the sex instincts of man, in any important way, is so far away from reality that it has to do only with the infinite."[150] If *The Masses'* radicals failed to fit free love into a socialist perspective, there was no denying the verdict of their own emotions; free love would not work on account of jealousy.

Monogamy and Marriage

The obvious alternative to free love was monogamous marriage. Although some radicals such as Dell and Eastman came to a belief in marriage and fidelity only after a period of personal struggle, many American socialists never wavered in their support for traditional social forms. They tended to emphasize economic conditions at the expense of considering problems of personal life and assumed that family relations were too subjective to be included in an analysis of social production.[151] It may simply be that in a period of rising socialist strength radicals did not wish to alienate potential converts within the middle class by endorsing offensive social views. At any rate, there was virtually no discussion among socialists who upheld marriage of the implications of monogamy in developing revolutionary consciousness. The conservative sociologist William Graham Sumner recognized the dilemma that such radicals preferred to evade: "Every socialist who can think is forced to go on to a war on marriage and the family, because he finds that in marriage and the family lie the strongholds of the 'individualistic vices' which he cannot overcome. He has to mask this battery, however, because he dare not openly put it forward."[152] As a result, William E. Carson was able to report in *The Marriage Revolt* (1915) that radical opinion was indistinguishable from conservative and liberal thought in upholding "the monogamic ideal of marriage."[153]

A popular socialist argument held that the economic freedom derived from socialism would bring about a truer form of monogamy than that existing under conditions of capitalism. American socialists were able to find ideological support for their position in the works of Friedrich Engels. In *The Origin of the Family, Private Property, and the State* Engels predicted that socialism would erase the economic considerations that forced women to tolerate the habitual infidelity of their mates; the resulting equality of women would tend to make men more truly monogamous.[154] American socialists disassociated themselves from the advocacy of free love and endorsed a social program that could appeal to the most conservative elements of the middle class and the labor movement. The president of the American Federation of Labor, Samuel Gompers, in arguing that "no program of life that threw overboard the family institution ever appealed to me" espoused sentiments that failed to distinguish him from many members of the Socialist party he opposed.[155] The ofttime party standard-bearer Eugene Debs couched an attack on capitalism in terms of the threat it posed to family life: "Capitalism is against homes. It makes it inexpedient for young workers to marry; that makes for prostitution, which is against the home. And so is the tenement system of housing, which is good for profits and rents, but bad for homes and—love. And so is marriage for money against love."[156] The lawyer Morris Hillquit argued that socialism would remove all mercenary motives for marriage and would foster unions based upon mutual love, which could be dissolved by the parties involved if that love ceased to exist. The result would be the introduction of "actual and lasting monogamy": "Just because under socialism marriage will be based on true love rather than economic considerations, the chances are that it will endure in undimmed and lifelong purity in a much larger number of cases than to-day."[157]

John Spargo was particularly interested in presenting a popularized version of socialist views on marriage in order to reassure socially conservative members of the proletariat and middle class. Spargo's first task was to obscure the aspects of Marxist ideology that would prove offensive. In *The Communist Manifesto*, hardly a minor work, Marx and Engels argued that the bourgeois family, with its attendant system of public and private prostitution, would vanish with the disappearance of capitalism and the arrival of communism.[158] Spargo decided to evade the issue by purposely confusing Marx's life with his views: "Those persons who regard socialism as being antagonistic to the marriage relation, and fear it in consequence, will find no suggestion of support for that view in the life of Marx. The love of Marx and his wife for one another was beautiful and idylic [sic]; a true account of their love and devotion would rank with the most beautiful love stories in literature."[159]

He attempted to disassociate the mainstream of socialism from the advocacy of free love, which he tried to ascribe alternately to the utopian stage of socialism that preceded the scientific approach of Marx and to anarchism.[160] Without adducing any evidence in support of his position, Spargo argued that there was "nothing in the philosophy or programme of socialism . . . incompatible with the maintenance of the private family based upon monogamic marriage."[161] He echoed the arguments of Debs and Hillquit that the economic equality of men and women ushered in by socialism would result in a truer form of monogamy, an end to prostitution, and the elevation of family life.[162]

Spargo's only major theoretical innovation involved his attempt to consider the implications of family life for the coming of socialism. He tried to portray the ideal home as a "microcosm of the ideal state" in which one could view the successful integration of collective and individual interests.[163] Hence socialism was merely the translation of family ideals to the social economy: "Socialism, then, is an attempt to realize in the larger life of the community that rational and fair adjustment of collective and individual power and responsibility which is exemplified by the family at its best."[164]

In addition to this rather straightforward defense of marriage, many radicals advocated reforms such as trial marriage and divorce that offended traditionalists but that were actually supportive of family life. Trial marriage, championed by Havelock and Edith Ellis from Britain and Judge Ben Lindsey in the United States, was predicated on the notion that a provisional arrangement would enhance the consideration given to women and remove the sense of compulsion that tended to produce dissatisfaction and revolt from formal marriage.[165] Divorce, too, could be used to buttress the institution of marriage. The social historian William L. O'Neill has argued convincingly: "If the married state was the most exalted to which man could aspire, if it was truly sacred, then those marriages which were substandard undermined the system and made a mockery of the connubial ideals that were the glory of Victorian civilization. Looked at in this manner, divorce was not antithetical to the dominant ideology of marriage, but stemmed . . . from a literal interpretation of its texts."[166]

Free access to divorce, radicals argued, would improve marital life. The popular Swedish feminist Ellen Key claimed that the availability of divorce would compel husband and wife to give each other the attentiveness and delicacy of conduct that characterized courtship.[167] Even those radicals who viewed divorce as a prelude to the free union of the future tended to champion a form of free love "that differed from the old slavery only in the forms surrounding it."[168] Others like Floyd Dell and Upton Sinclair, both divorced from their first wives, hoped to minimize the disruption entailed by the public nature of divorce to allow themselves and their mates to seek happiness elsewhere; they wished to remove the stigma from divorce in order to provide a second chance at personal fulfillment.[169]

Nevertheless, there was also a substantial body of opinion that represented a more fundamental dissatisfaction with the traditional institution of marriage. Some radicals viewed marriage as needlessly repressive, a result of the power of public opinion to suppress the search for individual happiness.[170] Harry Kemp held that it was wrong for the state and the church to restrain honest sex-expression by imposing oaths of eternal fidelity upon men and women. Such restrictions only complicated human relations without providing any stronger safeguards for family life than would result from the free exercise of the maternal and paternal instincts.[171] The anarchist Emma Goldman viewed marriage as positively inimical to love. She characterized it as primarily an economic arrangement that circumscribed woman's sphere by denying the female partner privacy and self-respect; the growing emancipation of women could not help but undermine marriage as an institution.[172]

Others tried to change the nature of marriage from within its confines. Both Max Eastman and Floyd Dell attempted to sustain marriages as fully egalitarian partnerships in which no breach of complete honesty would be tolerated.[173] However, both marriages foundered on the rock of marital infidelity and were wrecked for the reason that no amount of civility or understanding could assuage the hurt of jealousy.[174] Most attempts to bore at the institution of marriage from within failed to reckon with the staying power of emotions like jealousy and the desire for exclusiveness, emotions that could only be enhanced by the sense of proprietorship associated with marriage.

Others, particularly in the feminist camp, applauded the passing of the family as a necessary step in human progress.[175] Even in the late nineteenth century some advocates of women's rights began to recognize the importance of domestic feminism. In particular, the National Woman Suffrage Association admitted that woman's place in the family system, not her legal or political status, was the source from which her other inequities derived.[176] In championing the right to birth control information and economic equality with men, twentieth-century radicals hoped to free women from endless uncompensated childbearing and child-rearing. Some male feminists among them felt that children and family life impinged unduly upon their own right to undisturbed creativity. Upton Sinclair expressed this feeling in his semiautobiographical novel, *Love's Pilgrimage* (1911), the story of a young literary genius plagued by the twin burdens of matrimony and parenthood; his domestic arrangements robbed him of time vital for his artistic labors.[177] Floyd Dell, who later embraced marriage and domesticity, in the prewar period held that the artist must be absolved of family responsibilities in order to create. In a review of J. D. Beresford's *These Riese Lynnekers*, Dell wrote:

> The Hero must get free of his Family entanglements at the outset, if he is to be a real Hero. And I hope that Mr. Beresford, now that he has proved that he can write about ordinary people, will turn his attention to the Poet, the Artist, the Vagabond, the Criminal—anyone who has by hook or crook escaped, as Jacob Stahl did, the doom of being a member of a Family—anyone who shifts for himself.[178]

Whether objections to the family were motivated by feminism or by artistic expediency, there was a recognition of the need to provide an economically feasible alternative to marriage. Hence under the influence of H. G. Wells, Ellen Key, and Olive Schreiner, many American social critics proposed a government subsidy for motherhood so that women might be able to choose the nature of their domestic arrangements free from economic considerations.[179]

However, there was much less understanding of the psychological component of family life, a dimmer awareness of the need to provide similar emotional gratification in any alternative to marriage they might suggest. Although family life might be oppressive to women, work performed by women within the home brought immediate improvement to loved ones while wage work outside the home was likely to be more personally alienating. Creative artists were not likely to find any community more stable than the family to provide them with emotional sustenance. Although social evolution might provide viable alternatives to the family, for the radicals associated with *The Masses* the domestic ideal had lost none of its appeal. They might rebel for a time, but nearly all of them succumbed, for reasons more psychological than economic, to marriage and family life.

The Fight for Birth Control

By the late Victorian era the family had become a focus of emotional energy for its members, increasingly private and child-centered.[180] With urbanization and the corresponding breakdown of communal strictures, it became possible for couples to practice family limitation in order to improve the quality of family life and to offer greater opportunities to a dwindling number of offspring. Daniel Scott Smith has cited a steady decline in fertility in the nineteenth century: "The average number born to a white woman surviving to menopause fell from 7.04 in 1800 to 6.14 in 1840, to 4.24 in 1880, and finally to 3.56 in 1900. . . . The same decline is also apparent in U.S. Census data on completed fertility."[181] He attributes it to the increasing autonomy of women within the family, which allowed them to impose a demand for fewer children upon their husbands.[182]

Although there is some less than conclusive evidence of domestic feminism, it is interesting to note that many Victorian feminists themselves opposed birth control. In part, militant feminists were concerned that sexual intercourse would deplete their energies and, therefore, counseled continence instead of contraception.[183] Both suffragists and free-love advocates recognized the unilateral right of a woman to refuse sexual relations with her husband, an idea at the heart of voluntary motherhood.[184] Their refusal to condone the use of contraception was due to a desire to preserve the status of middle-class women. Respectable women disdained birth control because contraceptive techniques were viewed as the tools of prostitutes and were associated with sexual immorality.[185] Moreover, the likelihood that coitus would lead to conception was a guarantee that men would marry and thereby provide women with a family setting for motherhood, often the only creative and challenging career open to bourgeois women.[186] Finally, since Victorian women were economically and psychologically dependent upon men and much more so the victim of sexual taboos imposed by the community, legal, effective birth control would yield no benefit to them while increasing the freedom of their mates to stray.[187]

Handicapped by the double standard and by economic insecurity, Victorian feminists were forced into a socially conservative position despite their attempt to expand the sphere of women's rights: "Thus voluntary motherhood in this period remained almost exclusively a tool for women to strengthen their position within conventional marriages and families, not to reject them."[188] The actual advances in family limitation in the nineteenth century seem more an example of economics than of ideology; the rhetoric of the feminists lagged behind the practice of the people.

By the twentieth century conditions had changed sufficiently to sustain the open advocacy of birth control. Urbanization had proceeded to the point at which the family seemed to have lost its economic function and at which the large family was a definite liability.[189] The double standard weakened under the buffeting of the revolt against puritanism; in addition, women used their greater economic independence to demand greater sexual equality with men. Hence birth control became a social phenomenon that could no longer be ignored. Couples consciously chose to limit offspring to avoid the pinch of poverty, to permit upward mobility, and to provide a more supportive environment for fewer children: "The modern idea is decidedly against the large families which were once the fashion, the general opinion being that quality and not quantity should be the determining factor."[190] The increasing visibility of family limitation brought with it the specter of race suicide, the fear of

Family Limitation—Old Style

K. R. Chamberlain, "Family Limitation—Old Style,"
The Masses, May 1915
Courtesy Tamiment Library, New York University

depopulation in general and of the dwindling of superior stock in contrast to the profligacy of the poor and aliens in particular.[191] President Theodore Roosevelt led a crusade to encourage childbearing by pecuniary and honorific awards; he argued that family limitation, except for the most pressing reasons of economics or health, was shirking the most solemn of all duties to the state.[192] Moreover, medical opinion grew more concerned that "the increased avoidance of the natural consequences of married life" precipitated a drastic proliferation of nervous diseases among married women, a possible indication of the ill effects of the widespread practice of coitus interruptus.[193] To meet the objections of critics, birth control advocates would have to combat the racist assumptions of nativists, develop a social philosophy consistent with family limitation, and popularize new contraceptive devices that would not offend the average sensibility.

Margaret Sanger assumed most of the burdens of this crusade. Impelled by the tragedies of unwanted pregnancy that confronted her as a nurse on the Lower East Side of New York, she set out on a solitary struggle to unearth contraceptive information and disseminate it among the masses.[194] As a socialist she wished to provide lower-class women with the opportunities available to the wealthy to preserve their health and control their destinies. She arranged that the first birth control clinic be opened in Brownsville, a predominantly Jewish working-class tenement section of Brooklyn.[195] In her propaganda organ, *Woman Rebel*, Sanger linked contraception to social revolution; influenced by French and German Marxists who believed that workers should control their fertility to deny the military and industry a steady flow of exploited labor, she came to view birth control as a weapon in the class struggle.[196] She assumed that the only way for workers to improve their situation was for them to limit their numbers and demand higher wages, thereby rejecting any notion that only the increasing misery of the proletariat would spawn revolution.[197] Although her initial appeal through her articles in *The Call* and the publication of *Woman Rebel* was addressed primarily to lower-class women, Margaret Sanger bore a revolutionary message for the middle class as well.[198] Blending misconceptions of Freud with inspirations from Havelock Ellis, she urged women to use contraception to overcome repression in order more freely to express their distinctive feminine sexuality.[199] Rather than simply popularize the use of the condom and coitus interruptus, she scoured Europe to discover birth control devices like the cervical pessary that would be more psychologically acceptable to large numbers of people and that would not inhibit sexual spontaneity.[200]

However, Margaret Sanger's birth control ideas drew a mixed reception from radicals. Sympathizers in the Industrial Workers of the World offered her direct access to workingmen and their wives in her quest for facts on family limitation; Big Bill Haywood inspired her to carry her search to France to see for herself the benefits resulting from generations of birth control.[201] But support for her battles with Anthony Comstock and his fellow guardians of purity was not forthcoming from the source to which she turned expectantly for help. Progressives, socialists, and feminists urged upon her a course of caution and told her to await the dawning of a new day when women's suffrage, the coming of the socialist commonwealth, or some other pet panacea would permit the dissemination of birth control.[202] As a result, Margaret Sanger lost her faith in many of the social remedies of her day; she felt that socialists and feminists were too cowed by public prejudice to grapple with "so fundamental a need as sex."[203]

Only when her confrontations with the law dramatized the struggle did Margaret Sanger win a radical following in her fight for birth control. The indictment of Sanger on obscenity charges and the subsequent sentencing of her husband for distributing birth control information to a Comstock agent brought sympathetic editorials from Max Eastman and a letter of support from Upton Sinclair to the pages of *The Masses*.[204] However, the issues in the Sanger case were by no means clear. After her husband's conviction she decided to return from Europe to stand trial on obscenity charges stemming from articles in *Woman Rebel*. Even a favorable decision in her case would not have affected the prohibition against disseminating contraceptive information, and an unfavorable one would punish her for a crime that was merely incidental to the focus of her crusade.[205] Despite the advice of liberals like Leonard Abbott, Theodore Schroeder, and Gilbert Roe, as well as that of Max Eastman, that she plead guilty and accept a light sentence in order to continue her educational work, Margaret Sanger decided to maintain her innocence and stand trial.[206] The issue of trial strategy was never resolved because on 18 February 1916 the government unexpectedly entered a *nolle prosequi*, most likely to avert elevating Margaret Sanger to an unwelcome martyrdom.[207] Yet even the threat of martyrdom rallied radicals to her cause. During the trial preliminaries John Reed tried to persuade the *New York Times* and the *New Republic* to include news and editorials favorable to the birth control campaign.[208] A number of prominent left-wing women including Elsie Clews Parsons, Ida Rauh, Jessie Ashley, and Rose Pastor Stokes, as well as Bolton Hall, a leader of the single-tax movement, decided to risk arrest in order to win publicity for Margaret Sanger's struggles.[209]

However, it was difficult to measure the depth of their commitment. Ida Rauh later confessed that she and Jessie Ashley had courted arrest because of boredom with the less flamboyant tactics of the birth control advocates; borrowing a friend's chauffeured limousine, they went to Union Square to distribute birth control pamphlets with great flourish so that their arrest would be guaranteed.[210] Along with Bolton Hall both women decided to make test cases on the grounds that the denial of contraceptive information to women whose health might be endangered by pregnancy was a violation of the constitutional right to individual liberty. All three were convicted and elected to pay fines rather than face terms in prison. They all subsequently reneged on promises to appeal their cases, so much of the value of their activism either in terms of publicity or in terms of legal precedent was lost.[211] Margaret Sanger had failed to enlist the lower-class women she hoped to save in her crusade, and the radical women she inspired were in many cases merely temporary recruits. Therefore, it is no surprise that the birth control movement was left by default to the respectable women of the middle class who spurned activism, embraced eugenics, and heaved steadily to the legislative route.[212]

In the pre-World War I era the birth control movement had become associated in the public mind with one figure who had tremendous control over its destiny. Margaret Sanger was a woman convinced of her personal mission to spread the message of family limitation. At times her sense of self-importance caused her to be uncharitable to her coworkers in the field. During her summers in Provincetown and her years in Greenwich Village she had come under the influence of the anarchist Emma Goldman, who had been advocating contraception for well over a decade.[213] Nevertheless, Sanger refused to acknowledge Goldman's contribution to the movement and even left spiteful observations regarding her motivation to posterity:

> Emma Goldman and her campaign manager, Ben Reitman, belatedly advocated birth control, not to further it but strategically to utilize in their own program of anarchism the publicity value it had achieved. Earlier she had made me feel she considered it unimportant in the class struggle. Suddenly, when in 1916 it had demonstrated the fact that it was important, she delivered a lecture on the subject, was arrested, and sentenced to ten days.[214]

In fact, Emma Goldman's commitment to birth control had been both deeply personal and political for many years. In the 1890s she refused an operation that would have alleviated sharp recurrent pain by correcting an inverted womb. Rather than bear children she chose to bear pain in the service of anarchism.[215] Her experience as a nurse and a midwife on the Lower East Side had led Emma Goldman as it had Margaret Sanger to seek safe, cheap contraceptive methods to end involuntary motherhood among the poor.[216] After attending an international neo-Malthusian conference held in Paris in 1900, Emma Goldman added the subject of birth control to her lectures but did not discuss methods for fear of an arrest that would keep her from the rest of the social struggle.[217] Yet after the Sangers were threatened with legal reprisals for their involvement with birth control, she decided that she "must either stop lecturing on the subject or do it practical justice."[218] Committed to sharing with them the consequences of advocating birth control, on 28 March 1915, in an address to six hundred people in New York's Sunrise Club, Emma Goldman publicly explained for the first time in America how to use a contraceptive.[219] Following her arrest and a highly sensational trial, Goldman chose to spend fifteen days in the workhouse rather than pay a $100 fine. Margaret Anderson of *The Little Review* commented, "Emma Goldman was sent to prison for advocating that women need not always keep their mouths shut and their wombs open."[220] Her term in prison did not deter Emma Goldman from delivering similar speeches all over the country nor from turning her resulting courtroom appearances into public forums on the issue of birth control.[221] Her lover and manager Ben Reitman was sentenced to six months in the workhouse and to a $1,000 fine for distributing birth control information, "the heaviest penalty imposed for a birth-control offense."[222]

Protests were mounted on their behalf all over the country, but Margaret Sanger remained strangely silent. Although the maiden issue of *Woman Rebel* had contained an excerpt from Goldman's essay "Love and Marriage," which urged the right of women not to have children, Sanger refused to acknowledge any intellectual debt to anarchism.[223] She failed to come to Goldman's defense when the latter awaited trial, and she subsequently repudiated the birth control leagues organized by the anarchists, as well as their entire campaign for family limitation.[224] By severing her ties with the only segment of the left that had maintained a long-standing commitment to birth control, Margaret Sanger further insured that the movement would become the province of the middle class.

Although the medical profession in general shunned any public connection with the birth control movement, a socialist doctor, William J. Robinson, argued the case for family limitation through a proliferation of books and articles on the subject.[225] His approach was much less inflammatory than that of Margaret Sanger or Emma Goldman; he preferred to deal with the arguments of the critics of birth control through logic rather than by appealing to emotionalism. His work was a necessary supplement to their more ardent propaganda. Dr. Robinson tried to present his case for birth control from a socialist perspective. Like Margaret Sanger, he disputed the orthodox socialist belief in an "iron law of wages" whereby the prevailing wage would represent the minimum necessary to sustain life: "A strong union, a high standard of living and a scarce labor market can invert the iron law of wages into one of papier maché and tear it asunder with the greatest ease."[226] Therefore, he argued that workers could improve their standard of living by restricting the number of their offspring, thereby limiting the supply of labor and freeing themselves from an excessive burden of support that a large family would represent in times of strike or depression.[227]

But Robinson also went on to answer socialist objections to birth control neglected by Margaret Sanger. To those who argued that material improvement would sap the revolutionary fervor of the working class or that a numerically large proletariat was necessary to overthrow capitalism, Robinson argued that such a lumpenproletariat was often more antirevolutionary than the bourgeoisie and was the likely source of the "hired thugs, gunmen, hoodlums and hooligans, black hundreds, strikebreakers and other enemies of revolutionary or evolutionary progress."[228] If socialism were to commit itself to immediate improvement of working-class conditions, he argued, there was no more urgent task than "the *practical* propaganda of teaching the people the means of limiting the number of their offspring."[229]

Yet Robinson's socialist analysis shattered on the matter of simple arithmetic. He argued that working-class couples should limit their offspring to no more than two children in order to protect the health of the mother, insure adequate food and clothing to the children, and prevent the glutting of the labor market.[230] Although such a program of birth control has clear strategic advantages for the poor, such advantages are largely the product of their poverty. Robinson saw no class bias in permitting unlimited reproduction to the rich: "As far as couples are concerned who are well-to-do, who love children, and who are capable of taking care of a large number, we, that is, we American limitationists, would put no limit. On the contrary, we would say: 'God bless you, have as many children as you want to; there is plenty of room yet for all of you.' "[231]

Although a socialist, he failed to attack the allocation of resources under capitalism that permitted the luxury of large families to the rich while denying it to the poor. In his view contraception remained essentially a private matter with larger social implications. By failing to argue that the state had an obligation to support all children, Robinson reduced birth control to an option for the wealthy but a necessity for workers, an emblem of the class divisions he had come to accept rather than challenge. Although Robinson must be credited for his unflagging efforts to popularize birth control, his acceptance of class privileges and his own failure to disobey the law prohibiting "*practical* propaganda" undermined much of the revolutionary impact of his message.[232]

One might argue that for socialists like Margaret Sanger and William Robinson, people deeply committed to a single remedy for social ills, it was not easy to integrate the fight for birth control into a larger political perspective. However, such excuses do not apply in the case of the other radicals associated with *The Masses* who simply gave their uncritical support to the work of Sanger, Robinson, Goldman, and all the others who rallied to the cause.[233] They never attempted to yoke the fight for birth control with other socialist issues and never discussed the question in ecological terms. For them neo-Malthusianism was strictly the problem of the lower class. Only William English Walling raised the possibility that *"economic* evolution and social revolution"* might substantially alter the terms of the struggle. If a redistribution of wealth were to render birth control unnecessary for strictly economic reasons, it would also undermine the "authoritarian preachings" of the church, state, and industry that forbade any attempts at family planning.[234] In place of a sustained critique of everyday life, radicals turned to an ad hoc series of individual battles. Birth control, free love, Freudianism, and the assorted attempts at sexual experimentation all enriched the lives of the individuals who fought for them, but winning the sexual revolution did not mean winning the war. There was no concerted effort to view sex and family life in political terms. The link to socialism remained unforged.

Some Concluding Observations

The sexual revolution did not bring in its wake the social revolution. If anything, it proved injurious to political activism by encouraging a retreat to the haven of personal life. Yet this conclusion was not inevitable. As we have seen, a socialist critique of everyday life is possible, though difficult. Why did pre-World War I American radicals, like their postwar counterparts, the Bolsheviki in the Soviet Union, fail at integrating a sexual revolution into a larger movement of economic and political upheaval?

In part the failure is due to the fact that the radicals associated with *The Masses* lacked intellectual discipline. Most of them had read little of the works of Marx and Engels and so were easy victims of distortion and simplification. Although they tended to read more of Freud's works, they approached psychoanalysis more often with the zeal of converts than with any attempt at objectivity. The reason for their blindness was simple: they were more interested in personal salvation than in ascertaining truth. Hence they were likely to enlist in crusades for a favorite panacea, whether it be Freudianism, free love, or birth control.

Moreover, these crusades tended to be narrowly focused in such a way that they permitted little discussion of the implications for socialism of the individual remedy suggested. Because *The Masses'* radicals often lacked the kind of self-awareness that would permit them to see their own class bias, as when they neglected the burdens free love placed on the poor or when they allowed wealth to be a factor in determining family limitation, they convinced themselves that they were the leaders of the social revolution only to find themselves in the vanguard of middle-class reform. By failing to create a socialist critique of everyday life, they permitted the fatal distinction between the personal and the political to arise once more and to blight the budding sense of radical community. Because their vision was too weak, the left shattered after World War I into bohemians and radicals who could neither communicate nor cooperate in the interests of social change.

Chapter 6 The Road to Religion

The Social Gospel and Socialism

Pre-World War I American radicalism was eclectic and seldom doctrinaire. The European ideologies it imported, such as Freudianism and Marxism, it modified, often beyond recognition. The new radicals hoped to devise a left-wing philosophy that would meet their personal needs while responding to the peculiarities of American society. Hence Freud could be invoked to champion free love, Marx to buttress the family, and syndicalism to explain the Industrial Workers of the World in a veritable orgy of misinterpretation. No longer a matter of exegesis, ideology became the product of desire. Instead of shaping action to the dictates of doctrine, American radicals approached ideology as pragmatists who would employ practical results as a measure of value.

As a result, it is not surprising that many American socialists took the unorthodox position of embracing Christianity while rejecting its institutional embodiment, the church. Their departure from the Marxist view that all religion was simply an opiate to repress workers may be partly explained by the desire to attract the middle class, including churchgoers, to the Socialist party. But it also sprang from an equally powerful desire to tap religion as a vital source in American life.

In fact, American Christianity seemed to thrive on the problems that plagued the United States in the years following 1898. The church responded to urbanization, poverty, and social unrest by engaging in a wide variety of reform efforts. Its new commitments brought the church practical rewards: "Its membership increased by approximately sixteen million between 1900 and 1914, an advance which can be explained by its willingness to face squarely the problems of the new day."[1] Walter Rauschenbusch, a German-American Baptist who occupied the chair of church history at Colgate-Rochester Seminary, became the leading exponent of the Social Gospel in the United States. Rauschenbusch argued that fundamental moral, economic, and social reform, involving the overthrow of capitalism and its replacement by a

113

noncompetitive economic system, would have to precede the establishment of the Kingdom of God. His ideas provided a theological basis for social reform and served to restore faith in the continued vitality of religion.[2]

Although many liberals and new radicals could applaud the strength of the religious impulse, they remained skeptical of the church as an institution. Bouck White, a *Masses'* contributor and rector of Trinity House in New York, wrote that the rise of democracy was causally linked to the decline of ecclesiasticism; working people had come to identify organized religion with support of the propertied classes and hence believed that the church was doomed to pass away.[3] However, White noted that the antagonism toward the church in no way affected their affection and esteem for Jesus, "the Workingman of Nazareth."[4] The general formula adopted by radicals to explain their stance toward religion was to praise Christianity and condemn the church. Max Eastman denounced the Christian church as the "betrayer of Christ." He claimed that the very evils that roused Christ to invective—bigotry, self-righteousness, false piety—the church perpetuated in his name: "The Roman Catholic Church is the most tragically stupendous swindle that human and animal nature ever combined to produce."[5] William English Walling also attacked the Catholic church as a foe of socialism. He argued that since the highest church dignitaries had denounced women's suffrage, public education, the initiative and referendum, and state ownership, each victory for the democratic process would spell defeat for the hierarchy. The church gradually would lose its ability to mediate between labor and capital in the interest of the latter and would be faced with rapid decline in a workers' state.[6]

Radicals tended to ignore the reforms associated with the Social Gospel in order to concentrate on the reactionary nature of American Christianity. They pointed to the wealth and corruption of the church and to its failure to meet human needs with the riches at its disposal. In fact, *The Masses'* radicals documented these charges with attacks upon specific churches and clergymen. Maurice Becker drew a cartoon that portrayed a sumptuous banquet held by the Episcopal Convention at New York at which Christ on his crucifix hung unnoticed above the assemblage, and Art Young depicted Trinity Church dwarfed by the business buildings surrounding it in a cartoon cynically entitled "Nearer My God to Thee."[7] Trinity Church, the richest church in America, came to epitomize the decay of institutional religion. The progressive journalist Ray Stannard Baker did an exposé of Trinity as a slumlord that financed the worship of the wealthy through its exploitation of the poor. He found the church unresponsive to urban conditions and unable to meet its moral responsibilities, yet he refused to strike a note of doom for the religion it purported to represent: "But religion is not decaying; it is only the church. More religion is to be found in our life to-day than ever before, more hearts respond to its inspiration; it is found among common men and women everywhere. As ever, it demands, not observances, nor doctrines, nor a habitation in magnificent

Maurice Becker, "Their Last Supper," *The Masses*, December 1913
Courtesy Tamiment Library, New York University

temples—but self-sacrifice and a contrite heart."[8] In a poem that appeared in Upton Sinclair's anthology *The Cry for Justice*, the contemporary American poet Edwin Davies Schoonmaker condemned Trinity Church for sharing the venality of the marketplace, thereby leaving it powerless to rebuke other sinners and mocking the true religion of Christ.[9]

In attacking the hypocrisy of the church, radicals were implicitly asserting their belief in the meaning of the Christian ideal and in its ability to respond to the deepest human emotions. One cause célèbre among the new radicals was the case of Frank Tanenbaum, a youth imprisoned for leading a band of homeless, unemployed men to the Church of Alphonsius to ask for food and shelter. The fact that the church failed to give charity to the poor and even betrayed its supplicants by turning them over to the police meant that the church no longer had a sense of Christian mission and further that it stood athwart the expression of a new economic ideal.[10] Carl Sandburg satirized this commercialization of religion in his poem "To Billy Sunday." Sandburg viewed the evangelist as a tool of bankers, businessmen, and lawyers, who employed him to foster docility among the poor. In contrast, Jesus stood aloof from the business interests to cast his lot with the downtrodden; he was slain for his refusal to abide by the rules of the wealthy.[11]

If there were any doubts about the role of the church in America, these were erased by the support that most religious groups gave to World War I, a conflict many radicals viewed as a bankers' war. Church groups sold Liberty Bonds, operated canteens, entertained servicemen abroad, and provided educational and religious programs for the military as their contribution to the war effort. The Federal Council of Churches even founded a General Wartime Commission to coordinate those activities.[12] Max Eastman reviled the churches for permitting patriotism to become a new religion, one that would allow them to ignore the Gospels to preach hatred since no one would consider applying Christian ethics to international relations.[13] George Bellows contributed a drawing of a manacled Christ with bowed head in prison; the caption read:

> This man subjected himself to imprisonment and probably to being shot or hanged
>
> The prisoner used language tending to discourage men from enlisting in the United States Army
>
> It is proven and indeed admitted that among his incendiary statements were—
>
> Thou shalt not kill
> > and
> Blessed are the peacemakers.[14]

Thus Bellows, who actually supported the war, and other new radicals condemned the church for forgetting the pacifism of Christ in its desire to aid business and government in their conduct of the war.

Radical critics of Christianity found the church and its rituals devoid of personal meaning and, therefore, called for a more human-centered religion. The new radicals adopted a strange hero in their attack on religious orthodoxy. Ignoring his Republicanism and utter conventionality in all matters except religion, they chose for their champion the agnostic author and popular orator Colonel Robert Ingersoll. Isadora Duncan, influenced by her reading of Ingersoll, Darwin, and pagan philosophy, refused marriage, baptism for the children she conceived out of wedlock, and a funeral to mark their tragic death by drowning. As a bereaved mother, church rituals could not gratify her profound desire to transform the hideous death of her children into a thing of beauty.[15]

Sherwood Anderson also pointed to the failure of the church to make Christianity meaningful in the modern world in his depiction of Mike McCarthy, the hedonistic Irishman in *Windy McPherson's Son*. McCarthy, imprisoned for having killed a jealous husband, raves from within the jail and calls for a new Christ who would swear and knock the townspeople about until they accepted God's teachings. The hero, Sam McPherson, hears McCarthy's wild language and finds in his words inspiration that the church could not provide: "In the midst of the blasphemy of Mike McCarthy he had sensed a deep and abiding love of life. Where the church had failed the bold sensualist succeeded. Sam felt that he could have prayed in the presence of the entire town."[16]

The literary historian Walter B. Rideout has noted that in socialist novels of this period the attack on institutionalized Christianity rarely extended to include the religion itself. Radical writers tended to view Christianity as a religion of brotherly love, and in mentioning Christ himself who often was described as the "first Socialist," they emphasized "not his divinity, but his carpentry."[17] Thus radicals were able to create an intellectual distinction that would allow them to accept Christianity as a religion while rejecting its institutional embodiment, the church.

The Masses' radicals experienced no great difficulty in divorcing themselves from the church since many of them had been raised by free thinkers or had been troubled by religious doubts early in their lives. Max Eastman's mother, although a minister, was plagued by religious uncertainty, which she communicated to her son. As a result, both of them found that their spirituality changed from a concern with moral salvation to the millennial hope for a new society that would be more democratic in its values.[18] Similarly Hutchins Hapgood was influenced by the agnosticism of his father. The elder Hapgood removed all fear of theological punishment from his children and neglected all the positive aspects of religion. Therefore, his son Hutchins "became a skeptic at an early age" because he took his father's word as law.[19] Horace Traubel's father had been banished from his paternal home because he had refused to live according to Talmudic law; his mother was a former Christian who had renounced all church affiliations in her youth. Traubel and his siblings were raised in an atmosphere of complete religious liberty, and he formed his own beliefs free from dogma or the influence of churches.[20] Walter Lippmann's parents were agnostics, and he arrived at agnosticism without any attendant struggle; in fact, his own convictions merely expressed a family "tradition."[21] Claude McKay was influenced by a brother who was a free thinker and shared his beliefs by the time he was fourteen. Moreover, McKay was joined by a band of ten boys in his high mountain village in Jamaica who also believed in free thought.[22] Clarence Darrow's father had studied for the Methodist ministry but had given up that career for carpentry. He had concluded that the fear of God led men to foolishness and that the beginning of doubt spelled the onset of wisdom. Under such paternal influence, the younger Darrow naturally became an agnostic.[23]

Other radicals turned away from traditional religion during adolescence. Floyd Dell came from a family "only vaguely Christian." His decision to become an atheist resulted from an intellectual recognition of the falsity of proclaiming the Bible a true record of events. But the emotional alienation that had preceded his decision and made it possible derived from the church's identification with respectability. Since the Dell family was too poor to flaunt its prosperity in church on Sunday, Dell chose to identify with his parents and spurn organized, and ostentatious, religion.[24] Upton Sinclair at age fourteen became the protégé of a clergyman, the Reverend William W. Moir, who gave him volumes of Christian apologetics to assuage his doubts. These confirmed Sinclair in his apostasy since they revealed the weaknesses of the church's defense of religion.[25] Sinclair then repudiated the Christianity that he had outgrown intellectually that he might free himself from family obligations in order to write poetry. He invested the writing of poetry with a sense of religious mission that ascribed to his resulting poverty a quasi-divine sanction. He used his reading of Nietzsche to buttress his claim that Christianity taught a slave-morality of obedience; he would serve humanity by ignoring religious claims in order to produce art.[26]

The hostility that many of the new radicals expressed for church ritual and doctrine made sense within a world view that repudiated dogma in all forms. Moreover, the revolt against puritanism identified organized religion and big business as allies in securing the vested interests against any challenge to their power. Those who professed atheism did so out of profound bitterness at the ability of the church to prey upon the ignorance of the masses for its own profit. William D. Haywood had been indifferent to religion since his boyhood, but he rejected it utterly when he discovered that most churches stood in opposition to both his unionism and his radicalism. He became an unwilling victim of the church when his sickly wife, Nevada Jane, was converted to Christian Science in 1903. He tolerated her treatments at the hands of healers he dubbed charlatans in order to appease his wife, but he deeply resented the influence of the religion on his daughters.[27]

Several of the poets who contributed to *The Masses* sought to expose religious deception. Clement Wood composed a biting satire of the Psalm of David to reveal the true selfishness of the church's ministry. "Never the Shepherd watches the sheep for their good," warned Wood. The tender care offered to the flocks was merely a prelude to their delivery to the shearer or the butcher. Wood appealed to his readers not to accept like sheep the will of a Lord who would only rob them of their goods or lead them to slaughter: "If we are men, we will snatch His crook from the Shepherd's hands / And break it over His fleeing shoulders, and go on our way rejoicing."[28] And William Williams, soon to die in New York, alone and destitute, contributed the only poem he ever wrote to *The Masses*. Entitled "A Ballad," this satire of the Immaculate Conception caused Ward and Gow to remove the magazine from New York subway newsstands.[29] Using the language of the uneducated, Williams tried to demystify the Virgin Birth and to reduce the fundamental Christian myth to human terms by portraying Joseph as the true father of Christ. Although Joseph was shown sympathetically as a proud and tender father, the language the poet used to describe him was hardly calculated to please the orthodox: "God knows what he told th' neighbors, / But he knew it warn't no Ghost."[30] *The Masses* accepted such contributions as those of Wood and Williams in order to mount an attack upon church dogma at the same time that it printed articles and drawings glorifying Christ as a pacifist and rebel workman.

In contrast, Emma Goldman and her organ, *Mother Earth*, were violently anti-Christian. Goldman differentiated herself from other radicals who confused the teachings of Christ with the struggles for social and economic emancipation. She argued instead that Christianity preached the gospel of nonresistance, of slavish acceptance of the status quo; hence all true radicals were obliged to turn their backs on Christianity regardless of the form in which it was presented.[31] Goldman claimed that organized religion exploited the ignorant and the curious with the approval and support of businessmen and rulers of state who would profit thereby: "They know that capital invested in Billy Sunday, the Y.M.C.A., Christian Science, and various other religious institutions will return enormous profits from the subdued, tamed, and dull masses."[32] She urged mankind to free itself from the shackles of religion in the belief that only after the triumph of atheism could beauty and freedom be realized on earth.[33] Yet the religious impulse was not entirely absent in Goldman's life; it was transmuted into a humanitarian political philosophy that she preached with all the fervor of a recent convert. A popular portrait of Goldman in *Current Literature* described her devotion to the anarchist ideal: "To her, Anarchism is a religion—something to live for, if necessary to die for."[34]

In fact, although many radicals rejected traditional Christianity, they nevertheless shared a religious sensibility. In describing the anarchist community in Chicago, Hutchins Hapgood noted: "All the anarchists and social rebels I have known have, more or less, the religious temperament, although a large part of their activity is employed in scoffing at and reviling religion—as they think the God of theology has been largely responsible for the organisation of social and political injustice." Youthful exposure to latter-day puritanism in religion and community morals had left its mark on the social consciousness of an entire generation of prewar rebels. When *The Masses* was banned from New York subway newsstands for preaching "irreligion," Max Eastman asserted that the reason that the artists and writers contributed their best pieces gratis to the magazine was because they had a religion, not one concerned with moneymaking in this world followed by individual salvation in the next, but rather a social religion intent on providing humanity with more happiness and freedom.[35] In his semiautobiographical novel, *Venture*, Eastman described the poet Jo Hancock, in reality John Reed, as coming from "that rocky stock from which New England made her theologians," people who could resist the temptation to be human to stand by a dogma: "Jo's dogma was life, and he was living."[36] In Eastman's view, the artist, like the Puritan, tends toward a gospel of salvation by works, thus infusing an old ethic with new meaning. Greenwich Village artists and intellectuals attributed sanctity to the fervent living of everyday life.

The new radicals were capable of only limited rebellion; many of them were religious in spite of themselves. Floyd Dell, a committed atheist in his youth, confided to Bernard Shaw that the best theory he could devise to explain his behavior to himself was to admit that he was religious.[37] The adolescent Dell transferred his spiritual allegiance to the synagogue of Dr. William Fineshriber, a Davenport rabbi, because in this contact with Judaism he found intellectual satisfaction in the rabbi's sermons, cultural enrichment in the music of the choir, and, most important, a sense of community.[38] Similarly, the young Harry Kemp, convinced that he had ceased altogether to believe in orthodox Christianity, nevertheless, discovered that he still possessed "this all-pervasive need to pray to God. A need as strong as physical hunger."[39] Troubled by his awakening sexuality, Kemp sought refuge in prayer. Religion remained a balm for those poor in spirit. When Mabel Dodge found herself "perpetually unassuaged," unlucky in love, and unfulfilled by the power conferred upon her by public opinion, she thought to herself, "only religion will fill me, some day I will find God."[40] And religion could deepen the sense of purpose of those who had found personal meaning in rebellion. Isadora Duncan, who spurned the trappings of formal religion, demanded that the dance of the future "become again a high religious art as it was with the Greeks."[41] Duncan felt that all art had to be rooted in religion or it would be ignoble, a mere product of the mercantile spirit.[42] Thus Duncan, who despised the church, consecrated her life to an art that was profoundly religious in conception.

If historical Christianity had lost its meaning in the modern age, the spirit of religion had not. George Cram Cook had discarded the teachings of the church only to reinvent the religion of Jesus as proof that it was the inevitable expression of sorrow and love. Cook believed that even if every vestige of Christianity were destroyed, the faith itself would be reborn among the brokenhearted of the future. He found that he could attain a state of inner peace by secret acts of charity and self-sacrifice, that the practice of Christian virtues brought solace to his spirit.[43]

Randolph Bourne also found consolation in religion. Plagued by a sense of social guilt analogous to that of his Puritan ancestors, Bourne rejected the traditional pursuit of individual salvation to engage in a strenuous effort to criticize himself and the culture in which he lived.[44] He argued that agnosticism ought to be dead, that a philosophy of pure cognition was inadequate to explain human values and emotions. Although the church had become stultified and stereotyped, religion, like art, remained a valid attempt to fix and render intelligible life and life's meaning.[45] Bourne noted that the rising generation was demanding a "definite faith," one that would concern itself with social, rather than individual, salvation; such a humanitarian faith could be transfigured into a "Religion of Socialism."[46]

In seeking to present itself to the unconverted, the socialist movement had to develop a position on religion that would not alienate potential converts among churchgoing members of the middle class. Socialists maintained that freedom of religious belief was essential to democracy, and a large section of the American wing of the party even argued that only under socialism could the teachings of pure Christianity be realized.[47] As a further precaution against charges of promoting irreligion, the Socialist party inserted into its 1908 platform the following statement: "The Socialist Party is primarily an economic and political movement. It is not concerned with matters of religious belief."[48]

The prewar period saw numerous attempts to reconcile socialism and religion. Morris Hillquit insisted upon the socialist commitment to absolute religious freedom and argued that if the laws of gravitation and natural selection could be deemed compatible with the belief in a personal Creator and Ruler of the Universe, then the theory of economic determinism that underlay socialism should provide no greater challenge to a theistic faith.[49] John Spargo developed an elaborate set of socialist apologetics in his lectures before the People's Institute in Cooper Union, entitled *The Spiritual Significance of Socialism* (1908).[50] Spargo tried to present the class struggle not as an attempt to enthrone one class in place of another but as an effort to obliterate class rule; thus he could label it as "essentially a spiritual struggle."[51] He went on to argue that in subduing all racial and religious hatred and suspicion, in fighting to replace a system of privilege with equality of opportunity, socialists were helping to achieve economic justice, "the only basis upon which the divine fabric of human brotherhood can be raised!"[52] Max Eastman used the occasion of the second *Masses* trial to instruct the jury that socialism was in no way opposed to religion. He noted that the hundreds of millions of socialists all over the world must comprise among their numbers every kind of religion. And he closed this section of his speech by appropriating Jesus Christ for Socialist party purposes: "As for me, my father and mother were both ministers, and I was brought up with the utmost love for the character and the beauty of the teachings of Jesus of Nazareth, and I count Him much nearer in His faith and His influence to the message of the Socialists than to the message of any other political body of men."[53]

William English Walling was nearly alone among Socialist party leaders in announcing his opposition to religion, even in its so-called evolutionary forms. He claimed that humanity had passed beyond the point of having a psychological need for religion; the old habits of faith had been lost forever.[54] Although Walling did not believe that the ruling class had ever deliberately manufactured religion for its own purposes, he did contend that "every form of religion from the earliest times to the present has had its utility as a means of class rule."[55]

Apart from isolated notes of dissension, most socialists and certain progressive clerics tried to effect a reconciliation between socialism and religion. Eugene Debs Christianized the socialist movement and helped to invest it with respectability. For those socialists who clung to their old religious faith, Debs personified the Christ figure, the humble workman who sacrifices himself to bring salvation to the oppressed masses.[56] Debs advanced the claim that Christianity was impossible under capitalism, that only socialism could accomplish the economic changes needed to permit the reign of brotherly love.[57] Even for most Jewish party members, "socialism was Judaism secularized." The dissemination of socialism was seen as a "sacred duty," an obligation to enlighten and uplift fellow Jews who had not seen the light. Moreover, Jewish socialists hoped to provide for laboring humanity in this world a reward similar to that which Judaism promised to the righteous in the world to come.[58]

The invocation of Christianity in particular, with its pledge of ultimate redemption, injected a note of optimism into the socialist movement. Horace

Traubel fused Marx and Christ in *Chants Communal* to foretell "the first coming of the worker."[59] In this series of prose-poems Traubel implored his audience to ready itself for social salvation.[60] He affirmed an intimate connection between political commitment and religious faith: "God is not way off somewhere waiting to be worshiped. God is in the cause. And in the cause I worship God."[61] John Haynes Holmes tried to popularize the notion that the religion of the future would eschew ritual and dogma to emphasize moral development and social sympathy.[62] Christianity would change from a religion of charity to one of justice, and the church, therefore, would be compelled to deal not merely with individuals but with society itself, entering the fields of education, politics, and industry to preach the gospel of Christ.[63]

Among other *Masses'* contributors who concerned themselves with the application of Christianity to the social order were Lincoln Steffens, Charles Erskine Scott Wood, and Randolph Bourne. Steffens was in many ways the most naive because he was the most literal. He believed that the original muckrakers were the prophets of the Old Testament and thus viewed himself as merely a part of a vital religious tradition.[64] Unfortunately he decided to apply the "Golden Rule" to one of the most explosive political situations of his day. When the McNamara Brothers had been arrested for dynamiting the *Los Angeles Times* building, the Socialist Job Harriman was mounting a promising mayoralty campaign in that city. Steffens convinced Clarence Darrow, defense counsel for the McNamaras, to let him settle the case according to Christian principles since it had been tearing Los Angeles apart. He spoke to the leading capitalists, making them promise that they would not seek revenge and would negotiate with labor. The settlement was supposed to involve a confession from the McNamaras. The district attorney wanted a life term for J. B. McNamara plus some punishment for J. J. McNamara but agreed that there would be no denunciation of labor.[65] However, to Steffens's dismay, on Sunday the churches of Los Angeles preached "hate and disappointed revenge." Their sermons were reported across the United States, and other churches, equally incapable of recognizing applied Christianity, used the McNamara confession as a means of lambasting labor.

The results were an unmitigated disaster. In sentencing the McNamaras, Judge Bordwell denounced them and made a public statement that the little he had mitigated their punishment was the result of judicial discretion and bore no relation to any policy favored by Steffens, who, he noted, was a professed anarchist. Local citizens, shocked by revelations of labor violence, abandoned their support of the Socialist ticket, and Harriman was defeated. And finally the contract made between capital and labor to promote class harmony was broken on the part of the employers. Only then did Steffens learn the cynical truth that "the Christian churches would not recognize Christianity if they saw it," but the price of his enlightenment was draconian justice for the

McNamaras and major setbacks for both the Socialist party and organized labor.[66]

Both Wood and Bourne lacked Steffens's naive faith in the immediate application of Christianity to the solution of social problems. Wood contributed a series of comic dialogues on the subject of religion to *The Masses*; in 1927 these pieces and others were published under the title *Heavenly Discourse*.[67] Wood's approach was to people his Heaven with Mark Twain, Robert Ingersoll, Mary Wollstonecraft, Rabelais, Voltaire, and other favorites among the world's freethinkers and to allow them to discuss Comstockery, revivalism, Social Darwinism, free love, war, and temperance. His satires presented God and Christ as anarchists who had no use for the censorship and repression practiced in their name.[68] But Wood's solution to earthly misery was essentially socialist in nature. His God argues that war and poverty can end only when mankind loses its instinct for self-preservation and decides to end the private ownership of the great natural resources of the planet to free these resources for social use.[69] Randolph Bourne held a similar view of socialism as "applied Christianity."[70] Bourne hoped that a "Religion of Socialism" could move toward "an ever more socialized human life on earth."[71] Thus both he and Wood hoped that through education and inspiration mankind gradually could learn to view socialism as the ultimate expression of the Christian promise. Although they both acknowledged the reactionary power of the churches in their own time, they believed that the future belonged to socialism and Christian brotherhood.[72]

Christ as Revolutionary

In fusing Christianity and socialism, the new radicals had to devise a view of Jesus that would be consistent with socialist principles. They substituted a portrait of Christ as a revolutionary figure for the traditional notion that he had urged his followers to accept earthly deprivation in hope of salvation in the world to come. Eugene Debs claimed that twenty centuries of attempts by the ruling class to make Christ appear to be the divinely commissioned soother of the oppressed did not suffice to erase his revolutionary personality. To Debs Jesus remained "the greatest moral force in the world" and the economic and social gospel he preached one of pure communism.[73] John Spargo stated that socialists and progressive workers might hurl invectives against reactionary churches, but for Christ himself they felt only "reverence and love."[74] Lincoln Steffens compared Jesus to leading Progressives as an enemy of privilege and depicted the Apostles as "practicing communists." In what may have been an effort at self-justification for his own role in the McNamara affair, Steffens claimed that the churches subsequently had ignored Christ's teachings because he, presumably like Steffens, "had evidently tried not only to preach Christianity, but proposed also a scheme to make it possible!"[75]

The concept of Christ as a revolutionary was pervasive among the artists and intellectuals who contributed to *The Masses*. Charles P. Fagnan, a professor at the Union Theological Seminary in New York, submitted an article in which he argued that the "class consciousness" of Christ, here defined in non-Marxist terms as sympathy primarily with the whole human race and secondarily with the oppressed, enabled him to withstand the Temptation.[76] In his reminiscences Upton Sinclair claimed that as a little child he had imbibed the "spirit of social revolution" by reading the life of Jesus in the New Testament.[77] He later portrayed Christ as the founder of socialism, a tramp and an outcast who had died the death of a criminal that he might preach revolution to the dispossessed.[78] In a diary entry of 25 December 1909 the artist John Sloan explained his refusal to attend church on the grounds that it would be hypocritical to be present at services whose ideas contradicted the intentions of "that great Socialist Jesus Christ." Sloan viewed Christ as a "revolutionist" and the church as a reactionary servant of exploiters through its willingness to preach contentment to the victim.[79]

Bouck White devoted an entire book, *The Call of the Carpenter* (1912), to his exposition of Christ as a workman-agitator. White claimed that eighteen years of work as a day laborer caused Jesus to identify himself ever afterward with the working class in its struggle against the industrial despotism of Rome.[80] He saw Christ as a revolutionary figure who transformed the relation between religion and poverty. Christ recognized the power of charity to take the insurrectionary edge off poverty and, therefore, forebade it; charity was no substitute for justice.[81] White tailored his portrait of Christ to the contemporary scene. In an age of urbanization he claimed that Christ preached the civic ideal, "the holy city descending from God out of heaven." Christianity was no abstract ideal. By choosing to live in the city, the point of greatest economic pressure, Jesus translated religion into a social gospel fit for the multitudes.[82] White and other *Masses'* radicals attempted to enlist Christ in their own crusades. If Max Eastman and the magazine staff viewed churchdom as opposed to the struggle of the lower classes for liberty and a better world, they also surmised that Christ "was more than half in favor of these things."[83] Hence Jesus was adopted as an ally of the new radicalism.

Christ's image was projected through many prisms of desire. To Art Young Christ was a workingman-agitator who in Young's time would be one of the many itinerant speakers proclaiming the message of industrial democracy.[84] Such a view would enable Young to reconcile his youthful religion and the political faith that informed his later years. To Harry Kemp, the hobo poet, Christ was a "super-tramp," a "divine hobo" who consorted with outcasts and criminals.[85] Kemp emphasized the merciful qualities of Christ, his ability to forgive sinners. In "Impenitence" he rejoiced in his own life of sin, which allowed him to probe the mystery of good and evil, secure in the knowledge that Christ knew the human condition and would forgive all. In a sense, Christ pardoned Kemp the man and allowed Kemp the poet to "wax folly-wise."[86]

Hutchins Hapgood, a sympathetic chronicler of criminal life, portrayed Christ as "the greatest Reformer who ever lived," a figure who shared Hapgood's willingness to apply patience and charity in dealing with criminals.[87] In keeping with the cult of youth, Horace Traubel saw Jesus as "boyhood resisting the invasions of the Hebrew plutocracies," a figure too young to brook oppression without resistance.[88] Christ, therefore, was used to sanction the intemperance with which radicals approached social change. Similarly Margaret Sanger invoked Jesus as a supporter of birth control. She asserted that Christ, who associated with sinners and publicans, who paid little heed to sins of the flesh, would find his religion of love and brotherhood more truly expressed in the scientific research done in birth control clinics than in the opulent cathedrals or pompous rituals of the church.[89]

Floyd Dell epitomized the radical penchant for adapting Christ to personal needs. After reading the gospel of St. Mark, Dell conceived a qualified admiration for its protagonist. He found "a certain pith of wisdom" in Christ's statements: "He [Christ] resented family ties, like Samuel Butler; he was an impatiently hostile critic of marriage, like Ibsen; he had a deep contempt for work done not in joy but for bread and butter, just as William Morris had; and he believed that the kingdom of heaven is within us, like Bob Ingersoll, from whom I first learned that revolutionary doctrine."[90] In casting Christ as a revolutionary figure, radicals made him all things to all men. The first socialist, the friend of sinners and criminals, a workman-agitator, this Christ allowed radicals to fuse their old religious faith with their newly acquired political beliefs. Christianity, not church dogma but the living faith of Jesus, became a prop of socialism.

Chapter 7 The New Feminism

Stereotyping by Sex

The Victorian heritage of the new radicals was particularly evident with regard to their feminism. Although most of them campaigned actively for equality between the sexes, their view of sex roles was limited by stereotypes inherited from a previous age. The Victorians viewed the female body as a limited system that provided women with only enough energy for childbearing. Physicians advocated that young women limit their activities to a quiet regimen of domestic routine that would provide moderate exercise and permit the full development of the maternal organs.[1] Obviously such a view of women saw the maternal function as their transcendent purpose and designated the home as women's proper sphere. This Victorian view was reinforced for the new radicals by the writings of Sigmund Freud. From a Freudian perspective, women were *hommes manqués*, embittered for having been wronged from infancy, brought into the world as women instead of as men.[2] They were lesser beings of a different order from men. Sexual differentiation was reflected in personality type from infancy onward; females by nature tended toward passivity and sexual repression.[3]

Victorian stereotypes pervaded the writings of the new radicals on the subject of women. Charles Erskine Scott Wood viewed nature as a feminine principle, benevolent, soothing, a mother to a helpless child.[4] Wood viewed himself as that child, who rested his head in Nature's lap and there found ease and the succor of freedom.[5] This image also occurs during Floyd Dell's psychoanalysis. Dell composed four lines of verse about a dream in which he returned to a female figure and laid his head upon her knees to weep; the woman silently drew his hands into hers "for rest and keeping." In recalling the dream Dell realized that the woman in it had been his mother, a "very illuminating" thought for a man in analysis.[6] Both in Wood's poetic fancy and in Dell's dream-work women appear as maternal creatures who can bring rest and comfort to their troubled men-children.

127

Women are seen as aloof from the corruption and struggles of daily life. This idealization of women took many forms. In the dramatic romance written by Charles Eugene Banks and George Cram Cook, *In Hampton Roads* (1899), the reunion of the protagonists, Earl Hamilton and Virginia Eggleston, is portrayed as the infusion of feminine spirituality into the male: "The glory passed into his heart, the hush of worship came upon him, and he knew that here, shining in a woman's eyes, he beheld what men call God."[7] This worship of woman as a pure, sacred force also occurs in the love lyrics of Louis Untermeyer: "My Soul, how could you ever doubt / That she was less than all divine [?]"[8] Women were supposed to be too pure to be selfish, too sensitive to ignore the claims of justice. John Spargo argued that socialism appealed most strongly to women because their experience of motherhood allowed them a deeper understanding of the revolutionary demand that equality of opportunity be the birthright of every child. Men gave intellectual assent to socialism; women offered their hearts.[9]

Women belonged above the competitive struggle. Outside of the workplace it was possible to surround their image with an aura of romance, which faded when they won the equality of drudgery. Abraham Cahan wrote in *The Rise of David Levinsky* (1917): "The factory is scarcely a proper setting for romance. It is one of the battle-fields in our struggle for existence, where we treat woman as an inferior being, whereas in civilized love-making we prefer to keep up the chivalrous fiction that she is our superior."[10] Certainly *The Masses'* radicals tended to invest the women they knew with a natural superiority to men. We have seen the idealization of strong maternal figures that characterized many of the male radicals. This was coupled with the fact that these men formed friendships and love relationships with women in Greenwich Village or Provincetown, both oases from the degradations of the commercial world. Liberal opinion agreed that the increasing presence of women in public life was destined to work for the benefit of humanity because women were peculiarly suited for the task of social uplift.[11] The implicit assumption was that, by remaining aloof from competitive strife for so long, women then could enter civic life as disinterested public servants.

Work proved to be a touchstone of sexual behavior. In attitude and assignment, it was assumed that men and women approached work differently. John Dewey's influence helped to maintain orthodox social and economic roles for the sexes. Dewey expected the school to prepare children for their allotted tasks in life—"the girls to be more efficient house managers, if not actually cooks and sempstresses; the boys (were our educational system only adequately rounded out into trade schools) for their vocations."[12] Dewey presupposed that women would remain confined to the traditional careers arising out of their roles on the farm at a time when office and factory jobs were becoming more readily available to them. Moreover, although the male radicals had a true sense of vocation—here note Upton Sinclair's unfailing belief in his own genius or Floyd Dell's commitment to his first novel—the women, with the possible exceptions of Margaret Sanger and Elizabeth Gurley Flynn, had difficulty adjusting their work to meet the demands of their personal lives. For example, Isadora Duncan went to France with her patron-lover, Paris Singer, and in the villa they rented at Beaulieu, apart from her world of dance, she was able to ponder the division between art and life. She wondered "if a woman can ever really be an artist, since Art is a hard task-master who demands everything, whereas a woman who loves gives up everything to life."[13] Romance often eclipsed all other concerns in the lives of Emma Goldman and Mabel Dodge, and both Neith Boyce and Susan Glaspell adapted their careers to the needs of their more famous husbands.

A novel by Susan Glaspell, *The Glory of the Conquered* (1909), significantly subtitled *The Story of a Great Love*, provides detailed evidence of a belief that women's work is of negligible importance when compared with the work chosen by a man. Ernestine Stanley, an artist, weds Karl Hubers, a university professor engaged in cancer research. After a year's honeymoon in Europe, both return to their respective work, but Karl is suddenly blinded after carelessly rubbing a deadly germ into his eyes. Ernestine remains his faithful wife and even secretly gives up her own career in art to be Karl's "eyes" in the laboratory. She thinks of herself as the woman in the Gloria Victis, the Greek statue in which the winged warrior with broken sword is upheld by a woman. Karl eventually develops appendicitis and is rushed to the hospital while they are apart. Ernestine tries to save him by telling him of her laboratory preparations. He dies transfigured by her love. However, Ernestine finds herself despondent and bitter. She overcomes this resentment by dedicating years to painting a portrait of the transfigured Karl before death, which, after exhibition abroad, she donates to the University of Chicago, where he had performed his research. Thus she returns to art to express her love for Karl.[14]

The Glory of the Conquered is filled with blatant sexual stereotyping. Karl is portrayed as scientific, logical, engaged in the life-saving work of cancer research while Ernestine's work is emotional and of less importance. He is stoical and purposeful; she succumbs to her feminine weaknesses by fainting at Dr. Parkman's operation or by becoming hysterical upon learning that Karl is ill. She is passive while he thrusts marriage upon her and shapes her life. Even after his death, she resigns herself to celibacy for years and produces only work inspired by him. The novel assumes that only a man can have a true sense of vocation. When Ernestine asks Karl if his worst pain is the work he misses while blind, his affirmative response seems to release him from a long bondage: " 'Ernestine—no one but a man can quite see that. What *is* a man without a man's work? What is there for him to do but sit around in a namby-pamby fashion and be fussed over and coddled and cheered up! Lord'—he threw away her hands and turned his face from her—'I'd rather be dead!' "[15] Glaspell invests man's work with supreme importance while relegating women to a minor role as man's comforter. Although Glaspell herself was a feminist who produced a significant number of plays and novels, she assumed that few women could produce great art. A friend tells Ernestine that Mr. Ryan, an admirer of her work, was upset by her failure to paint: " 'He said you were *one* American woman who was an artist instead of a "woman who paints." ' "[16] Only the exceptional woman made a significant contribution to the world of art; most women produced ephemera.

If few women could engage in artistic creation, all women could serve as inspiration for the novels, paintings, poems, and dramas produced by their more gifted counterparts. Both Floyd Dell and Eugene O'Neill were haunted by childhood fantasies of a dream-girl who would be the perfect soul-mate for a young poet. Dell had a recurrent dream of an empty room in the top of a barn where he had a dream-companionship with an elusive girl. When he had that dream for the last time, the barn caught fire and vanished in flames, but he had no regrets because he had saved his dream-companion, who turned out to be his second wife, B. Marie Gage.[17] Dell considered the dream a good omen for their marital happiness, and it was this marriage that sustained him in his resolve to finally produce a novel.[18] Eugene O'Neill also had childhood dreams of an elusive companion who made him feel complete. When he met his first wife, Agnes Boulton, O'Neill recognized her as the other presence in his dreams. He wanted her alone "in an aloneness broken by nothing"—not even by their own children.[19] The portrait of Agnes Boulton that emerges from her autobiography is one of a self-effacing woman, who nursed O'Neill through bouts of drunkenness, shared his poverty and the bitter isolation of winters at Provincetown, at great expense to her own literary efforts.

The romantic notion that women lived primarily for love was fairly common. This idea was always present in the writings of Floyd Dell, but it became more pronounced after his *Masses* period. In his novel *Souvenir* (1929) the hero, Felix Fay, wants his son Prentiss to go to his sweetheart Betty Postgate to make up for his affair with Helen Dorsey. Fay muses that his son will think that his father failed to comprehend the situation: "He would think that a girl so young, so inexperienced, would be too deeply hurt ever to forgive him. As if forgiving a lover *anything* wasn't what made a girl happy, affording her a proof of her own love!"[20]

The notion that women found true happiness only in loving men was not merely a masculine form of self-flattery; it was shared by women themselves. Mary Heaton Vorse wrote a novel entitled *The Heart's Country* (1914) whose central idea was that women's true accomplishments lay in the quality of their loving. Roberta, the friend of the heroine, Ellen Payne, reflects on the pains and triumphs of Ellen's romantic life and decides that "this silent making and marring of the hearts of women means the fate of all men forever." Roberta concludes from her friend's bitter experiences, "I fancy that women will have another bar of judgment and that the question asked of us there will be: Have you loved well?"[21] Nor was this notion merely a romantic fiction; it shaped such lives as those of Isadora Duncan, Emma Goldman, and Mabel Dodge. All these women would disregard their other accomplishments when they felt themselves failures in love.

The woman who may have best exemplified the feminine cult of love was Mabel Dodge. Her four-volume autobiography can be read as a quest for sexual fulfillment; power and purpose derive from the relentless struggle between the sexes. Dodge admitted her utter dependence upon men to wrest her from the "fatal inner immobility" from which she had suffered since childhood. A brief separation from her lover sufficed to plunge her into emptiness. When she left John Reed in Provincetown to journey with Neith Boyce to Florence, where Reed would join them at her villa, Dodge complained: "I, myself, had sunk into the unrelated blankness from which I suffered when I found myself unattached to someone, and no longer borne up and supported by the male contiguity through which alone I seemed to become real to myself."[22] The affair with Reed caused her to discard the illusion that she was a maker of history and to give up all else for love.[23] Lacking other outlets for her energies and emotions, Dodge became consummately jealous of Reed and found release only when he fell ill with diphtheria. His illness created a sense of his helplessness and dependency that allowed her for a time the illusion of complete possession. She admitted that in attaining ascendancy over men in periods of illness, women gained possession not only of them, but of their own souls, once more.[24] Dodge philosophized that the only happy woman had no history, "for by happy we mean the loving and beloved, and by history we designate all those relatable occurrences on earth caused by the human energies seeking other outlets than the biological one."[25] Dodge dismissed her own role in shaping the cultural history of her day and stripped her autobiography of any wider significance by writing: "That I have so many pages to write signifies, solely, that I was unlucky in love."[26]

If women were to devote themselves to love, the care of the offspring of romantic unions acquired greater importance. In the nineteenth century both advocates of voluntary motherhood and free-love proponents clung to the cult of motherhood; they accepted the stereotypes of feminine passivity and domesticity in order to strengthen the position of women within the conventions of marriage and family life.[27] These notions were reinforced by the writings of European social radicals who gained an American audience in the early twentieth century. Despite pleas for a transformation in the relation between the sexes, these radicals helped to buttress the traditional concept of the feminine role.

Edward Carpenter, for example, in *Love's Coming-of-Age* (1896) argued that motherhood was "woman's great and incomparable work"; if properly fulfilled, such work engaged women in "the broadest and largest culture."[28] The argument, in short, is that creative motherhood can transform the home into an exciting microcosm of the larger society. This argument gained vogue again decades later when women threatened to remain in the workplace after their emergency employment during World War II and the Korean War. According to Betty Friedan in *The Feminine Mystique* (1963) male-dominated advertising then sought to portray housework as a science and an art in order to lure women back to their homes.[29] Moreover, Carpenter viewed women as closer to nature and hence more primitive and more emotional than men. This view also had economic implications. If woman confined herself to the universe of the child, she could provide the refuge and solace for her mate demanded by Victorian ideology, thereby fortifying him for his struggles in a Social Darwinist business world. These limitations on the woman were crucial to the preservation of the economic order: "it is to her that Man, after his excursions and wanderings, mental and physical, continually tends to return as to his primitive home and resting place, to restore his balance, to find his centre of life, and to draw stores of energy and inspiration for fresh conquests of the outer world."[30] Even if women were to share with men that wider sphere of activity, it was assumed that they would bring to it those feminine instincts nurtured by the home. In *The Marriage Revolt* (1915) William E. Carson wrote that as decreased family size and increased household efficiency freed more women from the home, these women extended their housekeeping instinct to the municipality and their maternal instinct to all the nation's children. Carson posited the maternal instinct as a fixed feature of feminine nature but one that could be adapted to the needs of the body politic.[31] In short, all of women's experience, whether domestic or worldly, was to be shaped by biological imperatives beyond their control.

Even the most advanced rhetoric could belie a traditional view of women's fate. The influential Swedish author Ellen Key in *Love and Marriage* (1911) championed free love but justified it on the grounds that women's desire to be made happy at any price through love unconsciously referred to a deeper longing for motherhood.[32] For Key the ultimate expression of the new womanhood was for women to regard men "merely as a means to the child." Women would hopefully restrain their temporary lust for vengeance for centuries of oppression at the hands of men to enlist the latter in the central task of child-rearing.[33] Key held that the greatest value of healthy womanhood lay in procreation; all other pursuits sapped women's strength and vitality from that essential function. She acknowledged that women experienced a momentous conflict between "two equally strong, healthy, and beautiful forms of life: the life of the soul or the life of the family."[34] But for Key there was clearly only one proper course in resolving the conflict, namely unselfish dedication to the demands of maternity: "But it may be—according to a very moderate calculation—that there are annually produced by the women of the world a hundred thousand novels and works of art, which might better have been boys and girls!"[35]

The Masses' radicals echoed the European social theorists in their romanticization of maternity. Even the ever-restless Mabel Dodge achieved perfect satisfaction in pregnancy. She found herself detached from worrisome social obligations while performing her supreme biological service to the race; she, therefore, commended the months of pregnancy to other women as a time especially precious and unique.[36] Socialist writers also emphasized the uniqueness of maternity, but their primary concern was social benefit, not individual satisfaction. William English Walling contended that even if pregnancy and childbirth were relieved of all of their terrors by medical progress, they would remain the most momentous events in a woman's life. In his view both celibacy and the childless life were inferior modes to a more normal existence and were justifiable only "if the fuller and more natural life is in some way cut off."[37] John Spargo went even further in his conscription of womanhood. He argued that there was no substitute for maternal affection and attention; hence all schemes for communal or cooperative child care were at best necessary evils suitable only for orphans and foundlings. During her child-raising years a woman's place remained the home and only the home: "Every human child needs and should have 'a pair of mother's arms all its own.'"[38]

And even a dreamer like Floyd Dell was to discover that women shared a deep, if sometimes unexpressed, longing for motherhood. Although Dell was an exponent of free love unencumbered by parental responsibilities, the notebook from his Chicago period contains a listing under B of stories concerning babies, all of which describe how women, whether single, married, or widowed, overcome obstacles to maternity.[39] As we have seen, Dell's flight from bohemia to suburbia confirmed him in the belief that women were designed for motherhood and, in fact, desired that end. By the time he wrote *Love in the Machine Age* (1930), Dell equated the acceptance of marriage and parenthood with maturity and adult responsibility. He repudiated the feminist notion of a career in favor of urging women to work for several years after marriage to prepare for the babies to come.[40] And he utterly disavowed the free-love ideal he had championed in his youth:

> *It needs to be said that useful wage-labor, enlivened by occasional secret sexual love-affairs, probably punctuated at intervals by abortions, without prospect of permanency and without hope of mutual responsi-*

ble parenthood, is not a glorious or even a satisfactory career for a young woman. It is merely a combination of patriarchal nunship with patriarchal hetairism.[41]

If Dell rejoiced in his discovery that women desired babies, Upton Sinclair faced that prospect with dismay. When the penniless poet found that his wife, presumed to be interested in nothing but inspiring and fostering his career, not only was pregnant but wanted the child, Sinclair reconciled himself to fatherhood at the expense of his art.[42]

Motherhood was not merely woman's true destiny; it also was supposed to determine her relentless opposition to war. The South African feminist Olive Schreiner argued that women would end war because they alone knew the history and cost of human flesh.[43] In America the new radicals, too, assumed that women were natural pacifists. John Spargo claimed that socialism and motherhood shared a common hatred of war and militarism; he urged the socialist movement to aim a special appeal to women on that account.[44] The actual coming of war merely provided the new radicals with additional proof of their beliefs. Art Young wrote a moving description of the ordeal of Jeanette Rankin, representative from Montana, who sobbing in despair cast her vote against American entry into World War I: "So Jeanette Rankin, in that nest of dominant males, made herself heard. If the manner was essentially feminine, nevertheless it was truly the voice of the maternal instinct which seeks to protect life rather than destroy it."[45]

The reports of the war abroad added strength to the argument. From her observation of the war in Italy, France, and England, Mabel Dodge concluded that women universally opposed war. They needed to be aroused and educated to make that opposition effective but were the only force that could resist war's appeal to men: "The only hope of permanent peace lies in a woman's war against war."[46] Mary Heaton Vorse reported from France that men viewed the war as adventure; it welded them into an engine of destruction while their women dedicated themselves to errands of mercy.[47] This divergence in attitude reflected profound differences in life experience. The most significant event for woman was the gift of life whereas for man the supreme adventure was life's destruction in warfare. The result was an unbridgeable gap in communication between the sexes.[48] Vorse noted the stirring of the women of France, which when self-conscious was dubbed feminism, and found that its roots lay "in women's age-old mute protest against war."[49] Although Young, Dodge, and Vorse found inspiration in women's pacifism, they concurred in portraying it as ineffectual in stemming the tides of war.

Some of the blame was placed on women's lack of familiarity with the political process. However, many of the new radicals also paid tribute to a modified version of the domestic ideal and thought that women could be truly effective only through their role in the home and the immediate community. We have already seen the impact of John Dewey's notions of progressive education, which relegated women to a domestic career while preparing men for work in a trade.[50] The home retained much of its Victorian sanctity, which partially explains all the efforts to reform rather than discard it. Mary Heaton Vorse expressed the centrality of the home to feminine experience in her chronicle of life at Provincetown: "Women are meant to have houses as they are meant to have children of their own."[51] Because the home did not mirror accepted social ideals for the new radicals but instead reflected individual rebellion, it required even more self-conscious effort to design and maintain. And the tendency was to enroll women in the task of reforming the home. In *Drift and Mastery* (1914) Walter Lippmann urged the theorists of feminism against encouraging more women to seek economic independence in the marketplace. He claimed that any further influx of female workers would only increase economic disorder, and he offered domesticity as a competing ideal: "For the great mass, women's work in the future will, I believe, be in the application of the arts and sciences to a deepened and more extensively organized home."[52]

Only an occasional voice was raised in protest against this stereotyping of women. In part the silence reflected favorable stereotypes; women were portrayed as more natural, emotional, loving, and peaceable than men. One commentator, June Sochen, has noted that the art and prose of *The Masses* consistently upheld feminine superiority: "The cartoons and the articles frequently portrayed men as ignorant, drunken, and cruel while the women were selfless and long suffering."[53] However, a few writers did speculate about the origins and importance of sexual differentiation. Floyd Dell posited that an early knowledge revolution led mankind to divide itself by sex. Young men were educated for war and the chase while young women were prepared for domestic duties. Dell argued that this division, substantially one of intellectual rather than physical labor, persisted to the modern age regardless of changing evolutionary conditions. Hence each sex encountered needless institutional and psychological barriers to learning how to perform those tasks traditionally designated as within the province of the opposite sex.[54] The separate treatment of the two sexes was not based upon simple physical differences. Eugene Wood in an article entitled "Foolish Female Fashions" noted that boys and girls of age eleven similarly attired had roughly comparable athletic abilities. However, seven or eight years later the female of the species found herself imprisoned in garments designed to render her immobile so that the easily discouraged male would encounter no obstacle to his pursuit.[55] William English Walling carried these speculations to their logical conclusion. He argued that it was ludicrous to apply the theory of sexual selection to mankind. Biological differences dwindled in importance with every advance of civilization. Therefore, Walling concluded: "The contrast between the men and women of our time is due infinitely more to differences of early training than it is to fundamental biological differences."[56] If environment did supersede heredity in determining sexual traits, it then became possible to create a new race of women capable of destroying the stereotypes that had shackled their predecessors.

The New Woman

Early twentieth-century feminism aimed at achieving equality between the sexes. One of its earliest and most fervent exponents, William Allen White, by 1914 ruefully concluded that he had "supposed 'feminism' meant giving a latch-key to mother" but found that it meant instead "taking the latch-key away from father."[57] For those most intimately connected with the feminist movement, it effected a revolution in their daily lives, upsetting traditional sex roles and disconcerting even its most committed adherents. Feminism was not reducible to a demand for the franchise, although many middle-class leaders of the suffrage movement tried to focus it on that narrow goal. Floyd Dell aptly noted that the modern women's movement benefited from the liberating influence of evolutionary science and psychology: "it is to the body that one looks for the Magna Charta of feminism."[58] Feminism promised to liberate the whole modern woman.

The Masses was in the vanguard of the feminist movement. Its contributors assumed that economic and political reform were insufficient goals, that women needed far more options than those traditionally available to them. Even the demands raised by proponents of middle-class reform fell far short of meeting feminine needs. In his unpublished study of *The Masses* John Waite commented: "Love and nature and children had as much claim to fulfillment for the individual woman as career and politics and the public life of society. The dearth of either kind of satisfaction proved the bitter need to revolutionize society."[59]

Greenwich Village provided a context of nurture for modern feminism. It offered freedom from the constraints of propriety. If the women of the Latin Quarter were victimized to gratify and amuse men, their counterparts in the Village retained all their rights and the full respect of the community. Even the most advanced thinkers among the men found themselves at a disadvantage under the new regime and suffered psychologically from women's full assumption of what were once exclusively male privileges.[60] The Village was able to provide feminists with a community receptive to their values, yet it was linked to American society at large.[61] Most of the Village feminists were successful in merging their personal and professional lives. Many combined marriage, motherhood, and a career, and none fit the mannish stereotypes that the opponents of feminism had created to describe and dismiss them.[62] Rose Pastor Stokes, Susan Glaspell, Neith Boyce, and Mary Heaton Vorse had husbands committed to feminism, and Emma Goldman's lover Alexander Berkman and Elizabeth Gurley Flynn's lover Carlo Tresca accepted women's equality as part of their revolutionary program.[63] As a result, Village feminists gladly welcomed male support.[64]

The Village was merely the headquarters for the new feminism, but its influence reached a much wider public. Margaret Deland served notice of a distinct change in the feminine ideal to a popular audience in her article for the *Atlantic Monthly* of March 1910. Deland claimed that modern women lacked the old-fashioned sense of duty to others regardless of the personal expense. Instead they grasped new experiences and opportunities. The new ideal emphasized individualism and relegated the family to secondary importance.[65] Modern women questioned the value of the old selflessness, which sacrificed the individual welfare and happiness of women to that of their husbands and families; they argued that while such women had grown in grace, their families had been rendered more selfish as a result.[66]

The new feminine ideal was unsettling; it challenged description. Even avowed feminists found it difficult to supply metaphors that would render the new woman intelligible to the unconverted. Max Eastman made a poetic attempt in "Child of the Amazons" (1913). His heroine, Thyone, is an Amazon who renounces her desire to live with the king, the man she loves, in order to prove herself equal to the world. Yet Thyone is no enemy of man; she prays for the day "when men shall cease / Their tyranny, Amazons their revolt," when both may unite to subdue the earth and share passionate love.[67] Eastman thus implies that any feminine stridency may be a temporary phenomenon preceding a new and healthier balance between the sexes. James Oppenheim used the frontier as a setting for his poetic drama, *The Pioneers* (1910). Conditions at the fringe of settlement demanded that a new woman arise equal to their challenge, manly in her freedom and strength yet imbued with the grace and beauty of eternal womanhood. A new manhood, heroic as the old yet unafraid of tenderness and emotion, would have to arise to mate her.[68] Oppenheim offers the hope that the new womanhood would retain all the virtues of the old in a synthesis more capable of meeting the demands of modern life.

Male radicals approached feminism with mixed motivation. In part, they viewed the liberation of women as simply a piece of their revolutionary program, but many of them cherished a personal interest in bestowing freedom upon women. For example, Randolph Bourne viewed feminism as a rejection of both puritanism and the conventions of romantic love; he hoped that it would inaugurate an era of freer relations between the sexes.[69] Disappointed by his realization that the new women he encountered were more interested in claiming privileges once monopolized by men than in developing the art of personal relations, Bourne grew increasingly cynical about feminism itself.[70] Under the pseudonym of Max Coe, Bourne left to posterity a biting portrait of a new woman and her coterie of feminist friends. Karen herself is described as incapable of fitting men into her carefully constructed Jamesian universe: "she has solved the problem by obliterating them." And her friends are seen as women whose feminism "had done little more for their emotional life than to make them acutely conscious of the cloven hoof of the male."[71] Bourne, who prized the intimacy of feminine friendship because he was so often denied the deeper intimacy of passion, sought personal solace as well as social benefit in feminism. When denied the former, he spurned the latter and turned his back upon the women's movement.

Male feminists found it difficult to discard the sense of their own superiority. Despite preachments of sexual equality, men preferred to view themselves as patrons of feminism. There is no trace of irony in David Karsner's praise of the pioneering efforts of Horace Traubel: "He took woman from her little sphere within four walls and placed her in the parliament of the world."[72] Walter Lippmann felt no awkwardness in detailing what he thought should be the proper aspirations of the women's movement.[73] Even in attacking the behavior of other less sensitive males, the note of noblesse oblige crept in. John Reed wrote a short story entitled "The Rights of Small Nations" (1915) in which the main character is an American living in Bucharest who deals with marriage strictly as a business proposition. Frank wants "a good-looker, with no scandal about her and a social pull that will help me in my job." Moreover, Frank prefers economic dependency in a wife, since a woman with a private income is likely to do as she pleases. The narrator, who clearly represents Reed's point of view, replies, "If I lived with a girl, whether we were married or not, I'd make her my equal, financially and every other way."[74] In his well-intentioned oblivion, the narrator ignores the fact that the female is as dependent in either case upon the good graces of her mate.

Floyd Dell also claimed to be aware of the failings of other males. He asserted that most men were afraid to face the implications of sexual equality, that they preferred an illusion to the task of living in the world of real women.[75] Yet Dell's primary interest in feminism appeared to be in the benefits it would derive for men. He baldly stated, "Feminism is going to make it possible for the first time for men to be free."[76] If men were exempt from the claims of economically dependent women and children, they would no longer be enslaved by the capitalist system.[77] In explaining why he, a male, wrote the articles on feminism that were later incorporated into *Women as World Builders* (1913), Dell noted that the modern women's movement was but another example of feminine willingness to adapt to masculine demand:

Men are tired of subservient women; or, to speak more exactly, of
the seemingly subservient woman who effects her will by stealth—the
petty slave with all the slave's subtlety and cleverness. So long as it
was possible for men to imagine themselves masters, they were satisfied.
But when they found out that they were dupes, they wanted a change.
If only for self-protection, they desired to find in woman a comrade and
an equal. In reality, they desired it because it promised to be more
fun.[78]

Most feminists accepted uncritically the inflated claims advanced on behalf
of the new woman by the women's movement, and most male radicals rested
smugly in the assumption that they were patrons of feminism. A lone voice,
the strident one of Emma Goldman, pierced their complacency and challenged
their beliefs. Goldman denounced the suffrage movement for accepting the
view of middle-class women that they were superior to men in purity, goodness, and morality; until women rid themselves of such delusions, Goldman
found no benefit in awarding them the vote.[79] In particular, Goldman resented
the tendency of her sex to ascribe all evil to the part of the male. If men were
as vile as such women were wont to portray them, it was only fair to place the
blame upon mothers, sisters, wives, and mistresses, who cultivated in men
the strength, egotism, and exaggerated vanity that helped to enslave them. If
such women wanted truly to be free, they would have to learn to be as self-
centered and as determined as men, to accept the risks as well as the benefits
of their newfound courage; only then could women achieve their liberation
and incidentally aid men in becoming free.[80] Goldman insisted that no one
could bestow meaningful privileges upon women, that independence and
development must come only from and through their own efforts. Goldman's
formula for the new woman demanded a far more radical break with convention than that which most of the Village feminists were willing to effect. The
modern woman was to achieve freedom:

First, by asserting herself as a personality, and not as a sex commodity.
Second, by refusing the right to anyone over her body; by refusing to
bear children, unless she wants them; by refusing to be a servant to God,
the State, society, the husband, the family, etc., by making her life
simpler, but deeper and richer. That is, by trying to learn the meaning
and substance of life in all its complexities, by freeing herself from
the fear of public opinion and public condemnation. Only that, and not
the ballot, will set woman free, will make her a force hitherto unknown
in the world, a force for real love, for peace, for harmony; a force
of divine fire, of life-giving; a creator of free men and women.[81]

This formula was intended to preserve the women's movement from devolving into a tool of middle-class reform, a danger in those years of ferment before the Great War but a reality in its aftermath.

The Political and Economic Emancipation of Woman

The American suffrage movement found inspiration abroad in the militant tactics of Sylvia Pankhurst and her supporters among British feminists.[82] The young Walter Lippmann applauded the British suffragettes for turning the question of the vote for women into a burning political issue.[83] He willingly excused their trampling of convention. If the suffragettes were unladylike, Lippmann noted, then the Boston Tea Party had been ungentlemanly and the Civil War bad form; good manners never settled momentous questions.[84] Randolph Bourne, too, was stirred by the forthright manner of the British suffragettes. He hoped that the American women's movement would emulate its freedom from cant, its willingness to discuss the hitherto taboo issues of birth control, prostitution, and venereal disease.[85]

Although American suffragettes proved eventually willing to adopt the militant tactics of their British counterparts, they shunned the more explosive social issues, which were left to a handful of Village feminists. They also tended to couch their arguments in terms acceptable to the Victorian view of womanhood. Rheta Childe Dorr argued that a thousand generations of unpaid, loving service had prepared women to apply the lessons of domesticity to political life.[86] Dorr denied that she was ascribing innate moral superiority to women; instead she argued that they were to be found supporting the new ideals of democracy and social service as a result of their intellectual youth.[87] She failed to deal with the prognosis for their maturity; would women remain a liberal influence years after they had achieved the vote?

The reigning assumption among many suffragists was that women were inherently more sensitive to social issues than were men. Helen Keller began her argument for suffrage with the contention that women should not have to rely upon men's chivalry to obtain justice; they should assert their right to protect themselves and relieve men of this "feudal responsibility."[88] Yet Keller concluded by claiming that women had a stronger social consciousness than men, that their experience of maternity would cause them to use the ballot to prevent war and to defeat militarist ideology.[89] Similarly Sarah N. Cleghorn noted that woman needed the franchise primarily to protect her home and children against exploitation and vice.[90] Walter Lippmann made this argument more explicit. He stated that the mass of women did not view the world as workers; in America their prime interest was as consumers.

Hence the impact of women's suffrage would be to render the consumer "the real master of the political situation."[91]

It was precisely because this view of women's suffrage as an extension of domesticity tended to make woman "a better Christian and homekeeper, a staunch citizen of the State" that Emma Goldman rejected it so vehemently. Such an approach to the ballot would merely strengthen the shackles that bound women to their assigned lot.[92] Floyd Dell managed to poke fun at the bloated claims of the suffrage movement with considerably less venom in his unpublished play "St. George of the Minute: A Comedy of Feminism." Dell's heroine, Priscilla, triumphantly assures her businessman-husband, St. George, that women are about to achieve "The Vote." He responds somewhat belligerently to her scolding by querying: "What are you going to do when you get the vote, my dear? I have a vote right now, and a fat lot of good it does me."[93] Actually Floyd Dell did have in mind a suitable use for the franchise. Like Emma Goldman, he hoped that women would use the ballot to win command over their bodies, to remove existing penalties against the spread of contraceptive information.[94] But both of them realized that such a result could proceed only from a fundamental change in women's consciousness.

Max Eastman held the reverse expectation. He believed that the ballot itself would serve to broaden women's experience and thus prepare them for political responsibility. When Mrs. Marshall, the wife of the vice-president, argued that current fashions were proof enough that women should be denied the vote, Eastman responded that such foolishness provided the main argument in favor of women's suffrage. If women were permitted to embark on a life of adventure and achievement, they would abandon their preoccupation with trivialities.[95] In fact, Eastman advanced the claim: "The great thing to my mind is not that women will improve politics but that politics will develop women."[96] He believed that the vote would also make women better mothers. Even those women who did not covet the vote would be led through its possession to exercise it and thereby broaden their perspective.[97] Eastman's outlook was definitely middle class. In "Confession of a Suffrage Orator" (1915) he wrote that he did not want women to control the milk supply and food laws for the sake of their children half so much as he wanted them to exert such control for the benefit they would gain by accruing the life-experience. Eastman cared less for the state of material conditions that mothers and their families might face than for the psychological welfare of women: "The babies of this world suffer a good deal more from silly mothers than they do from sour milk. And any change in political forms, however superficial from the standpoint of economic justice, that will increase the breadth of experience, the sagacity, the humor, the energetic and active life-interest of mothers, can only be regarded a profound historic revolution."[98]

Most progressive observers agreed that the status of women had changed irreversibly although they differed on the implications of that change. Citing the census of 1900, Rheta Childe Dorr noted that nearly six million American women were gainfully employed outside their homes, that between 1890 and 1900 their labor force participation rate increased faster than that of men, faster even than the birthrate. In 1910, she estimated, there were at least nine million women wage earners. Their very existence constituted a challenge to the Victorian social order: "Nine million women who have forsaken the traditions of the hearth and are competing with men in the world of paid labor means that women are rapidly passing from the domestic control of their fathers and husbands. Surely this is the most important economic fact in the world to-day."[99]

The increasing employment of women in the nation's economic life did not necessarily spell economic progress for those working women. As a result of the persistent sex typing of work, most women were confined to the lowest-paid occupations. According to the historian Harold U. Faulkner, between 1900 and 1910 "of the women sixteen years of age and over at work outside the home and professions, almost half earned less than six dollars a week in 1914 and approximately three fourths less than eight dollars."[100] Hence women could not be truly free economically until freedom to work was supplemented by equality of opportunity with male wage earners.

Upton Sinclair noted that historically the enslavement of women had been inextricably entwined with the enslavement of labor; as men were exploited as workers by the rising plutocracy, women were degraded to dependency on their sex function to win male support. Twentieth-century mechanization had permitted women to enter the work force, thereby stimulating their intelligence and the discovery of their chains. But freedom for women was linked with the emancipation of labor. Once the competitive wage system and the leisure-class tradition had been overthrown, women no longer would market their sexuality, whether in marriage or prostitution, and humanity would cease to be infected by female vice.[101] Equality of economic opportunity would pose a fundamental threat to the double standard. If women could earn their own living, they would not have to condone male philandering, and men finally would be forced to restrain themselves sexually.[102] Thus for Sinclair moral progress was predicated on women's economic liberation.

A leading feminist, Charlotte Perkins Gilman, in her pioneer study *Women and Economics* (1898) also had viewed women's economic inequality as a bar to social progress. In a male-dominated society men alone bore the full burden of all technological achievement; women lagged centuries behind and contributed only menial labor. The economic status of women was anachronistic, even atavistic:

> To take from any community its male workers would paralyze it economically to a far greater degree than to remove its female workers. The labor now performed by the women could be performed by the men, requiring only the setting back of many advanced workers into earlier forms of industry; but the labor now performed by the men could not be performed by the women without generations of effort and adaptation.[103]

Moreover, advanced industrial society failed to compensate women for the work they actually performed, domestic labor, and instead rewarded women of leisure for their idleness; class divisions separated women from one another and further degraded laboring women to poverty.[104] As long as women could not earn their freedom through their labor, they remained victims of male rapacity. Only when men had been stripped of the purchasing power with which they compassed their desires could women judge them on their merits in selecting mates.[105] For Gilman the economic emancipation of women would not merely improve public morality but the human race itself.

While Gilman called for an evolutionary change in relations between the sexes, *The Masses'* radicals predicted that women's economic freedom would lead to social revolution. William English Walling preached sexual equality in all realms of life and, in the words of his wife, Anna Strunsky Walling, "looked to a time when the home would follow the functions of the woman instead of the woman the functions of the home."[106] Women would not simply adapt themselves to male needs but would demand that society provide fulfillment for them as well. Women's newfound consciousness of their economic power is charmingly depicted in a cartoon drawn for *The Masses* by K. R. Chamberlain. It depicts a young woman worker with some plans in her hand talking to a startled soldier with a gun at rest. Around her are women workers engaged in building a city. The caption is:

> AFTERWARDS
> He: The War's Over. You can go home now, and
>   We'll run things.
> She: You go put up that gun, and perhaps
>   We'll let you help.[107]

The new woman presumably would lead in the task of social reconstruction by championing the positive, humanistic values bred in her sex through centuries of domesticity.

Social Freedom for Women

The Masses' radicals disagreed as to how much the new woman differed from her Victorian predecessor. Women clearly were demanding greater freedom and opportunity, but could such demands conflict with what were eternally feminine, the maternal instinct with its attendant domestic passivity? Respectable socialists clung to this view of the feminine psyche and were joined by a handful of new radicals resisting the tide of social revolution. John Spargo in *Socialism and Motherhood* (1914) argued that the coming of socialism would end prostitution and marriage for economic gain and thereby elevate traditional family life.[108] For Spargo women's consummate achievement was motherhood, and they could find no finer freedom than to be allowed to remain with their children through their years of dependency:

> Motherhood is not for all women, perhaps, but it is surely woman's highest and holiest mission. A curse rests upon the social system which tears millions of mothers from the cradles of their babies, from their true vocation as builders of the bodies and souls of their sons and daughters, and forces them into factories, workshops, stores, counting-houses and other women's kitchens to labor while their children are neglected.[109]

Whereas Spargo's solution would democratize motherhood by making it accessible to all women regardless of economic class, it failed to recognize that some women might find fulfillment in work or simply enjoy an escape from the drudgery of the individual home.[110]

Floyd Dell's socialism was even more muddled. Neither Spargo nor Dell dealt with Marx's attack on the bourgeois family and instead romanticized the virtues of the class Marx despised. In *Women as World Builders* (1913) Dell actually confessed to having "the greatest sympathy" for the young woman of the leisure class "in her endeavor to create a livelier, a more hilarious and human morale," which Dell believed was a genuine service to the cause of women's rights.[111] Instead of demanding greater class consciousness among women, Dell urged them to emulate the pseudo-aristocracy to rid themselves of all traces of middle-class morality; only thus could women learn to play. And to obtain his playmates the poet was willing to risk harm to an ethos of social responsibility: "And that celebrated 'public-be-damned' attitude of the pseudo-aristocracy is a great moral improvement over the cowardly, hysterical fear of the neighbors which prevails in the middle class."[112]

Dell's feminism was haunted always by the fear that women really did not want the freedom they claimed. In an unpublished novel entitled "Cynthia," whose action is set in 1916, Dell presents us with a wealthy heroine, Cynthia Flower, who rejects several intriguing marital prospects in order to wed Leslie Payton, a highly eligible but somewhat stuffy bachelor, viewing the whole thing as an adventure.[113] When Leslie asks her whether she has any interest in not marrying or in social freedom for women, her reply reveals the author's own suspicions: " 'No!' Cynthia cried passionately. 'I don't want to be free.' "[114]

As Dell himself settled into domesticity during his second marriage, his published novels reflected his belief that the fulfillment women truly desired was personal and best achieved through family life. Since these novels often were autobiographical, they shed light on Dell's earlier opinions. In *The Briary-Bush* (1921) the heroine, Rose-Ann Prentiss, is more a pagan than a radical. She explains to her husband Felix that she became a settlement worker because she could not abide the stuffy meetings of the socialists, failed to understand Marx, and had no interest in women's suffrage. "My life had to be centred around something personal," she confesses, "So. . . ." Her husband instantly recognizes the real meaning of her phrase: "So you taught those children how to play."[115] The novel upheld Dell's prewar belief that women were by nature practical (hence their solutions to problems were pragmatic ones) and that men were idealistic dreamers.[116] For Dell autobiography tended to masquerade as social theory.

In fact, the novels written in the 1920s can be viewed as a prelude to Dell's major attempt at sociological explanation of sexual relations, *Love in the Machine Age* (1930). In *Janet March* (1923) Dell assumes that sexual experimentation has for its goal marriage and family, that paganism is an illusion created by men unable to face sexual responsibilities.[117] In *Souvenir* (1929) Felix Fay discovers, after the breakup of his first marriage, that the women with whom he had had love affairs did not know their own minds, that they were secretly bewildered despite a veneer of complacency: "They had seemed creatures divided against themselves; they were fleeing from woman's traditional destiny as wife and mother, and yet at the same time they were seeking for an opportunity to accept that destiny."[118] By the time that Dell wrote *Love without Money* (1931), he no longer was the Village apostle of free love. His solution to the problems of young love was a highly personalistic one. The central figures of the novel, Gretchen Cedarbloom and Peter Carr, find respectable jobs, pretend to be married, and feel no need to proselytize free love: they even encourage the wedding of their friends Dick and Anne.[119] Although some hints of rebellion remain in the novels, Dell no longer is encouraging social apostasy for its own sake but only as preliminary to marriage and family life.

By the end of the decade, matured by his successful marriage and fatherhood, Dell felt ready to make serious pronouncements on the subject of sexual relations. So when *Love in the Machine Age* appeared in 1930, Dell propounded as his thesis that love has been evolving from infantile forms in patriarchal society (homosexuality, hetaerism, prostitution, polite adultery) to advanced modern forms of mating through romantic love-choice and child-bearing matrimony.[120] As in *Women as World Builders* (1913), Dell still assumes certain basic unchanged human characteristics and needs, which are defined by sex. Although Dell bases his arguments on Darwinian evolution, he exempts human beings from that process and ignores the possibility of psychic evolution. Furthermore, Dell contends that the only meaningful work for a sexually adult woman is "nestbuilding." Should she be shot after menopause? Is it contrary to woman's nature to desire independence or to derive satisfaction from work itself? In celebrating the monogamous family as the culmination of an evolutionary process, Dell enacted his own social statics, once more relegating women to a domesticity that they, in fact, were seeking to escape.

Most other new radicals proved more willing than Dell to challenge the domestic ideal. Christopher Lasch has noted that twentieth-century feminists viewed the passing of the family as both a necessary and desirable step in the social evolution of mankind; by the turn of the century the view that the family had lost its economic functions had become a sociological truism.[121] Proponents of women's rights hoped to modify the traditional family. According to June Sochen: "The feminists of the 1910 decade did not argue that the family unit should be changed because it was ineffective; they believed that it should be changed because it inhibited the woman's development."[122] Rheta Childe Dorr took heart from the fact that between 1890 and 1910 over six hundred thousand women successfully initiated suit for divorce, thereby repudiating the burden of unhappy wedlock. "Without any doubt," she concluded, "this is the most important social fact we have had to face since the slavery question was settled."[123]

Although Dorr was given to hyperbole, a redefinition of family relations and responsibilities was taking place. Feminists were beginning to demand that the home no longer reflect the dependency of one sex upon the other but that it be based upon egalitarianism and comradeship. Mrs. Lena Morrow Lewis, a suffragette and secretary of the National Socialist Association, told a *Masses* interviewer: "In the perfect marriage, man and woman will contribute equally to the home, spiritually, mentally and economically. The equal home is the dream of the future, as is the perfect romantic love."[124] Some new radicals recognized in domesticity a burden for the woman. Reviewing a performance of George Bernard Shaw's *Getting Married* at the Booth Theatre, Charles W. Wood wrote that if women realized the physical, social, economic, and psychological toll of marriage, with its end to the promise of romance, they might react like Shaw's heroine Lesbia, wanting children yet spurning the marital bond.[125]

Others saw that traditional family life could stifle women's growth and aspirations. In a complete reversal of her expectations of feminine self-sacrifice in *The Glory of the Conquered* (1909), Susan Glaspell in *Fidelity* (1915) presents us with Annie Morris, a former classmate of the heroine Ruth Holland. Annie is a mother who no longer believes that child-raising alone will suffice to fulfill her, who demands that her own needs be taken into account. Just as Randolph Bourne had criticized parental sacrifice for the burden of guilt it imposed upon offspring, Glaspell, too, saw that the traditional concept of motherhood was ultimately repressive to those it purportedly sought to protect, the children.[126] Annie Morris is intended as an example of the new woman whose influence will have a liberating effect on family life:

> Thinking back to that it seemed to Ruth a bigger mother feeling than the old one. It was not the sort of maternal feeling to hem in the mother and oppress the children. It was love in freedom—love that did not hold in or try to hold in. It would develop a sense of the preciousness of life. It did not glorify self-sacrifice—that insidious foe to the fullness of living.[127]

A corollary of the old mother feeling was the notion that women had no purpose beyond the years of child-raising. Hence there was a differential standard of aging for both sexes: men matured, women decayed. An elderly woman had no life of her own; at best she could wait patiently and quietly for her grandchildren to come home.[128] Writing anonymously and using as her persona an older woman, Mary Heaton Vorse detailed the unnecessary imposition of conventional behavior upon her kind. In fact, younger women, even those who considered themselves avant-garde, were most responsible for this tyranny: "But there is no reactionary older woman I know who holds as 'mediaeval' opinions as those which the ordinary younger women have about the older generation. The broadest-minded women I know are as tradition-bound as possible when it comes to what we older women may do."[129]

If women were to have aspirations beyond domesticity and motherhood, feminists realized, the home itself would have to be redefined to make it less restrictive of those ambitions. In her major theoretical work, *Women and Economics* (1898), Charlotte Perkins Gilman declared the traditional home outmoded as an economic form and argued for a cooperative alternative to it. The individual household was not even efficient at providing food for its members; a single large-scale purchaser could command much higher-quality food than housewives buying food for their respective homes.[130] Moreover, the home perpetuated inequality between the sexes by defining mutually exclusive economic roles; married lovers shared neither work nor household chores. Like Lena Morrow Lewis, Gilman saw this arrangement as a bar to marital communion: "Marriage is not perfect unless it is between class equals.

There is no equality in class between those who do their share in the world's work in the largest, newest, highest ways and those who do theirs in the smallest, oldest, lowest ways."[131]

Economically outmoded and personally destructive to women, the private home was viewed by Gilman as "the luxury of the rich."[132] In its place Gilman suggested the creation of cooperative apartment houses for professional women with families. Cooking would be performed in a central kitchen from which meals would be served to families either in their separate quarters or in a common dining room, according to individual preference. Workers hired by the central management would clean the rooms, and trained professional nurses and teachers would care for the children in the roof-garden, day nursery, and kindergarten provided for each house. Such a cooperative arrangement would represent "a permanent provision for the needs of women and children, of family privacy with collective advantage."[133]

Gilman hoped that economically free motherhood, allowing a woman to live in the world and to shape it, would improve society for her children.[134] Like Glaspell, Gilman saw the new maternal feeling as a vast improvement on the old. In an era that glorified childhood, Gilman was able to argue effectively for exempting some mothers from educating their own children on the grounds that they lacked the requisite talent, experience, and expertise. Human motherhood was by nature deficient: "No mother knows more than her mother knew: no mother has ever learned her business; and our children pass under the well-meaning experiments of an endless succession of amateurs."[135] By professionalizing child care, women would be freed for work in the world while the children would benefit from improved standards of care. Moreover, women would cease to consider themselves "mere fractions of families"; they would rest secure in their self-worth and purpose even if they did not marry and beyond the years of child-raising if they did.[136]

In the twentieth century Gilman's pleas for a new domestic order were echoed by Henrietta Rodman, a high school English teacher and ardent feminist. Rodman envisioned a totally mechanized apartment house with central kitchen in the basement and a rooftop kindergarten for preschool youngsters, both staffed strictly by professionals, in order to service the needs of professional women wishing to combine family and career.[137] To Rodman such an apartment house was essential to feminine equality.[138] Actually Rodman's scheme would free only those professional women who could afford it. Her social philosophy was fundamentally elitist. Rodman conceded that "the bringing up of a child is the greatest work of the average man or woman," but her emphasis lay on the word "average." She did not consider child-raising suitable life work for exceptional women.[139]

Advocates of women's rights consistently were unable to forge a link between feminism and socialism in their critique of domesticity. Few Village feminists had working-class contacts, and fewer still understood working-class aspirations. Like Gilman, they applied a mechanical solution to the problem of sexual relations, believing that revised domestic arrangements would free women for salaried work outside the home. Gilman, Rodman, and their supporters did not argue for a socialist order that would provide free public nurseries, paid maternity leaves, and other services essential to allow all women, regardless of means, to leave the home if they so desired. Instead they championed an aristocratic arrangement suitable only to professional women, one that envisioned a socialized home within a capitalist order.[140]

Emma Goldman was virtually alone in perceiving the superficiality of the economic critique of the Village feminists. As a midwife she noted a substantial increase of professional women among her patients. They had been emancipated in the sense of earning their own living but had gained no social freedom as a result: "Lacking the courage to tell the world to mind its own business, the emancipation of the women was frequently more of a tragedy than traditional marriage would have been. They had attained a certain amount of independence in order to gain their livelihood, but they had not become independent in spirit or free in their personal lives."[141] Economic independence brought no freedom from the tyranny of public opinion. Goldman blamed the absolute sexual continence imposed upon single women for their neuroses and mental inferiority to men. Citing Freudian psychology, Goldman attributed such intellectual inequality to the "inhibition of thought" imposed upon women for purposes of sexual repression.[142] Moreover, economic independence had little meaning for working women who did not belong to the small professional elite:

> As to the great mass of working girls and women, how much independence is gained if the narrowness and lack of freedom of the home is exchanged for the narrowness and lack of freedom of the factory, sweatshop, department store, or office? In addition is the burden which is laid on many women of looking after a "home, sweet home"—cold, dreary, disorderly, uninviting—after a day's hard work. Glorious independence! No wonder that hundreds of girls are so willing to accept the first offer of marriage, sick and tired of their "independence" behind the counter, at the sewing or typewriting machine. They are just as ready to marry as girls of the middle class, who long to throw off the yoke of parental supremacy.[143]

As long as the work available to women was both alienating and sex-typed, Goldman argued, it would replicate domestic drudgery.

What was needed was a new psychology, one that would not substitute one tyranny for another, but that would promote equality between the sexes. Goldman chastised those feminists who claimed the right to be self-supporting while demanding their husbands' support, who blamed men for their own failure to achieve greatness, who arrogated to their own sex privileges based on their supposedly superior virtue. Social freedom demanded an end to such hypocrisy: "The radicals, no less than the feminists, must realize that a mere external change in their economic and political status, cannot alter the inherent or acquired prejudices and superstitions which underlie their slavery and dependence, and which are the main causes of the antagonism between the sexes."[144] As long as female services were for sale, whether at home or on the market, economic independence was a mirage. To Goldman under capitalism all women were prostitutes and could win their freedom only by recognizing the true nature of their bondage and struggling to free themselves and all their sisters.[145]

Righteousness, Romance, Sex Drives, Hard Cash: Changing Views of Prostitution

Simply by discussing prostitution Victorian women took one small step in their personal liberation. Respectable women were able to break the bonds of reticence that rendered any mention of sexual conduct taboo by speaking in the interest of social purity. Egal Feldman has argued that the "preoccupation of long-sleeved spinsters with the reform of sexual perversions" lost some of its shock value because it upheld a crucial aspect of Victorian morality, its nativism. Native-born American women were believed to be superior to the degraded animal passions of males and hence were custodians of the nation's sexual purity. In cleansing society of sexual evil, in ending male exploitation of even the defenseless immigrant girl, respectable women would redeem America not only for themselves, but also for the menfolk who had been instrumental in causing social degradation in the first place.[146]

Victorian reformers had one decided advantage in attacking prostitution; they did not understand it, so they optimistically could look forward to its obliteration. Turn-of-the-century suffragists actually attributed prostitution to the exclusion of women from public affairs; once women obtained the vote, feminists believed, they consistently would vote for the elimination of vice.[147] Moreover, they held that enfranchised women would find more opportunities for work and would not be coerced into selling sexual favors to men, either within marriage or outside its bounds. Repelled by incessant, and obviously unreciprocated, male appetite, some feminists believed that eventually sexual expression would be limited to a small part of the year, as with lower animals.[148] To such women a female sex drive equal to that of men would have been inconceivable. They asked not for a reprieve from repression, as many twentieth-century feminists would do, but for release from unwanted sexual attention from males. And they extrapolated on the basis of their own experience to argue that prostitutes, too, were purely victims of male lust.

By the early twentieth century the agitation against prostitution became a national preoccupation. Mark Sullivan has noted that the exploitation of this theme was as commercial in motive as the traffic in women itself. The stage, press, and films offered sensational accounts of "white slavery." In the popular hysteria that followed the public came to believe that " 'white slavers' procured victims by carrying a 'poisoned needle' with which they stupefied young women beside whom they, in the artful pursuit of their business, seated themselves in street-cars."[149] Any male who offered the slightest civility to a person of the opposite sex with whom he was not acquainted was immediately suspect of the utmost evil. Finally the press itself became alarmed by the national paranoia induced by its propaganda and tried to stifle public suspicion by "procuring from physicians authoritative testimony to the practical impossibility of drugging an unwilling person by injection from a hypodermic needle in a crowded street-car."[150] The effect of such white-slavery campaigns was to reinforce the public in its unwillingness to recognize that women might turn to prostitution for money or for the freedom of its life-style or to support drug habits.

By systematically, if unconsciously, misinterpreting prostitution, progressive reformers could advance simple remedies for this social evil. Their campaign sprung from a relatively new assumption, namely that the behavior of both individuals and society could be controlled and regulated to achieve human and social perfectibility.[151] Such a rational calculus of human behavior lacked the complexity of the Freudian model of the mind, replete with subconscious drives, which held such an attraction for radical intellectuals of the period. If prostitution could be understood rationally, progressives argued, then it could be controlled legally. As a result, progressives mounted a statutory attack on prostitution that resulted in congressional passage of the Mann Act of 1910, forbidding the interstate transportation of women for use as prostitutes "or for any other immoral purpose," and segregation and control of prostitutes by the army during World War I.[152] Despite local efforts by Brand Whitlock, reform mayor of Toledo, to check prostitution by improving economic conditions and sex education for women, many cities sought to end prostitution altogether by wiping out their red-light districts through police action.[153] These progressive reforms pleased the public at the time, but there is little historical evidence that they reduced illicit sex. In fact, it appears that prostitution subsequently became more widespread, if less conspicuous, and that "call houses" and other methods were devised to evade the law.[154]

The progressive mind was ensnared by its own rationality and legalism. It could not solve the problem posed by prostitution because it failed to understand its complexity. Even in the nineteenth century novelists and social feminists began to pose an alternative view of prostitution to that of the purity crusaders. In 1889 Edgar Fawcett wrote a novel, *The Evil That Men Do*, describing the social and economic pressures that led working women to become prostitutes. He provided graphic details of oppression at work and the degradation of tenement life. Nevertheless, Fawcett's novel is a sentimental one. Although his heroine Cora chooses the life of sin after her seduction and betrayal, Fawcett shows that her choice must result in "disfigurement, dissipation, and death." But in the case of Em, the sewing girl who preserves her innocence, Fawcett provides much the same fate; the wages of virtue are misery, starvation, and death. Margaret Wyman argues: "This subsidiary lesson implied a practical justification of a deliberate choice of prostitution at the lowest-paid level of female labor."[155] In the early twentieth century Theodore Dreiser's *Sister Carrie* and David Graham Phillips's *Susan Lenox: Her Fall and Rise* exploded the sentimentalist view of prostitution to confront the public with heroines who escaped the harsh realities of a working-girl's life by selling their sex and who achieved success and glamor beyond that available to the average woman who preserved her virtue intact.[156]

Moreover, a handful of nineteenth-century social feminists challenged the prevailing view of prostitution. Among the most notorious of these was Victoria Woodhull, who with her sister, Tennessee Claflin, coedited the reform newspaper, *Woodhull and Claflin's Weekly*. Woodhull argued editorially that all women were prostitutes, whether married or not, as long as they were coerced economically into bestowing their sexual favors upon men. She mounted a frontal attack upon the double standard of moral conduct that established different systems of accountability for men and women in Victorian America. If prostitutes were to be condemned for disgracing public morality, then it was only fair to condemn equally the men who patronized them.[157] The double standard tacitly accepted prostitution not merely as a necessary evil, but also as a bulwark of the nuclear family because it allowed men to philander with prostitutes, who presumably had knowledge of effective contraception, instead of causing unwanted pregnancies in their wives, who did not.[158] Since the resulting sexual freedom for males was irresponsible and oppressive to women, most feminists were convinced that increasing, rather than releasing, the taboos against extramarital sex would enhance their position, and they fervently supported social purity campaigns.[159] In contrast, Woodhull favored licensed prostitution on strictly pragmatic grounds. Noting the failure by Boston women to redeem and reform prostitutes through either rehabilitation or suppression, she argued cogently for decriminalization. Efforts at rehabilitation seemed doomed to failure because of the difficulty of reversing an entire way of life while making prostitution a crime resulted only in blackmail and graft.[160] The weekly editorialized: "The only repressive agency admissible is a system of police licensing and rigorous visitation. This is not authorizing sin by statute, simply recognizing social and physiological facts. In this way, and in this way alone, until a wholesome moral sentiment can be induced can legislation deal with the subject."[161]

Despite the practical merits of her argument, Woodhull was relatively isolated among nineteenth-century reformers and was explicitly repudiated by suffragists hell-bent on winning respectability at any and all costs.[162] The development of a comprehensive radical critique of prostitution had to await the twentieth century and the post-Freudian "repeal of reticence" regarding the mention and practice of sex.[163] Despite a tendency to romanticize the prostitute herself, these radicals were willing to recognize the vital role of prostitution in American society and to analyze the social and economic forces behind it without wrapping themselves in their own righteousness.

Some radicals viewed prostitution as a social necessity and hence refused to condemn it out of hand. The lawyer Clarence Darrow himself never patronized brothels. "Why," he once said, "should I *pay* for it?"—but he felt a deep affinity for madams and prostitutes alike. "After all," he argued, "they're serving a good purpose and giving value for value received. What's so wrong about that?" Hence Darrow willingly came to their defense legally, feeling that they were, in fact, victims of circumstances.[164] Similarly the hobo poet Harry Kemp argued that prostitutes were free of divine censure because it was through their sacrifices that civic morality was preserved. Like Woodhull, Kemp held that prostitution served to sustain marriage and family life. In "The Painted Lady" the central figure of the poem, a prostitute who is at once heroine and victim, reveals the true nature of her social role:

And, maidens who boast the purest white,
'Tis I who save you from Lust's despite,
'Tis I preserve you without a flaw
Till you go and lie with a man by law.[165]

As victims of the double standard and of economic oppression, but also as symbols of freedom from the repression of Victorian America, prostitutes were romanticized by modern radicals. In a short story that appeared in *The Masses* of January 1915 James Henle described a prostitute named Marjorie as honest, giving value for value received. She is satisfied with what other women leave behind, is loyal to the man who dupes her if she loves him, and is not revolutionary in that she blames herself for her own weaknesses. For Henle such a woman is redeemed through suffering. The story concludes with the following bit of monologue:

"So Marjorie is Nobody's Sister. When you approach her you
lock your soul and open your purse. To that other world of womankind
she is a painted plague. She is cursed and hounded and mulcted and

jailed for earning her livelihood by the only means she knows. I wonder if God loves her the less for all this. Nobody's Sister."[166]

John Reed saw not only redemption but liberation in the prostitute's way of life. "A Daughter of the Revolution," which appeared in *The Masses* of February 1915, is the story of a French prostitute, Marcelle, daughter of a revolutionary family that was an economic failure. Her father, a union man, disowned her when she became a prostitute, but her brother, also a radical, was more tolerant. Once she visited him and unrecognized afterward on the street was solicited by her father. Marcelle admits to the Americans who interrogate her that she is bad but also states that she does not regret her life: " '*Dame*, no! I'm free.' " Reed concludes, "Here was the key to Marcelle, her weakness, her vileness. It was not vice, then, that had twisted her, but the intolerable degradation of the human spirit by the masters of the earth, the terrible punishment of those who thirst for liberty."[167] In an earlier story, "Where the Heart Is," which had appeared in *The Masses* of January 1913, Reed actually portrays prostitution as an attractive way of life with more allure than foreign travel. A Haymarket girl named Martha is seen as having normal aspirations to travel, learn, and grow. She takes a trip to London on her savings and is a proper tourist for a week. Then she uses her sexual allure to induce men to finance her travels through France, Belgium, Germany, and Brazil, but finally longs for her old life at the Haymarket in New York and returns voluntarily from her wanderings.[168]

Even when radicals provided an economic critique of prostitution, they did not reduce it to a simple matter of deprivation. For example, Max Eastman condemned the current vice-commission reports, which seemed to hold that prostitution could be eliminated by establishment of a national minimum wage for women. Eastman claimed that this solution was mean and niggardly: "This minimum wage once nationally established will give the moral people in the community a comfortable feeling (the same they had before vice was discovered by William Rockefeller in the year 1912) that if any girl goes wrong it's her own fault. She had a chance to go to heaven on a Minimum Wage and she went to hell on a toboggan."[169] Moreover, Eastman found the reformers' approach devoid of any appreciation for "individual temperament or the sacred love of life." The limits of sympathy were the living wage. Eastman balked at the narrow-mindedness of the progressive spirit: "If I were a girl working all day and suffering the imposition of a living wage in a rich country, I trust I would be either a prostitute or a thief."[170]

Similarly Hutchins Hapgood avoided the trap of pure economic determinism that plagued progressives and crude Marxists. Hapgood held that most prostitutes were victims of economic necessity and that they were as necessary to society as its reserve of miserably underpaid workers. Prostitutes deserved respect for the social service they rendered and sympathy for having been forced into a sex life that violated their deepest instincts. But Hapgood argued for nothing less than fundamental moral reform in dealing with the problem:

> It would seem that emancipation from the evils of the industrial system, and from a false and sentimental philosophy, would have two beneficent results: it would not only free those women who are economic prostitutes, but also set free the small minority of them who are like what the Greek hetaerae were supposed to be, women who treat their sex as a means of adding to the richness of life for themselves and their lovers, and increasing the temperamental understanding of erotic possibilities, which in the practical circumstances of married life generally does not obtain.[171]

In *A Preface to Politics* (1914) Walter Lippmann also contended that economic and legal reform by themselves were inadequate as means of abolishing prostitution: "Cities and factories, schools and homes, theaters and games, manners and thought will have to be transformed before sex can find a better expression. Living forces, not statutes or clubs, must work that change."[172]

The feminist arguments against prostitution advanced in the nineteenth century by Victoria Woodhull were reformulated in the twentieth by the anarchist Emma Goldman. Victorian morality was plagued by a fundamental contradiction, she argued. In suppressing all knowledge of sex, the prudish deprived young girls of the very knowledge necessary to guard themselves against unwittingly being lured into a life of sin. Reared as a sex commodity in order to be guaranteed the safety and economic security of marriage, the socially acceptable form of bartering sex for money, these girls remained in total ignorance of the meaning and importance of sex.[173] Goldman argued that in modern society women nowhere were treated according to the merit of their work; their true value lay in their sexual allure and availability. Legal distinctions were trivial in this regard, Goldman noted: "Thus it is merely a question of degree whether she sells herself to one man, in or out of marriage, or to many men. Whether our reformers admit it or not, the economic and social inferiority of women is responsible for prostitution."[174]

Blending Marx and Freud, arguing both for socialism and for feminism, the new radicals confronted the problem of prostitution in its true complexity. Only by coupling economic change with a transformation of consciousness could prostitution be wiped from the land.

Farewell to Feminism

The feminist ferment of the prewar years in Greenwich Village had produced a critique of American society that demanded not merely the vote for women but the extension of opportunity to them in many other realms. Changes in the social, political, and economic status of women were to be accompanied by a fundamental change in consciousness that would permit women the same quality of life experience as men. No longer sheltered and shackled by the home, women would emerge from centuries of enforced domesticity to tackle the world's problems from a fresh perspective. Socialists believed that their presence would hasten the coming of the cooperative commonwealth.

Yet, in fact, the feminist impulse waned sharply after World War I and left few solid accomplishments in its wake beyond the enfranchisement of women, which failed to insure the political millennium promised by the more ardent suffragists. The Village feminists had been isolated within the suffrage movement because their economic program attacked capitalism while their demands for sexual liberation offended respectability. In contrast, Aileen Kraditor has noted, the suffrage movement upheld orthodoxy: "Few suffragists were radicals; the vast majority of them simply wanted the right to participate more fully in the affairs of a government the basic structure of which they accepted."[175] Moreover, the Village feminists did not see the vote for women as a final goal but rather viewed it as an initial step toward a cultural transformation creating equality between the sexes.[176] They believed that such a transformation would accompany the cooperative commonwealth ushered in by the eventual success of socialism.[177]

Their espousal of socialism divided Village feminists from their counterparts in the suffrage movement, especially with the coming of World War I. Crystal Eastman gave up her suffrage work to become a leader in pacifist organizations. When in February 1917 the executive secretary of the Woman's Suffrage party pledged her half million members to supporting the government in case of American entry, Eastman vigorously repudiated her action: "I believe a great many suffragists, who are not pacifists, felt decidedly aggrieved that their services had been so lightly pledged to a government which has denied to them for forty years a fundamental democratic right."[178] When the United States joined the war, the most influential suffrage groups abandoned their agitation to rally to their country's support while radical feminists deserted their ranks in disgust.[179] Those who formed the Woman's Peace party, however, carried with them the sense that women derived from their maternal capability a deeper commitment to peace than men; neither pacifism nor socialism brought them to a belief in the fundamental equality of the sexes.[180] In fact, their belief in women's special mission as peacemakers splintered the effort to oppose the war. Crystal Eastman later explained the decision to form a separate female group:

> From the beginning it seemed to me that the only reason for having
> a Woman's Peace Party is that women are mothers, or potential mothers,
> therefore, have a more intimate sense of the value of human life and
> that, therefore, there can be more meaning and passion in the determina-
> tion of a woman's organization to end war than in an organization of
> men and women with the same end.[181]

Women who before the war had welcomed male support in their efforts to win the vote, birth control, and sexual equality suddenly isolated themselves when socialist opposition to the war had proved ineffectual by itself and when socialists themselves were under attack.

From the beginning the relation between feminism and socialism had lacked mutuality. We already have seen that although women theorists like Charlotte Perkins Gilman, Crystal Eastman, and Henrietta Rodman dubbed themselves socialists, their respective programs to achieve feminine equality could be enacted under capitalism.[182] Although they held that socialism would promote sexual equality, it is by no means clear that they viewed socialism as a pre-requisite for it. Max Eastman, prominent among male suffragists, even argued that socialism did not include sexual equality. In an article for *The Masses*, he noted that Wisconsin, the area of socialism's greatest success, voted against women's suffrage by a two-to-one margin while reactionary Michigan sup-ported it; hence, via some rather questionable logic, he argued that socialism and women's liberation were unrelated: "The question of sex equality, the economic, social, political independence of woman stands by itself, parallel and equal in importance to any other question of the day. The awakening and liberation of woman is a revolution in the very process of life. It is not an event in any class or an issue between classes. It is an issue for all humanity."[183]

Most other new radicals believed that feminism and socialism were linked, but they differed on the advances possible for women under capitalism. The Socialist party itself was hardly a haven for radical feminists. Most socialist leaders viewed the problem of women's rights as part of the "labor question" and argued that once capitalists were forced to pay their husbands living wages, "ninety-nine women out of every hundred would choose the lot of wife and mother."[184] Thus leading socialists celebrated the domesticity that many new radicals saw as women's bane. Women were relegated to a subsid-iary role in the struggle for socialism. Since the party emphasized political action, the disfranchised women were asked to create "a sentiment" in favor of establishing a socialist state.[185] Although the 1908 party platform demanded complete political and economic equality for women, such rights were to be won by males, who, in turn, would bestow them upon grateful but passive women. Ira Kipnis has noted the failure of the party to treat women seriously as a revolutionary force: "Of the 50,000 dues-paying Socialists in 1909, only 2,000 were women. A large proportion of party members apparently had not considered it worth their time to recruit even their wives and mothers."[186]

Finding no inspiration in the rhetoric of the Socialist party, most new radicals were confused as to the role women would play in achieving their own freedom and the parameters of reform possible under capitalism. Floyd Dell argued that socialists could not wait for "the natural downfall of capitalism" to reform working-class morality, especially its disregard for the corruption capitalism imposed upon working women as the price for keeping their jobs. If workers failed to commit themselves to the economic equality of women, if they failed to view prostitutes simply as degraded members of their own class, they would lack "sufficient moral integrity" to achieve their own liberation.[187] While Dell looked to the working class for leadership in the struggle for women's rights, *The Masses* editorialized that the true leaders of the feminist revolt were bourgeois women whose revolt was "not against capitalist society but merely against man's injustice to woman." However, their agitation failed to reach the mass of modern women who were not factory workers but rather remained isolated within their individual homes. The Socialist party consistently supported the enfranchisement of women as a first step toward their economic independence, but, the editorial argues, the proximity of the goal depended on the vigor of "the campaign carried to the women who keep home."[188] In short, women did not have to become proletarianized, to discover their class identity in the workplace, in order to struggle as socialists for their own liberation. In contrast, William D. Haywood and Frank Bohn, both leaders of the Industrial Workers of the World, viewed women primarily as workers and forecast that proletarian rule under socialism would be instrumental in women's liberation: "Socialist government will be a democratic government of industry by all the workers. Of course both men and women will work. Free people do not wish to be supported, nor support idlers and parasites. Therefore, when those who work rule, women will take part in government."[189] Thus the new radicals failed to agree on the relation of socialism to feminism.

Radical feminism did not outlive the war. Those who were pacifists like Crystal Eastman found themselves without any organizational base. The Woman's Peace party affiliated itself with the Women's International League for Peace and Freedom and remained exclusively pacifist instead of championing broader social reform.[190] Others, such as Elizabeth Gurley Flynn, Kate Richards O'Hare, and Rose Pastor Stokes, who believed that women never could achieve equality under capitalism, became devout Marxists and spent the rest of their lives organizing on behalf of communism.[191] For them feminism was subsumed within the wider struggle.[192] Moreover, those Village feminists who sought greater social freedom for women were too individualistic to leave viable organization in their wake. The young women who came to the Village in the 1920s were more interested in social rebellion than in social reform.[193] Sexual freedom became the sum total of feminism; the end product of the New Freedom was the flapper.

Chapter 8 The Exotic Other

Dress Rehearsal in Race Relations

At the turn of the century the promise of Reconstruction had been betrayed and long forgotten, and American blacks journeyed northward and into cities in the slimmer hope of economic betterment. Once again they impinged on the conscience of white radicals who felt compelled to protest the economic exploitation and cultural degradation of blacks in American society. Yet the drama played out in these prewar years, which was in many respects a dress rehearsal for the civil rights and black power movements of the 1950s and 1960s, was often no more than an expression of white sympathy and guilt. Few radicals sensed the immediacy of black problems or the difficulties of creating a new black culture free of the marks of white oppression. As a result, the alliance between white radicals and blacks was a tenuous one that began to fragment from its very inception.

The Socialist party, hoping for respectability and success, virtually ignored the plight of blacks. Center and Right-wing Socialist party members agreed that blacks and whites had no desire to live or work together; since capitalism forced them to do so against their will, socialism would solve the race question by complete segregation. Until the advent of socialism, Center and Right-wing party members raised no objection to separate black communities, schools, and Socialist party locals.[1] This indifference to racism as an issue dominated party policy regarding blacks for the early years of the twentieth century. Historian Ira Kipnis writes: "There is no record that the party ever actively opposed discrimination against Negroes from 1901 to 1912."[2] Although Left-wing Socialists were far less tolerant of all forms of racial discrimination and urged blacks to struggle for equality by joining the labor and socialist movements, they contributed little more than rhetoric in committing the party to fighting for the rights of blacks.[3] Even the party's most popular leader, Eugene Debs, who defied racial prejudice by refusing to speak before segregated audiences in the South, failed to see that poor blacks were more disadvantaged than poor whites and hence deserving of special consideration from the Socialist party. In 1903 Debs successfully opposed a proposal that the party make a special fight on behalf of black rights: "We have nothing special to offer the Negro, and we cannot make separate appeals to all the races. The Socialist party is the party of the whole working class, regardless of color— the whole working class of the whole world."[4] Those socialists who felt more poignantly the need for special work among minorities turned increasingly to the Industrial Workers of the World, which under the leadership of William D. (Big Bill) Haywood attacked the racial policies of the American Federation of Labor.[5]

More than a decade after the founding of the IWW in 1905, the Socialist party began active organizing among blacks and included civil rights demands in party platforms.[6] But this latter-day recognition of black needs came too late to offset suspicion among blacks that the socialists lacked a genuine concern for their plight. As early as 1913 W. E. B. Du Bois criticized socialist leaders who held that racial equality would have to await the coming of the cooperative commonwealth. Du Bois noted that the socialist program aimed at the creation of an industrial aristocracy that differed from its predecessors only in including a larger number of workers. Excluded from the revolutionary proletariat as they had been from the inner circles of craft unions, blacks remained suspicious of socialist sincerity. If socialists did not demonstrate an immediate commitment to civil rights, Du Bois argued, blacks might turn to the enemies of labor to better their lives.[7] Even the handful of black socialists who rallied around A. Philip Randolph's *Messenger* magazine split in 1919 over whether to support the Bolshevik Revolution, thereby causing destructive rivalry in Harlem's civil rights and labor movements.[8]

Apart from efforts within organized socialism, some party members played a leading role in the organization and activities of the National Association for the Advancement of Colored People (NAACP). William English Walling and Mary White Ovington were among its founders and along with Charles Edward Russell and Florence Kelley served as directors of the NAACP after 1914.[9] The NAACP was created by Walling in response to racial warfare in Springfield, Illinois, in 1908, during which six thousand innocent blacks had been victimized by mob attack; the new organization was intended to stop the spread of racism in American society.[10] Yet the NAACP inadvertently perpetuated racist practices within its own administration. Priding itself on never noting the racial composition of its membership, the organization, nevertheless, practiced de facto segregation on its executive board, with Du Bois its only nonwhite member. Mary White Ovington attempted to explain away this contradiction in her memoirs: "As our program was directed primarily against segregation, this almost exclusive employment of whites may sound out of place, but it was the result of circumstances. Few colored people were trained to take such executive positions as we had to offer, and also few had the leisure of our volunteer white workers."[11] The NAACP did mount a crusade against lynching, thereby winning the loyalty of blacks eager to fight racial oppression.[12] But the organization found itself divided by World War I. Pacifists Oswald Garrison Villard and John Haynes Holmes were joined in opposition by Ovington, who viewed the war as a struggle of competing imperialisms, but Du Bois supported American entry and waxed enthusiastic over the black officers' camp.[13] After the armistice, Du Bois went to France and discovered the blatant racism practiced by the American military. His documentary evidence was printed in *The Crisis* of June 1919; the edition of one hundred thousand sold out in a few days, awakening black and white liberal opinion to new dimensions of racial discrimination.[14] The NAACP did pathbreaking work on behalf of blacks without creating a true model of racial equality within its own organization; it strove sincerely and single-mindedly for civil rights without placing that struggle in a broader ideological context that would have unified its membership in face of new challenges like the war.

If the Socialist party viewed the blacks as workers to be organized and the NAACP viewed them as victims of American racism, the new radicals in Greenwich Village found in blacks a new cultural symbol. Villagers envied the paganism of blacks, believed them to be free of the puritanical repression that plagued whites. Hence for them blacks had to remain exotic and uncivilized, untouched by the modern world. Carl Van Vechten, a music critic, novelist, photographer, and art patron, established the first cultural link between artists in Harlem and Greenwich Village and subsequently became the leading white patron of black art during the height of the Harlem Renaissance of the 1920s.[15] His novels of the later period (*Nigger Heaven*, 1926; *Peter Whiffle*, 1929) celebrated black primitivism.[16] Reveling in the sex and spontaneity of blacks denied to whites by their puritanism, Van Vechten failed to question whether freedom and escapism should be equated, whether drunken revels could compensate for the deprivation and discrimination that blacks faced in their daily lives. During the 1930s, in celebrating proletarian literature, Mike Gold lambasted Van Vechten for misleading black intellectuals and perverting their talents:

> Gin, jazz and sex—this is all that stirs him in our world, and he had imparted his tastes to the young Negro literatuers [*sic*]. He is a white literary bum, who has created a brood of Negro literary bums. So many of them are now wasting their splendid talents on the gutter-life side of Harlem.
>
> What a crime against their race! This will lead the Negro nowhere. And what a slander against the majority of Negroes who must work so painfully in the mills, factories and farms of America. The Harlem

cabaret no more represents the Negro mass than a pawnshop represents the Jew, or an opium den the struggling Chinese nation.[17]

Even if one does not accept Gold's notion that art should be a weapon in the class struggle, there still remains the question of the degree to which black art in this period was an attempt to return to black roots or to devise an indigenous realistic tradition and the degree to which it was simply an expression of white cultural imperatives.

Blacks were exploited for their exotic value by white radicals. Perhaps the most famous instance of this exploitation was the "evening" at Mabel Dodge's salon for which Van Vechten had persuaded her to invite two black entertainers. The evening was an exercise in voyeurism, a vicarious participation in Harlem high life; it left its hostess filled with horror. Dodge consoled herself with the thought, "One must just let life express itself in whatever form it will."[18]

Dodge then joined the pro-Indian faction of Village intellectuals while others were left to patronize black art.[19] Emilie Hapgood produced *The Rider of Dreams*, *Granny Maumee*, and *Simon the Cyrenian*, three one-act plays by white dramatist Ridgely Torrence; Robert Edmond Jones designed the settings and costumes. Sculptor Maurice Sterne dubbed 5 April 1917 "the date of the most important single event in the entire history of the Negro in the American theatre"; for the first time black drama commanded serious attention from the white press and public.[20] Yet the "serious attention" these plays received was couched in terms more meaningful to white critics than to black audiences. Although all three plays deal with the thwarting of black hopes by racist oppression, Van Vechten reviewed the plays as universal dramas that transcended race. Of *Granny Maumee* he wrote:

> Mr. Torrence has taken the negro—just as Synge took the Irish
> peasant—to write about seriously and poetically and tragically, and he
> has written a great play. Like most great plays, it transcends its medium.
> Soon one forgets the negroes are speaking, and one becomes imbued
> with the universal philosophy and spirit of the piece, and the tremendous
> force with which the idea that mind and soul are stronger than matter
> is presented.[21]

Van Vechten had no sensitivity to the desire of black intellectuals to create racial identity through art. Even the Provincetown Players, creators of the little theater movement in modern drama, who dealt seriously with racial themes and sponsored Eugene O'Neill's *Emperor Jones* in the 1920s, the first all-black play with black actors in all the parts, saw its mission as creating an American community that transcended race.[22]

White radicals continually cast black aspirations into white molds. They expected black gratitude for their efforts and were mystified by its absence. Hutchins Hapgood counted as one of his disappointments as a journalist his failure to persuade W. E. B. Du Bois to introduce him to blacks so that he could write a series of articles on black life. "The Negroes," Du Bois said, "do not wish to be written about by white men, even when they know that they will be treated sympathetically. Perhaps especially then, they do not desire it."[23] Du Bois seemed so proud and earnest that Hapgood abandoned the project.[24]

Blacks felt similarly constrained by white aspirations in the literary field. In reviewing the poetry of James Weldon Johnson, Floyd Dell argued that blacks were instinctive poets whose words had "natural rhythmic grace and order," that they were closer to nature than whites, and they could reveal secrets of love yet unknown to the white world. Dell's comments might have been easily discounted as romantic effusions except for his insistence that there was "a peculiar racial way of writing poetry. Or—to fall back frankly upon dogma—there ought to be." Hence he dismissed Johnson's nondialect poetry as lacking in self-revelation because it bore no racial imprint.[25] Johnson replied by complaining that blacks had been confined to an artistic niche by whites who preferred to view blacks in Sambo-like contentment in a log cabin. White critics celebrated dialect poetry, but Johnson viewed the medium as too constricting: "Negro dialect is the natural instrument for voicing that phase of Negro life, but the poet finds it is too limited for any higher or deeper notes. It has but two main stops, humor and pathos."[26] Johnson valued growing black participation in American life and was willing to sacrifice dialect poetry to this wider aim: "The best that can be done will be to preserve it as a literary curiosity."[27]

White radicals were often insensitive to the fact that the cultural heritage of slavery was a bittersweet one for blacks. Radical artists might portray blacks as Sambos or savages with little feeling for black response. For example, John Sloan submitted an illustration entitled "Piddlin' Roun' 1904" for a poem by Paul Laurence Dunbar; it contained simian blacks hoeing on top, a border of kitchen implements, and an apelike mother and two sons. The drawing was so close to caricature and so offensive to public taste that it was rejected by Henry Fangel, the art editor of *Good Housekeeping*.[28] In the 1890s Art Young sketched famous persons and familiar scenes for a traveling show performed with the accompaniment of a Signor Tomaso on mandolin. Apart from historical scenes, Young noted, "I also made 'evolution sketches' —with a few swift strokes of my crayon. I rhythmically changed a watermelon into the face of a grinning darkey while the long-haired Signor obliged with the tune 'Dancing in the Barn.' "[29] Even contact with blacks through a subsequent trip to Alabama and his growing social consciousness did little to dispel the racial stereotypes through which Young viewed southern blacks:

And there was fine sketching material hereabouts, both in the landscape and among the primitive white folks and the happy-go-lucky Negroes (thus I thought of them then, not knowing of the hard lives
of which their apparently care-free attitude gave me no hint). We soon
got acquainted with the neighborhood pickaninnies. Some were named
after perfume brands and others after labels on package groceries. I liked
to talk with them, their vocal tones and their dreamy ideas about
life delighting me. The name of one little girl, so she insisted, was
Pickle Lily.[30]

Even Robert Minor, who years later abandoned art to work full time for the
Communist party, succumbed to the pervasive stereotyping of blacks with a
cartoon entitled "PUGILISM IN EXCELSIS: The Grinning Negro as He Appears
to Robert Minor," which appeared in *Current Literature* of October 1912.
The cartoon depicts the black boxing champion as a grinning cannibal surrounded by what are presumably human bones.[31] The most lurid southern
fantasies of blacks could do no worse.

The issue for white cultural radicals was, in part, one of artistic integrity.
Some artists consciously tried to support civil rights by casting a more favorable light on blacks in their portraits. Black poet Claude McKay commended
The Masses' cartoons of Stuart Davis: "I thought they were the most superbly
sympathetic drawings of Negroes done by an American. And to me they have
never been surpassed."[32] John Sloan called Davis "absolutely the first artist
. . . who ever did justice to the American Negro."[33] Yet a reader of *The
Masses*, Carlotta Russell Lowell, attacked the magazine for its degrading
portraits of blacks with their depressing effects on black audiences and their
tendency to confirm white racism. Editor Max Eastman replied by citing
cartoons that celebrated black militancy and protested a Supreme Court decision upholding Jim Crow laws. Eastman disclaimed any racist intentions in
Davis's drawings: "Stuart Davis portrays the colored people he sees with
exactly the same cruelty of truth with which he portrays the whites. He is so
far removed from any motives in the matter but that of art, that he cannot
understand such a protest as Miss Lowell's at all." Yet Eastman at least
acknowledged the claims of blacks to be spared racial slurs from their friends:

> Some of the rest of us, however, realize that because the colored
> people are an oppressed minority, a special care ought to be taken not to
> publish *anything* which their race-sensitiveness, or the race-arrogance
> of the whites, would misinterpret. We differ from Miss Lowell only in
> the degree to which a motive of art rather than of propaganda may
> control us.[34]

White radicals may have been afraid of the kind of demand for censorship mounted by blacks, the NAACP, and other white liberals as a result of the screening of D. W. Griffith's *Birth of a Nation* (1915) with its lurid portrait of black rapacity and corruption during Reconstruction. Although censorship boards did little to restrict showing of the film, public protest did have some result. The ultimate effect of liberal outcry, according to *Masses'* coeditor Floyd Dell, was "a trail of film censorships . . . which it will take twenty-five years to abolish!"[35] However, radicals were loathe to acknowledge even the legitimacy of demands for self-policing against racial slurs; their desire for "free expression" blinded them to the subtleties of racial oppression.

Although few white radicals could transcend racial limitations on their vision to respect black perspectives, their own point of view gradually gained sophistication as they began to view the black problem in an international context. When *The Masses* supported the NAACP crusade against lynching in 1916, the magazine urged the action as more beneficial to mankind "than merely giving relief to your feelings by denouncing atrocities which happen to be German or advocating that we send an army into Mexico to avenge the incidental killing of a few American citizens during a Mexican war for loyalty."[36] Eradicating racial inequality at home became for white radicals a potent antidote to the blandishments of Wilsonian democracy abroad.

Moreover, some white radicals came to an intuitive realization of the blacks' sense of desperation. In 1913 in response to a racial war in Georgia in which hundreds of blacks were driven from their homes, Max Eastman editorially urged blacks to arm themselves and fight back against their oppressors. He called for a Toussaint L'Ouverture to liberate southern blacks and permit the racial improvement rendered impossible by whites: "The possibilities of the black man have never been tested, and they never will be tested until after the wine of liberty and independence is instilled into his veins."[37] Eastman raised one of the first white calls for black power:

> We view the possibility of some concentrated horrors in the South with calmness, because we believe there will be less innocent blood and less misery spread over the history of the next century, if the black citizens arise and demand respect in the name of power, than there will be if they continue to be niggers, and accept the counsels of those of their own race who advise them to be niggers. When we speak for militant resistance against tyranny, we speak for democracy and justice. Everybody grants this as to the past, but few are bold enough to see it in the present.[38]

White radicals had groped along a tortuous route from ignoring blacks to patronizing them to calling for black power and pride. But they had erred too long to be readily forgiven. In the 1920s through the Harlem Renaissance blacks renewed their culture and forgot the whites. It was not until the Great Depression posed privation as a force for racial unity that white radicalism had any lasting appeal for blacks.

The Exotic Ethnic

Neither did organized socialism in the prewar period concern itself extensively with the plight of immigrants. Although the origins of the Socialist party lay among immigrant communities and although the party retained many immigrants in its membership, it virtually ignored their special needs and violations of their rights. Much of the socialist activity among immigrants was conducted by independent national socialist organizations with minimal contact with the Socialist party until 1910–12. In fact, the position taken by many socialists during the ongoing party debate over the immigrant question revealed a desire to placate the leaders of the American Federation of Labor by advocating restrictions on immigration and discouraging the foreign-born from joining the party.[39]

American socialists gradually differentiated themselves from their more orthodox Marxist counterparts in Europe. As early as the Stuttgart International Socialist Congress of 1907, Morris Hillquit refused to support the majority position on immigration. His stance subsequently received confirmation by the National Executive Committee and by a party referendum in a resolution opposing Oriental immigration to the United States because of its depressing effect on the living standard of workers.[40] American socialists remained divided on the issue, alternately espousing the international solidarity of all workers and exempting Orientals as unassimilable into the modern labor movement. In fact, Joshua Wanhope, writing in *The Masses* in 1912, suggested that the dilemma be resolved by ignoring European Marxists and viewing the immigration question solely in its American context.[41] In short, for much of the prewar period the American Socialist party either viewed the immigrant as a problem or ignored him entirely.

An exception to this generally bleak picture involved socialist activities on the Lower East Side of New York. Amid the squalor of the ghetto, Jews thirsting for education and improvement turned to the Socialist party and its experimental socialist Sunday Schools.[42] As early twentieth-century socialism grew increasingly synonymous with social reform, the socialism that flourished on the Lower East Side "acquired a native American air." A largely East Side audience was attracted to the lectures offered at the Rand School, where Charles Beard, Robert Bruere, Morris Hillquit, and John Spargo spoke on socialism, government, economics, American history, and urban problems. For decades the suffrage movement had emphasized its Americanism, even to the point of being nativistic, but in 1906 Harriot Stanton Blatch led the suffragette incursion into the district to win immigrant women to the cause.[43] Thus through socialism were the denizens of the Lower East Side initiated into the mainstream of American life.

Although their Americanization drew immigrants closer to native-run branches of the Socialist party, it ironically robbed them of the exotic qualities so attractive to the new radicals. The latter were largely white Anglo-Saxon Protestants, rebels against puritanism, seekers of new culture and fresh experience. Interlopers among the socially conservative Italians and Irish who inhabited the district, the newcomers to the Village generally ignored their neighbors to investigate the more colorful immigrant life of the Lower East Side.[44] These intellectuals' thirst for exoticism could not be satisfied within their own group. A handful of Jews belonged to the avant-garde Liberal Club, but these were "Westernized, sophisticated, cosmopolitan—Jews by origin but not by interests."[45] Similarly most of the Jews associated with *The Masses* had no personal experience of ghetto life. Maurice Becker came to America as a child not from a ghetto but from Nizhni Novgorod, a city in central Russia nearly devoid of Jews; Louis Untermeyer, a founding member of *The Masses'* staff, was born into a German-Jewish family in a genteel American neighborhood. Hence Village intellectuals, Jew and Gentile alike, had to venture out to the Lower East Side to capture the peculiar flavor of ghetto life before it withered in the process of Americanization.[46]

Their quest was a romantic one, a search for life more deeply felt, more richly textured than their own. Hutchins Hapgood befriended the colorful characters who captured the imagination of the poor: Chuck Connors, the "mayor of Chinatown," a former prizefighter who organized Bowery balls; John L. Sullivan, and Kid McCoy; and he found vicarious excitement in linking his life to theirs. Hapgood turned to the submerged tenth because they "laid themselves bare" to him, because through them he could live intensely and immediately in the realm of pure feeling.[47] Fascinated by the strange assortment of humanity that confronted him on his urban prowls, he dedicated an entire book, *Types from City Streets* (1910), to the delicious description of their habits. Hapgood presents a gallery of Lower East Side types: Bowery bums, ex-thieves, Tammany men, "spieler" girls, bohemians, and artists. In a paean to proletarianism, he assumes that "everything, in this time of democracy, leads to the people, even literature."[48] Hapgood finds an authenticity— what he dubs the real thing, living at "de limit"—among the lower classes that is absent among their bourgeois counterparts. Also, lacking social pressures toward conformity, their lives seem richer and deeper. Although he calls them "types," their characters sparkle with eccentricity, individuality, and uniqueness. But they also have wider meaning than their value as exemplars of nonconformity. Like Lincoln Steffens, who redeemed party bosses by

Hutchins Hapgood
Courtesy Beinecke Rare Book and Manuscript Library, Yale University

pointing to the efficiency of their efforts at relief, Hapgood saw these lower types as practicing a viable social morality far superior to the puerile philanthropy of reformers. They were living proof that bourgeois morality need not be the only norm. In resolving some of the tensions confronting Village intellectuals, their lives also reflected unresolved conflicts that were shared. In the chapter entitled "Life's Little Misfits," most of the misfits Hapgood presents are schizoid people torn between art and success, which was the problem faced by *The Masses'* staff whose success in commercial journalism supported more creative efforts for the magazine. Max Eastman discussed this conflict of the young and eager writer or artist in *Journalism versus Art.*[49]

Villagers were torn between a desire to celebrate the uniqueness of their rebellion against older values and their need to know that that rebellion was shared by others. The problems of youth were rendered only more poignant by the generational conflicts among immigrants on the Lower East Side. Infatuated by ghetto life, Lincoln Steffens was moved by the tragedy of medieval parents, living in a timeless spiritual world resisting assimilation or accommodation, unable to communicate with offspring shaped on New York City streets.[50] In contrast, Randolph Bourne saw this generational conflict as a sign of the spiritual health of modern youth. He viewed the restiveness of the young as "a desire to get away from the enervating and spiritual coddling and demands for an exaggerated affection" imposed by old-fashioned parents. The clearest evidence of this painful but "healthy insurgency" was to be found among Old World immigrants and their children: "You see much of it among the immigrant families whose sons and daughters go to Columbia or City College and become inoculated with new ideas that produce a constant guerrilla warfare with the irreconcilable traditions of the parents."[51]

But those more familiar with ghetto life knew that this "healthy insurgency" was but an ephemeral thing destined to pass with growing acculturation. Joseph Freeman, himself a product of ghetto life, saw the increasing reconciliation between parents and children within his own family, a resolution mirrored in other ghetto families of his generation. The four older children, born abroad, struggled "to overcome the prejudices of the vanquished village," the eldest girl to convince her father that acting was no "sin," Freeman himself to persuade his father that playing baseball did not make one a "bum." Yet once his father became affluent and had been Americanized, he permitted his younger daughter to dance in a professional ballet and his younger son to run on the track team, captain the football squad, and appear in the rotogravure as part of the all-scholastic nine. The tide of Old World prejudice had ebbed:

> In all the families I knew, the younger children did not have to fight
> for what they wanted as hard as we had, because the cultural distance be-

tween them and their parents had diminished. Wealth made the parents more generous; tragic experience with the older rebels who had stormed out the house in the name of their "sacred principles" made them more tolerant. On the other hand, the younger children had also learned from their rebellious and romantic elders; they were more detached from the home and had acquired an adroit technique of carrying out their "principles" on the sly. Their adolescence was different from ours because time and circumstances had altered.[52]

But most Villagers sought evidence of conflict rather than of reconciliation in ghetto life because they needed proof that their own rebellion would not also be eroded by "time and circumstances."

In seeking ethnic exoticism in the ghetto, the new radicals ignored a growing similarity of value and belief between themselves and the erstwhile objects of their curiosity. The pristine quality of ghetto life, its asceticism, its commitment to saving and self-denial, had been eroded by newfound affluence. The wealthier set frequented Catskills' resorts and mimicked Protestant wealth in their gaudy finery. Abraham Cahan, speaking through the protagonist in *The Rise of David Levinsky* (1917) wrote: "Prosperity was rapidly breaking the chains of American Puritanism, rapidly 'Frenchifying' the country, and the East Side was quick to fall into line."[53] But radical rebels against puritanism preferred to spurn the Jewish nouveaux riches and celebrate the impoverished poets, artists, and scholars of the ghetto, who either by conviction or fate remained practitioners of the ascetic life.

The younger ghetto women, influenced both by socialism and by avantgarde Russian ideology, abandoned orthodoxy to become fiercely intellectual and often to become as well "new women," asserting in particular their economic independence of men.[54] But although new radicals might admire their seriousness of purpose, they felt that they lacked the charm and femininity of their American sisters.[55] Nor was there any radical appreciation of the older, unassimilated Jewish women with a tradition of independence and strength stemming back to shtetl days when many of them had been sole or principal breadwinners in their families as their menfolk devoted themselves to Talmudic study.[56] Instead of recognizing the crude vitality of these women whose resourcefulness contrasted strikingly with the plaintive weakness of the Victorian ideal of the lady, radicals tended to dismiss them as quaint oddities, corsetless and periwigged.

Villagers never quite realized the patronizing nature of their position as interlopers, voyeurs, cognoscenti of ghetto curiosities. They profited from their exposure to new cultures without recognizing that the price of this experience was condemning other peoples to remain mired in what in America must remain the culture of poverty, for in the prewar era there were no economic rewards for maintaining one's ethnic identity. Nor was there any promise of genuine equality between Villager and immigrant because the intellectual bore no gifts comparable to the authenticity of experience he sought to take away with him.

The truest measure of respect and admiration was paid to Jewish realism and to the productions of the Yiddish theater. As artists and writers Villagers and immigrants could find an equality lacking on the level of chance encounter. Unable to find a market for his realistic portraits of ghetto life among Jews themselves, Abraham Cahan resigned his post on the *Forward* and turned to the English press, where Lincoln Steffens, assistant city editor of the *Evening Post* and an admirer of Cahan's first novel, *Yekl*, accepted several of his articles and introduced him to the editor of the *Commercial Advertiser*, which printed character sketches and human interest features by Cahan.[57] In turn, Cahan guided his colleagues to the Canal Street cafés where Jews heatedly debated the merits of realism in the arts and to Bowery theaters where audiences split into factions to discuss the plays. Encouraged by Cahan, Hutchins Hapgood produced the series of articles later assembled in his 1902 classic, *The Spirit of the Ghetto*.[58]

The vigor of the Yiddish theater attracted intellectuals interested in experimental modern drama: "The neighborhood Playhouse on Grand Street was the meeting place of the two elements: the Village and the East Side."[59] George ("Jig") Cram Cook of the Provincetown Players ventured into the ghetto for inspiration. He wrote enthusiastically of the Grand Street Players: "Full of a strong inherited religious feeling beyond the command of any commercial manager, danced the Jewish youths and maidens of that neighborhood, their drama, much of it taken from the Hebrew ritual, full of feeling immeasurably old, the tribal religious feeling of the ancient Jews still a living thing to some of the Jews of Henry Street."[60] The excitement of the Yiddish theater bridged the ancient and modern worlds and effaced their separate realities. Susan Glaspell described the moment of contact: "That night, before the glowing grate in Milligan Place, we talked of what the theatre might be. It is one of the mysterious and beautiful things of the world, if you are true to the thing you feel, across gulfs of experience you find in another the thing he feels."[61]

Villagers cherished and wished to preserve the integrity of ethnic cultures; they numbered among the earliest exponents of cultural pluralism, which they substituted for old-fashioned patriotism. Elizabeth Gurley Flynn noted that the majority of the American working class consisted of foreigners, one or two generations removed, bound to their old homelands by ties of affection yet shaped by their American environment; hence internationalism became "the logical patriotism of a heterogeneous population."[62] She feared the creation of a single national culture that would demand conformity of the immigrants and their offspring and instead proposed her own version of cultural pluralism: "America—not as a melting pot that produces a jingoistic, mercenary, one-mold type, but as a giant loom weaving into a mighty whole the song, the poetry, the traditions, and the customs of all races, until a beautiful human fabric, with each thread intact, comes forth—would stretch forth a myriad hands of brotherhood to the four quarters of the globe."[63] For Flynn cultural pluralism was intimately linked to her socialist hopes for international class solidarity.

In propagandizing a new American culture, Randolph Bourne arrived at a similar vision. Bourne had repudiated the notion of Americanization publicized by Israel Zangwill's play *The Melting Pot* and in its place supported the notion of a "federation of nationalities," or "cultural pluralism," as developed by Horace Kallen. Bourne placed great faith in the cosmopolitanism developing in American cities with their burgeoning ethnic populations. Writing from Europe, he observed that "the good things in the American temperament and institutions are not English . . . but are the fruit of our far superior cosmopolitanism."[64] Like Flynn, Bourne, too, feared that the melting pot ideal might be a ploy to achieve cultural and economic imperialism by rendering the public more manipulable:

> I feel so strongly on this subject that I am willing to believe that the so-called "hyphenate," by keeping us from being swept into a premature and nebulous cohesion, has actually been our salvation. I believe that almost anything that keeps us from being welded together into a terrible national engine which powerful political or financial interests may wield at will, flinging the entire nation's strength in a moment to any cause or movement that seems to advance their will or their private class-sense of honor or justice—I say that anything that keeps us from being thus used is a salvation.[65]

But Bourne's vision was not merely a defense against jingoism; he longed for America to become a transnationality, a cosmopolitan interweaving of distinctive ethnic cultures to produce a sense of world citizenship.[66] Creating this new transnational community was a task worthy of the finest spirits of the younger generation: "To make real this striving amid dangers and apathies is work for a younger intelligentsia of America. Here is an enterprise of integration into which we can all pour ourselves, of a spiritual welding which should make us, if the final menace ever came, not weaker, but infinitely strong."[67] Ultimately the fascination with immigrant cultures was no mere flirtation with ethnicity but yet another attempt by young radicals to create a new American culture more democratic and cosmopolitan than the genteel tradition.

The Cult of the Criminal

As with blacks and immigrants, new radicals achieved a peculiar blend of sympathy for criminals as society's victims and envy of their freedom from the traditional restraints of bourgeois culture. By viewing crime as the product of economic exploitation, they blamed capitalism for its existence rather than the individual criminal. Although Eugene Debs conceded that at best the convict remained a scourge to himself and to society, he also noted that reformation of the criminal was impossible as long as thousands of free laborers innocent of any wrongdoing were unable to find work; in fact, their enforced idleness might drive them, too, into a life of crime.[68] Debs reversed traditional wisdom in his attack upon unthinking advocates of law and order: "It is popular to say that society must be protected against its criminals. I prefer to believe that criminals should be protected against society, at least while we live under a system that makes the commission of crime necessary to secure employment."[69] From his own youthful experiences in New York when he and other boys would "swipe" potatoes from local groceries to roast them in bonfires on vacant lots, Upton Sinclair reached similar conclusions regarding the origins of crime and the means of eradicating it: "And just as we can stop getting alcohol by not mixing a mash, so we can stop crime by not permitting exploitation and economic inequality."[70]

No longer would new radicals accept Lombroso's nineteenth-century theory of "the criminal type," which assumed a hereditary basis for crime, nor earlier explanations attributing it to moral depravity; instead they placed the major blame on environmental influences. John Haynes Holmes wrote: "There are plenty of criminals, of course, who are physically and mentally defective, just as there is a sprinkling of criminals in every prison who are out-and-out moral perverts. But the average criminal is a perfectly normal man, whose fate is wholly to be explained by the fact that he has never had a chance, or has been led astray by degrading and corruptive influences."[71] Emma Goldman confirmed Holmes's theory through personal experience. Jailed for her antiwar activities in the penitentiary at Jefferson City, Missouri, she observed that her fellow inmates there, like those incarcerated with her at Blackwell's Island off New York, were recruited from the poorest classes: "Coloured or white, most of them had been driven to crime by conditions that had greeted them at birth."[72] Her twenty-one months of daily contact with the inmates only strengthened her initial belief: "The contention of criminal psychologists notwithstanding, I found no criminals among them, but only unfortunate, broken, hapless, and hopeless human beings."[73]

Not only did new radicals see criminals as victims of society, but they began to view crime itself as socially defined and hence arbitrary. The law, they noted, did not apply equally to rich and poor alike. Robert Minor caricatured the problem in his cartoon "The Sifter" on 19 October 1911. It depicts a huge sieve labeled "Law Enforcement" held up by the hands of Uncle Sam. The fat capitalist figures named "Trust Magnate" and "$1,000,000 Law Breaker" stay above the sieve while a variety of petty crooks fall through to a funnel labeled jail to a prison below.[74] Clarence Darrow explained the problem to criminals themselves when he addressed the prisoners of the Chicago County Jail. He noted the arbitrary nature of a definition of crime that included pickpockets and thieves yet excluded gas company executives who gouged the public by charging exorbitant prices. The latter were respectable pillars of society, but their victims went straight to jail.[75] Moreover, the wealthy were responsible for creating much of what society dubbed crime because as each monopoly raised the price of essentials like gas, oil, and meat, those who could no longer afford them were driven to commit crimes.[76] The true distinction lay between those criminals who were caught and those who escaped punishment altogether, the latter including many who could afford the services of a good lawyer.[77] "There is no very great danger of a rich man going to jail," Darrow noted, ". . . first and last, people are sent to jail because they are poor."[78] Hence the only means of abolishing crime was to destroy special privileges, curtail the private ownership of land, end monopoly, and place all goods and services in common ownership; only equality would wipe out crime.[79]

As an interim solution new radicals demanded the reform or even the abolition of existing prisons. They found these institutions incapable of either meting out fair punishment or rehabilitating those consigned to them. In a cartoon captioned "No Individual Criminal Has Ever Equaled the Crime Committed on Men by Prisons Themselves," appearing in the *New York Call* of 17 July 1915 Robert Minor leveled a visual attack on the prison system. The cartoon depicts a gap-toothed monster-like bully in the uniform of a prison guard with a cap labeled "N.Y. Prisons." About him are iron bars, men on racks, chained, or sprawled in agony.[80] Nor was the brutality practiced in prison purely physical. Prisons broke inmates of their will, thwarted all their natural inclinations, and sent them back into the world bereft of all hope and purpose, fit only to sink back into crime. Emma Goldman was so disturbed by the role prisons played in perpetuating the cycle of crime that she concluded: "Society might with greater immunity abolish all prisons at once, than to hope for protection from these twentieth-century chambers of horrors."[81] Clarence Darrow's years of experience as a criminal lawyer did nothing to deter him from arriving at the same conclusion:

> There should be no jails. They do not accomplish what they pretend to accomplish. If you would wipe them out, there would be no more criminals than now. They terrorize nobody. They are a blot upon any

civilization, and a jail is an evidence of the lack of charity of the people on the outside who make the jails and fill them with the victims of their greed.[82]

Hence jails were viewed not as society's defenses but rather as evasions of social responsibility for crime. By calling for the abolition of false solutions, new radicals were demanding that the public refocus its attention on the true causes of crime: inequality and exploitation.

Their interest in crime, however, was no mere scholarly product of their socialism; it engaged them emotionally as well. Intellectuals in the prewar era were alienated as a class from the dominant values of American society and preferred to level their critique of that society from an alternate vantage point. As Christopher Lasch has noted: "The intellectual in his estrangement from the middle class identified himself with other outcasts and tried to look at the world from their point of view."[83] Whether by fate or by choice, new radicals consorted far more with criminals than their bourgeois counterparts. Alexander Berkman was cast in among criminals when he was imprisoned for his unsuccessful *Attentat* against Henry Clay Frick. At first he found them distasteful, not truly belonging to "the People" for whom he had consecrated his life, victims of social injustice who remained so loathsome to him that he could offer them only his intellectual sympathy: "they touch no chord in my heart."[84] Gradually Berkman's prison experiences overcame his chill revolutionary intellectuality as he developed friendships with other criminals based on their common misery: "The touch of sympathy had discovered the man beneath the criminal; the crust of sullen suspicion has melted at the breath of kindness, warming into view the palpitating human heart."[85] For the first time he could see the shattered nobility of his comrades in jail and feel a genuine sense of "kinship with the humanity of *les misérables*, whom social stupidity has cast into the valley of death."[86] Berkman began his internment by feeling only pity and contempt for criminals; he ended it by announcing his solidarity with them. That same sense of kinship with criminals developed more readily in the more humane and tolerant faith of Eugene Debs. In his Canton, Ohio, statement to the court after his conviction for having violated the Espionage Act, Debs affirmed his solidarity with criminals and the downtrodden in a speech imbued not only with socialism but with Christian humility: "Your Honor, years ago I recognized my kinship with all living beings, and I made up my mind that I was not one bit better than the meanest on earth. I said then, and I say now, that while there is a lower class, I am in it, while there is a criminal element, I am of it, and while there is a soul in prison, I am not free."[87]

Moreover, just as new radicals had flirted with black and immigrant culture to enrich their own experience, so did they consort with underworld types to make their own lives more exciting. Hutchins Hapgood once asked a sculptor who also frequented the Bowery why they preferred low life to the company of respectable people. The sculptor replied that well-bred people bored him because they never grew oblivious enough of their personal dignity to reveal their emotions and interests or to break with conventionality. In contrast, on the Bowery one encountered men and women "who talk in terms of immediate emotion and passion, who lay themselves bare, who exhibit the 'real thing' in human character," in short, who vivify the human drama for artist and writer.[88] Speaking quasi-autobiographically through the character of Terry in *An Anarchist Woman* (1909), a man, like the author, widely experienced, who "had rejected society, but not the ideal," who "consorted with thieves, prostitutes, with all low human types," Hapgood revealed his own "deep sympathy and even an aesthetic appreciation" for the criminals he had chosen to befriend.[89] He claimed always to have valued God's creatures far more than man-made laws and convictions and so could care for criminals more than for their ethics: "A man might be a thief and a woman a prostitute, but these have seemed to me more or less accidental and unimportant aspects, not affecting deeply their essential natures, which might be beautiful."[90] Yet Hapgood took far more trouble to discover and portray publicly the essential humanity of the ordinary criminal than he did to unearth the same quality in his bourgeois counterpart. Although he might argue that common criminals were too frivolous and vain to pose a genuine threat to society, Hapgood seems to wish that they were more effective in their rebellion.[91] Hapgood's attitude toward criminals is at its very base contradictory: he cherishes both their common humanity and their rebellious individuality, both the immaturity that renders them harmless and the implicit critique that their lives provide of prevailing bourgeois mores.

It was the society of criminals, not merely individual friendship, that certain new radicals sought. They recognized in the underworld a viable social order, a brotherhood bound together more firmly than society itself was yoked together by law. John Reed actually implies that its solidarity transcended culture and nationality. When as a reporter he covered the Mexican Revolution, he had been warned by Americans that the Mexicans were "fundamentally dishonest" and that he should expect to be robbed of his outfit on the first day out. Reed traveled with a rough band of ex-outlaws, undisciplined, uneducated, many of them "Gringohaters." Unpaid for six weeks, some were so impoverished that they lacked sandals or serapes. Nevertheless, not only did they fail to take advantage of an unarmed stranger with a good outfit, but they refused to let him pay for food or tobacco and considered every suggestion from him that he do so an insult.[92] In contrast to orthodox socialists who held that the lumpenproletariat was incapable of achieving true socialism, Reed saw in this motley crew of Mexican ex-outlaws true practitioners of communal ideals.

Like Hapgood and Reed, other *Masses'* radicals found more genuine honesty, sincerity, humanity among criminals than among the pious and respectable. In Harry Kemp's *Tramping on Life: An Autobiographical Narrative* (1922), Bud and John Gregory (Kemp's persona) are cast in jail for breaking and entering with intent to rob, although their only true crime was to have been apprehended as tramps sleeping in a cotton-seed warehouse. The local sheriff detained them in jail to make a profit on his feeding contract. The days spent in jail deepened the two tramps' understanding of their shared humanity with their fellow inmates: "But on Saturday morning he came to turn us loose. By this time we seemed blood brothers to the others in the cage . . negro . . mulatto . . white . . criminal and vicious . . weak, and victims of circumstance . . everything sloughed away. Genuine tears stood in our eyes as with strong hand-grips we wished the poor lads good luck!"[93] Similarly, black poet Claude McKay befriended a white thief, Michael, and sheltered him in his Harlem hideout while he continued his petty tricks downtown.[94] The relationship was a kind of symbolic doubling: a white man who lived by his wits paired to a black man who lived by his art; together they seemed more whole than apart.

Although McKay's friendship with a criminal eluded public detection, other new radicals, especially Hapgood, Reed, and Steffens, consorted publicly with criminals, in part to gain literary insight into the underside of life but also, no doubt, to twit bourgeois mores. This playful intention clearly informs Charles Erskine Scott Wood's "Heavenly Discourse" in which the revivalist preacher Billy Sunday visits Heaven, expecting to be greeted by his old cronies from earth, and instead finds all the people he had consigned to Hell in his sermons. He is appalled to see Herman Morgenstern, the keeper of a family beer garden on Fourth Avenue, and protests to Jesus the presence of a saloonkeeper among the Heavenly host. Jesus replies that he liked the man, found him "a gentle, charitable soul." When Sunday insists that the man is unworthy, Jesus cites his own example: "I lived with Publicans and Sinners." Sunday becomes increasingly distressed as he sees himself surrounded by "harlots, saloonkeepers, infidels"—even agnostic Bob Ingersoll has been angelicized because "he fought superstition all his life." Finally the preacher begs to be released from Heaven because it fails to meet his lofty expectations.[95] Wood implies that Sunday himself is not worthy of Heaven—God asks Gabriel to check if a sudden stench is caused by a malfunction in the sewer to Hell—but the reader feels confident that Heavenly housekeeping will improve when Sunday takes his leave.[96] In Wood's view, and implicit also in the view of other new radicals who emphasized the spirit of Christianity rather than its ritual or dogma, criminals were more fit for the company of Heaven than the wealthy and respectable people whose profiteering drove the exploited to a life of crime.[97]

Moreover, the temptation to criminality, or even the mere mention of it, added romantic color to the seemingly drab life of artists and writers subtly resisting their own latent tendencies toward the bourgeois. Clearly Floyd Dell remained in perpetual turmoil, desiring both the security and respectability of the middle class and the ascetic commitment of the true disciple of socialism.[98] Although presumably socialists should condemn train robbers for threatening the worldly goods of the poor, in Dell's "Keep Your Eyes on the Sidewalk" (1913) the narrator attends a missionary meeting where a reformed train robber discourses on his salvation: "I lost much of my respect for train-robbery on the spot." Longing for a brief entrée into a forbidden world, he is disappointed:

> I had hoped for a flash at least of the old bandit fire—a touch of unconscious pride in the narration of his former wickedness. He might have brought into that overheated room, filled with old and ugly women, a breath of beauty—for life is always beautiful. But no—he brought nothing that was not already there. He repeated to them the phrases which they had taught him. The familiar accents of piety came smoothly from his lips, like a well-learned lesson, and all the old and ugly women nodded approval.[99]

Dell never quite grew up, although he did finally assume the adult responsibilities of marriage and fatherhood. His later novels only thinly disguise the moon-calf of his youth. In *The Golden Spike* (1934), Dell writes of Harvey Claymore, a small-town reporter who, while morally condemning them, drew comfort from the existence of local facilities for devilment:

> He could never feel himself an alien when he touched the fringes of lawlessness—instead, he felt at ease, as if he were coming home. But he suspected that if he once started cutting loose, he would like it altogether too well—and perhaps not be able to come back to the narrow path—or he might have let himself take a holiday from duty when he was bored and discouraged. And sometimes it seemed that he must bust loose. Oh, God! if there were just some excitement in his life.[100]

Lawlessness, then, was a touchstone for the confused rebellion of a new radical like Dell. Throughout his lifetime he remained uncertain whether lawbreaking, the illicit pursuit of pleasure, was the mark of the respectable burgher above the law or of a cultural rebel who attacked society by defying its laws.

Radicals longed for a vacation from responsibility, for the carefree existence of the vagabond who lived on society's margins. They celebrated the image of the proletarian hero as hobo, tramp, wanderer, Wobbly—"a portrait that was captured in Hutchins Hapgood's *The Spirit of Labor* and personified in the life of John Reed."[101] Jack London, too, spent part of his life as a tramp, belonging at once "to the tradition of Walt Whitman, the social outcast, the prophet, and the bard" and to the spirit of vagabondage that permeated the Western states in the 1890s.[102] To wander freely was to burst the ties of responsibility and respectability, to sever the rigid cash nexus imposed by capitalism in order to be the slave of many masters, taking a series of menial jobs, as Piet Vlag did, or living by one's wits.[103] Harry Kemp was known as the "hobo poet," Claude McKay interrupted his college career to wander abroad, and even Max Eastman gleefully inflated a critic's insult by dubbing himself a "Professional Hobo" so that he could rank with other rebel luminaries such as Pancho Villa, William D. Haywood, and Wild Joe O'Carroll.[104]

As romantic rebels the new radicals often effaced the distinction between the individual defiance of tramps and outlaws and the serious, disciplined nature of the class struggle. At times they seemed to feel that any tilting at respectability might serve to topple the structure of capitalism. Intellectuals themselves, nevertheless they feared the academic critique alone as ineffectual. In *Chants Communal* (1904) Horace Traubel dismissed the possibility that writers, scholars, or scientists could cure social ills. Only society's outcasts and failures, its outlaws and rebels, could foment the final storm that would destroy the corrupt old civilization and replace it with a freer, healthier social order.[105] The Wobblies, too, believed that bums or bindle stiffs were potential revolutionaries because they lacked a stake in preserving the inequities of the status quo. Wobbly poet Arturo Giovannitti wrote his own paean to "The Bum" from Salem Jail on 20 November 1912. The poem was an invocation to the "bummery" to arise in protest against its oppressors, to use its own scorn and hatred as weapons of liberation.[106]

Even more respectable rebels like Upton Sinclair liked to think of themselves as capable of criminality in support of "the cause." After publishing *The Jungle* Sinclair publicly proclaimed: "I would cheerfully have sandbagged a capitalist or robbed a bank to accomplish my purpose, had it been impossible any other way. I wanted a point of vantage from which to begin the agitation of my cause."[107] Floyd Dell agreed that any self-respecting radical would resort to crime to awaken the class-consciousness of the workers.[108] Sinclair believed that criminality might be the crucible in which socialism could be created. He suspected that the extraordinary social progress of New Zealand was the result of its convict-settlement. He found that "the men whom capitalism makes into criminals" were "for the most part a very superior class of people, active, independent, and impatient of injustice.

Transported to a new land, and given a fair chance, I should think that a burglar or a highwayman ought to make a very excellent Socialist."[109]

Max Eastman took the next logical step of demanding an end to the punishment of the evildoer. Instead, society should foster in him the pride of rebels:

> But we ought to give him all possible opportunity to escape from
> the prison of his own misfortune—whether that be sickness, or reckless
> good health mixed with poverty. To teach criminals to escape from
> prison—that will be the aim of prison reformers. And as they learn to
> adopt that aim, may they borrow at least this much from the creed
> of revolution—not to demand from their prisoners humbleness, and
> gratitude, and goodness, and other stultifications of spirit, but to wel-
> come from prisoners an arrogant *demand* for even better justice than
> they so benevolently hand down. For without that, without both pride
> and power from below, neither the system nor the spirit of the sys-
> tem, will ever be completely changed.[110]

"Pride and power"—whether of race, ethnicity, or even criminality—new radicals saw as essential to freedom not as a privilege but as a birthright. They wished to establish popular entitlement as firmly as the a priori claims of natural law had done during the Enlightenment. As Freudians they recognized the importance of self-awareness for the individual; as socialists they understood the importance of self-respect for the group. "Pride and power" could set a people free.

Chapter 9 Art in the Class Struggle: The Personal Politics of *The Masses'* Radicals, 1911–1917

As a socialist literary and political magazine, *The Masses* (1911–17) claimed to be heir to the Marxist tradition of using art as a weapon in the class struggle. It accepted the goal of consciousness-raising and repudiated any pretensions to "art for art's sake." Its members rushed to the battlefronts and picket lines to report the ebb and flow of socialist success; they, too, marched, were jailed and martyred. But their commitment to socially conscious art was tentative at best. *The Masses* remained a magazine of "free expression," open to a wide range of opinion, much of it bearing little resemblance to orthodox socialism.

The Masses was heir to the muckraking movement, a phenomenon so brief and transitory that it scarcely could be called a tradition. Turn-of-the-century journalists like Ida Tarbell, Lincoln Steffens, Ray Stannard Baker, and others leveled their attack not on capitalism per se but on its individual corruptions. Their discontent was reflected in the novels of Booth Tarkington, Frank Norris, David Graham Phillips, Winston Churchill, and Upton Sinclair. In both reportage and fiction, according to Joseph Freeman, the younger generation of intellectuals grew accustomed to two powerful ideas: "first, that American capitalism was corrupt from top to bottom; second, that art and politics were closely related."[1] Since the muckrakers were native-born Americans, their limited social critique could lay the foundations for an indigenous radicalism.[2]

Like the muckrakers, a number of new radicals embraced journalism as the best available means of bringing their message to a mass audience. Jack London pioneered "the alliance of realism in literature and socialism"—what Floyd Dell dubbed the "journalistic" trend—and John Reed, Arturo Giovannitti, and Michael Gold refined the genre:

> Such journalism was radical, even revolutionary, because it implied
> that the journalist must not merely be the mirror of events, but a partici-

pant in their outcome. The works of Lincoln Steffens and John Reed exemplify this journalism pushed to its revolutionary limits—the promotion of social change by fixing upon what were considered the radical implications of reality, the facts that cried out for change.[3]

Their journalism laid the foundations of the documentary style of the 1930s with its on-the-spot reportage, its discovery of an underworld of poverty, and its artistic handling of fact. Moreover, it served to resolve personal role ambivalence as new radicals refused to be defined strictly by their profession: "the radical did not want to be *just* a novelist, for that was to be circumscribed and limited, but to be a novelist *and* an adventurer *and* a bohemian. In the figure of the journalist the radical was able to combine these four roles into one eclectic hero."[4] As a journalist, the rebel intellectual could be engagé.

The Masses was a product of both the failures of commercial journalism and the experiments of the little magazines. The magazine argued that the repressive nature of capitalism extended to art and that its own function was to lead the revolt against commercial control of editorial content.[5] Perhaps as a result, its members were equally unwilling to subject themselves to revolutionary discipline. Daniel Aaron has noted that *The Masses'* radicals differed from subsequent Marxists "in their insistence that the writer as *writer* was beyond social criticism," that only when he launched into social commentary could he be chided for improper views.[6] Max Eastman and Floyd Dell were eager to print good revolutionary verse, but neither would have based editorial judgment on a writer's political affiliations: "It took World War I and the Russian revolution to induce some of them, like the cartoonist Robert Minor, the reporter Jack Reed, and (to a lesser extent) the poets Eastman and Dell to renounce poetry for revolution."[7]

The undisciplined nature of *The Masses* evoked criticism that its contributions were self-concerned and lacked seriousness. Hutchins Hapgood complained that many of the illustrators were more concerned to achieve dramatic effect than to raise consciousness, that the magazine itself "consistently lacked an objective revolutionary quality."[8] Despite its admixture with socialism, *The Masses'* revolt yet seemed personalistic, ego-gratifying, seeking refuge from conflict in art and psychoanalysis.[9] Moreover, the magazine was good-humored, gay, impertinent in tone, qualities that Richard Drinnon believes may have been essential to "any real fusion of social and artistic rebellion."[10] But the very humor that enhanced the rebel spirit also confined it to its class of origin. "When *The Masses* advertised, *The Masses* has a sense of humor. . . . Enjoy the Revolution," orthodox socialists like William J. Ghent were appalled. No matter how rich the response from middle-class intellectuals, such an appeal was meaningless to those most oppressed by capitalism, the starving strikers at Lawrence or the miners gunned down at Ludlow.[11] Genevieve Taggard explained the difficulty:

Because this magazine of rebellion was edited, in spite of its title, for the bourgeois liberal, to give him the freedom he had grown needy of, and because, although it did talk in a very specific and realistic tone of voice about the proletariat, it did not talk *to* the proletariat.
Scoffers said, rightly enough:
They draw nude women for the *Masses*,
Thick, fat, ungainly lasses—
How does that help the working classes?[12]

According to Louis Untermeyer, all of *The Masses'* contributors were plagued by a fear that they were not activists, not truly "makers of revolution." They led a schizophrenic existence, constantly torn between their art and the practical necessities of politics. Martha Sonnenberg concluded from her interview with Untermeyer: "These artists did not conceive of a synthesis between art and politics, of art as a form of revolutionary activity, or of radical consciousness as a liberated aesthetics."[13] In the absence of a Marxist theory of art, *The Masses'* radicals could find no synthesis, no truly socialist expression. Would democratic art free them from market constraints to develop their individual styles, or would it compel them to serve the cause of the workers? Would it promote experimentation or enforce uniformity through the imposition of the collective will? Was the place of the artist more secure in the interstices of an imperfect capitalist system than it would be in the monolithic structure of the cooperative commonwealth? And, most important, was rebellion the lifeblood of art?

The artistic rebellion led by *The Masses'* radicals aimed at a revolution in content, not in form. The magazine attempted to provide a forum for art and writing too stark, too realistic, too obviously socialist to achieve commercial acceptance. But little of the material that appeared in *The Masses* was truly innovative or experimental in form. In fact, there appeared to be a direct correlation between radicalism in politics and conservatism in style: "The same poet or painter who condoned sabotage might hate imagism or free verse or cubism. Neither Floyd Dell nor Eastman, for example, were drawn to experimentation in the arts and, later, remained hostile to [T. S.] Eliot and his poetic posterity, to 'obscurity,' and to modish European importations."[14]

Despite their aversion to modernism, in the prewar period Dell, Eastman, cartoonist Art Young, and others in *The Masses'* group avowed their commitment to a journal of free expression for radical ideas. They condemned rigidity and dogma in others yet enshrined them in their own style. The same men and women who gleefully confessed each sexual peccadillo to their analysts and to one another, who publicly explored their conflicts as artists and radicals, who aired their most intimate anxieties without shame or hesitation, were singularly inarticulate on the subject of style. They dismissed their predilection for older forms as a gut reaction, a feeling too deep and irrational to be communicated adequately in intelligible prose. In fact, the problem of style posed a fundamental challenge to the radicals' self-image. In place of spontaneity and authenticity, the art produced by a greater concern with style would be crafted and highly self-conscious. It would demand deferred gratification, the middle-class mode, to be born. Instead of on-the-spot reportage of direct experience, documentary as propaganda, journalism, art as adventure, a self-aware art would demand a kind of reflection and premeditation inimical to bohemian élan.

Meshing form and content required a commitment to theoretical work uncommon among new radicals and implied an organic view of the universe that demanded complete dedication from the radical artist. His person no longer would be exempt from social criticism; his art could not flourish apart from the cause it should serve. The bohemian artist-rebel who dabbled in reform, whose art was spontaneous and free, would have to give way to the disciplined socialist creating a revolutionary *oeuvre*. However, a few prewar radicals were prepared to depart their bohemian grove for the front lines of the class struggle.

The loyalties of prewar radicals undermined their commitment to a socialist art. As Freudians who initially embraced psychoanalysis as a tool of personal liberation, they also confronted the Freudian dogma that art was intimately linked to neurosis, that a healthy adjustment to one's environment would obviate the need for the sublimation that produced art.[15] Hence radical art would be proof of failure in what F. H. Matthews has termed "a morality of mental health."[16] Ironically enough, when radicals like Dell, Eastman, and James Oppenheim resorted to psychoanalysis to overcome their writer's blocks and release creativity, they inadvertently were adopting an ideology that implied conformity, adjustment, acceptance of the status quo.[17]

In contrast, as Marxists prewar radicals were supposed to assume that capitalist society was diseased and that their discontent was a purgative force that would restore their own psychic health and redeem that society. They were to abjure personal solutions and instead build the cooperative commonwealth on a base of class solidarity. In place of an ethos of adjustment, Marxist ideology demanded a commitment to social reconstruction. Hence rather than emphasize the uniqueness of the creative process and grant the artist privileged status on account of his gift, Marxists argued that artists should identify themselves with other workers and share in their struggles. In the early twentieth century sophisticated journalistic production techniques robbed the individual artist of his sense of status and craftsmanship. The proletarianization of newspaper art as a result of mass production journalism probably served as much as ideology to induce radical artists to identify themselves as workers.

Nevertheless, new radicals retained a certain skepticism regarding their effectiveness as revolutionaries. They wondered about their dedication, their forcefulness, their ability to lead in time of crisis. And for many of the writers this ambivalence was compounded by an inability to immerse themselves in work that demanded total commitment. Robert Post has noted the striking absence of radical novels produced by rebels in the prewar period and their fascination with a more ephemeral form, namely journalism.[18] Carl Van Vechten, through the persona of Peter Whiffle, epitomized this indecision.[19] The radical writer in this period had lost the sense of his vocation as predominantly, or at least exclusively, literary. Thus John Reed worked for the Paterson strike and for the Russian Revolution, Randolph Bourne involved himself in educational reform, Max Eastman gave antiwar lectures, and Floyd Dell promoted psychoanalysis. As a result, the failure to achieve a genuinely socialist art could be mitigated by accomplishments in the nonliterary world. A series of ad hoc commitments could substitute for a more durable literary one. Writing came to be viewed as self-definition and hence intimidating. In a playful twist on reality, Peter Whiffle writes a letter of 17 June 1917 to Carl Van Vechten, appointing the latter his executor. In it he confesses his dedication to drift:

> . . . If there has been one set purpose in my life, it has been not to have a purpose. That, you alone, perhaps, understand. You know how I have always hesitated to express myself definitely, you know how I have refrained from writing, and you also know, perhaps, that I can write; indeed, until recently, you thought I was writing or would write. But, I think you realize now what writing has come to mean to me, definition, constant definition, although it is as apparent as anything can be that life, nature, art, whatever one writes about, are fluid and mutable things, perpetually undergoing change and, even when they assume some semblance of permanence, always presenting two or more faces.[20]

Journalism, or more drastically, the failure to write at all, implied an evasion of responsibility, an escape from permanent commitment. Like Peter Whiffle, new radicals preferred a full life to a disciplined art. [21]

Living before the Bolshevik Revolution, at a time when radical ideas were in perpetual flux, Villagers lacked a sure sense of political direction. Yet the burgeoning strength of American socialism and the crisis of the war gave an urgency to their debates on the nature of radical art. Whereas the Victorians sharply distinguished between the realms of art and politics, "the *Masses*, however, and the *Liberator* (through 1922) simply *assumed* art and socialism complemented one another."[22] *The Masses'* founder, Piet Vlag, demanded that art live with the people and struggle on their behalf. The American artist was to be twice a rebel, shedding both the dead hand of Europe and his own snobbery. Socialism would permit the artist to escape the stultifying sense of self and to participate in the destruction of the old order and the creation of the new.[23] *The Masses'* early editor, Thomas Seltzer, argued the compatibility of art and socialism from another perspective. He claimed that a novel need not have an explicitly political purpose in order to foster the eventual triumph of socialism, that, in fact, too crude an exposition of ideology, by distorting the life it purported to represent, might render that particular analysis of socialism ridiculous and unpersuasive. Repudiating "art for art's sake" in literature, Seltzer also challenged the validity of writing popular editions of Marx, Engels, and Kautsky in novelistic form: "Socialism has more to gain from a free, artistic literature reflecting life as it actually is, than from an attempt to stretch points in order to make facts fit the Socialist theory. Socialism has nothing to fear from a true reproduction of life, because life is never opposed to Socialism."[24]

Despite Vlag and Seltzer's optimism, certain *Masses'* radicals emphasized free expression, even at the expense of politically conscious art. After the Paterson Pageant, John Reed reassured his mother that he would not join the Industrial Workers of the World by stating: "I am not a socialist temperamentally any more than I'm an Episcopalian. I know now that my business is to interpret and live life, wherever it may be found—whether in the labor movement or out of it."[25] Would a magazine of free expression serve socialist ends? Would mere compatibility with socialism suffice, or were artists obliged to produce work inspiring socialist thought and deed? One critic of the magazine, E. Ralph Cheney, argued that *The Masses'* predilection for the picturesque might be "an amiable weakness . . . in a mere Bohemian" but that it was "distinctly reprehensible in a revolutionist."[26]

Two decades after Cheney's reproach, Max Eastman still was responding to the charges of "mere Bohemianism" that had been leveled against *The Masses.* He saw the commitment of young rebels against bourgeois conventions to a free and candid mode of life as exemplary, even to the revolutionary intellectuals who repudiated it: "A Bohemian life, in this good sense, is precisely the kind of life that they hope to make natural to the race of man after the artificialities that spring out of our money culture are removed."[27] Only "mere Bohemianism" masquerading as "serious social thought and action" deserved the revolutionary's disdain. Eastman claimed to have engaged in a constant editorial battle against the substitution of a personal revolt for the practical scientific work critical to revolutionary survival: "Against Greenwich Villagism in that sense my editorship of *The Masses* and *The Liberator* was a continual struggle—a struggle in which I was at times resisted, not only by men like George Bellows and Stuart Davis, whose interest in art is obviously primary, but by John Reed and Robert Minor."[28]

New radicals felt a constant tension between aesthetics and ethics, between artistic complexity and political purpose. Robert Minor resolved that tension by eradicating it completely. A successful artist, he gave up a lucrative position on the *New York World* for a twenty-five-dollar-a-week job on the socialist daily *Call*, to free his artistic energies for the class struggle.[29] Yet when his art seemed to interfere with his political activism, Minor abandoned it to become a Communist party functionary. For Minor, Marxism was a scientific faith, altogether precise and objective. Waldo Frank reminisces: "I recall an argument with him on the beach of Truro on Cape Cod. We were talking about the 'certain' Marxist future; and I cried: 'But the imponderables, Bob! The imponderables—.' His smile was somewhat a sneer: 'There are no imponderables,' he said."[30]

In sharp contrast to Minor's single-mindedness was Randolph Bourne's speculations about the relationship between aesthetics and social reform. His travels on the Continent had awakened Bourne to the significance of civic art, town planning, and modern architecture in enriching European life and to the perils of their absence, as reflected in the drab and brutalized life of the English people. Hence the promotion of artistic sensitivity among the people became the intellectual's contribution to the task of social reform: "Any general improvement in taste means a demand for a rise in the standard of living, and this rise is *the* great fulcrum, I am convinced, in social progress. Until people begin really to *hate* ugliness and poverty and disease, instead of merely pitying the poor and the sick, we shall not have, I fear, any great social advance."[31] As Carl Resek has noted, Bourne saw art and politics as so intertwined that they were separable only at each other's perils. For Bourne, the artist who educated was the true revolutionary; the cultural leader would direct popular desire toward radical ends. Whereas Minor abandoned art for politics, Bourne created a politics of aesthetics: "From Nietzsche he learned that desire could be transformed into a 'will to power,' and the shaping of desire therefore became a political as well as artistic duty."[32] Thus Bourne's cultural radicalism allowed him to reconcile art and politics by discovering a revolutionary function of aesthetics.

New radicals lived in an era of growing awareness of popular culture. Unlike many Victorians who sought to employ elite culture as a means of disciplining the masses, early twentieth-century radicals sought to create a culture that would serve the needs of the proletariat. Their mission embraced contradiction. Did the masses need more cultured spokesmen? If they did, would not that need betray a fatal weakness in their class? Did proletarian art demand greater simplicity and directness than elite culture, or were such gestures patronizing proof of condescension by the intellectuals who produced it?

The proponents of popularization differed markedly in their view of the masses. James Oppenheim believed that few had ascended so high in the evolutionary scale as to dispense with popular superstition; most people remained so enslaved to childish desire that conscious maturation was beyond their ken: "let a Billy Sunday appear, or a Bill Haywood, or the Day of Armageddon, or Defense of Liberty and England or the Fatherland, and they will flock to the dream."[33] Unlike Walter Lippmann, a "strong young modern" who would abolish more remote symbols in favor of greater conscious evolution, Oppenheim felt that only a tiny elite was capable of such effort. Most people depended upon their delusions for support even within the most gradual process of evolution: "Utopia-vision and the fairy-tale belong to the same category, and spring from the same needs. For the truth of the matter is that most people are childish and undeveloped, and you can no more take their utopias, heavens, holy Maries, resurrections and immortality from them, than you can ask them to write H. G. Wells novels. Their real need produces the symbol which sustains them, and not only sustains them, but is actually a bridge toward maturity."[34] Despite his condescension, James Oppenheim had produced one of the song classics of the labor movement, "Bread and Roses," in response to a banner inscribed, "We Want Bread, and Roses too!," carried by young girls in a parade of the strikers of Lawrence, Massachusetts.[35] These girls complained of cultural as well as of physical starvation, evincing an artistic sensitivity that intellectuals like Bourne had thought *they* would have to awaken in the masses.

Other new radicals felt that exposition alone would not suffice to propagandize the mass. Many Wobblies, especially after 1912, argued that the best educational material for their movement appeared in *The Little Red Song Book*, some even recommending that the IWW cease publishing pamphlets and other economic literature to concentrate exclusively on the *Song Book*. Although Joe Hill himself did not subscribe to this position, he did argue that "if a person can put a few cold, common-sense facts into a song and dress them (the facts) up in a cloak of humor to take the dryness out of them, he will succeed in reaching a great number of workers who are too unintelligent or too indifferent to read a pamphlet or an editorial on economic science."[36] There seemed to be little questioning of the value of such facilely formed commitments. New radicals transformed the drama into little theater and pageant; they turned magazine art into a vehicle for political propaganda; they made traditional arts serve radical ends. The mass evacuation of starving children from Lawrence, hunger strikes in prison in support of the public right to birth control became early media events as radicals learned to harness the publicity machine for their own purposes. Even after Floyd Dell had left the Village, he remained conscious of the need for radicals to control the mass media. Joseph Freeman wrote: "Although he had already begun his self-imposed exile in the suburbs, he retained a keen intellectual interest in the revolutionary movement, and said that art, to be vital, must reflect that movement. He believed that the artist, in order to reach the masses of the proletariat, would someday have to resort to the poster, the billboard, the movie and the radio, then beginning to roar its inanities through America's cities."[37] The Freudian revolution had made radicals aware of subconscious levels of manipulation, hence their receptivity to nondiscursive means of persuasion and propaganda.

Yet the contradictions in early radical conceptions of proletarian art were most clearly embodied in the thought of Emma Goldman. Once Goldman and Alexander Berkman got into a furious argument with Margaret Anderson over the value of the poetry of Oscar Wilde and the Imagists. Whereas Anderson argued for the universal appeal of the "eternal human emotions" as expressed in poetry, her anarchist adversaries championed a revolutionary art that would reflect directly working-class experience.[38] Nevertheless, although Goldman called for literary content meaningful to a working-class audience, she despaired of the forms used to convey radical propaganda. Herself a charismatic speaker, she came to realize the inadequacy of the spoken word "to awaken thought, or even emotion." Oral propaganda might shake people from their lethargy, but it left no lasting impression. The written mode of expression had more permanent powers of persuasion, but it was inherently flawed: "No one, unless intensely interested in progressive ideas, will bother with serious books. That leads me to another discovery made after many years of public activity. It is this: All claims of education notwithstanding, the pupil will accept only that which his mind craves."[39] Hence Goldman posited a situation in which it was theoretically impossible for a radical intellectual to enlighten the masses since the latter would be receptive only to familiar ideas.

Despite her commitment to the masses, Goldman remained strongly individualistic, claiming that only an elite cadre could bring progress. She held the mass itself responsible for its own suffering and exploitation: "It clings to its masters, loves the whip, and is the first to cry Crucify! the moment a protesting voice is raised against the sacredness of capitalistic authority or any other decayed institution. Yet how long would authority and private property exist, if not for the willingness of the mass to become soldiers, policemen, jailers, and hangmen."[40] Whereas "Socialist demagogues" might celebrate the mythical virtues of the majority in order to cling to power, Goldman insisted that the will of the majority was always inimical to individuality, free initiative, and originality. Like Ralph Waldo Emerson, who sought to divide masses, to draw out individuals, Goldman, too, deplored the evils of mass society. For her, true democracy existed apart from the will of the masses she sought to serve: "In other words, the living, vital truth of social and economic well-being will become a reality only through the zeal, courage, the noncompromising determination of intelligent minorities, and not through the mass."[41] Could an intelligent minority adequately serve its inferiors? Would both groups be yoked by a common class interest? Could they ultimately share a *Weltanschauung*? Would there be limits on their powers of communication?

In contrast, Claude McKay escaped these problems by identifying himself with the black workers about whom he wrote. He came to his knowledge of unskilled black laborers through his work as a porter, longshoreman, and railroad waiter, sharing their life and aspirations. His was an empathy denied to the scholars, lecturers, and bohemians whose curiosity regarding black life lacked insight or familiarity: "So when I came to write about the low-down Negro, I did not have to compose him from an outside view. Nor did I have to write a pseudoromantic account, as do bourgeois persons who become working-class for a while and work in shops and factories to get material for writing dull books about workers, whose inner lives are closed to them."[42] McKay's own impeccable working-class credentials enabled him to resist Michael Gold's pressure to transform *The Liberator* into "a popular proletarian magazine, printing doggerels from lumberjacks and stevedores and true revelations from chambermaids." McKay contended that only proletarian writing of quality deserved to find its way into print. Sympathetic to the pathetic efforts of working people struggling toward adequate literary expression, yet he abjured Gold's mawkishness:

> Because I was also an ordinary writer, without benefit of a classic education. And I had had the experience of the hard struggle and intellectual discipline and purposefulness that were necessary to make a fine stanza of verse or a paragraph of prose. And Michael Gold also knew. He was still intellectually battling up from the depths of proletarian starvation and misery. And like myself he was getting hard criticism and kind encouragement from Max Eastman. But Michael Gold preferred sentimentality above intellectuality in estimating proletarian writing and writers.[43]

McKay accepted the need for politically conscious art, but he demanded that that art be comparable to other work in its clarity and expressiveness.

This respect for the technical aspect of art eluded Robert Minor, who even as a radical cartoonist at age twenty-seven on the *St. Louis Post-Dispatch* had come to champion art as a weapon in the class struggle. Joseph North wrote of the young artist: "He had never received an hour of formal training in an art school; how could he truly have mastered his techniques? He had no reverence for art as an end in itself. Art, to him, was a means of waging the war of politics."[44] Minor's art was blunt, simple, direct, its emphasis on message rather than on medium. In repudiating the principle of "art for art's sake," he and others of his generation created a new genre of politically conscious art intended as a weapon in the class struggle. His biographer described Minor at a 1946 memorial meeting for John Reed: "He must have thought of the companions of his youth and, later, men like Art Young, Boardman Robinson, Theodore Dreiser, Mike Gold, William Gropper, Fred Ellis, Rockwell Kent, Hugo Gellert, when he put down on paper that among his generation Reed pioneered 'in applying the principle that art is a fighting instrument in the great affairs of men.' "[45]

These debates about the nature of proletarian art among prewar radicals were to be recapitulated during the Great Depression by the contributors to *The New Masses* and *Partisan Review*. But the general structure of the debates had been set by the time of the Great War. The tension between aesthetics and politics, the alternation between disdain and empathy for the mass, the intellectual's fear of popular superstition and his attraction to proletarian vigor, the questioning of whether it was enough that art be true to life for it to promote socialism or whether it had to be explicitly political in order to achieve that purpose, all these ambiguities and more had been explored by prewar radicals. Virtually all of them agreed on the compatibility of art and politics, but only a handful of the most dedicated revolutionaries accepted the notion of art as a weapon in the class struggle.

Chapter 10 Life-style and Radicalism

As social and cultural rebels *The Masses'* radicals faced the difficulties of integrating their political commitments into their lives. More moderate socialists might lead lives of impeccably bourgeois respectability, but new radicals scorned their Victorian past to dabble in bohemian ways. As rebels against both convention and capitalism, they found themselves caught in contradiction. Was not bohemianism inimical to the ascetic discipline demanded of a dedicated revolutionary? Would it not alienate its Village practitioners from the workers they sought to reach? Yet if their radicalism were rooted in their rejection of Victorianism, could they successfully sever that rebellion from its roots? Were true revolutionaries to be spartan and self-disciplined, soldier-like in their struggles, or were they, by their example, to teach others to live as if the revolution already had occurred? What personal succor would they need to sustain their political commitments? As Freudians as well as Marxists, these radicals lived at a pitch of heightened self-consciousness. Theirs was an introspective rebellion, marked by constant analysis and confessional. And the challenge that they posed for themselves as artists and as radicals involved the creation of a life-style appropriate to both commitments. Living itself demanded an artistry that could challenge the complacency of others. In Sherwood Anderson's *Windy McPherson's Son* (1916) John Telfer boasts to Sam McPherson: " 'I do not paint pictures; I do not write books; yet am I an artist,' declared Telfer, proudly. 'I am an artist practising the most difficult of all arts—the art of living. Here in this western village I stand and fling my challenge to the world. "On the lip of not the greatest of you," I cry, "has life been more sweet." ' "[1]

The link between the art of life and radical artistry, however, remained elusive. The prewar radicals believed that their lives should be a testament to a postcapitalist world, yet they remained uncertain whether their bohemian life-styles detracted from their efficacy as revolutionaries. They longed to achieve the mystical unity of the trinity, integrating art, politics, and personal life, and they found only relentless doubt. Living before the Bolshevik Revolution, their lives lacked revolutionary focus. There was no single standard by which they might judge themselves, no sense of urgency or immediacy that would demand more than temporary sacrifice in the face of a fight for civil liberties, a labor struggle, or the war itself. Even when prewar rebels chose downward mobility, their economic deprivation need only be temporary; their literacy and charm, combined with clearly marketable skills, assured their return to middle-class status at will.

Unconventionality proved no defense against the most bourgeois emotions, particularly feminine romanticism. Despite the advent of the "new woman," female radicals felt traditional vulnerability in matters of the heart. Isadora Duncan periodically interrupted her struggles to liberate the world of dance by taking refuge in love. When she returned to her art, her work seemed only a sublimation of emotionality denied: "My life has known but two motives— Love and Art. And often Love destroyed Art—and often the imperious call of Art put a tragic end to Love—for these two have known no accord but constant battle."[2] Nor was a more consciously political rebel like Emma Goldman any less prone to find love subversive of her radical commitments. She longed to find permanency in love yet suspected that the price of her ideal was to find satisfaction only in fleeting attachments.[3] For seven years she had a torturous affair with photographer and Austrian anarchist Edward Brady, a man who held that political agitation was a career unnatural to woman. Goldman was repelled by his patriarchal attitude, his desire that she devote herself to him exclusively, become his wife and bear him a child. Brady was convinced that his lover's political dedication was no more than the result of her thwarted impulse toward motherhood. For years Goldman resisted his demand to choose between her work and their love, and the resulting tension ultimately led to the dissolution of their union.[4] Goldman's inability to reject his imperious demands outright reveals her susceptibility to traditional romantic appeals. She felt shamed by the superior dedication of male anarchists. To her the figure of Alexander Berkman, imprisoned for his heroic *Attentat*, was a glowing but elusive ideal:

> The spirit of the boy of twenty-three was extraordinary. It shamed me for my own faint heart. Yet I knew that the personal would always play a dominant part in my life. I was not hewn of one piece, like Sasha [Berkman] or other heroic figures. I had long realized that I was woven of many skeins, conflicting in shade and texture. To the end of my days I should be torn between the yearning for a personal life and the need of giving all to my ideal.[5]

Many of the male radicals were dreamers who had difficulty enough adjusting to adult responsibility and so had little surplus energy to devote to reconciling politics and life-style. In his autobiographical novel *Love's Pilgrimage*

(1911) Upton Sinclair describes the havoc his work as a radical artist wreaked on his family life. Rather than deny his literary ambition, Sinclair removed his family to an island and lived in a tent. When his wife fell ill, he would take their baby to his own tent, "where he would draw a chalk-line across the floor. One-half of the forty-nine square feet of space was his; and in it he would sit and read and study; in the other half the baby would play. After long experience he came to realize that at such times Papa would not pay any attention to him, and that crossing the chalk-line involved getting one's 'mungies' [fingers] spanked."[6] The reader is left to wonder how a man who cannot provide for the elemental physical and psychological needs of his own wife and child can fancy himself an architect of social reconstruction. In desperation Sinclair clung to the romantic conception of the artist as a creature transcending the claims of ordinary responsibility: "Here again was the torment of this matrimonial bond to a man who wished to be an artist. He had to live two lives, when one was more than he could attend to; he had to be always aware of another soul yearning for him, reaching out to him and craving his attention."[7] When Sinclair in reality sought to dissolve this unwanted bond by obtaining a Dutch divorce from his first wife in order to wed Mary Craig Kimbrough, he still had not reconciled his personal and political loyalties. En route to Holland to obtain the divorce, he visited England during the miners' strike and as the guest of labor leader John Burns heard Asquith versus Balfour on the floor of Parliament, "or rather both of them versus the working masses of Britain." The spectacle threw Sinclair into confusion and turmoil: "When the great lawyer Asquith was in the midst of his sophistries, the young American could stand no more; he half rose from his seat, with his mouth open to say what he thought of these starvers of British labor. Half a dozen times he rose, with words starting from his throat; and half a dozen times he sank back again. They could have arrested him, no doubt, and his protest would have been heard. But it would also have gone to Amsterdam, where the polite judge had still to decide the problem of the custody of Thyrsis' [Sinclair's] son!"[8] Having an exaggerated sense both of his own importance and of the likelihood of socialist revolution in his lifetime, Sinclair's alternating willingness to sacrifice the personal and the political seems all the more inadequate a response to the demands placed upon him.

A fellow dreamer, Floyd Dell, also devoted an inordinate amount of energy to his quest for personal fulfillment. An apostle of both Freud and Marx, Dell had come to the Village to find sexual liberation and socialist solidarity. In fact, he set the local standard for bohemianism before his remarriage and produced little explicitly political writing. Most of his work concerned itself with love and art; his radicalism was always fashionable and eclectic. In 1919 Dell projected a volume of book reviews for Alfred A. Knopf on the literary treatment of politics and love by eminent authors of the Victorian age, such as

H. G. Wells, George Bernard Shaw, Chesterton, Galsworthy, Theodore Dreiser, Frank Norris, Robert Herrick, Sherwood Anderson, D. H. Lawrence, Arnold Bennett, and J. D. Beresford. The aim of this work was "to show how far each of these people succeeded or failed in preparing us to face the Bolshevik reconstruction of the world."[9] Dell's ambition to be a communist literary critic came to naught, but it had foundered on his own inability to accept the demands of scientific socialism.[10] In his autobiographical novel *The Briary-Bush* (1921) Dell's hero Felix Fay confides to his wife Rose-Ann that being an artist has robbed him of his humanity: "There are two kinds of people in the world—artists and human beings. I've never been a human being; so I must have been an artist. And I don't want to be any longer!"[11] Dell's position and that of many of his fellow bohemians placed them in a prison of their own making. On the one hand, they condemned puritanism for severing the link between art and normality, and, on the other, they embraced Freudianism, which did the same by branding art neurotic. If Dell truly had adhered to the Marxian synthesis, he would have been able to ascribe the artist's failure to achieve full humanity to the alienation produced by modern capitalism. Instead he adopted a Freudian world view, which mandated his retreat from art and politics into the satisfactions of personal life. Although Dell never abandoned his writing, he did restrain his political activities, and his work reflected intimate personal concerns.

Another writer who was to use the artist's claims to exemption from human responsibility was Sherwood Anderson. Reviewing Anderson's *Memoirs* in 1942, Dell described his friend's Chicago advertising period as a time of increasing resentment against the world's demands that he be a businessman, husband, and father when he longed to devote himself to his writing. As a result, Anderson excluded his family from his inner life and experienced the same inner turmoil described by Upton Sinclair. After his marriage crumbled, Anderson tried to resolve his conflicts by becoming a socialist but found no relief in political commitment. Verging on nervous collapse, he "pretended to be going crazy, or else suffered a genuine amnesia (his subsequent accounts varied); at any rate, he walked out of his business one day and never came back."[12] This pattern of flight from domesticity and responsibility was to recur in Anderson's life. Former moon-calf Floyd Dell could understand Anderson's marital failures because they mirrored the problems that had caused his own first marriage to dissolve: "In his memoirs Sherwood does not say much of anything about his various marriages; and I shall follow his example. He had tried being grown up and responsible—a husband, a father, a provider—and he had failed at it dismally because his heart was never in it. He wanted to be in life what he was in his writing, a child—a more than ordinarily self-centered child. He wanted to be loved and believed in and encouraged, and allowed to love only his dreams and the words he put on paper."[13] Hence for men like Sinclair, Dell, and Anderson, their ability to reconcile art, politics, and personal life foundered on the rock of their own narcissism.

Clement Wood's flirtation with socialism merely arrested his search for personal fulfillment. Born in Tuscaloosa, educated at Yale, a practicing lawyer in the South, he came to New York at age twenty-five to seek adventure. Wood described himself as "a talkative Socialist then, a youthful error it took some years to overcome."[14] His life in New York was wracked by contradiction. At first he waited table at a socialist restaurant, scribbling his poems at stolen intervals between his duties. Then he worked at night for the Rockefeller Vice Investigation and by day for Upton Sinclair while each battled furiously against the other. Then Wood became teacher and later vice-principal at a conservative boy's preparatory school while at night he "soapboxed the East Side as a Socialist candidate for alderman or something equally cosmic." Wood's entire life as a socialist was marked by this extreme schizophrenia. Only by abandoning his socialism and achieving literary success and romantic fulfillment in a second marriage was he able to lead an integrated and satisfying existence.[15] In time Dell and Eastman's lives followed a similar pattern.

Another who found the emotional demands of socialism excessive was the novelist Hutchins Hapgood, who felt temperamentally unequal to the task of dedicating his life to left-wing causes. In his autobiography, *A Victorian in the Modern World* (1939), Hapgood complained that throughout the years many of his friends had criticized him for his steadfast refusal to work on labor-defense committees or strikers' fund-raising committees despite their recognition of the value of his writing to labor's cause: "I remember how scornful of me Mary Heaton Vorse and Joe O'Brien were when they were so active in work connected with the I.W.W., the unemployed riots, and all that. Mary forgot that she had told me repeatedly years before, that I was doing more for the cause of labor through my writing than any of her acquaintances. This is typical of the sort of misunderstanding active people have for those who are contemplative and expressive."[16]

Hapgood found revolutionists as a breed insensitive to human emotional needs. When he first had lost his son Boyce to influenza in New Mexico in 1918, John Reed telephoned some conventional words of sympathy but urged Hapgood to go to Russia. Needing time to mourn, the latter turned Reed down, refusing his friend's demand for sacrifice. Hapgood felt that if the purpose of the labor movement was "to make it possible for more human beings to devote themselves largely to simple life, to love, to friendship, to family, and to poetic contemplation," the genuine reformers and revolutionaries who were willing to sacrifice their own fulfillment for the cause should not demand such sacrifice of others, as Reed had of him. Those who chose to live simply and happily, he held, did not interfere with or oppose the liberation of those still oppressed.[17] Hapgood's analysis of the situation was hence a nonrevolutionary one since he refused to recognize the polarities of the Marxist world view: as an artist and a humanist Hapgood believed in the possibility of neutrality in the class struggle. In fact, Hapgood's personal experience led him to despair of the humanity of most rebels:

> But, as I have said, the greater number of revolutionists I have known, and I have known many in the last forty years, are somewhat below the standard of good human conduct. And I know many who, because they are working for the revolution, think they thereby are allowed to be especially egoistic, selfish, and unfeeling in their human relations. It is a kind of asylum, a sort of church, in which they can take refuge and avoid the claims of their fellow-men. If they only knew, they would see that this is one of the main reasons why the revolution is so periodically retarded. But, even if they realized this, it would probably have very little effect on their conduct; for they are with the revolution either because it is an easy substitute for unexciting, painstaking, unheralded, and unnoticed sobriety in life and work, or because it is the only way they see to feed their ego.[18]

The novelist found it strangely suspicious that those most dedicated to revolution would most resolutely oppose those who attempted to live in the present the kind of liberated lives that only revolution would make possible for all.

Hapgood was by no means alone in his suspicions. All too often radical activities proved a compensation for failures in personal life. Nevada Jane Haywood, the wife of the union leader, blamed Big Bill's political activities for the disruption of their marriage. Haywood's biographer, Joseph R. Conlin, viewed Haywood's "total immersion in work for unionism and socialism" as partly an escape from unhappiness at home; his work, in turn, only exacerbated his marital difficulties. Nevada Jane failed to share her husband's radicalism and hence could not comprehend his rejection of a lucrative speaking career after his exoneration in the Idaho murder trial.[19] In later life she confided to Ralph Chaplin, an old Wobbly friend of her husband, her disillusionment with the personal consequences of Big Bill's radicalism. "I once thought the world of that man," she told Chaplin, "but nothing meant as much to him as the labor movement. For it he gave up his God, his country, his wife and two children—everything."[20]

Like Haywood, Upton Sinclair, too, took refuge from personal failure in socialism. While writing *The Journal of Arthur Stirling*, Sinclair had lived in the woods with his baby and invalid wife. Despairing of his personal ability to cope with adversity, Sinclair found new strength in socialism: "My nightmare experience had to continue until I discovered the Socialist movement, until I had learned to identify my own struggle for life with the struggle for life of humanity."[21] Just as Floyd Dell had found socialism personally therapeutic, allowing him to resolve his own oedipal feelings and shame at poverty, so did Sinclair turn to it to be healed: "It was a wonderful discovery when I made it, for it gave me the key to all my problems. I discovered that I did not have to carry the whole burden of the world's woe upon my shoulders; that I had comrades and allies in the fight. I was no longer obliged to think of civilization as a place where wild beasts fought and tore one another without purpose and without end; I saw the anguish of the hour as the first pang of the great world-birth that is coming."[22]

Although Sinclair might find solace in a revolution to come, Claude McKay took a far more jaundiced view of actual revolution once it had occurred. McKay resembled Hapgood in his thirst for excitement and adventure to fuel his talent. Visiting Russia in the wake of the Bolshevik victory, McKay refused Zinoviev's request that he speak at the opening of the Communist International in the Bolshoi Theater in Moscow: "I told Zinoviev that I came to Russia as a writer and not as an agitator." McKay had no difficulty brooking Zinoviev's anger. The black poet was cynically aware that the mulatto delegate to the congress had proved a washout—"he was too yellow"—and he was confident of the appeal of his own African features to the Russian masses. If the president of the Third International was using McKay as popular entertainment, the American knew that Zinoviev could offer him nothing once the sideshow had ended: "I could never be a radical agitator. For that I was temperamentally unfit. And I could never be a disciplined member of any communist party, for I was born to be a poet."[23] McKay, like Hapgood, felt compelled to subordinate revolution to his art, since only through their art could both men find personal fulfillment.

Prewar rebels were in a quandary regarding the political implications of personal behavior. Many of them were Freudians uncertain of the relationship between art, normality, and rebellion. At the Clark University conference in September 1909, again in 1917, and still later in *Civilization and Its Discontents*, Freud had argued that neurotics were ineffectual rebels, victims of their incapacity to repress, sublimate, or fulfill their powerful sexual drives.[24] Would sexual fulfillment then lead to conformity and adjustment or to effective rebellion? Floyd Dell, an early popularizer of Freudianism, at first thought that psychoanalytic insights would strengthen his socialism. But gradually he came to reject the callousness and inhumanity with which he sacrificed others to his own idealism. Dell dismissed his five years of bohemian life in Chicago as a time in which he unconsciously inflicted cruelty on everyone who cared for him in the service of "an arrogant and ignorant idealism." En route to a new life in New York in the fall of 1913, Dell wrote to Rabbi William Fineshriber in Davenport: "If my five years had done nothing else for me, it [*sic*] would have freed me from the superstitious reverence which I paid to reason

Photograph of Floyd Dell from lecture poster labeled "Leigh-Emmerich Lecture Bureaus, Inc., presents FLOYD DELL/Novelist, Essayist, Editor"
Courtesy Floyd Dell Papers, The Newberry Library

and logic. I hope I shall never use them in the future save as tools and weapons in the service of my enthusiasm and instincts."[25] By identifying political radicalism with a too vigilant superego and normality with his repressed libido, Dell came to view Freudianism as a more liberating ideal than Marxism could offer. He assured Fineshriber that he no longer could be a single-minded revolutionary careless of the personal consequences of belief: "It is then, if I have succeeded in showing you what I mean, a rather different person going to New York than came to Chicago five years ago. I am not so much of an idealist. I would not hurt anybody's feelings to prove the most beautiful theory ever invented. I care a great deal more than I did about how to go about making other people happy."[26] By the beginning of the 1920s Dell openly confessed his unconscious allegiance to utopian fantasies of luxury, sensuality, and self-indulgence; communism seemed too much like work.[27] By 1930 he had rationalized his preference for Freudianism in theoretical terms. In *Love in the Machine Age* Dell used the Freudian notion of transference as the litmus test by which any therapy might be judged. Psychoanalysis was deemed successful only if the analyst could state that transference had been dissolved and that the patient no longer remained in an infantile state of emotional bondage; hence analysis had as its twin objects maturity and independence. According to Dell no ideology could offer the same promise of liberation to its followers:

> How far politics and military "science" and ethics are from this modern notion is obvious. Can political leaders ever be expected to train their constituencies to get along without them? Can generals train their armies to dispense with commands? Can religious and ethical leaders train their followers to decide questions of behavior for themselves? If not, then this is a confession that politics, war and ethics all belong to an infantile stage of our human development; and however long we may remain in this stage, nothing is clearer than that the institutions which such kinds of leadership represent will have no place in the affairs of a socially adult and self-determining humanity.[28]

Since Dell's Marxism and Freudianism both were employed in his quest for adulthood, it offers no surprise that he ultimately embraced the philosophy that contributed most to his own maturation. In his "Psycho-Analytic Confession" Dell had recognized that his unconscious was unrepentantly capitalistic, and others came to a parallel recognition.[29] As much a moon-calf in many ways as Dell, the hobo poet Harry Kemp confessed to being grateful that his individualism kept him from abandoning poetry for revolution. An avowed socialist who wrote much verse for the cause, Kemp harbored inner reservations about the innocence of the proletariat and the certain coming of the socialist millennium. He suspected that capitalism owed its continued existence to the would-be capitalist in every worker, and he feared that the rule of the proletariat might exceed the atrocities committed under the current system of exploitation.[30] Even as devout a lifelong socialist as Art Young despaired of the continued evidence of a capitalist disposition in his own psyche, with its chastening implications for a socialist future: "There is no hope for us except by rebirth. I am a believer in the brotherhood of man, social common-wealths and international good will. But with all my idealism I know that I am tainted with capitalism. I don't fool myself. To be the kind of man I should like to be, with noble qualities and helpfulness toward others, I would have to come to life again into a more just and harmonious world."[31] Only an occa-sional figure like Randolph Bourne would argue that radicalism might be fully compatible with human sensitivity even in a corrupt world.[32]

A more ardent Marxist like Joseph Freeman was skeptical of the emotional reservations of many Village radicals. He dismissed them as mere bohemians whose radicalism consisted of eccentricities with which they might shock the bourgeoisie until they saw fit to return as prodigal sons to their middle-class existence, being richly rewarded for discarding the trappings of their Village days. Longing for self-expression, bohemians hated not only capitalism, but the responsibilities that any highly developed social system, including a com-munist one, might impose on its members.[33] Freeman denigrated the bohe-mian revolt for its individualism: "Against the pressure of business ideals in work and puritan standards in personal conduct, sensitive individuals, mostly from the middle classes, demanded the right to pursue art, to experiment sexually, and to absorb political ideas which came to them partly from books, and partly from such influence as the revolutionary movement exercised on its literary fellow travellers."[34] Hence the bohemian could not be trusted not to return to a more tolerant bourgeois order nor could he be expected to over-come his "deep sentimental attachment to barbarism and savagery, preferably of a nomadic sort," in order to practice the dull, sober virtues demanded of revolutionaries building a new order.[35]

Only a handful of *The Masses'* radicals could match the exalted standards of conduct set by Freeman. For some, like John Reed, revolutionary discipline came only at a tremendous price. Floyd Dell had told Freeman that he "only knew Jack as a playboy, in his off hours."[36] Dell delighted in his memory of Reed as a dilettante, adventurer, and lover of the insatiable Mabel Dodge, an episode in his hero's life with which Reed's biographer Granville Hicks dealt with "evident proletarian reluctance."[37] His colleagues on *The Masses* re-membered Reed for his humor and enthusiasm. Art Young recalled Reed writing the libretto for an opera at the Dutch Treat Club in the same spirit of fun with which he led a polyglot chorus of hundreds of Paterson silk workers in the Internationale at the Madison Square Garden Pageant; to Young, Reed's "fun was doing."[38] Max Eastman viewed Reed primarily as a poet for whom poetry "was not only a matter of writing words but of living life."[39] According to Eastman, "Reed had come to *The Masses* from the evangelical and rebel, not the proletarian and revolutionary, side," hence his need, even more than men like Art Young and John Sloan, to prove himself adult and serious about his beliefs.[40] Reed redeemed himself as a revolutionary by sacrificing the pride of his youth, his poetry. Although he confessed to George Cram Cook that he really wanted to write poetry, by the summer of 1918, in the wake of the Bolshevik Revolution, his political commitments restrained him.[41] Upon his return from Russia, Reed met Eastman, who questioned him about his political work. "It's all right," Reed said. "It's going all right. . . . You know this class struggle plays hell with your poetry!"[42]

Revolutionary success rendered personal concerns irrelevant. At the moment of commitment to the cause itself rather than to a specific battle, the future of the individual self seemed petty in importance. The Lawrence strike of 1912 proved a critical intersection in the lives of Mary Heaton Vorse and Joe O'Brien, as it had for writers as different as Lincoln Steffens, William Allen White, and Fremont Older: "For Joe and myself it was decisive and he threw himself into the labor movement, working in it until he died, and I followed him."[43] Lawrence transformed both of them: "We knew now where we belonged—on the side of the workers and not with the comfortable people among whom we were born. We knew, although at the time our personal lives seemed incidental, that we wanted to go on together and work together."[44] But even Vorse, who like Reed was later to become a communist, did not wrench herself as dramatically from her former life as Reed had: "I could not be an organizer or a labor leader; I was too impatient of results to work for a possibly perfect society."[45] Vorse could rationalize her continued career as a writer through her espousal of an essentially Progressive notion of the function of propaganda: "I believed then that if enough people saw what I had seen they would get so angry that conditions such as those in Lawrence could not exist for the very force of public opinion."[46] Truth could be power only in a world exempt from class struggle, a world in which Mary Heaton Vorse presumably no longer believed.

Those who most valued personal life left the movement. Floyd Dell took refuge in marriage, novel-writing, and country life in Croton-on-Hudson as "barring the trifle of a mortgage . . . a landed proprietor."[47] Fellow poet Clement Wood explained his own retreat from radicalism in verse. In "Comradeship" he complained that his life as a revolutionary had failed to yield genuine human intimacy and spiritual companionship; his poetic nature remained unslaked.[48] Wood felt that peddlers of radical nostrums submerged themselves in mass movements because they feared self-knowledge; their hunger for community concealed an escape from self: "If you do not understand yourself, one atom of reality, / How can you know the whole?"[49] His chosen remedy was a return to earth, to the kind of primitive existence Freeman had accused mere bohemians of preferring, and a retreat from socialist revolution.[50] As Malcolm Cowley shrewdly noted, it was impossible to be both a bohemian and a rebel in Mr. Wilson's world.[51] The charming elixir of social and political rebellion that had lent its magic to the prewar Village lost its potency in a world of repression and reaction.

Those who remained dedicated revolutionaries did so at great personal sacrifice. Emma Goldman renounced her chance for motherhood to "find an outlet for [her] mother-need in the love of all children."[52] She was to end her days in exile from her adopted land, estranged from many of her former comrades, having seen the future fail as Bolshevism betrayed its promise. Nor was the American who came to symbolize that revolution to end his days in peace with the new order. John Dos Passos may have praised John Reed for abandoning his privileged life as a bohemian poet to ally himself with the soldiers and peasants who built the Russian Revolution.[53] Mike Gold made Reed the sole proletarian hero among *The Masses'* rebels, the only one who could capture the romance of the revolution and combine intellect and activism in the service of the working class.[54] His biographer Granville Hicks memorialized Reed for dedicating his talent selflessly to the communist cause: "We think of Reed then as one who did for the cause all that he was highly trained to do as a journalist and also turned himself over to the service of the cause in any capacity that the leaders could find for him."[55] Yet Reed himself regretted the loss of his art, and the debate still rages as to whether he recoiled at the excesses of the dictatorship of the proletariat. Robert Minor had no such hesitation. For several years Minor found himself poised between demands of cartooning and direct political agitation until in 1926 "he laid aside his crayon and pencil, not gladly, and yet without brooding frustration. He made no fanfare of the occasion. More important than his individual inclination, he felt, was the common job that had to be done."[56] He became an editor of the Communist party *Daily Worker* and drew no more.[57]

The war and the Bolshevik Revolution forced radicals to choose between bohemianism and political commitment, yet the fundamental questions remained unresolved. Could revolutionary discipline permit tilting at bourgeois convention? Did bohemianism offer a genuine critique of bourgeois life compatible with a Marxist one? Could rebels who had renounced the satisfactions of art and personal life be trusted to preserve humane values in a revolutionary world? Was the failure of the Bolshevik Revolution to sustain its initial vision proof that ascetic discipline could destroy the very values that revolution was intended to preserve?

Chapter 11 The End of Radical Innocence

The radical renaissance of the prewar years in Greenwich Village was a time of great promise both in culture and politics. Those who participated in it or who were affected by its fervor believed in the possibility of transforming society within their own lifetime, in a revolution of consciousness that would transcend any change in political rule. The new radicals existed in that special time before the revolution when one's goals seem tantalizingly near, when excitement adds spice to commitment, when the personal and the political fuse to release new sources of human energy. Nevertheless, the promise of these years died with the Great War and the Russian Revolution. What happened to the vision of new radicals? Why did they fail and their dream die?

For many of them the revolt was too personal; it lacked sufficient commitment to party or ideology to survive the vicissitudes of time. As they matured (or adapted) and their individual problems became less pressing, such new radicals turned away from the discipline and sacrifice of political work to seek refuge in private life. For example, Floyd Dell valued his literary career more highly than his political obligations. Richard Fitzgerald has noted: "When John Reed, home from the Soviet Union in 1918, told Floyd Dell he would organize a communist party in the United States, a disciplined party of professional revolutionaries, Dell replied that he would not join it because he was a 'professional writer'; thus Dell expressed the very bourgeois egotism that he later criticized in his 1923–1924 *Liberator* articles."[1] Boardman Robinson retreated to a studio in an old barn near Croton-on-Hudson next to that of Max Eastman; he enjoyed his solitude and the opportunity "to read and make a great many drawings which did not sell."[2] Mabel Dodge looked back nostalgically upon her affair with John Reed and his revolutionary charm. She gave up all sense of her personal power to undermine the status quo: "My young lover was gone, and, it seemed, gone with him were the younger hopes of change. With a world at war, one somehow ceased to war with systems and circumstances. Instinctively I turned once more to nature and art and tried to live in them."[3] As a result, she gave up her famous salon at 23 Fifth Avenue and abandoned her interest in anarchists and other radicals, like Robinson seeking refuge in the bucolic life by moving to Finney Farm in Croton, New York.[4] Art Young, who had pursued bulging capitalists through the pages of *The Masses*, became "a quiet country gentleman, cultivating his potatoes and pruning his hedges near Danbury, Connecticut," while Floyd Dell, former free-love advocate and antiwar agitator, flourished in his newfound respectability. Happily married, Dell raised a family, wrote a stream of novels for the bourgeoisie he once had scorned, and even worked for the government on the Federal Writers' Project.[5] The quest for personal fulfillment could be realized short of revolution.

Moreover, the transition to bourgeois life proved relatively simple. Ideas that had been avant-garde in the prewar years—Freudian psychology, birth control, bohemianism—became the clichés of the postwar era. The ex-Villagers ceased to be social outcasts. In the words of Joseph Freeman: "The bourgeois world overtook and surpassed them; it absorbed their talents and expropriated their poses."[6] During the 1920s the prosperous scorned respectability to pursue bohemianism on a large scale; the speakeasy captured the Village manners and mores for the middle class. Once radical writers and artists were recruited by enterprising businesses to spread the new taste in salable form throughout the land. The accommodation was a happy one: "The prosperous middle classes needed a little bohemianism to spend their money in ways not sanctioned by the puritan tradition; the bohemians needed a little puritanism to go with their newly acquired money."[7]

Some, like Floyd Dell and Louis Untermeyer, exchanged their socialism for a vague humanitarianism while others, like Max Eastman and Walter Lippmann, repudiated it altogether.[8] Few of *The Masses'* radicals ever became "thoroughgoing Marxists."[9] Most of these entered the newly formed Communist party that emerged in the United States in the aftermath of the Bolshevik Revolution. As American socialism, disrupted by the wartime persecutions, entered a period of decline, these radicals turned to Bolshevism for inspiration. Joseph Freeman later wrote: "We concentrated our hopes on the Russian Revolution in direct proportion as American socialism became more confused."[10]

John Reed journeyed to Russia and stayed there six months, throwing himself into a frenzied round of political activity and for the first time in his life committing himself fully to the cause.[11] His activism restored him and gave him new faith: "As in the case of so many middle-class intellectuals, the revolution had integrated a mind divided against itself."[12] Nevertheless, Reed never succumbed to the political discipline demanded by the Bolsheviki; more a pragmatist than an ideologue, emotionally bound to the IWW although

Lenin had designated the AFL the place of true revolutionaries, Reed challenged his superiors with an audacity that soon would find no place within organized communism.[13]

Reed and Robert Minor proved inspirational to younger radicals by choosing to abandon literature and art in favor of active participation in the communist movement.[14] Minor's decision was a personal one rather than a political one; in fact, the Communist party persistently encouraged Minor to return to his drawing to no avail. Minor felt the need for complete concentration in his work and preferred to dedicate himself exclusively to organizing.[15]

As *The Masses'* radicals went their separate ways, the magazine itself underwent several transformations that fundamentally altered its substance and style. *The Liberator*, its first successor, appeared on Lincoln's birthday in 1918 and was less revolutionary, accepting the Wilsonian program for peace. Although John Reed's article on the Bolshevik Revolution had appeared in the maiden issue, he resigned from *The Liberator* shortly thereafter, claiming that he could not take editorial responsibility for a magazine that existed by permission of the postmaster general.[16] In 1924 *The Liberator* merged with *The Labor Herald* to form *The Workers' Monthly*. The closing chapter for the magazine remains a matter of debate. Louis Untermeyer noted wryly: "Neither *The Masses* nor *The Liberator* would have recognized its final left-handed—or should I say left-winged?—offspring, *New Masses*."[17] Although some of the founders—Joseph Freeman, Mike Gold, Susan Glaspell, Eugene O'Neill, Carl Sandburg, and Sherwood Anderson—had been associated in friendship with *The Masses'* group or had contributed to the magazine itself, they did not preserve the old *Masses* in the new.[18] The lighthearted wit, the bohemianism, the stubborn refusal to be bound by ideology all were gone and in their place was much more pedestrian proletarian art and prose. A magazine of free expression was resurrected as a vehicle for party dogma. The descent, if it existed at all, certainly was not linear.

Why did so little of *The Masses* survive to take root in another soil? Why did its spirit wither and decay? Those who viewed their radicalism as a panacea for personal problems drifted away when those problems could be resolved without its aid. Welcomed by a bourgeoisie seeking bohemian delights, they found a refuge in private life. A handful of others became committed Communists; they joined the party but never were genuine Marxists. For them Marxism was an ideology, not a methodology, and their idealization of the Soviet Union blinded them both to the betrayal of the revolution in that country and to the irrelevance of much of Bolshevik dogma to their own. The pragmatism that had tempered the socialism of *The Masses* had vanished. Gone, too, was the unflinching ability of a John Reed to face the reality of American politics, to recognize the conservatism of the labor movement as a truth to be changed rather than dismissed as a fiction because it did not accord with party dogma.

The Masses' radicals had existed in a special time. For them life had urgency, and the personal and the political could be fused. They attempted a revolutionary transformation of consciousness that would prepare them for the cooperative commonwealth to come. To live as one did before the revolution after the revolution has come truly is to be blessed.

Notes

Chapter 1: The Cradle of Radical Culture

1. Christopher Lasch, *The New Radicalism in America, 1889–1963*, pp. xiv–xv and passim.

2. Philip Rieff, "Introduction" to Sigmund Freud, *Delusion and Dream and Other Essays*, pp. 10, 11; Sigmund Freud, "The Relation of the Poet to Daydreaming," ibid., pp. 122–33; Nathan Hale, Jr., *Freud and the Americans*, p. 230.

3. F. H. Matthews, "The Americanization of Sigmund Freud," p. 53.

4. Ibid.; Alfred Booth Kuttner, "The Artist," pp. 409–10.

5. Ibid., pp. 411, 412; Alfred Booth Kuttner, "The Artist (A Communication)," p. 550.

6. Ibid., p. 551.

7. J[ames] O[ppenheim], "Editorials," *Seven Arts* 1 (February 1917): 393–94.

8. Robert E. Humphrey, *Children of Fantasy*. Cf. especially pp. 5–11, 251–53.

9. Robert Cantwell, "Upton Sinclair," in Malcolm Cowley, ed., *After the Genteel Tradition*, p. 39.

10. Van Wyck Brooks, *John Sloan*, p. 4.

11. Richard Fitzgerald, *Art and Politics*, pp. 8–10.

12. Margaret Sanger, *My Fight for Birth Control*, pp. 5–7.

13. Louis Filler, *Crusaders for American Liberalism*, pp. 114–15.

14. Joseph North, *Robert Minor*, p. 14.

15. Joseph Freeman, *An American Testament*, pp. 7, 25–27, 29–34.

16. Moses Rischin, Introduction to Hutchins Hapgood, *The Spirit of the Ghetto*, p. xii.

17. Elizabeth Gurley Flynn, *The Rebel Girl*, pp. 45, 47.

18. Carl Resek, Introduction to Randolph S. Bourne, *War and the Intellectuals*, p. viii; Sherman Paul, *Randolph Bourne*, p. 7; Carl Resek, "The New Radicalism," pp. 68–69.

19. Max Eastman, *Enjoyment of Living*, pp. 50, 51, 68–71.

20. Floyd Dell, *Homecoming*, pp. 4, 5, 12, 13, 23, 55, 56.

21. Stephen Marion Reynolds, "Life of Eugene V. Debs," in Eugene V. Debs, *Debs*, p. 58; Ray Ginger, *Eugene V. Debs*, pp. 41, 56, 240.

22. Carl Van Vechten, "The Reminiscences of Carl Van Vechten," pp. 1, 40.

23. Albert Christ-Janer, *Boardman Robinson*, pp. 1–2.

24. Flynn, *The Rebel Girl*, pp. 29–30.

25. Ernest Poole, *The Bridge*, pp. 5, 102, 195.

26. Dell, *Homecoming*, pp. 6, 82–83, 101, 252–53, 257.

27. Max Eastman, *Great Companions*, pp. 304, 306–7; Eastman, *Enjoyment of Living*, pp. 316, 341, 349, 362.

28. North, *Robert Minor*, p. 14.

29. Poole, *The Bridge*, p. 170.

30. Margaret Sanger, *An Autobiography*, p. 16.

31. Eastman, *Enjoyment of Living*, p. 23.

32. Claude McKay, *A Long Way from Home*, p. 12.

33. Flynn, *The Rebel Girl*, pp. 41–42.

34. North, *Robert Minor*, pp. 13–14.

Chapter 2: *The Masses*: A Socialist Magazine of "Free Expression"

1. Walter B. Rideout, *The Radical Novel in the United States, 1900–1954*, pp. 292–94.

2. Moses Rischin, *The Promised City*, p. 233.

3. Lillian Symes and Travers Clement, *Rebel America*, pp. 270–71.

4. Mabel Dodge Luhan, *Intimate Memories*, 3:85.

5. Symes and Clement, *Rebel America*, pp. 270–71.

6. "The Younger Generation," p. 324.

7. Margaret Anderson, *My Thirty Years' War*, p. 49.

8. James Oppenheim, "The Story of the *Seven Arts*," p. 156.

9. "The Seven Arts," pp. 52–53.

10. Oppenheim, "The Story of the *Seven Arts*," pp. 163–64.

11. Daniel Aaron, *Writers on the Left*, p. 18.

12. Ibid., p. 19; James Gilbert, *Writers and Partisans*, p. 10.

13. "Greeting," p. 12.

14. Rideout, *The Radical Novel in the United States, 1900–1954*, pp. 22–23; Gilbert, *Writers and Partisans*, p. 10.

15. Rideout, *The Radical Novel in the United States, 1900–1954*, p. 22.

16. Aaron, *Writers on the Left*, p. 19; "Editorial Notice," *Masses* 4 (December 1912): 3.

17. John Stuart, "The Education of John Reed," in John Reed, *The Education of John Reed*, p. 20.

18. Art Young, *On My Way*, pp. 274–75.

19. Floyd Dell, "Memories of the Old Masses," pp. 485–86.

20. Piet Vlag, "A Knock, a Boost, and a Bet," *Masses*, 1 (July 1911): 8.

21. George Thomas Tanselle, "Faun at the Barricades," pp. 160–61; Louis Untermeyer, *From Another World*, pp. 44, 63; Max Eastman, *Enjoyment of Living*, p. 444.

22. Young, *On My Way*, p. 275.

23. This is the formulation given in Art Young's *On My Way*, p. 276, and in Max Eastman's *Enjoyment of Living*, p. 394. Louis Untermeyer in *From Another World*, p. 42, gives the message as "Dear Eastman: We have just elected you editor of *The Masses* at no salary per annum."

24. "Purely Personal," Editorials, *Masses* 1 (July 1911): 3; [Editors], "A Crisis in the Socialist Party," *Masses* 3 (February 1912): 3.

25. Frederick J. Hoffman, Charles Allen, and Carolyn F. Ulrich, *The Little Magazine*, p. 29.

26. "Editorial Notice," *Masses* 4 (December 1912): 3.

27. [Editorial: "This magazine is a success . . ."], *Masses* 4 (January 1913): 2.

28. Eastman, *Enjoyment of Living*, pp. 414, 420.

29. Floyd Dell, "Affidavit Concerning Max Eastman and Communism" (1925), Dell Papers, p. 3.

30. Young, *On My Way*, p. 293; Eastman, *Enjoyment of Living*, p. 474.

31. Ibid., p. 464; Floyd Dell errs in *Homecoming*, p. 250, in attributing the suit to a charge that the AP suppressed news of the Colorado strike.

32. Eastman, *Enjoyment of Living*, p. 474; Young, *On My Way*, pp. 32–33.

33. Eastman, *Enjoyment of Living*, pp. 467–68.

34. Floyd Dell to Arthur Davison Ficke, 8 December 1913, Dell Papers, p. 3.

35. Eastman, *Enjoyment of Living*, pp. 468–69.

36. Ibid., pp. 469–70; Young, *On My Way*, p. 33.

37. Eastman, *Enjoyment of Living*, pp. 470–73.

38. Young, *On My Way*, pp. 33–34.

39. Eastman, *Enjoyment of Living*, p. 474.

40. " 'Suppressed,' " *Masses* 8 (February 1916): 14.

41. "Messrs. Ward and Gow . . . ," pp. 318–19.

42. " 'Suppressed,' " *Masses* 8 (February 1916): 14.

43. Tanselle, "Faun at the Barricades," p. 177; Max Eastman, "An Important Announcement," *Masses* 8 (August 1916): 5.

44. Max Eastman, *Journalism versus Art*, pp. 7, 49–50, 79.

45. Dell, *Homecoming*, pp. 250–51.

46. Untermeyer, *From Another World*, pp. 48–49.

47. Eastman, *Enjoyment of Living*, p. 548.

48. Max Eastman, "Bunk about Bohemia," p. 207.

49. Eastman, *Enjoyment of Living*, pp. 549–52, 554; Dell, *Homecoming*, p. 251.

50. Eastman, *Enjoyment of Living*, pp. 554–55, 558.

51. Max Eastman, *Love and Revolution*, p. 26.

52. See Zechariah Chafee, Jr., *Freedom of Speech*, and H. C. Peterson and Gilbert C. Fite, *Opponents of War, 1917–1918*, for details of the government prosecutions and the flimsiness of the evidence offered.

53. Zechariah Chafee, Jr., "Freedom of Speech," pp. 66–69; M. G. Wallace, "Constitutionality of Sedition Laws," pp. 389, 390.

54. Espionage Act of 1917, tit. I, § § 3, 4, and 5, 40 STAT. 219 (1917), reprinted in part in Fund for the Republic, *Digest of the Public Record of Communism in the United States*, pp. 188–89.

55. Untermeyer, *From Another World*, pp. 66–67. Untermeyer is incorrect in claiming that the August 1918 issue was the one suppressed. In fact, the August 1917 issue was denied access to the mails. Cf. Peterson and Fite, *Opponents of War, 1917–1918*, pp. 96–97; Chafee, Jr., *Freedom of Speech*, pp. 47–48.

56. Untermeyer, *From Another World*, p. 67.

57. Dell, *Homecoming*, pp. 298, 313.

58. Ibid., p. 313; Young, *On My Way*, p. 293; Untermeyer, *From Another World*, pp. 69–70.

59. Dell, *Homecoming*, pp. 313–14, 316.

60. Ibid., p. 314; Untermeyer, *From Another World*, p. 69.

61. Untermeyer, *From Another World*, p. 71; Dell, *Homecoming*, p. 317.

62. Joseph Freeman, *An American Testament*, pp. 163–64.

63. Untermeyer, *From Another World*, pp. 69–70; Young, *On My Way*, pp. 293–94.

64. Young, *On My Way*, pp. 294, 296–97; Untermeyer, *From Another World*, pp. 71–72.

65. Dell, *Homecoming*, p. 319.

66. Young, *On My Way*, p. 297.

67. Untermeyer, *From Another World*, p. 73.

68. Freeman, *An American Testament*, pp. 164–65; Untermeyer, *From Another World*, p. 74.

69. Aaron, *Writers on the Left*, p. 41; John Dos Passos, "Playboy," in *Nineteen Nineteen, U. S. A.*, p. 16; Eastman, *Love and Revolution*, p. 105.

70. Freeman, *An American Testament*, p. 165; Dell, *Homecoming*, p. 326.

71. Untermeyer, *From Another World*, p. 76; *New York Times*, 6 October 1918, p. 9, col. 6.

72. Peterson and Fite, *Opponents of War, 1917–1918*, p. 97; Chafee, Jr., *Freedom of Speech*,

pp. 47–48; *Masses Publishing Company* v. *Patten*, 244 *Federal Reporter*, 535–45, District Court, S.D., New York, 24 July 1917.

73. Chafee, Jr., *Freedom of Speech*, pp. 47, 107.

74. *Masses Publishing Company* v. *Patten*, 245 *Federal Reporter*, 102–6, Circuit Court of Appeals, Second Circuit, 6 August 1917.

75. *Masses Publishing Company* v. *Patten*, 246 *Federal Reporter*, 24–39, Circuit Court of Appeals, Second Circuit, 2 November 1917; Socialist Party, *Court Rulings Upon Indictments . . . Growing Out of Alleged Offenses Against Draft and Espionage Acts*, pp. 40–41; Peterson and Fite, *Opponents of War, 1917–1918*, p. 97; Chafee, Jr., *Freedom of Speech*, p. 54.

76. Chafee, Jr., *Freedom of Speech*, pp. 55, 118.

77. Young, *On My Way*, p. 298.

78. Eastman, *Love and Revolution*, p. 103.

79. Dell, *Homecoming*, p. 327.

80. Max Eastman, *Enjoyment of Laughter*, pp. 73–74.

81. Eastman, *Love and Revolution*, p. 598; Eastman, *Enjoyment of Living*, p. 415 n; Eastman, "Bunk about Bohemia," pp. 200–208; Max Eastman, "New Masses for Old," pp. 292–300; Michael Gold, "John Reed and the Real Thing," p. 7.

Chapter 3: Cracks in the New American Culture

1. Arthur Frank Wertheim, *The New York Little Renaissance*.

2. Ibid., pp. 243–46 and passim.

3. William L. O'Neill, *Divorce in the Progressive Era*, p. 202.

4. Floyd Dell, *Women as World Builders*, pp. 19–20.

5. James Burkhart Gilbert, *Writers and Partisans*, p. 20.

6. Sherwood Anderson, *Sherwood Anderson's Memoirs*, p. 277.

7. Gilbert, *Writers and Partisans*, p. 20.

8. H. L. Mencken, *A Book of Prefaces*, pp. 232, 233, 243, 250; "Sex O'Clock in America," p. 113; "Morals Efficiency," *Masses* 5 (February 1914): 19.

9. Heywood Broun and Margaret Leech, *Anthony Comstock*, pp. 15, 24–25.

10. Mencken, *A Book of Prefaces*, p. 254.

11. Ibid., pp. 265–66. Mencken cites an impressive battery of legal decisions in support of his allegations.

12. Broun and Leech, *Anthony Comstock*, pp. 249–50.

13. [Floyd Dell], "Why People Go to Brick Munro's," p. 3.

14. Walter Lippmann, *A Preface to Politics*, pp. 42–43; Frederick J. Hoffman, *Freudianism and the Literary Mind*, pp. 52–53.

15. Mabel Dodge Luhan, *Intimate Memories*, 1:5–6.

16. Theodore Dreiser, "Life, Art, and America," pp. 364–65.

17. Hutchins Hapgood, *A Victorian in the Modern World*, p. 19.

18. Dreiser, "Life, Art, and America," pp. 375, 376.

19. Agnes Repplier, "The Repeal of Reticence," p. 298.

20. William E. Carson, *The Marriage Revolt*, p. 86.

21. Randolph S. Bourne, "The Puritan's Will to Power," pp. 631–37.

22. Henry F. May, "The Rebellion of the Intellectuals, 1912–1917," pp. 116–17.

23. Frederick J. Hoffman, Charles Allen, Carolyn F. Ulrich, *The Little Magazine*, pp. 72–73.

24. Upton Sinclair, *American Outpost*, pp. 122–23; Upton Sinclair, "The Reminiscences of Upton Sinclair," pp. 147–49; May, "The Rebellion of the Intellectuals, 1912–1917," p. 116.

25. Randolph Bourne, "Denatured Nietzsche," p. 390.

26. George H. Daughtery, "Anderson, Advertising Man," in *Sherwood Anderson Memorial Number*, pp. 30–38.

27. Mabel Dodge Luhan, *Intimate Memories*, 2:445.

28. Heinz Eulau, "Mover and Shaker," pp. 302–3.

29. Emily Taft Douglas, *Margaret Sanger*, pp. 58–59.

30. Isadora Duncan, *My Life*, p. 341.

31. George Cram Cook, "Polemic/*Against the Dominant Idea*," in George Cram Cook, *Greek Coins*, pp. 117–18.

32. Susan Glaspell, *The Road to the Temple*, p. 298.

33. Agnes Boulton, *Part of a Long Story*, p. 61.

34. Doris Alexander, "Eugene O'Neill as a Social Critic," in O. Cargill, N. B. Fagin, and W. J. Fisher, eds., *Eugene O'Neill and His Plays*, p. 399.

35. Richard Drinnon, *Rebel in Paradise*, p. 103.

36. William English Walling, *The Larger Aspects of Socialism*, p. 227.

37. Van Wyck Brooks, *The Confident Years, 1885–1915*, pp. 461–62.

38. Gilbert, *Writers and Partisans*, p. 24.

39. Max Eastman, *Understanding Germany*, pp. 65–66.

40. May, "The Rebellion of the Intellectuals, 1912–1917," pp. 116–17.

41. Nathan Hale, Jr., *Freud and the Americans*, p. 242.

42. Edwin Björkman, "The Immortality of Bernard Shaw," *Masses* 1 (April 1911): 16, 18; Randolph Bourne, "Some Pre-War Letters, 1912–1914," pp. 79–102; Floyd Dell, "Shaw and Religion," pp. 82–88.

43. Douglas, *Margaret Sanger*, pp. 60, 78–79; Hale, Jr., *Freud and the Americans*, pp. 265–66.

44. Margaret Sanger, *My Fight for Birth Control*, pp. 57, 101–2.

45. George Santayana, *The Genteel Tradition in American Philosophy: The Annual Public Address before the Philosophical Union of the University of California*, p. 16.

46. Van Wyck Brooks, *America's Coming-of-Age*, p. 112.

47. Randolph Bourne, *History of a Literary Radical and Other Essays*, pp. 29–30.

48. Harry Kemp, *Tramping on Life*, pp. 43, 167–68.

49. David Karsner, *Horace Traubel, His Life and Work*, p. 70.

50. Dell, *Women as World Builders*, pp. 48–49.

51. Duncan, *My Life*, pp. 30–31, 340–41; Isadora Duncan, *The Art of the Dance*, pp. 47–48.

52. Drinnon, *Rebel in Paradise*, p. 161.

53. Anderson, *Sherwood Anderson's Memoirs*, p. 522.

54. Hutchins Hapgood, *The Spirit of Labor*, p. 386.

55. Walling, *The Larger Aspects of Socialism*, p. vii.

56. Sigmund Freud, *Leonardo da Vinci*, pp. 56–57.

57. Bouck White, *The Call of the Carpenter*, p. 347.

58. Lincoln Steffens, Max Eastman, and Floyd Dell, "The First Few Books," *Masses* 6 (February 1915): 17.

59. Floyd Dell, *Runaway, A Novel*, p. 98.

60. Floyd Dell, *The Briary-Bush*, p. 194.

61. Floyd Dell, "A Psycho-Analytic Confession," p. 18.

62. Brooks, *The Confident Years*, p. 540.

63. Duncan, *My Life*, p. 254.

64. Max Eastman, *Heroes I Have Known*, p. 86.

65. Brooks, *The Confident Years*, p. 223; Louis Untermeyer, *Challenge*, pp. 83–87; Floyd Dell, *Looking at Life*, p. 49; Floyd Dell, "On Seeing Isadora Duncan's School," p. 8.

66. Duncan, *My Life*, pp. 340–41; Duncan, *The Art of the Dance*, pp. 47–48.

67. Claude McKay, *A Long Way from Home*, p. 212.

68. Carl Van Vechten, *Nigger Heaven*, p. 59.

69. Ibid., p. 226.

70. Mabel Dodge Luhan, *Intimate Memories*, 3:79–80.

71. Van Vechten, "The Reminiscences of Carl Van Vechten," pp. 25–26.

72. Carl Van Vechten, *Peter Whiffle*, pp. 208, 210–13.

73. Luhan, *Intimate Memories*, 3:265–79; Max Eastman, *Enjoyment of Living*, pp. 522–26.

74. Ralph Waldo Emerson, *Selections from Ralph Waldo Emerson*, p. 153.

75. Randolph Bourne, *History of a Literary Radical and Other Essays*, p. 40.

76. Waldo Frank, "Vicarious Fiction," pp. 302–3.

77. Alfred Kazin, *On Native Grounds*, p. 135.

78. John Dewey, "In a Time of National Hesitation," p. 5.

79. James Oppenheim, "The Story of the *Seven Arts*," p. 156.

80. "The Seven Arts," p. 53.

81. J[ames] O[ppenheim], "Editorials," *Seven Arts* 1 (January 1917): 267.

82. James Oppenheim, "America," p. 471.

83. J[ames] O[ppenheim], "Editorials," *Seven Arts* 1 (April 1917): 629–30.

84. Van Wyck Brooks, *Emerson and Others*, pp. 127–29.

85. Randolph Bourne, "Letters, 1913–16," pp. 88–89.

86. Randolph Bourne, *History of a Literary Radical and Other Essays*, pp. 296–99.

87. Randolph Bourne, *War and the Intellectuals*, p. 52.

88. Brooks, *Emerson and Others*, pp. 139–40.

89. Van Wyck Brooks, *Fenellosa and His Circle with Other Essays in Biography*, p. 274.

90. Randolph Bourne, *Youth and Life*, p. 167; Randolph Bourne, *Education and Living*, p. 236.

91. Randolph Bourne, "The Cult of the Best," p. 276; Bourne, *Education and Living*, pp. 51, 53–54.

92. Robert Henri, "The New York Exhibition of Independent Artists," p. 161; "The Seven Arts," p. 53.

93. Henri, "The New York Exhibition of Independent Artists," p. 161.

94. John Sloan, *John Sloan*, p. [2]; A. E. Gallatin, ed., *John Sloan*, pp. 11–12, 14.

95. J[ames] O[ppenheim], "Editorials," *Seven Arts* 1 (December 1916): 154.

96. Sherwood Anderson, "An Apology for Crudity," pp. 437–38.

97. Harold Stearns, "A Poor Thing, But Our Own," pp. 517–18, 520.

98. Arthur E. Waterman, *Susan Glaspell*, p. 48; Floyd Dell, "A Seer in Iowa," in Cook, *Greek Coins*, p. 16.

99. Duncan, *My Life*, pp. 340–42; Duncan, *The Art of the Dance*, p. 133.

100. Arthur W. Calhoun, *A Social History of the American Family from Colonial Times to the Present*, 3:157–58.

101. J[ames] O[ppenheim], "Editorials," *Seven Arts* 1 (January 1917): 267.

102. Henri, "The New York Exhibition of Independent Artists," p. 167.

103. Duncan, *My Life*, p. 176.

104. Brooks, *Emerson and Others*, p. 126.

105. Randolph S. Bourne to Prudence Winterrowd, 5 February 1913, Bourne Papers, p. 1.

106. Randolph S. Bourne to Prudence Winterrowd, 18 May 1913, Bourne Papers, p. 1; reprinted in Randolph Bourne, "Letters, 1913–1916," p. 85.

107. Randolph Bourne, *Youth and Life*, pp. 15–16.

Chapter 4: Greenwich Village—Home as Bohemia

1. Christopher A. Kent, "The Idea of Bohemia in Mid-Victorian England," pp. 360–61.
2. William Dean Howells, *The Coast of Bohemia*.
3. Anna Alice Chapin, *Greenwich Village*, p. 278.
4. Floyd Dell, "Rents Were Low in Greenwich Village," p. 663.
5. Genevieve Taggard, *May Days*, p. 2.
6. Van Wyck Brooks, *The Confident Years*, p. 371.
7. Allen Churchill, *The Improper Bohemians*, p. 28.
8. Edmund T. Delaney, *New York's Greenwich Village*, p. 104.
9. Ibid.
10. Mary K. Simkhovitch, *My Story of Greenwich House*, quoted in ibid.
11. John Reed, *The Day in Bohemia*.
12. Mary Heaton Vorse, *Time and the Town*, pp. 82–83.
13. This discussion owes much of its conceptualization to Rosabeth Moss Kanter's *Commitment and Community*, but Kanter's theoretical framework is meant to apply to intentional communities such as communes and utopias and must be modified with reference to bohemias; see also Floyd Dell, *Homecoming*, p. 272.
14. Floyd Dell to Arthur Davison Ficke, 5 September 1913, Dell Papers, p. 2.
15. Floyd Dell, *This Mad Ideal*, p. 119.
16. Harry Kemp, *More Miles*.
17. Joseph Freeman, *An American Testament*, pp. 283–84.
18. Frederick J. Hoffman, Charles Allen, and Carolyn F. Ulrich, *The Little Magazine*, pp. 28–29.
19. Ibid.
20. Max Eastman, "Bunk about Bohemia," pp. 200–201.
21. Ibid., p. 201.
22. Joseph Freeman, "Greenwich Village Types," pp. 18–20.
23. Albert Parry, *Garrets and Pretenders*, p. 272.
24. Interview by a Mrs. Pearson with Mabel Dodge, quoted in Mabel Dodge Luhan, *Intimate Memories*, 3:82.
25. Kanter, *Commitment and Community*, pp. 129–30.
26. Dell, *Homecoming*, pp. 279–80.
27. Vorse, *Time and the Town*, pp. 117–18.
28. Reed, *The Day in Bohemia*, p. 33.
29. Sinclair Lewis, "Hobohemia," pp. 3–5, 121, 122, 125, 126, 129, 130, 133.
30. Floyd Dell, *Love in Greenwich Village*, pp. 320–21.
31. Floyd Dell, "The Rise and Fall of Greenwich Village—II: Its Fall," p. 51.
32. Malcolm Cowley, *Exile's Return*, pp. 60–61.
33. Ibid., p. 61.
34. Ibid., pp. 66–67.
35. Henry F. May, *The End of American Innocence*, p. 32.
36. Chapin, *Greenwich Village*, pp. 244–45.
37. May, *The End of American Innocence*, p. 32.
38. Roger Garaudy, *Humanisme Marxiste*, pp. 28, 40.
39. Ibid., pp. 43, 44.
40. Ibid., p. 58.
41. Charles Forcey, *The Crossroads of Liberalism*, pp. 38–39, 47.
42. Ibid., p. 39.
43. John Dewey, *Democracy and Education*, pp. 36–37.

44. Ibid., p. 304.

45. Ibid., pp. 36–37.

46. Ibid., p. 367.

47. Emma Goldman, *Anarchism and Other Essays*, p. 75.

48. Hutchins Hapgood, *The Spirit of Labor*, p. 388.

49. Hutchins Hapgood, *An Anarchist Woman*, p. 224.

50. Dell, *Homecoming*, p. 87.

51. "Sally Thompson" [Floyd Dell], "A Candy Factory from the Inside," pp. 17–20.

52. Floyd Dell, *Love in the Machine-Age*, p. 350.

53. Barnet G. Braverman, "College Proletarians," p. 16.

54. Susan Glaspell, *The Road to the Temple*, pp. 235–36, 256.

55. Hapgood, *The Spirit of Labor*, p. 388.

56. Walter Lippmann, *A Preface to Politics*, pp. 288–89.

57. Melvyn Dubofsky, *We Shall Be All*, pp. 81, 84–86, 106, 132.

58. Quoted in Granville Hicks, *John Reed*, pp. 346–47.

59. Churchill, *The Improper Bohemians*, p. 329. While Kenneth S. Lynn in "The Rebels of Greenwich Village," pp. 338, 362–63, indicates that many of the Village rebels had been born in large cities or had emigrated to them before coming to New York, some of the most influential members of *The Masses'* group either were born and raised in the country—Max Eastman, Floyd Dell, Art Young, Lincoln Steffens, Margaret Sanger—or returned there for refuge like George Cram Cook.

60. Max Eastman, *Venture*, pp. 33–34.

61. Dell, *Homecoming*, pp. 155–56.

62. Ibid., pp. 346–47.

63. Clement Wood, *The Earth Turns South*, pp. 117–18.

64. Glaspell, *The Road to the Temple*, pp. 120–21.

65. Ibid., p. 132. Brook Farm was a Transcendentalist utopian community, 1841–47.

66. Sherwood Anderson, "Mid-American Prayer," p. 190.

67. Ibid., p. 191.

68. Sherwood Anderson, *Marching Men*, p. 156.

69. Egal Feldman, "Prostitution, the Alien Woman, and the Progressive Imagination, 1910–1915," p. 194.

70. Upton Sinclair, *The Metropolis*, pp. 354, 355.

71. Ibid., pp. 180–81.

72. Max Eastman, *Enjoyment of Living*, pp. 489–90.

73. Art Young, *Art Young*, pp. 229, 243–44.

74. Ibid., pp. 244–45.

75. "Settlement Work" from *A Man's World* by Albert Edwards [pen-name of Arthur Bullard], quoted in Upton Sinclair, ed., *The Cry for Justice*, p. 208.

Chapter 5: The Sexual Revolution

1. Eli Zaretsky, "Capitalism, the Family, and Personal Life: Part 1," pp. 87, 112.

2. James R. McGovern, "The American Woman's Pre-World War I Freedom in Manners and Morals," pp. 318–19.

3. Ibid., p. 333.

4. Agnes Repplier, "The Repeal of Reticence," pp. 297, 298.

5. "Sex O'Clock in America," p. 113. William Marion Reedy was editor of the St. Louis *Mirror*.

6. Sherwood Anderson, *Sherwood Anderson's Memoirs*, p. 343.

7. Ibid., pp. 342–43.

8. Mary Heaton Vorse, *The Heart's Country*, p. 217.

9. Sondra R. Herman, "Loving Courtship or the Marriage Market?," p. 242.

10. Linda Gordon, "Voluntary Motherhood," p. 11; Charles E. Rosenberg, "Sexuality, Class, and Role in Nineteenth-Century America," p. 145.

11. Susan Glaspell, *The Visioning*, pp. 200–201.

12. Ibid., pp. 268–69.

13. Allen Churchill, *The Improper Bohemians*, p. 24.

14. William E. Carson, *The Marriage Revolt*, p. 409.

15. Quoted in Mark Sullivan, *Our Times*, 4:282–83.

16. Lincoln Steffens, *Upbuilders*, pp. 160–61.

17. Ibid.

18. James Oppenheim, *Wild Oats*.

19. Ibid., p. 74.

20. William English Walling, *The Larger Aspects of Socialism*, pp. 292–93.

21. Emma Goldman, *The Social Significance of the Modern Drama*, pp. 119–20.

22. Olive Schreiner, *Woman and Labour*, p. 25.

23. Nathan G. Hale, Jr., *Freud and the Americans*, pp. 265, 266.

24. Margaret Sanger, *My Fight for Birth Control*, pp. 101–2.

25. Ibid., p. 101.

26. Mabel Dodge Luhan, *Intimate Memories*, 3:69–70.

27. Churchill, *The Improper Bohemians*, p. 52.

28. Susan Glaspell, *The Game*, in Eugene O'Neill, Louise Bryant, and Floyd Dell, *The Provincetown Plays*, p. 38.

29. Floyd Dell, *Homecoming*, pp. 212–16, 240; Max Eastman, *Enjoyment of Living*, pp. 483–87, 517–18, 573.

30. Hutchins Hapgood, *A Victorian in the Modern World*, p. 587.

31. William L. O'Neill, *Divorce in the Progressive Era*, p. 202.

32. Joseph Freeman, *An American Testament*, pp. 244–45.

33. O'Neill, *Divorce in the Progressive Era*, pp. 202–3.

34. Elsie Clews Parsons, "Privacy in Love Affairs," p. 12.

35. Gordon, "Voluntary Motherhood," p. 7.

36. Ibid.

37. Advertisement, *Masses* 9 (May 1917): 37.

38. Floyd Dell, "I Doubted Not" and Notes on Poem, in a file labeled Poems and Notes, vol. 2, pp. 140–41, Dell Papers.

39. Ibid., p. 140.

40. Anderson, *Sherwood Anderson's Memoirs*, pp. 521–22. In this connection, it is interesting to note that Floyd Dell readily confessed his unconscious homosexuality to this psychoanalyst during an analysis which lasted from 1917 to 1918. Cf. Dell, *Homecoming*, p. 295.

41. Emma Goldman, *Living My Life*, 2:555–56.

42. "The Mother: Observations Made by Our Travelling European Representative," *Masses* 3 (April 1912): 9; Max Eastman, "Natural Eugenics," in "Knowledge and Revolution," *Masses* 4 (September 1913): 7; Isadora Duncan, *My Life*, pp. 17, 18, 186–87; Rose Pastor Stokes, *The Woman Who Wouldn't*, p. 180.

43. Charles W. Wood, "Is Seeing Believing, and Other Questions," *Masses* 9 (January 1917): p. 32.

44. Sanger, *My Fight for Birth Control*, pp. 25–28.

45. Mabel Dodge Luhan, *Intimate Memories*, 1:31–33, 184–85, 208, 216, 261–66.

46. Ibid., *Intimate Memories*, 2:221, 277–78.

47. John Chynoweth Burnham, "Psychiatry, Psychology, and the Progressive Movement," pp. 459–61.

48. Ibid., p. 465.

49. Ibid., pp. 462–63; Hale, Jr., *Freud and the Americans*, pp. 223, 472, 480.

50. Burnham, "Psychiatry, Psychology, and the Progressive Movement," pp. 462–63; Hale, Jr., *Freud and the Americans*, pp. 223, 472.

51. Philip Rieff, *Freud*, p. 6n.

52. Sigmund Freud, *The History of the Psychoanalytic Movement and Other Papers*, pp. 63–64.

53. G[ranville] Stanley Hall, *Life and Confessions of a Psychologist*, pp. 332–33.

54. Sullivan, *Our Times*, 4:168.

55. Ibid., 4:168–69.

56. A. A. Brill, "The Introduction and Development of Freud's Work in the United States," p. 323.

57. Sullivan, *Our Times*, 4:170–71.

58. Hale, Jr., *Freud and the Americans*, p. 399.

59. Frederick J. Hoffman, Charles Allen, and Carolyn F. Ulrich, *The Little Magazine*, p. 69.

60. Anna Alice Chapin, *Greenwich Village*, pp. 264–65.

61. Luhan, *Intimate Memories*, 3:142; Brill, "The Introduction and Development of Freud's Work in the United States," pp. 322–23; Churchill, *The Improper Bohemians*, pp. 54–55.

62. Brill, "The Introduction and Development of Freud's Work in the United States," p. 323; Churchill, *The Improper Bohemians*, p. 55.

63. Frederick J. Hoffman, *Freudianism and the Literary Mind*, p. 50.

64. Max Eastman, "Mr. -er -er -Oh! What's his Name?," p. 103.

65. Max Eastman, "Fake Oracles" in "Knowledge and Revolution," *Masses* 5 (October 1913): 6.

66. M[ax] E[astman], "A New Journal," *Masses* 5 (April 1914): 9; Max Eastman, "The First Few Books," *Masses* 6 (April 1915): 22.

67. Floyd Dell, "Speaking of Psycho-Analysis," p. 53.

68. Floyd Dell, "The Science of the Soul," *Masses* 8 (July 1916): 31.

69. Dell, *Homecoming*, pp. 293–96, 322, 338, 344–47, 354, 363.

70. Hoffman, *Freudianism and the Literary Mind*, pp. 77–78.

71. F. H. Matthews, "The Americanization of Sigmund Freud," p. 53.

72. Susan Sontag, *Against Interpretation and Other Essays*, pp. 16–17.

73. Philip Rieff, *The History of the Psychoanalytic Movement and Other Essays*, pp. 15–16.

74. Rieff, *Freud*, p. 261.

75. Eli Zaretsky, "Capitalism, the Family, and Personal Life: Part 2," pp. 68–69. Floyd Dell in *Homecoming*, pp. 293–94, claimed to have viewed Freudianism as a supplement to the Marxian world view, but most of Dell's discussion of personal life occurs later, e.g., in *Love in the Machine Age*.

76. My discussion of Freudianism and Marxism has been aided by suggestions from Mark Gould.

77. For the notions of the European Freudo-Marxists see Bruce Brown, *Marx, Freud, and the Critique of Everyday Life*, especially pp. 60–61, 104–5, 157.

78. Hale, Jr., *Freud and the Americans*, p. 230.

79. Hoffman, *Freudianism and the Literary Mind*, p. 55.

80. Ibid.; Luhan, *Intimate Memories*, 3:439, 506.

81. Floyd Dell to Frederick J. Hoffman, 17 September 1942, quoted in Hoffman, *Freudianism and the Literary Mind*, p. 56.

82. Ibid.; Hoffman, *Freudianism and the Literary Mind*, p. 70; Frederick Hoffman is mistaken in believing that Dell was "in the midst of his first novel." The Floyd Dell Papers at the Newberry Library in Chicago substantiate the existence of at least two or three novels that had been destroyed. See Floyd Dell to Arthur Davison Ficke, [5 June 1913], Dell Papers; Floyd Dell, Notes on "Where I Have Not Been for a Long Time," Poems and Notes (Washington, D.C.), Dell Papers. Regarding the analysis also see Dell, *Homecoming*, pp. 293–95; John E. Hart, *Floyd Dell*, pp. 152–53; Floyd Dell, "How It Feels to be Psycho-Analyzed," [no date], Dell Papers.

83. Dell, *Homecoming*, p. 293.

84. Ibid., p. 295; Eastman, *Enjoyment of Living*, p. 491.

85. Dell, *Homecoming*, p. 295.

86. Ibid., pp. 293–94.

87. Ibid., pp. 294, 298; Dell, "How It Feels to be Psycho-Analyzed," Dell Papers.

88. Freeman, *An American Testament*, p. 244.

89. Floyd Dell to Elizabeth Lancaster, [1937], Dell Papers, quoted in George Thomas Tanselle, "Faun at the Barricades," p. 445.

90. Dell, *Love in the Machine Age*, pp. 396–97.

91. Dell, *Homecoming*, pp. 346–47.

92. Duncan, *My Life*, pp. 74–75.

93. Upton Sinclair, *American Outpost*, pp. 64–66.

94. James Burkhart Gilbert, *Writers and Partisans*, p. 24.

95. Hale, Jr., *Freud and the Americans*, p. 385; Eastman, *Enjoyment of Living*, pp. 490–94.

96. Eastman, *Enjoyment of Living*, p. 495.

97. Max Eastman, *Understanding Germany*, pp. 27, 131, 132; Max Eastman, "War Psychology and International Socialism," *Masses* 8 (August 1916): 27–28.

98. Eastman, "War Psychology and International Socialism," p. 28.

99. Sigmund Freud, *On Creativity and the Unconscious*, p. 211.

100. Ibid., pp. 211–12.

101. Max Eastman, *Great Companions*, pp. 175–76.

102. Hoffman, *Freudianism and the Literary Mind*, pp. 51–52; Heinz Eulau, "Mover and Shaker," pp. 299–300; Charles Forcey, *The Crossroads of Liberalism*, p. 109.

103. Walter Lippmann, "Freud and the Layman," pt. 2, pp. 9–10.

104. Hoffman, *Freudianism and the Literary Mind*, pp. 51–53; Eulau, "Mover and Shaker," pp. 300–301.

105. Randolph S. Bourne to Alyse Gregory, 8 September 1913, Bourne Papers, p. 3.

106. Beulah Amidon to Alyse Gregory, 4 October 1948, Bourne Papers.

107. Floyd Dell, *The Angel Intrudes*, in George Cram Cook and Frank Shay, *The Provincetown Plays*; Floyd Dell, *King Arthur's Socks*, in O'Neill, Bryant, and Dell, *The Provincetown Plays*.

108. Helen Deutsch and Stella Hanau, *The Provincetown*, p. 8.

109. Ibid., p. 26.

110. George Cram Cook and Susan Glaspell, *Suppressed Desires*, in John Reed, Neith Boyce, Hutchins Hapgood, George Cram Cook, and Susan Glaspell, *The Provincetown Plays*, Second Series (New York: Frank Shay, 1916).

111. Ibid., p. 141; Hoffman, *Freudianism and the Literary Mind*, pp. 60–64.

112. S. B. Randolph [Randolph Bourne], "Sophronisba," pp. 41–43; Randolph Bourne, *Youth and Life*, p. 37.

113. Bourne, *Youth and Life*, p. 37.

114. Randolph Bourne, *The History of a Literary Radical and Other Papers*, p. 195.

115. Walter Lippmann, *A Preface to Politics*, pp. 84–85.

116. Ibid., p. 51.

117. Ibid., pp. 214–15.

118. Ibid., pp. 51, 168.

119. Arlene Kisner, ed., *Woodhull and Claflin's Weekly*, p. 28.

120. "On the Reprinting of the Steinway Hall Speech," *Woodhull and Claflin's Weekly*, 16 August 1873, reprinted in ibid., p. 29.

121. Ibid.

122. "The Beecher-Tilton Scandal Case/The Detailed Statement of the Whole Matter by Mrs. Woodhull," *Woodhull and Claflin's Weekly*, 18 May 1873, quoted in ibid., pp. 39–40.

123. Frederick Engels, *The Origin of the Family, Private Property, and the State in the Light of the Researches of Lewis H. Morgan*, p. 10; ibid., pp. 27–28.

124. Ibid., p. 31.

125. O'Neill, *Divorce in the Progressive Era*, pp. 138–39.

126. Ellen Key, *Love and Marriage*, p. 176.

127. Ibid., pp. 176–77.

128. O'Neill, *Divorce in the Progressive Era*, p. 117; Edward Carpenter, *Love's Coming-of-Age*, p. 61.

129. Ibid., p. 63.

130. Ibid., p. 54.

131. "The Mother: Observations Made by Our Travelling European Representative," p. 9; Charles Erskine Scott Wood, *The Poet in the Desert*, pp. 45–47.

132. "The Mother: Observations Made by Our Travelling European Representative," p. 9.

133. Stokes, *The Woman Who Wouldn't*, esp. pp. 172, 180.

134. Clement Wood, *Glad of Earth*, pp. 72–73.

135. Floyd Dell, "The Book of the Month," *Masses* 9 (April 1917): 26. This was a review of *The Sexual Crisis: A Critique of Our Sex Life*, by Grete Meisel-Hess.

136. Ibid.

137. Harry Kemp, *More Miles*, pp. 362–63.

138. Dell, *Homecoming*, pp. 338, 344–45.

139. Neith Boyce to Mabel Dodge Luhan, quoted in June Sochen, " 'Now Let Us Begin,' " p. 38.

140. Luhan, *Intimate Memories*, 3:46.

141. Ibid., 3:49.

142. Duncan, *My Life*, pp. 186–87.

143. Victor Seroff, *The Real Isadora*, pp. 99–100.

144. Emily Hahn, *Romantic Rebels*, pp. 181–83.

145. Ibid., pp. 236–37.

146. Floyd Dell, "Babes in the Wood," [no date], Dell Papers; Floyd Dell, "The Perfect Husband: An Extravagant Comedy," [no date], Dell Papers.

147. Floyd Dell to Upton Sinclair presumably [1923?], Dell Papers.

148. Kemp, *More Miles*, p. 206; Max Eastman, *Venture*, pp. 266–67.

149. Hapgood, *A Victorian in the Modern World*, p. 202.

150. Ibid., p. 225; Hutchins Hapgood, *An Anarchist Woman*, p. 191.

151. Zaretsky, "Capitalism, the Family, and Personal Life: Part 2," p. 23.

152. William Graham Sumner, *Folkways*, pp. 376–77.

153. Carson, *The Marriage Revolt*, p. 435.

154. Engels, *The Origin of the Family, Private Property, and the State*, pp. 72–73.

155. Samuel Gompers, *Seventy Years of Life and Labor*, 1:56.

156. Eugene V. Debs quoted in Lincoln Steffens, "Eugene V. Debs on What the Matter Is in America and What to Do About It," p. 469.

157. Morris Hillquit, "Socialism and Morality," in Morris Hillquit and John A. Ryan, *Socialism*, p. 163.

158. Karl Marx and Frederick Engels, *The Communist Manifesto*, quoted in *The Woman Question*, pp. 34–35.

159. John Spargo, *Socialism*, pp. 171–72.

160. John Spargo, *The Spiritual Significance of Modern Socialism*, p. 68; John Spargo, *Socialism and Motherhood*, pp. 109–10.

161. Spargo, *Socialism and Motherhood*, p. 110; see also Spargo, *The Spiritual Significance of Modern Socialism*, pp. 69–70.

162. Spargo, *Socialism and Motherhood*, pp. 110–11, 118.

163. Ibid., pp. 52–53.

164. Ibid., pp. 53–54.

165. O'Neill, *Divorce in the Progressive Era*, pp. 106, 227; Carson, *The Marriage Revolt*, pp. 425–26.

166. O'Neill, *Divorce in the Progressive Era*, p. 12.

167. Key, *Love and Marriage*, p. 299.

168. O'Neill, *Divorce in the Progressive Era*, pp. 90–91.

169. Floyd Dell to Arthur Davison Ficke, [13 May 1913], Dell Papers; Sinclair, *American Outpost*, pp. 245–46.

170. Susan Glaspell, *Fidelity*, pp. 180–81; Susan Glaspell, *The Road to the Temple*, p. 139 (refers to opinion of George Cram Cook).

171. Kemp, *More Miles*, pp. 228–29.

172. Emma Goldman, *Marriage and Love*, pp. 3–4, 6; Emma Goldman, *Anarchism and Other Essays*, p. 234.

173. Eastman, *Enjoyment of Living*, pp. 379–82; Dell, *Homecoming*, pp. 198, 232.

174. Eastman, *Enjoyment of Living*, pp. 483–89, 517–21, 572–73; Dell, *Homecoming*, pp. 240–43; Tanselle, "Faun at the Barricades," p. 133.

175. Christopher Lasch, *The New Radicalism in America, 1889–1963*, p. 47.

176. William L. O'Neill, *Everyone Was Brave*, p. 21.

177. Upton Sinclair, *Love's Pilgrimage*, pp. 444–45, 451–52, 468.

178. [Floyd Dell], "Mr. Beresford and the Hero," *Masses* 9 (January 1917): 31. This was a review of *These Riese Lynnekers: A Novel*, by J. D. Beresford.

179. Carson, *The Marriage Revolt*, pp. 76, 428; Eastman, "Natural Eugenics," p. 7.

180. David M. Kennedy, *Birth Control in America*, pp. 49–50, 68.

181. Daniel Scott Smith, "Family Limitation, Sexual Control, and Domestic Feminism in Victorian America," pp. 42–43.

182. Ibid., p. 48.

183. O'Neill, *Everyone Was Brave*, pp. 31–32.

184. Gordon, "Voluntary Motherhood," p. 11.

185. Ibid., p. 15.

186. Ibid., p. 16.

187. Ibid.

188. Ibid., p. 19.

189. Lasch, *The New Radicalism in America, 1889–1963*, p. 47.

190. Carson, *The Marriage Revolt*, p. 27.

191. Ibid.; John Higham, *Strangers in the Land*, pp. 147–48.

192. Theodore Roosevelt, "A Premium on Race Suicide," pp. 163–64.

193. Carson, *The Marriage Revolt*, p. 27.

194. Margaret Sanger, *An Autobiography*, pp. 86–105.

195. Ibid., pp. 211–15.

196. Kennedy, *Birth Control in America*, pp. 21–23.

197. Ibid., pp. 21–22; June Sochen, *Movers and Shakers*, p. 105.

198. Emily Taft Douglas, *Margaret Sanger*, p. 41.

199. Kennedy, *Birth Control in America*, pp. 126, 131, 134.

200. Sanger, *An Autobiography*, pp. 96–105, 121–78.

201. Douglas, *Margaret Sanger*, pp. 37–38; Sanger, *My Fight for Birth Control*, p. 61.

202. Sanger, *An Autobiography*, pp. 93, 108; Sanger, *My Fight for Birth Control*, pp. 57, 61, 79–80.

203. Sanger, *An Autobiography*, p. 109; Sanger, *My Fight for Birth Control*, pp. 61, 79–80.

204. "Margaret Sanger," *Masses* 6 (November 1914): 20; Upton Sinclair, "From Upton Sinclair," *Masses* 6 (April 1915): 24; Max Eastman, "Is the Truth Obscene?," *Masses* 6 (March 1915): 6; "Birth Control," *Masses* 8 (April 1916): 21; "Birth Control" in *Masses* 8 (July 1916): 27.

205. Sanger, *An Autobiography*, pp. 176–80; Kennedy, *Birth Control in America*, pp. 78–79.

206. Sanger, *An Autobiography*, pp. 182–85; Kennedy, *Birth Control in America*, pp. 78–79.

207. Kennedy, *Birth Control in America*, p. 80.

208. Sanger, *My Fight for Birth Control*, p. 136.

209. Ibid., pp. 132–35, 150; Sanger, *An Autobiography*, p. 207.

210. Sochen, " 'Now Let Us Begin,' " p. 98.

211. Sanger, *An Autobiography*, p. 207.

212. Kennedy, *Birth Control in America*, pp. 112–26, 218–71.

213. Ibid., pp. 18–19; Hapgood, *A Victorian in the Modern World*, p. 170; Richard Drinnon, *Rebel in Paradise*, pp. 169–70.

214. Sanger, *An Autobiography*, p. 207.

215. Emma Goldman, *Living My Life*, 1:57–61.

216. Ibid., pp. 185–87; Drinnon, *Rebel in Paradise*, p. 166.

217. Goldman, *Living My Life*, 2:552–53.

218. Ibid., p. 553.

219. Alix Shulman, "The Most Dangerous Woman in the World," Introduction to Emma Goldman, *The Traffic in Women and Other Essays in Feminism*, p. 13.

220. Ibid.; Goldman, *Living My Life*, 2:570.

221. Alix Shulman, "The Most Dangerous Woman in the World," p. 13.

222. Goldman, *Living My Life*, 2:590.

223. Drinnon, *Rebel in Paradise*, p. 170.

224. Goldman, *Living My Life*, 2:590–91.

225. Kennedy, *Birth Control in America*, pp. 172–76; "The Question of Birth-Control," *Masses* 6 (June 1915): 21.

226. William J. Robinson, "The Prevention of Conception," p. 197; William J. Robinson, *Birth Control or the Limitation of Offspring by Prevenception*, pp. 90–91.

227. Robinson, "The Prevention of Conception," p. 197; Robinson, *Birth Control*, pp. 90–91.

228. Robinson, "The Prevention of Conception," p. 197; Robinson, *Birth Control*, pp. 92–93.

229. Robinson, "The Prevention of Conception," p. 198.

230. Robinson, *Birth Control*, p. 34.

231. Ibid., pp. 26–27.

232. "The Question of Birth-Control," p. 21.

233. "Margaret Sanger," p. 20; Sinclair, "From Upton Sinclair," p. 24; "The Question of Birth-Control," pp. 21–22; Eastman, "Is the Truth Obscene?," pp. 5–6; "To the School Board,"

Masses 6 (December 1914): 18; "Birth Control," *Masses* 7 (October-November 1915): 21; "Birth Control," *Masses* 8 (April 1916): 21; "Birth Control," *Masses* 8 (July 1916): 27.
 234. Walling, *The Larger Aspects of Socialism*, p. 351.

Chapter 6: The Road to Religion

 1. Harold U. Faulkner, *The Quest for Social Justice, 1898–1914*, pp. 204–5.
 2. Clifton E. Olmstead, *Religion in America Past and Present*, p. 129.
 3. Bouck White, *The Call of the Carpenter*, pp. x, xviii.
 4. Ibid., p. xxi.
 5. Max Eastman, "Jesus Christ," *Masses* 5 (December 1913): 5.
 6. William English Walling, "The Church in Politics," *Masses* 5 (December 1913): 22.
 7. Maurice Becker, "Their Last Supper," and Art Young, "Nearer My God to Thee," in William L. O'Neill, ed., *Echoes of Revolt: "The Masses," 1911–1917*, pp. 219, 222.
 8. Ray Stannard Baker, "The Downtown Church Arraigned: A Study of Trinity—the Richest Church in America, 1910," p. 95.
 9. Edwin Davies Schoonmaker, "Trinity Church," in Upton Sinclair, ed., *The Cry for Justice*, pp. 392–93.
 10. Max Eastman, "The Tanenbaum Crime," *Masses* 5 (May 1914): 6–8.
 11. Carl Sandburg, "To Billy Sunday," *Masses* 6 (September 1915): 11.
 12. Olmstead, *Religion in America*, pp. 137–38.
 13. Max Eastman, "The Religion of Patriotism," *Masses* 9 (July 1917): 8.
 14. George Bellows, "This Man Subjected Himself to Imprisonment . . . ," *Masses* 9 (July 1917): 4.
 15. Henry F. May, *The End of American Innocence*, p. 172; Isadora Duncan, *My Life*, p. 276.
 16. Sherwood Anderson, *Windy McPherson's Son*, pp. 44–46.
 17. Walter B. Rideout, *The Radical Novel in the United States, 1900–1954*, pp. 77–78.
 18. Max Eastman, *Enjoyment of Living*, pp. 50, 212–13, 277.
 19. Hutchins Hapgood, *A Victorian in the Modern World*, pp. 15–16.
 20. David Karsner, *Horace Traubel*, pp. 41, 44.
 21. Walter Lippmann, "The Reminiscences of Walter Lippmann," p. 39.
 22. Claude McKay, *A Long Way from Home*, p. 12.
 23. Alan Hynd, "Defender of the Damned," p. 93.
 24. Floyd Dell, *Homecoming*, pp. 68–73.
 25. Floyd Dell, *Upton Sinclair*, p. 39.
 26. Ibid., pp. 51–52.
 27. Joseph R. Conlin, *Big Bill Haywood and the Radical Union Movement*, p. 105.
 28. Clement Richardson Wood, "A Psalm Not of David," in Clement Wood, *Glad of Earth*, p. 96.
 29. "Williams" [William Williams], "A Ballad," *Masses* 8 (January 1916): 13; "Messrs. Ward and Gow . . . ," pp. 318–19; Eastman, *Enjoyment of Living*, pp. 474–75, 593–94.
 30. "Williams," "A Ballad," p. 13.
 31. Richard Drinnon, *Rebel in Paradise*, p. 103; Emma Goldman, "The Failure of Christianity," in *"The Philosophy of Atheism" and "The Failure of Christianity*," pp. [9–10].
 32. Emma Goldman, "The Philosophy of Atheism," in *"The Philosophy of Atheism" and "The Failure of Christianity*," p. [3].
 33. Goldman, "The Philosophy of Atheism," p. [6].
 34. "Emma Goldman's Faith," p. 178.
 35. Hutchins Hapgood, *An Anarchist Woman*, pp. 202–3; Max Eastman, "The Masses versus

Ward & Gow" (Statement of Max Eastman before the Senator Thompson Legislative Committee), *Masses* 8 (September 1916): 5.

36. Max Eastman, *Venture*, p. 72.

37. Floyd Dell to Bernard Shaw, [16 May 1908], Dell Papers.

38. Floyd Dell, "Dr. William Fineshriber" [lecture], [no date], Dell Papers.

39. Harry Kemp, *Tramping on Life*, p. 34.

40. Mabel Dodge Luhan, *Intimate Memories*, 3:264.

41. Isadora Duncan, *The Art of the Dance*, p. 62.

42. Ibid.; see also p. 135.

43. Susan Glaspell, *The Road to the Temple*, p. 155.

44. Max Lerner, "Randolph Bourne and Two Generations," pp. 61–62.

45. Randolph Bourne to Prudence Winterrowd, 16 January 1913, Bourne Papers.

46. Ibid.; Randolph Bourne, *Youth and Life*, p. 48; ibid., p. 355.

47. Jessie Wallace Hughan, *American Socialism of the Present Day*, pp. 160–61.

48. Ibid., pp. 161–62.

49. Morris Hillquit, "Socialism and Religion," in Morris Hillquit and John A. Ryan, *Socialism*, pp. 210, 225.

50. Louis Filler, *Crusaders for American Liberalism*, p. 298.

51. John Spargo, *The Spiritual Significance of Modern Socialism*, pp. 24–25.

52. Ibid., p. 30.

53. Max Eastman, *Max Eastman's Address to the Jury in the Second Masses Trial*, pp. 14–15.

54. William English Walling, *The Larger Aspects of Socialism*, p. 238.

55. Ibid., p. 242.

56. Melvyn Dubofsky, *We Shall Be All*, pp. 63–64.

57. Lincoln Steffens, "Eugene V. Debs on What the Matter Is in America and What to Do About It," p. 469.

58. Moses Rischin, *The Promised City*, pp. 166–67.

59. Karsner, *Horace Traubel*, pp. 117–18.

60. Horace Traubel, *Chants Communal*, pp. 176–77.

61. Ibid., pp. 179–80.

62. John Haynes Holmes, *Religion for To-day*, pp. 14–15, 68–69.

63. Ibid., pp. 99–100.

64. Lincoln Steffens, *The Autobiography of Lincoln Steffens*, p. 357.

65. Ibid., pp. 688–89.

66. Ibid.

67. Floyd Dell, Foreword to Charles Erskine Scott Wood, *Heavenly Discourse*, p. v; Charles Erskine Scott Wood, Introduction to ibid., p. vii.

68. Ibid., pp. 134–35.

69. Ibid., pp. 137–38.

70. Randolph Bourne, "Letters, 1913–1916," p. 78.

71. Ibid., p. 79.

72. Ibid.; Wood, *Heavenly Discourse*, pp. 137–38.

73. Eugene V. Debs, *Labor and Freedom*, pp. 23–24, 26; Eugene V. Debs, "Jesus," in Sinclair, ed., *The Cry for Justice*, p. 345.

74. Spargo, *The Spiritual Significance of Modern Socialism*, p. 33.

75. Steffens, *The Autobiography of Lincoln Steffens*, p. 526.

76. "The Temptation of Jesus: A Bible Lesson by Professor Charles P. Fagnan of the Union Theological Seminary, New York," *Masses* 3 (May 1912): 10.

77. Upton Sinclair, "The Reminiscences of Upton Sinclair," p. 194.

78. Upton Sinclair, *Love's Pilgrimage*, pp. 67–68; Upton Sinclair, *The Industrial Republic*, p. 253.

79. Diary entry, 25 December 1909, in John Sloan, *John Sloan's New York Scene*, p. 364. See also Van Wyck Brooks, *John Sloan*, p. 87.

80. White, *The Call of the Carpenter*, pp. 39–40, 41.

81. Ibid., p. 137.

82. Ibid., p. 312.

83. Max Eastman, "Churchly Rockefeller," *Masses* 8 (June 1916): 8.

84. Art Young, "One of Those Damned Agitators," *Masses* 5 (December 1913): 3.

85. Harry Kemp, *More Miles*, p. 378; Harry Kemp, *The Cry of Youth*, p. 4.

86. Kemp, *The Cry of Youth*, pp. 62, 75, 102–3.

87. Hutchins Hapgood, *Types from City Streets*, p. 49.

88. Horace Traubel, *Chants Communal*, p. 15.

89. Margaret Sanger, *My Fight for Birth Control*, p. 348.

90. Floyd Dell, "Shaw and Jesus," *Masses* 8 (September 1916): 33. This was a review of *Androcles and the Lion*, *Overruled* and *Pygmalion*, by Bernard Shaw.

Chapter 7: The New Feminism

1. Carroll Smith-Rosenberg, "Puberty to Menopause," p. 62.

2. Sigmund Freud, *On Creativity and the Unconscious*, p. 89.

3. Sigmund Freud, *Three Contributions to the Theory of Sex*, pp. 76–77.

4. Charles Erskine Scott Wood, *The Poet in the Desert*, pp. 22–23, 44.

5. Ibid., p. 57.

6. Floyd Dell, *Homecoming*, p. 324.

7. Charles Eugene Banks and George Cram Cook, *In Hampton Roads*, p. 285.

8. Louis Untermeyer, *First Love*, pp. 19, 26.

9. John Spargo, *Socialism and Motherhood*, p. 12.

10. Abraham Cahan, *The Rise of David Levinsky*, p. 155.

11. William E. Carson, *The Marriage Revolt*, pp. 14–15.

12. John Dewey, *The School and Society*, pp. 26–27.

13. Isadora Duncan, *My Life*, p. 245.

14. Susan Glaspell, *The Glory of the Conquered*.

15. Ibid., p. 182.

16. Ibid., p. 268.

17. Dell, *Homecoming*, p. 338.

18. Ibid., pp. 338–39.

19. Agnes Boulton, *Part of a Long Story*, pp. 67–68.

20. Floyd Dell, *Souvenir*, p. 257.

21. Mary Heaton Vorse, *The Heart's Country*, p. 3.

22. Mabel Dodge Luhan, *Intimate Memories*, 3:285–86.

23. Ibid., 3:215.

24. Ibid., 3:228.

25. Ibid., 3:263.

26. Ibid.

27. Linda Gordon, "Voluntary Motherhood," pp. 17, 18, 19.

28. Edward Carpenter, *Love's Coming-of-Age*, p. 54.

29. Betty Friedan, *The Feminine Mystique*, pp. 28–61 passim.

30. Carpenter, *Love's Coming-of-Age*, pp. 39–40.

31. Carson, *The Marriage Revolt*, p. 54.

32. Ellen Key, *Love and Marriage*, p. 124.

33. Ibid., p. 175.

34. Ibid., p. 216.

35. Ibid., pp. 216–17.

36. Mabel Dodge Luhan, *Intimate Memories*, 2:45, 47, 48.

37. William English Walling, *The Larger Aspects of Socialism*, p. 342.

38. Spargo, *Socialism and Motherhood*, pp. 30–31.

39. Floyd Dell, Notebook, 1913, Dell Papers.

40. Floyd Dell, *Love in the Machine Age*, pp. 353–54.

41. Ibid., p. 142. Italics in original.

42. Floyd Dell, *Upton Sinclair*, pp. 76–77.

43. Olive Schreiner, *Woman and Labour*, p. 167.

44. Spargo, *Socialism and Motherhood*, pp. 62–63.

45. Art Young, *Art Young*, pp. 313–14.

46. Mabel Dodge, "The Secret of War," *Masses* 6 (November 1914): 9.

47. Mary Heaton Vorse, "The Sinistrées of France," p. 449.

48. Ibid., p. 450.

49. Ibid.

50. Dewey, *The School and Society*, pp. 26–27.

51. Mary Heaton Vorse, *Time and the Town*, pp. 32, 33.

52. Walter Lippmann, *Drift and Mastery*, pp. 222–23.

53. June Sochen, " 'Now Let Us Begin,' " p. 74.

54. Floyd Dell, *Were You Ever a Child?*, pp. 55–56.

55. Eugene Wood, "Foolish Female Fashions," *Masses* 4 (December 1912): 7.

56. Walling, *The Larger Aspects of Socialism*, p. 52.

57. Mark Sullivan, *Our Times*, 4:130.

58. Floyd Dell, *Women as World Builders*, pp. 44–45, 48–49.

59. John A[lan] Waite, "*Masses*, 1911–1917," p. 146.

60. Hutchins Hapgood, *A Victorian in the Modern World*, p. 320.

61. Sochen, " 'Now Let Us Begin,' " p. 16. Sochen claims that the Village was unique in providing such a community, but she neglects the bohemian community in Chicago.

62. Ibid., p. 178.

63. Ibid., p. 90.

64. Ibid., pp. 58–59.

65. Margaret Deland, "The Change in the Feminine Ideal," pp. 291, 293.

66. Ibid., p. 292.

67. Max Eastman, *Child of the Amazons and Other Poems*, pp. 10, 15, 23–24.

68. James Oppenheim, *The Pioneers*, pp. 34–36.

69. Randolph Bourne to Mary Messer, 28 December 1913, in Randolph Bourne, "Letters, 1913–1914," p. 87; Christopher Lasch, *The New Radicalism in America, 1889–1963*, pp. 93, 95.

70. Lasch, *The New Radicalism in America*, p. 95.

71. Ibid.; Max Coe [Randolph Bourne], "Karen," p. 188.

72. David Karsner, *Horace Traubel*, p. 121.

73. Walter Lippmann, *A Preface to Politics*, pp. 91–92.

74. John Reed, "The Rights of Small Nations," pp. 94–96.

75. Floyd Dell, "Fairy Gold—The hill of dreams—The shadow mistress," [no date], Dell Papers.

76. Floyd Dell, "Feminism for Men," *Masses* 5 (July 1914): 19.

77. Ibid., pp. 14–15.

78. Dell, *Women as World Builders*, pp. 19–20.

79. Emma Goldman, *Anarchism and Other Essays*, p. 214; Emma Goldman, *Living My Life*, 2:556.

80. Goldman, *Living My Life*, 2:556–57.

81. Goldman, *Anarchism and Other Essays*, pp. 216–17.

82. Rheta Childe Dorr, *What Eight Million Women Want*, pp. 296–97.

83. Walter Lippmann, "In Defense of the Suffragettes," pp. 65–66.

84. Ibid., p. 67.

85. Randolph S. Bourne to Alyse Gregory, 1 November 1913, Bourne Papers; Randolph S. Bourne to Carl [Zigrosser], 16 November 1913, Bourne Papers.

86. Dorr, *What Eight Million Women Want*, pp. 11–13, 327, 330.

87. Ibid., pp. 12–13.

88. Helen Keller, *Helen Keller*, pp. 64–65; ibid., p. 87.

89. Ibid., p. 67.

90. Sarah N. Cleghorn, "The Mother Follows," in Genevieve Taggard, ed., *May Days*, pp. 188–89.

91. Lippmann, *Drift and Mastery*, p. 72.

92. Goldman, *Anarchism and Other Essays*, p. 203; Richard Drinnon, *Rebel in Paradise*, p. 153.

93. Floyd Dell, "St. George of the Minute: A Comedy of Feminism," [no date but c. 1914], Dell Papers.

94. Floyd Dell, "Socialism and Feminism," pp. 285–87.

95. Max Eastman, "Knowledge and Revolution: Starting Right," *Masses* 4 (September 1913): 5.

96. Max Eastman, as quoted in Ida Husted Harper, ed., *History of Woman Suffrage*, 5:285–86, cited in Aileen S. Kraditor, *The Ideas of the Woman Suffrage Movement, 1890–1920*, p. 60n.

97. Max Eastman, *Is Woman Suffrage Important?*, p. 20; William L. O'Neill, *Everyone Was Brave*, p. 68.

98. Max Eastman, "Confession of a Suffrage Orator," *Masses* 7 (October-November 1915): 7–9.

99. Dorr, *What Eight Million Women Want*, pp. 2–3.

100. Harold U. Faulkner, *The Quest for Social Justice, 1898–1914*, p. 153.

101. Upton Sinclair, *Love's Pilgrimage*, pp. 561–63.

102. Upton Sinclair, "The Double Standard—A Parable of the Ages," *Masses* 4 (August 1913): 7.

103. Charlotte Perkins Gilman, *Women and Economics*, p. 8.

104. Ibid., p. 14.

105. Ibid., p. 315.

106. Anna Strunsky Walling, *William English Walling*, pp. 13–14.

107. K. R. Chamberlain, "Afterwards," *Masses* 6 (October 1914): 12–13.

108. Spargo, *Socialism and Motherhood*, p. 118.

109. Ibid., pp. 25–26.

110. Ibid., p. 24.

111. Dell, *Women as World Builders*, p. 13.

112. Ibid., pp. 13–14.

113. Anthony Crone [Floyd Dell], "Cynthia," Dell Papers.

114. Ibid., pp. 136–37.

115. Floyd Dell, *The Briary-Bush*, p. 194.

116. Dell, *Women as World Builders*, p. 8.

117. Floyd Dell, *Janet March*.

118. Dell, *Souvenir*, pp. 153–54.

119. Floyd Dell, *Love without Money*.

120. Dell, *Love in the Machine Age*, passim.

121. Lasch, *The New Radicalism in America*, p. 47.

122. Sochen, " 'Now Let Us Begin,' " p. 175.

123. Dorr, *What Eight Million Women Want*, p. 3.

124. Ethel Lloyd Patterson, "Lena Morrow Lewis, Agitator: Something About Her Wonderful Work for the Socialist Party," *Masses* 1 (July 1911): 13.

125. Charles W. Wood, "Is Seeing Believing and Other Questions," *Masses* 9 (January 1917): 32.

126. Randolph S. Bourne to Prudence Winterrowd, 5 February 1913, Bourne Papers; Randolph S. Bourne to Prudence Winterrowd, 18 May 1913, Bourne Papers.

127. Susan Glaspell, *Fidelity*, pp. 272–73.

128. [Mary Heaton Vorse], *Autobiography of an Elderly Woman*, p. 59.

129. Ibid., pp. 63–64.

130. Gilman, *Women and Economics*, p. 228.

131. Ibid., pp. 219–20.

132. Ibid., p. 258.

133. Ibid., p. 242.

134. Ibid., p. 269.

135. Ibid., pp. 283, 293.

136. Ibid., pp. 299–300.

137. June Sochen, *Movers and Shakers*, pp. 19, 37–38.

138. Ibid., p. 37.

139. Ibid., p. 40.

140. Ibid.; O'Neill, *Everyone Was Brave*, pp. 132–33.

141. Emma Goldman, *Living My Life*, 1:371.

142. Emma Goldman, *Anarchism and Other Essays*, pp. 177–78.

143. Ibid., p. 222.

144. Emma Goldman, *The Social Significance of the Modern Drama*, pp. 66–67.

145. Emma Goldman, *Anarchism and Other Essays*, p. 185.

146. Egal Feldman, "Prostitution, the Alien Woman, and the Progressive Imagination, 1910–1915," pp. 205–6.

147. Robert E. Riegel, "Changing American Attitudes toward Prostitution, 1800–1920," p. 442.

148. Ibid.

149. Sullivan, *Our Times*, 4:134.

150. Ibid.

151. Feldman, "Prostitution, the Alien Woman, and the Progressive Imagination, 1910–1915," p. 192.

152. Ibid.; Sullivan, *Our Times*, 4:135; Riegel, "Changing American Attitudes toward Prostitution, 1800–1920," p. 452.

153. Riegel, "Changing American Attitudes toward Prostitution, 1800–1920," p. 452.

154. Ibid.; Sullivan, *Our Times*, 4:135–36.

155. Margaret Wyman, "The Rise of the Fallen Woman," pp. 174–76.

156. Ibid., p. 176.

157. "Sixteenth Amendment—Women as Social Element," in Arlene Kisner, ed., *Woodhull and Claflin's Weekly*, p. 22.

158. Gordon, "Voluntary Motherhood," p. 15.

159. Ibid., p. 16.

160. O'Neill, *Everyone Was Brave*, p. 27.

161. "The Social Evil," quoted in ibid.

162. Kraditor, *The Ideas of the Woman Suffrage Movement, 1890–1920*, p. 93.

163. Cf. Agnes Repplier, "The Repeal of Reticence," pp. 297–98, for an account of the startling new frankness of public discourse.

164. Alice Hynd, "Defender of the Damned," p. 98.

165. Harry Kemp, *The Cry of Youth*, pp. 30–31.

166. James Henle, "Nobody's Sister," *Masses* 6 (January 1915): 10.

167. John Reed, "A Daughter of the Revolution," *Masses* 6 (February 1915): 5–8. The first quotation appears on p. 8, second on p. 6.

168. John Reed, "Where the Heart Is," *Masses* 4 (January 1913): 8–9.

169. Max Eastman, "Knowledge and Revolution: Investigating Vice," *Masses* 4 (May 1913): 5.

170. Ibid.

171. Hapgood, *A Victorian in the Modern World*, pp. 136–37.

172. Lippmann, *A Preface to Politics*, pp. 134, 156, 160. Quote appears on p. 156.

173. Emma Goldman, *Anarchism and Other Essays*, pp. 190–91.

174. Ibid., p. 185.

175. Kraditor, *The Ideas of the Woman Suffrage Movement, 1890–1920*, p. 26.

176. Sochen, " 'Now Let Us Begin,' " pp. 3–4.

177. Ibid.

178. Crystal Eastman to Mrs. Leigh French, 28 February 1917, quoted in ibid., pp. 47–48.

179. Sochen, " 'Now Let Us Begin,' " pp. 47–48.

180. O'Neill, *Everyone Was Brave*, p. 176.

181. Crystal Eastman to Jane Addams, 16 January 1915, quoted in ibid.

182. Here June Sochen errs in assuming that Crystal Eastman and Henrietta Rodman symbolized "the most radical feminist position" in arguing that society be reorganized along socialist lines with cooperative nurseries and communalization of the home. Eastman and Rodman believed that such cooperatives could be run as businesses under capitalism; moreover, such enterprises were especially suited to professional women and did not meet the needs of women who had jobs rather than careers or who desired domesticity. See Sochen, " 'Now Let Us Begin,' " p. 9.

183. Max Eastman, "Knowledge and Revolution," *Masses* 4 (January 1913): 5.

184. *The Worker*, 28 April 1901, quoted in Ira Kipnis, *The American Socialist Movement, 1897–1912*, pp. 260–61.

185. Kipnis, *The American Socialist Movement, 1897–1912*, p. 261.

186. Ibid., p. 262.

187. [Floyd Dell], "The Salvation of the Working Class," pp. 9–10.

188. "Women and Socialism" [editorial], *Masses* 1 (December 1911): 3.

189. William D. Haywood and Frank Bohn, *Industrial Socialism*, p. 63.

190. Sochen, " '*Now Let Us Begin*,' " p. 94.

191. Sochen, *Movers and Shakers*, pp. 54–55.

192. Ibid., p. 55.

193. Sochen, " '*Now Let Us Begin*,' " pp. 94–95.

Chapter 8: The Exotic Other

1. Ira Kipnis, *The American Socialist Movement, 1897–1912*, pp. 130–32.

2. Ibid., p. 133.

3. Ibid., pp. 133–34.

4. Ibid., p. 133; Ronald Radosh, ed., *Debs*, pp. 62–63, 156–57. The quotation appears on p. 156.

5. Kipnis, *The American Socialist Movement, 1897–1912*, p. 134; James Weinstein, *The Decline of Socialism in America, 1912–1925*, p. 69.

6. Weinstein, *The Decline of Socialism in America, 1912–1925*, pp. 71–72.

7. W. E. B. Du Bois, "Socialism and the Negro Problem," pp. 138–41.

8. Harold Cruse, *The Crisis of the Negro Intellectual*, p. 40.

9. Weinstein, *The Decline of Socialism in America, 1912–1925*, pp. 69–70; Mary White Ovington, "How the National Association for the Advancement of Colored People Began," pp. 185–86.

10. William English Walling, "The Race War in the North," *The Independent*, pp. 529–34; see also the account of William English Walling by Charles Edward Russell in Anna Strunsky Walling, ed., *William English Walling*, pp. 77–78.

11. Mary White Ovington, *The Walls Came Tumbling Down*, p. 111.

12. James Weldon Johnson, "What the Negro Is Doing for Himself," p. 30.

13. Ovington, *The Walls Came Tumbling Down*, pp. 133–34, 144.

14. Ibid., pp. 144–46.

15. Cruse, *The Crisis of the Negro Intellectual*, p. 26.

16. Carl Van Vechten, *Nigger Heaven*; Carl Van Vechten, *Peter Whiffle*.

17. Michael Gold, "Notes of the Month: Negro Literature," p. 3.

18. Mabel Dodge Luhan, *Intimate Memories*, 3:80.

19. Cruse, *The Crisis of the Negro Intellectual*, p. 31.

20. Ibid.

21. Ridgely Torrence, *Granny Maumee, The Rider of Dreams, and Simon the Cyrenian*; "Beginnings of a Negro Drama," p. 114.

22. Van Wyck Brooks, *The Confident Years, 1885–1915*, pp. 544–45; Allen Churchill, *The Improper Bohemians*, p. 286; Helen Deutsch and Stella Hanau, *The Provincetown*, pp. 63–65; Susan Glaspell, *The Road to the Temple*, p. 289.

23. Hutchins Hapgood, *A Victorian in the Modern World*, pp. 344–45.

24. Ibid., p. 345.

25. F[loyd] D[ell], "Books: *Fifty Years and Other Poems* by James Weldon Johnson," pp. 32–33.

26. James Weldon Johnson, "Negro Poetry—A Reply," p. 41.

27. Ibid.

28. David W. Scott and E. John Bullard, *John Sloan, 1871–1951*, p. 80.

29. Art Young, *Art Young*, pp. 139–40.

30. Ibid., p. 200.

31. Robert Minor, "Pugilism in Excelsis," p. 460.

32. Claude McKay, *A Long Way from Home*, pp. 28–29.

33. Carlotta Russell Lowell and Max Eastman, "The Masses and the Negro: A Criticism and a Reply," *Masses* 6 (May 1915): 6.

34. Ibid.

35. Ovington, *The Walls Came Tumbling Down*, pp. 127–30; "A Liberal Censorship," *Masses* 6 (May 1915): 15; F[loyd] D[ell], "Intolerance," *Masses* 9 (November 1916): 18.

36. "An American Holiday," *Masses* 8 (September 1916): 12.

37. Max Eastman, "Niggers and Night Riders," *Masses* 4 (February 1913): 6.

38. Ibid.

39. Kipnis, *The American Socialist Movement*, p. 130.

40. Jessie Hughan, *American Socialism of the Present Day*, pp. 178–79.

41. Joshua Wanhope, "Asiatic Immigration: How About It?," *Masses* 3 (June 1912): 12.

42. Moses Rischin, *The Promised City*, p. 108.

43. Ibid., pp. 219–20.

44. Edmund T. Delaney, *New York's Greenwich Village*, p. 104; Albert Parry, *Garrets and Pretenders*, pp. 84–85.

45. Parry, *Garrets and Pretenders*, p. 84.

46. Ibid., pp. 84–85.

47. Brooks, *The Confident Years*, p. 123.

48. Hutchins Hapgood, *Types from City Streets*, p. 27.

49. Ibid., passim.

50. Brooks, *The Confident Years*, p. 123.

51. Randolph Bourne, "Letters, 1913–16," p. 85.

52. Joseph Freeman, *An American Testament*, p. 235.

53. Abraham Cahan, *The Rise of David Levinsky*, p. 429.

54. Hutchins Hapgood, *The Spirit of the Ghetto*, p. 79.

55. Ibid., pp. 71–72.

56. Ibid., pp. 72–74. I also profited from remarks made by Sonya Michel at the annual conference of the American Studies Association, San Antonio, Texas, November 1975.

57. Ibid., pp. 233, 239; Rischin, *The Promised City*, pp. 124–25.

58. Rischin, *The Promised City*, p. 125.

59. Parry, *Garrets and Pretenders*, p. 85.

60. George Cram Cook, quoted in ibid.

61. Susan Glaspell, quoted in ibid.

62. Elizabeth Gurley Flynn in Elizabeth Gurley Flynn et al., "Do You Believe in Patriotism?," *Masses* 8 (March 1916): 12.

63. Ibid.

64. Paul Sherman, *Randolph Bourne*, p. 33.

65. Randolph Bourne, *War and the Intellectuals*, p. 125.

66. Randolph Bourne, *History of a Literary Radical and Other Essays*, pp. 296–97.

67. Ibid., p. 299.

68. Eugene V. Debs, *Debs*, pp. 348–49.

69. Ibid., p. 349.

70. Upton Sinclair, *American Outpost*, pp. 36–37.

71. John Haynes Holmes, *Religion for To-day*, pp. 225–26.

72. Emma Goldman, *Living My Life*, 2:652–53.

73. Ibid., p. 653.

74. Robert Minor, "The Sifter," 19 October 1911, Minor Papers.

75. Clarence Darrow, *Crime and Criminals*, pp. 6–7.

76. Ibid., p. 9.

77. Ibid., p. 8.

78. Ibid., pp. 8, 10.

79. Ibid., pp. 15–16.

80. Robert Minor, "The Crime of the Law," *New York Call* 17 July 1915, in Minor Papers.

81. Emma Goldman, *Anarchism and Other Essays*, p. 126.

82. Darrow, "Crime and Criminals," p. 16.

83. Christopher Lasch, *The New Radicalism in American Life, 1889–1963*, p. xv.

84. Alexander Berkman, *Prison Memoirs of an Anarchist*, pp. 141–42.

85. Ibid., p. 394.

86. Ibid.

87. Eugene V. Debs, "Statement to the Court," in Radosh, ed., *Debs*, p. 82.

88. Hapgood, *Types from City Streets*, p. 375.

89. Hutchins Hapgood, *An Anarchist Woman*, p. 100.

90. Hapgood, *A Victorian in the Modern World*, pp. 22–23. The quotation appears on p. 23.

91. Ibid., p. 171.

92. John Reed, *Insurgent Mexico*, pp. 46–47.

93. Harry Kemp, *Tramping on Life*, p. 152.

94. McKay, *A Long Way from Home*, p. 50.

95. C[harles] E[rskine] S[cott] Wood, "Heavenly Discourse," *Masses* 9 (January 1917): 14–15.

96. Ibid., p. 15.

97. Ibid., p. 14.

98. Floyd Dell, "A Psycho-Analytic Confession," pp. 15–19.

99. Floyd Dell, "Keep Your Eyes on the Sidewalk," 1913, in Dell Papers.

100. Floyd Dell, *The Golden Spike*, p. 87.

101. James Burkhart Gilbert, *Writers and Partisans*, p. 13.

102. Ibid., pp. 13–14.

103. Piet Vlag, "The Worst Trade in the World," *Masses* 4 (August 1912): 10.

104. McKay, *A Long Way From Home*, p. 4; Max Eastman, *Colors of Life*, p. 79.

105. Horace Traubel, *Chants Communal*, pp. 110–11.

106. Arturo Giovannitti, *The Collected Poems of Arturo Giovannitti*, p. 167.

107. [Floyd Dell], "Editorial Comments," pp. 11–12. The quotation appears on p. 12.

108. Ibid., p. 12.

109. Upton Sinclair, *The Industrial Republic*, p. 190.

110. Max Eastman, "Riot and Reform at Sing Sing," *Masses* 6 (June 1915): 5–6. The quotation appears on p. 6.

Chapter 9: Art in the Class Struggle

1. Joseph Freeman, *An American Testament*, pp. 34–35.

2. Ibid., p. 35.

3. James Burkhart Gilbert, *Writers and Partisans*, p. 14.

4. Robert Charles Post, "The Absence of Radical Novels, 1910–1918," pp. 55–56. The quotation appears on p. 56.

5. John A. Waite, *"Masses, 1911–1917,"* p. 210.

6. Daniel Aaron, *Writers on the Left*, p. 217.

7. Ibid., p. 25.

8. Hutchins Hapgood, *A Victorian in the Modern World*, p. 313.

9. Frederick J. Hoffman, Charles Allen, and Carolyn F. Ulrich, *The Little Magazine*, pp. 28–29.

10. Richard Drinnon, *Rebel in Paradise*, p. 100.

11. Post, "The Absence of Radical Novels," pp. 15–16.

12. Genevieve Taggard, " 'May Days,' " p. 354.

13. Martha Sonnenberg, "Left Literary Notes," p. 71. Martha Sonnenberg interviewed Louis Untermeyer, 12 February 1968, Berkeley, California.

14. Aaron, *Writers on the Left*, p. 24.

15. F. H. Matthews, "The Americanization of Sigmund Freud," p. 53.

16. Ibid.

17. Nathan Hale, Jr., *Freud and the Americans*, p. 230.

18. Post, "The Absence of Radical Novels," passim.

19. Carl Van Vechten, *Peter Whiffle*, pp. 85–86.

20. Ibid., p. 3.

21. Ibid., p. 244.

22. Richard Fitzgerald, *Art and Politics*, p. 27.

23. Louis Untermeyer, *From Another World*, p. 38.

24. Thomas Seltzer, ed., "Socialism and Fiction," *Masses* 1 (February 1911): 3.

25. Granville Hicks, *John Reed*, p. 107.

26. E. Ralph Cheney, "Costly Luxuries," *Masses* 8 (May 1916): 22.

27. Max Eastman, "Bunk about Bohemia," pp. 200–201.

28. Ibid., p. 201.

29. Emma Goldman, *Living My Life*, 2:567.

30. Waldo Frank, *Memoirs of Waldo Frank*, p. 188.

31. Randolph Bourne to Carl Zigrosser, 3 November 1913, in Randolph Bourne, "Some Pre-War Letters, 1912–1914," p. 83.

32. Carl Resek, Introduction to Randolph S. Bourne, *War and the Intellectuals*, pp. xii–xiii. The quotation appears on p. xiii.

33. James Oppenheim, "The Strong Young Modern," p. 195.

34. Ibid., pp. 194–95. The quotation appears on p. 195.

35. James Oppenheim, "Bread and Roses," in Upton Sinclair, ed., *The Cry for Justice*, pp. 247–48.

36. *Solidarity*, 23 December 1911; 13, 30 January 1912; 19 December 1914, cited in Philip S. Foner, *The Case of Joe Hill*, p. 11.

37. Freeman, *An American Testament*, p. 245.

38. Margaret Anderson, *My Thirty Years' War*, pp. 133–34. The quotation appears on p. 134.

39. Emma Goldman, *Anarchism and Other Essays*, pp. 47–48.

40. Ibid., p. 83.

41. Ibid., p. 84.

42. Claude McKay, *A Long Way from Home*, p. 228.

43. Ibid., p. 139.

44. Joseph North, *Robert Minor*, p. 60.

45. Ibid., p. 265.

Chapter 10: Life-style and Radicalism

1. Sherwood Anderson, *Windy McPherson's Son*, p. 8.

2. Isadora Duncan, *My Life*, pp. 74–75, 143, 245. The quotation appears on p. 143.

3. Emma Goldman, *Living My Life*, 1:343.

4. Ibid., p. 151; Richard Drinnon, *Rebel in Paradise*, p. 64.

5. Goldman, *Living My Life*, 1:152–53.

6. Upton Sinclair, *Love's Pilgrimage*, pp. 444–45.

7. Ibid., p. 452.

8. Upton Sinclair, *American Outpost*, p. 250.

9. Floyd Dell, Manuscript beginning "Alfred A. Knopf wants to bring out a book of mine," 1919, Dell Papers. ["Draft of letter to (probably) Louis Untermeyer—it wd have been kept for my own use and shown to Louis at lunch. F.D."]

10. Floyd Dell, "A Psycho-Analytic Confession," pp. 15–19.

11. Floyd Dell, *The Briary-Bush*, p. 213.

12. Floyd Dell, Review of Sherwood Anderson's autobiography, undated, in manuscript, Dell Papers. This may be "How Sherwood Anderson Became an Author," *New York Herald Tribune Books*, 12 April 1942, pp. 1–2, which was a review of Sherwood Anderson's *Memoirs*.

13. Ibid., p. 8.
14. Clement Wood, *The Glory Road*, p. 13.
15. Ibid., pp. 13–14.
16. Hutchins Hapgood, *A Victorian in the Modern World*, p. 355.
17. Ibid., p. 443.
18. Ibid., p. 581.
19. Joseph R. Conlin, *Big Bill Haywood and the Radical Union Movement*, p. 106.
20. Ralph Chaplin, *Wobbly*, pp. 289–90, cited in ibid.
21. Upton Sinclair, "What Life Means to Me," p. 592.
22. Ibid.
23. Claude McKay, *A Long Way from Home*, p. 173.
24. Nathan G. Hale, Jr., *Freud and the Americans*, p. 13.
25. Floyd Dell to William Fineshriber, Fall of 1913 [copy], Dell Papers. ["Rabbi Fineshriber, in 1921, copied here and sent to me the letter I sent him in 1913 when I was on my way to New York. (F.D.)"].
26. Ibid., p. 3.
27. Dell, "A Psycho-Analytic Confession," pp. 15–18.
28. Floyd Dell, *Love in the Machine Age*, pp. 396–97. The quotation appears on p. 397.
29. Dell, "A Psycho-Analytic Confession," p. 18.
30. Harry Kemp, *More Miles*, pp. 272–73.
31. Art Young, *On My Way*, p. 113.
32. Randolph Bourne to Prudence Winterrowd, 16 January 1913, Bourne Papers.
33. Joseph Freeman, "Greenwich Village Types," *New Masses*, 8 (May 1933): 19.
34. Ibid., p. 18.
35. Ibid., pp. 19–20.
36. Floyd Dell to Joseph Freeman, [Fall 1929], Dell Papers.
37. Floyd Dell, "The Scent and Flavor of a Lost World," p. 3.
38. Young, *On My Way*, pp. 110–11.
39. Max Eastman, *Heroes I Have Known*, p. 213.
40. Ibid., p. 220.
41. Susan Glaspell, *The Road to the Temple*, p. 302; Granville Hicks, *John Reed*, p. 57; Richard O'Connor and Dale L. Walker, *The Lost Revolutionary*, p. 250.
42. Eastman, *Heroes I Have Known*, p. 223.
43. Mary Heaton Vorse, *Time and the Town*, pp. 94–95.
44. Mary Heaton Vorse, *A Footnote to Folly*, p. 14.
45. Ibid., p. 21.
46. Ibid.
47. Floyd Dell to Arthur Davison Ficke, [28 October 1919], Dell Papers.
48. Clement Wood, *Glad of Earth*, pp. 122–23.
49. Ibid., pp. 126–27. The quotation appears on p. 126.
50. Clement Wood, *The Earth Turns South*, pp. 117–18.
51. Malcolm Cowley, *Exile's Return*, pp. 66–67.
52. Goldman, *Living My Life*, 1:61.
53. John Dos Passos, *U.S.A.*, pp. 12–17; John Dos Passos, "Jack Reed," pp. 6–7.
54. Daniel Aaron, *Writers on the Left*, p. 214; Michael Gold, "Jack Reed and the Real Thing," pp. 7–8.
55. Granville Hicks, "John Reed," p. 24.
56. Joseph North, *Robert Minor*, p. 168.
57. Albert Parry, *Garrets and Pretenders*, p. 300.

Chapter 11: The End of Radical Innocence

1. Richard Fitzgerald, *Art and Politics*, p. 24.
2. Albert Christ-Janer, *Boardman Robinson*, p. 31.
3. Mabel Dodge Luhan, *Intimate Memories*, 3:303.
4. Ibid., p. 425.
5. Louis Untermeyer, *From Another World*, p. 78.
6. Joseph Freeman, "Greenwich Village Types," pp. 18–19.
7. Ibid., p. 19; Floyd Dell, in *Homecoming*, p. 360, expresses virtually the same ideas in similar prose.
8. Dell, *Homecoming*, pp. 346–47; Untermeyer, *From Another World*, p. 79; Fitzgerald, *Art and Politics*, p. 15; David Elliot Weingast, *Walter Lippmann*, pp. 12–13; Heinz Eulau, "Man Against Himself," p. 301.
9. Donald Drew Egbert, "Marxism, Reformism, and American Art before the Bolshevik Revolution," p. 99.
10. Joseph Freeman, *An American Testament*, p. 100.
11. Theodore Draper, *The Roots of American Communism*, pp. 119–20.
12. Freeman, *An American Testament*, p. 303.
13. Draper, *The Roots of American Communism*, pp. 133–36, 282, 283. Max Eastman later wrote a poem entitled "To John Reed," which appeared in *Poems of Five Decades* (New York: Harper & Brothers, 1954). He eulogizes Reed as a "young lion" whose god was not communism but life itself. Eastman viewed the poem as a protest against what he felt was "a pious falsification, or at least distortion" of Reed's true nature. Subsequent to writing the poem, Eastman discovered that Reed had spent his last days rebelling against his bureaucratic superiors in the Soviet Union: "A prior loyalty to life and truth makes accommodations to the bigotry of a developing police state difficult" (p. 56).
14. Fitzgerald, *Art and Politics*, p. 112; Freeman, *An American Testament*, p. 308; Michael Gold, "John Reed and the Real Thing," p. 7.
15. Freeman, *An American Testament*, p. 308; Fitzgerald, *Art and Politics*, pp. 100–101, 112.
16. Untermeyer, *From Another World*, pp. 76–77.
17. Ibid., p. 77.
18. Waldo Frank, *Memoirs of Waldo Frank*, p. 193.

Bibliography

Unpublished Sources

PERSONAL PAPERS

Cambridge, Mass.
  Houghton Library, Harvard University
    John Reed Papers.
Chicago, Ill.
  Newberry Library
    Floyd Dell Papers.
New York, N.Y.
  Special Collections, Butler Library, Columbia University
    Randolph Bourne Papers.
    Robert Minor Papers.
  Tamiment Institute Library
    Morris Hillquit Papers.

INTERVIEWS

New York, N.Y.
  Oral History Research Office, Columbia University
    Walter Lippmann. "The Reminiscences of Walter Lippmann." 1964. Interviews
      conducted on a wire recorder by Allan Nevins and Dean Albertson with Walter
      Lippmann at Lippmann's home in Washington, D.C., in 1950. The interviews were
      never completed or edited by Lippmann.
    Upton Sinclair. "The Reminiscences of Upton Sinclair." 1963. Tape-recorded interviews
      conducted by Ronald Gottesman of Indiana with Upton Sinclair in December 1962.
    Carl Van Vechten. "The Reminiscences of Carl Van Vechten." 1960. Tape-recorded
      interviews with Carl Van Vechten by William T. Ingersoll in March, April, and May
      1960 in New York City.

DISSERTATIONS AND OTHER TYPESCRIPTS

Egbert, Donald Drew. "Marxism, Reformism, and American Art before the Bolshevik
  Revolution." Chapter 6 of "Communism, Radicalism, and the Arts: American Developments in Relation to the Background in Western Europe and in Russia from the Seventeenth

Century to 1959." 121 pp. Four-volume typescript in the possession of Daniel Aaron, Harvard University, Cambridge, Mass.

Lloyd, Stanton Whitney. "Max Eastman: An Intellectual Portrait." An Honors Essay Presented in Partial Fulfillment of the Requirements for the Degree of Bachelor of Arts. The Committee on Degrees in American History. Harvard University, Cambridge, Massachusetts, 1965.

Post, Robert Charles. "The Absence of Radical Novels, 1910–1918: The Case of the Anomalous Hiatus; Suggestions on the Moral Implications of Literary Form." An Honors Essay Presented in Partial Fulfillment of the Requirements for the Degree of Bachelor of Arts. The Committee on Degrees in American History. Harvard College, Cambridge, Massachusetts, 1969.

Sochen, June. " 'Now Let Us Begin': Feminism in Greenwich Village, 1910–20." Ph.D. dissertation, Northwestern University, 1967.

Stricker, Frank. "Feminism for Men: Floyd Dell on Love, Marriage, and Feminism." Typescript, Los Angeles, California, 1971.

Tanselle, George Thomas. "Faun at the Barricades: The Life and Work of Floyd Dell." Ph.D. dissertation, Northwestern University, 1959.

Waite, John A[lan]. "*Masses*, 1911–1917: A Study in Rebellion." Ph.D. dissertation, University of Maryland [College Park], 1951.

Wertheim, Arthur Frank. " 'The Fiddles are Tuning': The Little Renaissance in New York City, 1908–1917." Ph.D. dissertation, New York University, 1970.

LETTERS

Maurice Becker to the author, 30 March 1970.
Helen Farr Sloan to the author, 4 July 1974.

Newspapers

The New York Times, 2 October 1918.
The New York Times, 6 October 1918.

Court Cases

Debs v. *United States*. 249 U.S. 211, 217. 10 March 1919.

Haywood v. *United States*. 268 *Federal Reporter*, 795, 808. Circuit Court of Appeals, Seventh Circuit. 5 October 1920. Rehearing denied 9 December 1920.

Masses Publishing Company v. *Patten*. 244 *Federal Reporter*, 535, 545. District Court, S.D., New York, 24 July 1917.

Masses Publishing Company v. *Patten*. 245 *Federal Reporter*, 102, 106. Circuit Court of Appeals; Second Circuit, 6 August 1917.

Masses Publishing Company v. *Patten*. 246 *Federal Reporter*, 24, 39. Circuit Court of Appeals, Second Circuit, 2 November 1917.

United States v. *Eastman et al.* 252 *Federal Reporter*, 232, 233. District Court, S.D., New York, 2 August 1918.

Books and Pamphlets

Aaron, Daniel. *Writers on the Left: Episodes in American Literary Communism*. New York: Harcourt, Brace & World, 1961.

Adamic, Louis. *Dynamite: The Story of Class Violence in America*. 1931. Reprint. New York: Chelsea House Publishers, n.d.

Aldred, Guy A. *Convict 9653: America's Vision Maker*. Glasgow: Strickland Press, n.d. [1942?].

Anderson, Margaret. *My Thirty Years' War: An Autobiography*. London: Alfred A. Knopf, 1930.

Anderson, Sherwood. *Marching Men*. New York: John Lane Company, 1917.

————. *Sherwood Anderson's Memoirs: A Critical Edition*. Edited by Ray Lewis White. Chapel Hill: University of North Carolina Press, 1969.

————. *Windy McPherson's Son*. Introduction by Wright Morris. 1916. Reprint. Chicago: University of Chicago Press, 1965.

The Appeal's Socialist Campaign Book, 1916. Girard, Kan.: Appeal to Reason, 1916.

Baker, Ray Stannard. "The Downtown Church Arraigned; A Study of Trinity—the Richest Church in America, 1910." In *The Spiritual Unrest*, by Ray Stannard Baker, pp. 1–48, 1910. Reprint. In *The Church and the City 1865–1910*, edited by Robert D. Cross, pp. 69–95. Indianapolis: Bobbs-Merrill Company, 1967.

Banks, Charles Eugene, and Cook, George Cram. *In Hampton Roads: A Dramatic Romance*. Chicago: Rand McNally & Company, 1899.

Baur, John I. H. *Revolution and Tradition in Modern American Art*. 1951. Reprint. New York: Frederick A. Praeger, 1967.

Bell, Daniel. "The Background and Development of Marxian Socialism in the United States." In *Socialism and American Life*, edited by Donald Drew Egbert and Stow Persons, 1:215–405. Princeton, N.J.: Princeton University Press, 1952.

————. "The Failure of American Socialism." In *The End of Ideology: On the Exhaustion of Political Ideas in the Fifties*, by Daniel Bell, pp. 265–85. Glencoe, Ill.: Free Press of Glencoe, Ill., 1960.

Berkman, Alexander. *Prison Memoirs of an Anarchist*. New York: Mother Earth Publishing Association, 1912.

Bimba, Anthony. *The History of the American Working Class*. New York: International Publishers, 1927.

Boulton, Agnes. *Part of a Long Story*. Garden City, N.Y.: Doubleday & Company, 1958.

Bourne, Randolph. *Arbitration and International Politics*. No. 70. New York: American Association for International Conciliation, 1913.

————. *Education and Living*. New York: Century Company, 1917.

————. *History of a Literary Radical and Other Essays*. Edited with an introduction by Van Wyck Brooks. New York: B. W. Huebsch, 1920.

————. *The History of a Literary Radical and Other Papers*. With an introduction by Van Wyck Brooks. New York: S. A. Russell, 1956.

————. *The Tradition of War*. No. 79. New York: American Association for International Conciliation, 1914.

————. *Untimely Papers*. Foreword by the editor James Oppenheim. New York: B. W. Huebsch, 1919.

————. *War and the Intellectuals: Collected Essays, 1915–1919*. Edited with an introduction by Carl Resek. New York: Harper & Row, 1964.

————. *Youth and Life*. 1913. Reprint. Freeport, N.Y.: Books for Libraries Press, 1967.

Boyce, Neith. *The Folly of Others*. New York: Fox, Duffield & Company, 1904.

Brissenden, Paul Frederick. *The I. W. W.: A Study of American Syndicalism*. Studies in History,

Economics and Public Law. Edited by the Faculty of Political Science of Columbia University. Vol. 83. Whole Number 193. 2d ed. New York: Columbia University, 1920.

Brooks, John Graham. *American Syndicalism: The I. W. W.* New York: Macmillan Company, 1913.

Brooks, Van Wyck. *America's Coming-of-Age*. New York: B. W. Huebsch, 1915.

_____. *The Confident Years, 1885–1915*. New York: E. P. Dutton & Company, 1952.

_____. *John Sloan: A Painter's Life*. New York: E. P. Dutton & Company, 1955.

_____. "Randolph Bourne." In *Emerson and Others*, by Van Wyck Brooks, pp. 123–45. New York: E. P. Dutton and Company, 1927.

Broun, Heywood, and Leech, Margaret. *Anthony Comstock: Roundsman of the Lord*. New York: Literary Guild of America, 1927.

Brown, Bruce. *Marx, Freud, and the Critique of Everyday Life: Toward a Permanent Cultural Revolution*. New York: Monthly Review Press, 1973.

Bryant, Louise. *Six Red Months in Russia: An Observer's Account of Russia before and during the Proletarian Dictatorship*. New York: George H. Doran Company, 1918.

Bullard, Arthur [pseud. Albert Edwards]. *Comrade Yetta*. New York: Macmillan Company, 1913.

_____. *Mobilising America*. New York: Macmillan Company, 1917.

Burgess, Gelett. *A Gage of Youth: Lyrics from The Lark and Other Poems*. Boston: Small, Maynard & Company, 1901.

_____. *Lady Méchante, or Life As It Should Be*. 1901. Reprint. New York: Frederick A. Stokes Company, 1909.

Cabell, James Branch. *Jurgen: A Comedy of Justice*. New York: Robert M. McBride & Co., 1919.

Cahan, Abraham. *The Rise of David Levinsky*. New York: Harper & Brothers, 1917.

Calhoun, Arthur W. *A Social History of the American Family from Colonial Times to the Present*. Vol. 3. *Since the Civil War*. Cleveland: Arthur H. Clark Company, 1919.

Cannon, James P. *The I. W. W.* 1956. Reprint. New York: Pathfinder Press, 1971. First appeared in the Summer 1955 issue of *Fourth International* (now *International Socialist Review*).

Cargill, O.; Fagin, N. B.; and Fisher, W. J., eds. *Eugene O'Neill and His Plays*. London: Peter Owen, 1964.

Carpenter, Edward. *Love's Coming-of-Age: A Series of Papers on the Relations of the Sexes*. Manchester, England: Labour Press, 1915.

Carson, William E. *The Marriage Revolt: A Study of Marriage and Divorce*. New York: Hearst's International Library Company, 1915.

Chafee, Zechariah, Jr. *Freedom of Speech*. New York: Harcourt, Brace and Howe, 1920.

Chamberlain, John. *Farewell to Reform: Being a History of the Rise, Life, and Decay of the Progressive Mind in America*. New York: Liveright, 1932.

Chapin, Anna Alice. *Greenwich Village*. New York: Dodd, Mead and Company, 1917.

Christ-Janer, Albert. *Boardman Robinson*. With chapters by Arnold Blanch and Adolf Dehn. Chicago: University of Chicago Press, 1946.

Churchill, Allen. *The Improper Bohemians: A Re-creation of Greenwich Village in Its Heyday*. New York: E. P. Dutton & Company, 1959.

Coleman, McAlister. *Eugene V. Debs, A Man Unafraid*. New York: Greenburg Publisher, 1930.

Conlin, Joseph R. *Big Bill Haywood and the Radical Union Movement*. Syracuse, N.Y.: Syracuse University Press, 1969.

Cook, George Cram. *The Chasm*. New York: Frederick A. Stokes Company, 1911.

_____. *Greek Coins*. With memorabilia by Floyd Dell, Edna Kenton, and Susan Glaspell. New York: George H. Doran Company, 1925.

_____. *Roderick Taliaferro: A Story of Maximilian's Empire*. New York: Macmillan Company, 1903.

_____, and Shay, Frank, eds. *The Provincetown Plays*. With a foreword by Hutchins Hapgood. Cincinnati: Stewart Kidd Company, 1921.

Cowley, Malcolm. *Exile's Return: A Literary Odyssey of the 1920's*. 1934. Reprint. New York: Viking Press, 1969.

_____, ed. *After the Genteel Tradition: American Writers Since 1910*. 1936. Reprint. Gloucester, Mass.: Peter Smith, 1959.

Cruse, Harold. *The Crisis of the Negro Intellectual*. New York: William Morrow & Company, 1967.

Darrow, Clarence S. *Crime and Criminals: An Address Delivered to the Prisoners in the Chicago County Jail*. Chicago: Charles H. Kerr, 1902.

Day, Dorothy. *The Long Loneliness: The Autobiography of Dorothy Day*. New York: Harper & Brothers, 1952.

Debs, Eugene V. *Debs: His Life, Writings and Speeches; With a Department of Appreciations*. Chicago: Charles H. Kerr & Company, 1908.

_____. *The Growth of Socialism*. Chicago: Charles H. Kerr & Company, n.d. [1905?].

_____. *Labor and Freedom: The Voice and Pen of Eugene V. Debs*. St. Louis: Phil Wagner, 1916.

_____. *Writings and Speeches of Eugene V. Debs*. Introduction by Arthur M. Schlesinger, Jr. New York: Hermitage Press, 1948.

_____, and Russell, Charles Edward. *Danger Ahead for the Socialist Party in Playing the Game of Politics*. Chicago: Charles H. Kerr & Company, n.d. [post 1911].

Delaney, Edmund T. *New York's Greenwich Village*. Barre, Mass.: Barre Publishers, 1968.

Dell, Floyd. *The Briary-Bush*. New York: Alfred A. Knopf, 1921.

_____. *Diana Stair*. New York: Farrar and Rinehart, 1932.

_____. *The Golden Spike*. New York: Farrar & Rinehart, 1934.

_____. *Homecoming: An Autobiography*. New York: Farrar and Rinehart, 1933.

_____. *Intellectual Vagabondage: An Apology for the Intelligentsia*. New York: George H. Doran Company, 1926.

_____. *Janet March*. New York: Alfred A. Knopf, 1923.

_____. *Looking at Life*. New York: Alfred A. Knopf, 1924.

_____. *Love in Greenwich Village*. New York: George H. Doran Company, 1926.

_____. *Love in the Machine Age: A Psychological Study of the Transition from Patriarchal Society*. New York: Farrar & Rinehart, 1930.

_____. *Love without Money*. New York: Farrar & Rinehart, 1931.

_____. *Moon-Calf*. New York: Alfred A. Knopf, 1921.

_____. *An Old Man's Folly*. New York: George H. Doran Company, 1926.

_____. *Runaway: A Novel*. New York: George H. Doran Company, 1925.

_____. *Souvenir*. Garden City, N.Y.: Doubleday, Doran and Company, 1929.

_____. *This Mad Ideal*. New York: Alfred A. Knopf, 1925.

_____. *An Unmarried Father*. New York: George H. Doran Company, 1927.

_____. *Upton Sinclair: A Study in Social Protest*. Long Beach, Calif.: George H. Doran Company, 1927.

_____. *Were You Ever a Child?* New York: Alfred A. Knopf, 1919.

_____. *Women as World Builders: Studies in Modern Feminism*. Chicago: Forbes and Company, 1913.

Deutsch, Helen, and Hanau, Stella. *The Provincetown: A Story of the Theatre*. New York: Farrar & Rinehart, 1931.

Dewey, John. *Democracy and Education: An Introduction to the Philosophy of Education*. 1916. Reprint. New York: Macmillan Company, 1924.

————. *The School and Society*. Supplemented by a statement of the University Elementary School. Chicago: University of Chicago Press, 1913.

Dorr, Rheta Childe. *What Eight Million Women Want*. Boston: Small, Maynard & Company, 1910.

Dos Passos, John. *U. S. A.* 3 vols. Vol. 1. *The 42nd Parallel*; Vol. 2. *Nineteen Nineteen*; Vol. 3. *The Big Money*. 1930. Reprint. New York: Modern Library, 1937.

Douglas, Emily Taft. *Margaret Sanger: Pioneer of the Future*. New York: Holt, Rinehart and Winston, 1970.

Draper, Theodore. *The Roots of American Communism*. 1957. Reprint. New York: Viking Press, 1966.

Drinnon, Richard. *Rebel in Paradise: A Biography of Emma Goldman*. Chicago: University of Chicago Press, 1961.

Dubofsky, Melvyn. *We Shall Be All: A History of the Industrial Workers of the World*. Chicago: Quadrangle Books, 1969.

Duncan, Isadora. *The Art of the Dance*. Edited with an introduction by Sheldon Cheney. 1928. 2d ed. New York: Theatre Art Books, 1969.

————. *My Life*. New York: Boni and Liveright, 1927.

Eastman, Max. *Child of the Amazons and Other Poems*. New York: Mitchell Kennerley, 1913.

————. *Colors of Life: Poems and Songs and Sonnets*. New York: Alfred A. Knopf, 1918.

————. *Enjoyment of Laughter*. New York: Simon and Schuster, 1936.

————. *Enjoyment of Living*. New York: Harper & Brothers, 1948.

————. *Enjoyment of Poetry*. New York: Charles Scribner's Sons, 1922.

————. *Great Companions: Critical Memoirs of Some Famous Friends*. New York: Farrar, Straus and Cudahy, 1959.

————. *Heroes I Have Known: Twelve Who Lived Great Lives*. New York: Simon and Schuster, 1942.

————. *Is Woman Suffrage Important?* New York: Men's League for Woman Suffrage, n.d. [1912?].

————. *Journalism versus Art*. New York: Alfred A. Knopf, 1916.

————. *Love and Revolution: My Journey through an Epoch*. New York: Random House, 1964.

————. *Max Eastman's Address to the Jury in the Second Masses Trial: In Defense of the Socialist Position and the Right of Free Speech; Summation for the Defense, Friday, 4 October 1918*. Liberator Pamphlet no. 1. New York: Liberator Publishing Company, n.d. [1918].

————. *Poems of Five Decades*. New York: Harper & Brothers, 1954.

————. *The Sense of Humor*. New York: Charles Scribner's Sons, 1921.

————. *Understanding Germany: The Only Way to End War and Other Essays*. New York: Mitchell Kennerley, 1916.

————. *Venture*. New York: Albert & Charles Boni, 1927.

Emerson, Ralph Waldo. *Selections from Ralph Waldo Emerson: An Organic Anthology*, edited by Stephen E. Whicher. 1957. Reprint. Boston: Houghton Mifflin, Riverside Editions, 1960.

Engels, Frederick. *The Origin of the Family, Private Property and the State in the Light of the Researches of Lewis H. Morgan*. 1884. Reprint. New York: International Publishers Company, 1970.

Faulkner, Harold U. *The Quest for Social Justice, 1898–1914*. Vol. 11 of *A History of American Life*. 1931. Reprint. Chicago: Quadrangle Books, Quadrangle Paperbacks, 1971.

Filler, Louis. *Crusaders for American Liberalism*. 1939. Reprint. Yellow Springs, Ohio: Antioch Press, 1950.

————. *Randolph Bourne*. Introduction by Max Lerner. Washington, D.C.: American Council on Public Affairs, 1943.

Fine, Nathan. *Labor and Farmer Parties in the United States, 1828–1928*. New York: Russell & Russell, 1961.

Fitzgerald, Richard. *Art and Politics: Cartoonists of the "Masses" and "Liberator."* Westport: Conn.: Greenwood Press, 1973.

Flynn, Elizabeth Gurley. *Debs, Haywood, Ruthenberg*. New York: Workers Library Publishers, 1939.

———. *The Rebel Girl: An Autobiography; My First Life (1906–1926)*. 1955. First published under the title *I Speak My Own Piece: Autobiography of "The Rebel Girl."* Revised. New York: International Publishers, 1973.

Foner, Philip S. *The Case of Joe Hill*. New York: International Publishers Company, 1965.

———. *The Industrial Workers of the World, 1905–1917*. Volume 4 of *History of the Labor Movement in the United States*. 1965. Reprint. New York: International Publishers Company, 1973.

Forcey, Charles. *The Crossroads of Liberalism: Croly, Weyl, Lippmann, and the Progressive Era, 1900–1925*. New York: Oxford University Press, 1961.

Foucault, Michel. "Nietzsche, Freud, Marx" and "Discussion." In *Nietzsche: Cahiers de Royaumont Philosophie No. 6*, pp. 183–92, 193–200. Paris: Les Éditions de Minuit, 1967.

Frank, Waldo. *Memoirs of Waldo Frank*. Edited by Alan Trachtenberg. [Amherst]: University of Massachusetts Press, 1973.

Freeman, Joseph. *An American Testament: A Narrative of Rebels and Romantics*. New York: Farrar & Rinehart, 1936.

Freud, Sigmund. *Delusion and Dream and Other Essays*. Edited and with an introduction by Philip Rieff. 1917. Reprint. Boston: Beacon Press, 1972.

———. *The History of the Psychoanalytic Movement and Other Papers*. Edited with an introduction by Philip Rieff. New York: Collier Books, 1963.

———. *Leonardo da Vinci: A Study in Psychosexuality*. Authorized translation by A. A. Brill. 1916. Reprint. New York: Random House, Vintage Books, n.d.

———. *On Creativity and the Unconscious: Papers on the Psychology of Art, Literature, Love, Religion*. Selected with an introduction and annotations by Benjamin Nelson. New York: Harper & Row, Harper Torchbooks, 1958.

———. *On Dreams*. Translated by James Strachey. [1901]. Reprint. New York: W. W. Norton & Company, The Norton Library, 1952.

———. *Three Contributions to the Theory of Sex*. Translated from the German by A. A. Brill. [1910]. Reprint. New York: E. P. Dutton & Company, 1962.

Friedan, Betty. *The Feminine Mystique*. 1963. Reprint. New York: Dell Publishing Company, 1965.

Fund for the Republic. *Digest of the Public Record of Communism in the United States*. New York: Fund for the Republic, 1955.

Gallatin, A. E. *John Sloan*. New York: E. P. Dutton & Company, 1925.

Garaudy, Roger. *Humanisme Marxiste: Cinq Essais Polémiques*. Paris: Éditions Sociales, 1957.

Gelb, Barbara. *So Short a Time: A Biography of John Reed and Louise Bryant*. New York: W. W. Norton & Company, 1973.

Gilbert, James Burkhart. *Writers and Partisans: A History of Literary Radicalism in America*. New York: John Wiley and Sons, 1968.

Gilman, Charlotte Perkins. *Women and Economics: A Study of the Economic Relation between Men and Women as a Factor in Social Evolution*. 1898. Reprint. Edited by Carl N. Degler. New York: Harper & Row, Harper Torchbooks, 1966.

———. *The Yellow Wallpaper*. 1899. Reprint. Afterword by Elaine R. Hedges. New York: Harper & Row, Harper Torchbooks, 1966.

Ginger, Ray. *Eugene V. Debs: A Biography*. 1949. First appeared as *The Bending Cross: A*

Biography of Eugene Victor Debs. Reprint. New York: Collier Books, 1966.

Giovannitti, Arturo. *The Collected Poems of Arturo Giovannitti*. Introduction by Norman Thomas. Chicago: E. Clemente & Sons, 1962.

Glaspell, Susan. *Fidelity*. Boston: Small, Maynard and Company, 1915.

———. *The Glory of the Conquered: The Story of a Great Love*. New York: Frederick A. Stokes Company, 1909.

———. *"The People" and "Close the Book."* New York: Frank Shay, 1918.

———. *The Road to the Temple*. New York: Frederick A. Stokes Company, 1927.

———. *The Visioning*. New York: Frederick A. Stokes Company, 1911.

Goldman, Emma. *Anarchism and Other Essays*. With a biographic sketch by Hippolyte Havel. New York: Mother Earth Publishing Association, 1910.

———. *Living My Life*. 2 vols. New York: Alfred A. Knopf, 1931.

———. *Marriage and Love*. New York: Mother Earth Publishing Association, 1911.

———. *Patriotism: A Menace to Liberty*. New York: Mother Earth Publishing Association, n.d. [1908?].

———. *"Philosophy of Atheism" and "The Failure of Christianity."* New York: Mother Earth Publishing Association, 1916.

———. *Preparedness: The Road to Universal Slaughter*. New York: Mother Earth Publishing Association, n.d. [1916?].

———. *The Psychology of Political Violence*. New York: Mother Earth Publishing Association, 1911.

———. *The Social Significance of the Modern Drama*. Boston: Richard G. Badger, 1914.

———. *The Traffic in Women and Other Essays on Feminism*. Introduction, "The Most Dangerous Woman in the World," by Alix Shulman. New York: Times Change Press, 1970.

Gompers, Samuel. *Seventy Years of Life and Labor: An Autobiography*. 2 vols. New York: E. P. Dutton & Company, 1925.

Goodrich, Lloyd. *John Sloan*. Published for the Whitney Museum of American Art. New York: Macmillan Company, 1952.

Hahn, Emily. *Romantic Rebels: An Informal History of Bohemianism in America*. Boston: Houghton Mifflin Company, 1966.

Hale, Nathan G., Jr. *Freud and the Americans: The Beginnings of Psychoanalysis in the United States, 1876–1917*. New York: Oxford University Press, 1971.

Hall, G[ranville] Stanley. *Life and Confessions of a Psychologist*. 1923. Reprint. New York: D. Appleton and Company, 1927.

Hapgood, Hutchins. *An Anarchist Woman*. New York: Duffield & Company, 1909.

———. *Fire and Revolution*. New York: Free Speech League, 1912. Republished for the (New York) *Globe*, 11 July 1912.

———. *The Spirit of the Ghetto*. Edited by Moses Rischin. 1902. Reprint. Cambridge, Mass.: Belknap Press of Harvard University Press, 1967.

———. *The Spirit of Labor*. New York: Duffield & Company, 1907.

———. *Types from City Streets*. New York: Funk & Wagnalls Company, 1910.

———. *A Victorian in the Modern World*. New York: Harcourt, Brace and Company, 1939.

Hart, John E. *Floyd Dell*. New York: Twayne Publishers, 1971.

Haywood, William D. *Bill Haywood's Book: The Autobiography of William D. Haywood*. 1929. Reprint. New York: International Publishers Company, 1969.

———. *Evidence and Cross-Examination of William D. Haywood in the Case of the U.S.A. vs. Wm. D. Haywood et al*. Chicago: General Defense Committee, n.d.

———, and Bohn, Frank. *Industrial Socialism*. Chicago: Charles H. Kerr & Company, 1911.

Herrick, Robert. *The Conscript Mother*. New York: Charles Scribner's Sons, 1916.

Hicks, Granville. *John Reed*. New York: Macmillan Company, 1936.

_____. *One of Us: The Story of John Reed*. New York: Equinox Cooperative Press, 1935.

Higham, John. *Strangers in the Land: Patterns of American Nativism 1860–1925*. 1955. Reprint. New York: Atheneum, 1965.

Hillquit, Morris. *Loose Leaves from a Busy Life*. New York: Macmillan Company, 1934.

_____. *Socialism Summed Up*. New York: H. K. Fly Company, 1913.

_____, and Ryan, John A. *Socialism: Promise or Menace*. New York: Macmillan Company, 1914. Originally appeared in *Everybody's Magazine*. Debate between Morris Hillquit, New York lawyer and Socialist delegate, and John Augustine Ryan, D.D., professor of moral theology and economics at St. Paul Seminary, St. Paul, Minnesota, liberal Catholic theologian.

Hoffman, Frederick J. *Freudianism and the Literary Mind*. Baton Rouge, La.: Louisiana State University Press, 1945.

_____; Allen, Charles; and Ulrich, Carolyn F. *The Little Magazine: A History and a Bibliography*. Princeton, N.J.: Princeton University Press, 1947.

Holmes, John Haynes. *Religion for To-day: Various Interpretations of the Thought and Practise of the New Religion of our Time*. New York: Dodd, Mead and Company, 1917.

Houghton, Walter E. *The Victorian Frame of Mind, 1830–1870*. 1957. Reprint. New Haven: Yale University Press, 1964.

Howe, Irving. *Sherwood Anderson*. 1951. Reprint. Stanford, Calif.: Stanford University Press, 1966.

_____, and Coser, Lewis, with the assistance of Julius Jacobson. *The American Communist Party: A Critical History, 1919–1957*. Boston: Beacon Press, 1957.

Howells, William Dean. *The Coast of Bohemia*. 1893. Reprint. New York: John Lane Company, 1911.

Hughan, Jessie Wallace. *American Socialism of the Present Day*. New York: John Lane Company, 1911.

Humphrey, Robert E. *Children of Fantasy: The First Rebels of Greenwich Village*. New York: John Wiley & Sons, 1978.

Hunter, Robert. *Violence and the Labor Movement*. New York: Macmillan Company, 1914.

James, William. *Essays on Faith and Morals*. Selected by Ralph Barton Perry. 1962. Reprint. Cleveland: World Publishing Company, Meridian Books, 1967.

Kanter, Rosabeth Moss. *Commitment and Community: Communes in Sociological Perspective*. Cambridge, Mass.: Harvard University Press, 1972.

Kaplan, Justin. *Lincoln Steffens: A Biography*. New York: Simon and Schuster, 1974.

Karsner, David. *Debs: His Authorized Life and Letters*. New York: Boni and Liveright, 1919.

_____. *Horace Traubel: His Life and Work*. Published at the Washington Square Book Shop, New York, 1919.

Kazin, Alfred. *On Native Grounds: An Interpretation of Modern American Prose Literature*. 1942. Reprint. Garden City, N.Y.: Doubleday & Company, 1956.

Keefer, Truman Frederick. *Ernest Poole*. New York: Twayne Publishers, 1966.

Keller, Helen. *Helen Keller: Her Socialist Years*. Writings and speeches, edited with an introduction by Philip S. Foner. New York: International Publishers Company, 1967.

Kemp, Harry. *The Cry of Youth*. New York: Mitchell Kennerley, 1914.

_____. *More Miles: An Autobiographical Novel*. New York: Boni and Liveright, 1926.

_____. *The Thresher's Wife*. New York: Albert and Charles Boni, 1914.

_____. *Tramping on Life: An Autobiographical Narrative*. New York: Boni and Liveright, 1922.

Kennedy, David M. *Birth Control in America: The Career of Margaret Sanger*. 1970. Reprint. New Haven: Yale University Press, 1971.

Key, Ellen. *Love and Marriage*. Translated from the Swedish by Arthur G. Chater. With a critical and biographical introduction by Havelock Ellis. New York: G. P. Putnam's Sons, Knickerbocker Press, 1911.

Kipnis, Ira. *The American Socialist Movement, 1897–1912*. 1952. Reprint. New York: Monthly Review Press, 1972.

Kisner, Arlene, ed. *Woodhull and Claflin's Weekly: The Lives and Writings of Notorious Victoria Woodhull and Her Sister Tennessee Claflin*. Washington, N.J.: Times Change Press, 1972.

Kraditor, Aileen S. *The Ideas of the Woman Suffrage Movement, 1890–1920*. 1965. Reprint. Garden City, N.Y.: Doubleday & Company, Anchor Books, 1971.

Kubie, Lawrence S., M.D. *Neurotic Distortion of the Creative Process*. 1958. Reprint. New York: Noonday Press, 1971.

Lasch, Christopher. *The New Radicalism in America, 1889–1963: The Intellectual as a Social Type*. New York: Alfred A. Knopf, 1965.

Lewis, Sinclair. *The Job: An American Novel*. New York: Harper & Brothers, 1917.

Lippmann, Walter. *Drift and Mastery: An Attempt to Diagnose the Current Unrest*. New York: Mitchell Kennerley, 1914.

———. *A Preface to Politics*. 1913. Reprint. New York: Mitchell Kennerley, 1914.

London, Jack. *War of the Classes*. 1905. Reprint. New York: Grosset & Dunlap, 1908.

Luhan, Mabel Dodge. *Intimate Memories*. 4 vols. Vol. 1. *Background*. Vol. 2. *European Experiences*. Vol. 3. *Movers and Shakers*. Vol. 4. *Edge of Taos Desert*. New York: Harcourt, Brace and Company, 1933–36.

McKay, Claude. *A Long Way from Home*. New York: Lee Furman, 1937.

———. *Songs of Jamaica*. With an introduction by Walter Jekyll. 1912. Reprint. Miami, Fla.: Mnemosyne Publishing, 1969.

Marot, Helen. *American Labor Unions*. New York: Henry Holt and Company, 1914.

Maurice, Arthur Bartlett. *The New York of the Novelists*. New York: Dodd, Mead and Company, 1916.

May, Henry F. *The End of American Innocence: A Study of the First Years of Our Own Time, 1912–1917*. 1959. Reprint. Chicago: Quadrangle Books, 1964.

Mencken, H. L. *A Book of Prefaces*. New York: Alfred A. Knopf, 1917.

Miller, Perry, ed. *The American Transcendentalists: Their Prose and Poetry*. Garden City, N.Y.: Doubleday & Company, Anchor Books, 1957.

Moss, Arthur H., ed. *Greenwich Village Anthology of Verse: Being a Compilation of Poetry from the Pages of the First Year's Issue of "The Quill," a Magazine of Greenwich Village*. New York: Arthur H. Moss, 1918.

Nomad, Max (pseud.). "William Z. Foster—Apostle in the Land of the Infidels." In *Rebels and Renegades*, by Max Nomad, pp. 338–91. New York: Macmillan Company, 1932.

North, Joseph. *Robert Minor, Artist and Crusader: An Informal Biography*. New York: International Publishers Company, 1956.

O'Connor, Richard, and Walker, Dale L. *The Lost Revolutionary: A Biography of John Reed*. New York: Harcourt, Brace & World, 1967.

O'Hare, Kate Richards. *Socialism and the World War*. St. Louis, Mo.: Frank P. O'Hare, n.d. [1919?]. An address delivered over 140 times in 1917 from coast to coast throughout the United States, and at Bowman, N.D., on 17 July 1917.

Olmstead, Clifton E. *Religion in America Past and Present*. Englewood Cliffs, N.J.: Prentice-Hall, 1961.

O'Neill, Eugene; Bryant, Louise; and Dell, Floyd. *The Provincetown Plays*. First Series. New York: Frank Shay, 1916.

O'Neill, William L. *Divorce in the Progressive Era*. New Haven: Yale University Press, 1967.

———. *Everyone Was Brave: The Rise and Fall of Feminism in America*. Chicago: Quadrangle Books, 1969.

————, ed. *Echoes of Revolt: "The Masses," 1911–1917*. Chicago: Quadrangle Books, 1966.

Oppenheim, James. *Night: A Poetic Drama in One Act*. New York: Published by Egmont Arens at the Washington Square Bookshop, 1918. *Night* was first produced by the Provincetown Players on 2 November 1917.

————. *The Nine-Tenths*. New York: Harper & Brothers, 1911.

————. *The Pioneers: A Poetic Drama in Two Scenes*. New York: B. W. Huebsch, 1910.

————. *Wild Oats*. With a foreword by Edward Bok. New York: B. W. Huebsch, 1910.

Ovington, Mary White. *The Walls Came Tumbling Down*. 1947. Reprint. With a new introduction by Charles Flint Kellogg. New York: Schocken Books, 1970.

Parry, Albert. *Garrets and Pretenders: A History of Bohemianism in America*. 1933. Revised edition, with a new chapter, "Enter Beatniks," by Harry T. Moore. New York: Dover Publications, 1960.

Paul, Sherman. *Randolph Bourne*. Pamphlets on American Writers, no. 60. Minneapolis: University of Minnesota Press, 1966.

Peterson, H. C., and Fite, Gilbert C. *Opponents of War, 1917–1918*. 1957. Reprint. Seattle: University of Washington Press, 1968.

Pierre, C. Grand. *The Fascinating History of Fourth Street Greenwich Village: The Street with "a Past."* New York: Greenwich Village Weekly News, 1939?.

Poole, Ernest. *The Bridge: My Own Story*. New York: Macmillan Company, 1940.

————. *The Harbor*. New York: Macmillan Company, 1915.

Pouget, Emile. *Sabotage*. Translated from the French, with an introduction by Arturo M. Giovannitti. Chicago: Charles H. Kerr & Company, 1913. Arturo M. Giovannitti's introduction written from Essex County Jail, Lawrence, Mass., August 1912.

Pound, Ezra. *Patria Mia*. 1913. Reprint. Chicago: Ralph Fletcher Seymour, 1950.

Preston, William, Jr. *Aliens and Dissenters: Federal Suppression of Radicals, 1903–1933*. Foreword by Oscar Handlin. 1963. Reprint. New York: Harper & Row, Harper Torchbooks, 1966.

Radosh, Ronald, ed. *Debs*. Englewood Cliffs, N.J.: Prentice-Hall, Spectrum Book, 1971.

Raskin, Jonah. *The Mythology of Imperialism*. 1971. Reprint. New York: Dell Publishing Company, Delta Book, 1973.

Reed, John. *Adventures of a Young Man: Short Stories from Life*. Berlin: Seven Seas Publishers, 1966.

————. *Daughter of the Revolution and Other Stories*. Edited with an introduction by Floyd Dell. 1927. Reprint. New York: Books for Libraries Press, 1970.

————. *The Day in Bohemia, or Life Among the Artists*. New York: Printed for the Author, 1913. Five hundred copies of this book were printed at Hillacre, Riverside, Connecticut, during the month of January 1913.

————. *The Education of John Reed: Selected Writings*. With an introductory essay by John Stuart. 1955. Reprint. New York: International Publishers Company, 1972.

————. *Insurgent Mexico*. New York: D. Appleton and Company, 1914.

————. *Ten Days That Shook the World*. 1919. Reprint. New York: Vintage Books, 1960.

————. *The War in Eastern Europe*. Pictured by Boardman Robinson. New York: Charles Scribner's Sons, 1916.

————; Boyce, Neith; Hapgood, Hutchins; Cook, George Cram; and Glaspell, Susan. *The Provincetown Plays*. Second Series. New York: Frank Shay, 1916.

Rideout, Walter B. *The Radical Novel in the United States, 1900–1954: Some Interrelations of Literature and Society*. Cambridge, Mass.: Harvard University Press, 1956.

Rieff, Philip. *Freud: The Mind of the Moralist*. 1959. Reprint. Garden City, N.Y.: Doubleday & Company, Anchor Books, 1961.

Rischin, Moses. *The Promised City: New York's Jews, 1870–1914*. Cambridge, Mass.: Harvard University Press, 1962.

Robinson, William J., M.D. *Birth Control or the Limitation of Offspring by Prevenception*. With an introduction by A. Jacobi, M.D., LL.D. 31st ed. 1916. Reprint. New York: Eugenics Publishing Company, 1928.

Rosenfeld, Paul. *Port of New York: Essays on Fourteen American Moderns*. New York: Harcourt, Brace and Company, 1924.

Rosenstone, Robert A. *Romantic Revolutionary: A Biography of John Reed*. New York: Alfred A. Knopf, 1975.

St. John, Vincent. *The I. W. W.: Its History, Structure, and Methods*. Cleveland: I. W. W. Publishing Bureau, 1913.

Sanger, Margaret. *An Autobiography*. 1938. Reprint. New York: Dover Publications, 1971.

———. *My Fight for Birth Control*. New York: Farrar & Rinehart, 1931.

Santayana, George. *The Genteel Tradition: Nine Essays by George Santayana*. Edited by Douglas L. Wilson. Cambridge, Mass.: Harvard University Press, 1967.

———. *The Genteel Tradition in American Philosophy: The Annual Public Address before the Philosophical Union of the University of California*. [Reprint from the *University of California Chronicle*, vol. 13, no. 4 (1911)] Berkeley, Calif.: University Press, [1911].

———. *The Genteel Tradition at Bay*. New York: Charles Scribner's Sons, 1931.

———. *Winds of Doctrine*. In *Winds of Doctrine and Platonism and the Spiritual Life*, by George Santayana, pp. 1–215. New York: Harper & Brothers, 1957.

Schapiro, Meyer. "Rebellion in Art." In *America in Crisis*, edited by Daniel Aaron, pp. 203–42. New York: Alfred A. Knopf, 1952.

Schlissel, Lillian, ed. *The World of Randolph Bourne*. New York: E. P. Dutton & Co., 1965.

Schmalhausen, Samuel D., and Calverton, V. F., eds. *Woman's Coming of Age: A Symposium*. New York: Horace Liveright, 1931.

Schreiner, Olive. *Woman and Labour*. Leipzig: Bernhard Tauchnitz, 1911.

Scott, David W., and Bullard, E. John. *John Sloan, 1871–1951: His Life and Paintings*, by David W. Scott; *His Graphics*, by E. John Bullard. Boston: Boston Book & Art, n.d. [1972 or 1973].

Seroff, Victor. *The Real Isadora*. New York: Dial Press, 1971.

Simonson, Lee. *Minor Prophecies*. New York: Harcourt, Brace and Company, 1927.

Sinclair, Upton. *American Outpost: A Book of Reminiscences*. New York: Farrar & Rinehart, 1932.

———. *A Captain of Industry: Being the Story of a Civilized Man*. 2 vols. Edited by E. Haldeman-Julius. Little Blue Books nos. 634 and 635. Girard, Kan.: Haldeman-Julius Company, n.d. [1924]. First appeared in *Appeal to Reason* (1906). Written, according to July 1924 preface, by Upton Sinclair, c. 1900.

———. *The Industrial Republic: A Study of the America of Ten Years Hence*. New York: Doubleday, Page & Company, 1907.

———. *The Jungle*. 1906. Reprint. [Pasadena, Calif.]: Upton Sinclair, 1920.

———. *King Coal*. With an introduction by Dr. Georg Brandes. 1917. Reprint. [Pasadena, Calif.]: Upton Sinclair, 1930.

———. *Love's Pilgrimage*. New York: Mitchell Kennerley, 1911.

———. *The Metropolis*. New York: Moffat, Yard & Company, 1908.

———, ed. *The Cry for Justice: An Anthology of the Literature of Social Protest*. With an introduction by Jack London. Philadelphia: John C. Winston Company, 1915.

Sloan, John. *Etchings*. Columbia, Mo.: University of Missouri Press, 1967.

———. *John Sloan*. New York: American Artists Group, 1945.

———. *John Sloan's New York Scene: From the Diaries, Notes, and Correspondence, 1906–*

1913. Edited by Bruce St. John, with an introduction by Helen Farr Sloan. New York: Harper & Row, 1965.

Sochen, June. *Movers and Shakers: American Women Thinkers and Activists, 1900–1970*. New York: Quadrangle/The New York Times Book Company, 1973.

Socialist Party. *Court Rulings Upon Indictments, Search Warrants, Habeas Corpus, Mailing Privileges, Etc., Growing Out of Alleged Offenses Against Draft and Espionage Acts*. Chicago: Socialist Party, n.d.

_____. *National Constitution and Platform of the Socialist Party, 1917*. Chicago: National Office, Socialist Party, 1917.

_____. *Socialist Hand Book, Campaign 1916*. Chicago: Published by the Socialist Party, 1916.

Sontag, Susan. "Against Interpretation" and "On Style." In *Against Interpretation and Other Essays*, by Susan Sontag, pp. 13–23, 24–25, 1961. Reprint. New York: Dell Publishing Company, Laurel Edition, 1969.

Spargo, John. *Socialism: A Summary and Interpretation of Socialist Principles*. New York: Macmillan Company, 1906.

_____. *Socialism and Motherhood*. New York: B. W. Huebsch, 1914.

_____. *The Spiritual Significance of Modern Socialism*. New York: B. W. Huebsch, 1908.

Spiro, Melford E. *Kibbutz: Venture in Utopia*. 1956. Reprint. New York: Schocken Books, 1963.

Steffens, Lincoln. *The Autobiography of Lincoln Steffens*. New York: Harcourt, Brace and Company, 1931.

_____. *Upbuilders*. Introduction by Earl Pomeroy. 1909. Reprint. Seattle: University of Washington Press, 1968.

Stokes, Rose Pastor. *The Woman Who Wouldn't*. New York: G. P. Putnam's Sons, 1916.

Sullivan, Mark. *Our Times: The United States, 1900–1925*. Vol. 4. *The War Begins, 1909–1914*. New York: Charles Scribner's Sons, 1932.

Sumner, William Graham. *Folkways: A Study of the Sociological Importance of Usages, Manners, Customs, Mores, and Morals*. Boston: Ginn and Company, 1906.

Symes, Lillian, and Clement, Travers. *Rebel America: The Story of Social Revolt in the United States*. New York: Harper & Brothers, 1934.

Taft, Henry W. *Freedom of Speech and the Espionage Act*. Plainfield, N.J.: New Jersey Law Journal Publishing Company, 1921.

Taft, Philip, and Ross, Philip. "American Labor Violence: Its Causes, Character, and Outcome." In *Violence in America: Historical and Comparative Perspectives: A Report Submitted to the National Commission on the Cause and Prevention of Violence*, edited by Hugh David Graham and Ted Robert Gurr, pp. 281–388. 1969. Revised ed. New York: Bantam Books, 1970.

Taggard, Genevieve, ed. *May Days: An Anthology of Verse from "Masses-Liberator."* New York: Boni & Liveright, 1925.

Thomas, Norman. *The Conscientious Objector in America*. New York: B. W. Huebsch, 1923.

Torrence, Ridgeley. *Granny Maumee, The Rider of Dreams, Simon the Cyrenian: Plays for a Negro Theater*. New York: Macmillan Company, 1917.

Traubel, Horace. *Chants Communal*. Boston: Small, Maynard & Company, 1904.

Trilling, Lionel. *Freud and the Crisis of Our Culture*. Boston: Beacon Press, 1955.

_____. "Freud and Literature" and "Art and Neurosis." In *The Liberal Imagination: Essays on Literature and Society*, by Lionel Trilling, pp. 32–54, 155–75. 1950. Reprint. Garden City, N.Y.: Doubleday & Company, Anchor Books, 1953.

United States Department of Justice. *Annual Report of the Attorney General of the United States for the Year 1918*. Washington: Government Printing Office, 1918.

Untermeyer, Louis. *Challenge*. New York: Century Company, 1914.

_____. *First Love: A Lyric Sequence*. Boston: Sherman, French & Company, 1911.

_____. *From Another World*. New York: Harcourt, Brace and Company, 1939.

_____. *These Times*. New York: Henry Holt and Company, 1917.

Van Vechten, Carl. *Nigger Heaven*. New York: Alfred A. Knopf, 1926.

_____. *Peter Whiffle*. 1922. Reprint. New York: Modern Library, 1929.

[Vorse, Mary Heaton]. *Autobiography of an Elderly Woman*. Boston: Houghton Mifflin Company, 1911.

Vorse, Mary Heaton. *A Footnote to Folly: Reminiscences of Mary Heaton Vorse*. New York: Farrar & Rinehart, 1935.

_____. *The Heart's Country*. Boston: Houghton Mifflin Company, 1914.

_____. *Time and the Town: A Provincetown Chronicle*. New York: Dial Press, 1942.

Walling, Anna Strunsky. *William English Walling: A Symposium*. New York: Stackpole Sons, 1938.

Walling, William English. *The Larger Aspects of Socialism*. New York: Macmillan Company, 1913.

_____. *Socialism As It Is: A Survey of the World-Wide Revolutionary Movement*. New York: Macmillan Company, 1912.

Waterman, Arthur E. *Susan Glaspell*. New York: Twayne Publishers, 1966.

Weinberger, Harry. *Emma Goldman: Speech Delivered at Her Funeral, Chicago, 17 May 1940*. Berkeley Heights, N.J.: Published privately by the Oriole Press, 1940.

Weingast, David Elliott. *Walter Lippmann*. New Brunswick, N.J.: Rutgers University Press, 1949.

Weinstein, James. *The Decline of Socialism in America, 1912–1925*. New York: Monthly Review Press, 1967.

_____. "Gompers and the New Liberalism, 1900–1909," pp. 101–14; Reply: "Historical Materialism and Labor History," by Philip S. Foner, pp. 115–20; Reply by James Weinstein, pp. 120–24. In *For a New America: Essays in History and Politics from "Studies on the Left," 1959–1967*, edited by James Weinstein and David W. Eakins. New York: Random House, 1970.

Weiss, Richard. *The American Myth of Success from Horatio Alger to Norman Vincent Peale*. New York: Basic Books, 1969.

Weitenkampf, F. *American Graphic Art*. New York: Henry Holt and Company, 1912.

Werstein, Irving. *Pie in the Sky: An American Struggle; The Wobblies and Their Times*. New York: Delacorte Press, 1969.

Wertheim, Arthur Frank. *The New York Little Renaissance: Iconoclasm, Modernism, and Nationalism in American Culture, 1908–1917*. New York: New York University Press, 1976.

White, Bouck. *The Call of the Carpenter*. 1911. Reprint. Garden City, N.Y.: Doubleday, Page & Company, 1912.

White, Morton. *Social Thought in America: The Revolt against Formalism*. 1947. Reprint. Boston: Beacon Press, 1963.

_____, and White, Lucia. "The American Intellectual versus the American City." In *The Future Metropolis*, edited by Lloyd Rodwin, pp. 214–32. New York: George Braziller, 1961.

The Woman Question: Selections from the Writings of Karl Marx, Frederick Engels, V. I. Lenin, Joseph Stalin. 1951. Reprint. New York: International Publishers Company, 1970.

Wood, Charles Erskine Scott. *Heavenly Discourse*. 1927. Reprint. New York: Vanguard Press, 1928.

_____. *The Poet in the Desert*. [A New Version]. Portland, Ore.: [Press of F. W. Baltes and Company], 1918.

Wood, Clement. *The Earth Turns South*. New York: E. P. Dutton and Company, 1919.

_____. *Glad of Earth*. New York: Laurence J. Gomme, 1917.

———. *The Glory Road: An Autobiography*. New York: Poets Press, 1936.

Young, Art. *Art Young: His Life and Times*. Edited by John Nicholas Beffel. New York: Sheridan House, 1939.

———. *The Best of Art Young*. With an introduction by Heywood Broun. New York: Vanguard Press, 1936.

———. *On My Way: Being the Book of Art Young in Text and Picture*. New York: Horace Liveright, 1928.

Articles

"The American." *Seven Arts* 1 (April 1917): 555–57.

"American Independence and the War: A Supplement with the April Issue." *Seven Arts* 1 (April 1917): 1–9.

Anderson, Sherwood. "An Apology for Crudity." *Dial* 63 (8 November 1917): 437–38.

———. "From Chicago." *Seven Arts* 2 (May 1917): 41–59.

———. "Mid-American Prayer." *Seven Arts* 2 (June 1917): 190–92.

———. " 'Mother.' " *Seven Arts* 1 (March 1917): 452–61.

———. " 'Queer.' " *Seven Arts* 1 (December 1916): 97–108.

———. "The Untold Lie." *Seven Arts* 1 (January 1917): 215–21.

Baury, Louis. "The Message of Bohemia." *Bookman* 34 (November 1911): 256–66.

"Beginnings of a Negro Drama." *Literary Digest* 48 (9 May 1914): 114.

"Boardman Robinson's Work as a Cartoonist: The Cartoon as a Means of Artistic Expression." *Current Literature* 53 (October 1912): 461–64.

Bodenheim, Maxwell. "The Unimagined Heaven." *Seven Arts* 2 (June 1917): 193–98.

Bourne, Randolph. "Below the Battle." *Seven Arts* 2 (July 1917): 270–77.

———. "The Cult of the Best." *New Republic* 5 (15 January 1916): 275–77.

———. "Denatured Nietzsche." *Dial* 63 (25 October 1917): 389–91. Review of *The Will to Freedom* by John Neville Figgis.

———. "Desire as Hero." *New Republic* 5 (20 November 1915): 5–6. Review of *The Genius* by Theodore Dreiser.

———. "Diary for 1901." *Twice a Year* 5–6 (Fall-Winter 1940; Spring-Summer 1941): 89–98.

———. "The Heart of the People." *New Republic* 3 (3 July 1915): 233.

———. "The Idea of a University." *Dial* 63 (22 November 1917): 509–10.

——— [pseud. Max Coe]. "Karen: A Portrait." *New Republic* 8 (23 September 1916): 187–88.

———. "A Letter to Van Wyck Brooks, March 27, 1918." *Twice a Year* 1 (Fall-Winter 1938): 50–55.

———. "Letters, 1913–1914." *Twice a Year* 5–6 (Fall-Winter 1940; Spring-Summer 1941): 79–88.

———. "Letters, 1913–1916." *Twice a Year* 7 (Fall-Winter 1941): 76–90.

———. "A Modern Mind." *Dial* 62 (22 March 1917): 239–40. Review of *Social Rule* by Elsie Clews Parsons.

———. "New Ideals in Business." *Dial* 62 (22 February 1917): 133–34. Reviews of: *New Ideals in Business*, by Ida M. Tarbell; *An Approach to Business Problems*, by A. W. Shaw; and *America and the New Epoch*, by Charles P. Steinmetz.

———. "The Puritan's Will to Power." *Seven Arts* 1 (April 1917): 631–37.

———. "Some Pre-War Letters, 1912–1914." *Twice a Year* 2 (Spring-Summer 1939): 79–102.

——— [S. B. Randolph]. "Sophronisba." *New Republic* 5 (13 November 1915): 41–43.

———. "A Stronghold of Obscurantism." *Dial* 62 (5 April 1917): 303–5. Review of *Problems of Secondary Education*, by David Snedden.

———. "The Two Generations." *Atlantic Monthly* 107 (May 1911): 591–98.

———. "War and the Intellectuals." *Seven Arts* 2 (June 1917): 133–46.

Brill, A. A., M.D. "The Introduction and Development of Freud's Work in the United States." *American Journal of Sociology* 45 (November 1939): 318–25.

Brooks, Van Wyck. "The Culture of Industrialism." *Seven Arts* 1 (April 1917): 655–66.

———. "Enterprise." *Seven Arts* 1 (November 1916): 57–60.

———. "Our Awakeners." *Seven Arts* 2 (June 1917): 235–48.

———. "Our Critics." *Seven Arts* 2 (May 1917): 103–16.

B[rooks], V[an] W[yck]. "Sinclair Lewis and Others." *Seven Arts* 2 (May 1917): 121–22.

———. "The Splinter of Ice." *Seven Arts* 1 (January 1917): 270–80.

———. "Toward a National Culture." *Seven Arts* 1 (March 1917): 535–47.

Bullard, Arthur. "America and the World's Peace." *Century Magazine* 90 (August 1915): 591–96.

Burnham, John Chynoweth. "Psychiatry, Psychology, and the Progressive Movement." *American Quarterly* 12 (Winter 1960): 457–65.

Burrow, Trigant, M.D., Ph.D. "Psychoanalytic Improvisations and the Personal Equation." *Psychoanalytic Review* 13 (April 1926): 173–86. Paper read at the Fifteenth Annual Meeting of the American Psychoanalytic Association, Richmond, Va., 12 May 1925.

Carroll, Thomas F. "Freedom of Speech and of the Press in War Time: The Espionage Act." *Michigan Law Review* 17 (June 1919): 621–65.

Chafee, Zechariah, Jr. "Freedom of Speech." *New Republic* 17 (16 November 1918): 66–69.

Coates, Robert M. "Profiles: After Enough Years Have Passed." *New Yorker* 25 (7 May 1949): 36–40, 42, 44–48, 51. Portrait of John Sloan.

Conlin, Joseph R. "Wobblies and Syndicalists." *Studies on the Left* 6 (March–April 1966): 81–91. Review of *The Industrial Workers of the World, 1905–1917*, vol. 4 of *History of the Labor Movement in the United States*, by Philip S. Foner.

Deland, Margaret. "The Change in the Feminine Ideal." *Atlantic Monthly* 105 (March 1910): 289–302.

D[ell], F[loyd]. "Books: *Fifty Years and Other Poems*, by James Weldon Johnson." *Liberator* 1 (March 1918): 32–33.

Dell, Floyd. "The Builders." *Tri-City Workers Magazine* 1 (November [1905]): 24.

[Dell, Floyd]. "A Candy Factory from the Inside." *Tri-City Workers Magazine* 1 (January 1906): 17–20. Signed "Sally Thompson."

———. "Change in American Life and Fiction." *New Review* 3 (May 1915): 13–15.

[Dell, Floyd]. "The Children vs. the Library Board." *Tri-City Workers Magazine* 1 (February 1906): 16–17. Signed "Thersites."

———. "Creators." *International* 5 (March 1912): 51–53.

[Dell, Floyd]. "The Davenport Public Schools." *Tri-City Workers Magazine* 1 (January 1906): 11–14. Signed "John Smith, Sr."

[Dell, Floyd]. "Diphtheria in Davenport." *Tri-City Workers Magazine* 1 (December 1905): 5–6. Signed "Thersites."

———. "The Drama of Dynamite." *New Review* 2 (July 1914): 404–10.

[Dell, Floyd]. "Editorial Comments." *Tri-City Workers Magazine* 1 (August 1906): 10–13.

———. "The 'Genius' and Mr. Dreiser." *New Review* 3 (15 December 1915): 362–63.

———. "The Littlest Theater: Chicago's Experiment in the Production of Poetic Drama." *Harper's Weekly* 58 (29 November 1913): 22–24.

———. "A Long Time Ago." *Forum* 51 (February 1914): 261–77.

———. "Memories of the Old Masses." *American Mercury* 68 (April 1949): 481–87.

[Dell, Floyd]. "The Only Original Socialist." *Tri-City Workers Magazine* 1 (January 1906): 10–11. Signed "Thersites."

_____. "On Seeing Isadora Duncan's School." *New York Tribune*, 4 February 1915, p. 8 [in "The Conning Tower"]. Reprinted in Floyd Dell, *Homecoming: An Autobiography*, p. 275. New York: Farrar & Rinehart, 1933.

[Dell, Floyd]. "Our Autocratic School Board." *Tri-City Workers Magazine* 1 (May 1906): 13–14. Signed "Vesurius."

_____. "The Passionate Friends: An Indictment of Jealousy and the Romantic Ideal of Love." *Harper's Weekly* 58 (13 December 1913): 25. Review of H. G. Wells's *The Passionate Friends*.

_____. "A Psycho-Analytic Confession." *Liberator* 3 (April 1920): 15–19.

_____. "Rents Were Low in Greenwich Village." *American Mercury* 65 (December 1947): 662–68.

_____. "The Rise and Fall of Greenwich Village—I: Its Rise." *Century Magazine* 110 (October 1925): 643–65. Reprinted in Floyd Dell, *Love in Greenwich Village*, pp. 13–44. New York: George H. Doran Company, 1926.

_____. "The Rise and Fall of Greenwich Village—II: Its Fall." *Century Magazine* 111 (November 1925): 48–58. Reprinted in Floyd Dell, *Love in Greenwich Village*, pp. 295–321. New York: George H. Doran Company, 1926.

[Dell, Floyd]. "The Salvation of the Working Class." *Tri-City Workers Magazine* 1 (July 1906): 8–10. Signed "Thersites."

_____. "The Scent and Flavor of a Lost World: When Mabel Dodge and John Reed Fell in Love and Discovered Art, Sex, and Revolution." *New York Herald Tribune Books*, 22 November 1936, p. 3. Review of Mabel Dodge Luhan's *Movers and Shakers*, vol. 3 of *Intimate Memories*.

_____. "Shaw and Religion." *Seven Arts* 1 (November 1916): 82–88.

_____. "Socialism and Feminism: A Reply to Belfort Bax." *New Review* 2 (June 1914): 349–53. Reply to Belfort Bax's "Socialism and the Feminist Movement." *New Review* 1 (May 1914): 285–87.

_____. "Socialists and Kindergarten." *Tri-City Workers Magazine* 1 (February 1906): 7–11.

[Dell, Floyd]. "Socialists and Their Critics." *Tri-City Workers Magazine* 1 (December 1905): 11–13. Signed "Thersites."

_____. "Speaking of Psycho-Analysis: The New Boon for Dinner-Table Conversationalists." *Vanity Fair* 5 (December 1915): 53.

[Dell, Floyd]. "Why People Go to Brick Munro's." *Tri-City Workers Magazine* 1 (September 1906): 1–4. Signed "Thersites."

Deutsch, Babette, et al. "A Group of Lyrics." *Seven Arts* 2 (June 1917): 185–89.

Dewey, John. "In a Time of National Hesitation." *Seven Arts* 2 (May 1917): 3–7.

Diggins, John P. "Getting Hegel Out of History: Max Eastman's Quarrel with Marxism." *American Historical Review* 79 (February 1974): 38–71.

Dos Passos, John. "Jack Reed." *New Masses* 6 (October 1930): 6–7.

Dreiser, Theodore. "Life, Art, and America." *Seven Arts* 1 (February 1917): 363–89.

Du Bois, W. E. B. "Socialism and the Negro Problem." *New Review* 1 (1 February 1913): 138–41.

Eastman, Max. "Bunk about Bohemia." *Modern Monthly* 8 (May 1934): 200–208.

_____. "Mr. -er -er —Oh! What's His Name?" *Everybody's Magazine* 33 (July 1915): 95–103.

_____. "New Masses for Old." *Modern Monthly* 8 (June 1934): 292–300.

_____. "Science and Free Verse." *Seven Arts* 1 (February 1917): 426–29.

_____. "The Will to Live." *Journal of Philosophy, Psychology, and Scientific Methods* 14 (15 February 1917): 102–7.

"Editorials." *Seven Arts* 1 (March 1917): 504–6.

Ellis, Havelock. "Freud's Influence on the Changed Attitude toward Sex." *American Journal of Sociology* 45 (November 1939): 309–17.

"Emma Goldman." *American Magazine* 69 (March 1910): 605, 608.

"Emma Goldman's Faith." *Current Literature* 50 (February 1911): 176–78.

Eulau, Heinz. "Man against Himself: Walter Lippmann's Years of Doubt." *American Quarterly* 4 (Winter 1952): 291–304.

———. "Mover and Shaker: Walter Lippmann as a Young Man." *Antioch Review* 11 (September 1951): 291–312.

———. "Wilsonian Idealist: Walter Lippmann Goes to War." *Antioch Review* 14 (March 1954): 87–108.

Feldman, Egal. "Prostitution, the Alien Woman, and the Progressive Imagination, 1910–1915." *American Quarterly* 19 (Summer 1967): 192–206.

Ficke, Arthur Davison. "The Headland." *Seven Arts* 1 (December 1916): 123–29.

"The Fifth-Month Poet." *Seven Arts* 2 (May 1917): 117–19.

Fox, Richard W. "The Paradox of 'Progressive' Socialism: The Case of Morris Hillquit, 1901–1914." *American Quarterly* 26 (May 1974): 126–40.

Frank, Waldo. "Bread-Crumbs." *Seven Arts* 2 (May 1917): 24–40.

———. "Concerning a Little Theatre." *Seven Arts* 1 (December 1916): 157–64.

———. "Emerging Greatness." *Seven Arts* 1 (November 1916): 73–78.

F[rank], W[aldo]. "The German Theatre in New York." *Seven Arts* 1 (April 1917): 676–77.

F[rank], W[aldo]. "Playing a Joke on Broadway." *Seven Arts* 2 (May 1917): 125–27.

———. "A Prophet in France." *Seven Arts* 1 (April 1917): 638–48.

———. "Vicarious Fiction." *Seven Arts* 1 (January 1917): 294–303.

Freeman, Joseph. "Greenwich Village Types." *New Masses* 8 (May 1933): 18–20.

Frost, Robert. "The Bonfire." *Seven Arts* 1 (November 1916): 25–28.

———. "A Way Out." *Seven Arts* 1 (February 1917): 347–62.

Gold, Michael. "John Reed and the Real Thing." *New Masses* 3 (November 1927): 7–8.

———. "Notes of the Month: Negro Literature." *New Masses* 5 (February 1930): 3.

Gordon, Linda. "Voluntary Motherhood: The Beginnings of Feminist Birth Control Ideas in the United States." *Feminist Studies* 1 (Winter-Spring 1973): 5–19.

"Greeting." *Comrade* 1 (October 1901): 12. Reprint. Westport, Conn.: Greenwood Reprint Corporation, 1970.

Hapgood, Hutchins. "Emma Goldman's Anarchism." *Bookman* 32 (February 1911): 639–40.

Haywood, William D. "Socialism, the Hope of the Working Class." *International Socialist Review* 12 (February 1912): 461–71. Speech delivered in New York City, at Cooper Union, under the auspices of the local New York Socialist party.

———, and Bohn, Frank. "The Problem and Its Solution: From McClure's Magazine and 'Industrial Socialism.' " *International Socialist Review* 12 (December 1911): 365–68.

Henri, Robert. "The New York Exhibition of Independent Artists." *Craftsman* 18 (May 1910): 160–72.

Herman, Sondra R. "Loving Courtship or the Marriage Market? The Ideal and Its Critics, 1871–1911." *American Quarterly* 25 (May 1973): 234–52.

Herrick, Robert. "Recantation of a Pacifist." *New Republic* 4 (30 October 1915): 328–30.

Hicks, Granville. "John Reed." *New Masses* 8 (December 1932): 24.

Hynd, Alan. "Defender of the Damned." *True* (August 1952): 37–39, 92–103.

Johnson, James Weldon. "Negro Poetry—A Reply." *Liberator* 1 (April 1918) 40–41, 43.

———. "What the Negro Is Doing for Himself." *Liberator* 1 (June 1918): 29–31.

Kent, Christopher A. "The Idea of Bohemia in Mid-Victorian England." *Queen's Quarterly* 80 (Autumn 1973): 360–69.

Kuttner, Alfred Booth. "The Artist." *Seven Arts* 1 (February 1917): 406–12.

———. "The Artist (A Communication)." *Seven Arts* 1 (March 1917): 549–52.

———. "The Freudian Theory." *New Republic* 2 (24 April 1915): 182–83.

———. "A Note on Forgetting." *New Republic* 1 (28 November 1914): 15–17.

Kwiat, Joseph J. "Dreiser and the Graphic Artist." *American Quarterly* 3 (Summer 1951): 127–41.

Lerner, Max. "Randolph Bourne and Two Generations." *Twice a Year* 5–6 (Fall-Winter 1940; Spring-Summer 1941): 54–78.

Lewis, Sinclair. "Hobohemia." *Saturday Evening Post* 189 (7 April 1917): 3–6, 121, 122, 125, 126, 129, 130, 133.

Lippmann, Walter. "The Case for Wilson." *New Republic* 8 (14 October 1916): 263–64.

———. "The Discussion of Socialism: Politics and Meta-Politics." *Harvard Illustrated Magazine* 11 (April 1910): 231–32.

———. "Freud and the Layman." *New Republic* 2 (17 April 1915), pt. 2, pp. 9–10.

———. "In Defense of the Suffragettes." *Harvard Monthly* 49 (November 1909): 64–67.

———. "Legendary John Reed." *New Republic* 1 (26 December 1914): 15–16.

———. "Life Is Cheap." *New Republic* 1 (19 December 1914): 12–14.

———. "A Reply." *Seven Arts* 1 (January 1917): 304–5.

———. "Socialism at Harvard." *Harvard Illustrated Magazine* 10 (March 1909): 137–39.

Lorwin, Lewis L. (pseud. Louis Levine). "The Development of Syndicalism in America." *Political Science Quarterly* 28 (September 1913): 451–79.

Lynn, Kenneth. "The Rebels of Greenwich Village." *Perspectives in American History* 8 (1974): 333–77.

M'Cormick, William B. "The Realism of John Sloan." *Arts and Decoration* 5 (August 1915): 390–91.

McGovern, James R. "The American Woman's Pre-World War I Freedom in Manners and Morals." *Journal of American History* 55 (September 1968): 315–33.

McKay, Claude. "Garvey as a Negro Moses." *Liberator* 5 (April 1922): 8–9.

Masses. Vol. 1, no. 1–vol. 10, no. 2 (1911–17).

Matthews, Brander. "Are the Movies a Menace to the Drama?" *North American Review* 205 (March 1917): 446–54.

Matthews, F. H. "The Americanization of Sigmund Freud." *Journal of American Studies* 1 (April 1967): 39–62.

May, Henry F. "The Rebellion of the Intellectuals, 1912–1917." *American Quarterly* 8 (Summer 1956): 114–26.

"Messrs. Ward and Gow . . ." *New Republic* 5 (29 January 1916): 318–19.

Milner, Lucille B. "Freedom of Speech in Wartime." *New Republic* 103 (25 November 1940): 713–15.

Minor, Robert. "Pugilism in Excelsis" and "The New Joss": "A Cartoon That Made Its Creator Famous." *Current Literature* 53 (October 1912): 460.

Myers, Gustavus. "Why Idealists Quit the Socialist Party." *Nation* 104 (15 February 1917): 181–82.

"The New Poetry." *Seven Arts* 2 (May 1917): 119–20.

Oneal, James. "The Socialists in the War." *American Mercury* 10 (April 1927): 418–26.

O'Neill, Eugene G. "Tomorrow." *Seven Arts* 2 (June 1917): 147–70.

Oppenheim, James. "America." *Seven Arts* 1 (March 1917): 462–71.

———. "Art, Religion, and Science." *Seven Arts* 2 (June 1917): 229–34.

O[ppenheim], J[ames]. "The Creative Will." *Seven Arts* 1 (April 1917): 671–73.

———. "Editorials." *Seven Arts* 1 (December 1916): 152–56.

———. "Editorials." *Seven Arts* 1 (January 1917): 265–69.

———. "Editorials." *Seven Arts* 1 (February 1917): 390–94.

———. "Editorials." *Seven Arts* 1 (April 1917): 627–30.

———. "Editorials." *Seven Arts* 2 (May 1917): 68–71.

———. "Editorials." *Seven Arts* 2 (June 1917): 199–201.

———. "'Lazy' Verse." *Seven Arts* 1 (November 1916): 66–72.

———. "Memories of Whitman and Lincoln." *Seven Arts* 2 (May 1917): 3–7.

———. "Prelude (to 'Creation'—a Drama)." *Seven Arts* 1 (January 1917): 240–59.

———. "The Shadow in the White House." *Seven Arts* 2 (July 1917): 263–69.

———. "The Story of the *Seven Arts*." *American Mercury* 20 (June 1930): 156–64.

———. "The Strong Young Modern." *Seven Arts* 1 (December 1916): 193–95.

Ovington, Mary White. "How the National Association for the Advancement of Colored People Began." *Crisis* 8 (August 1914): 184–88.

Phillips, William L. "How Sherwood Anderson Wrote *Winesburg, Ohio*." *American Literature* 23 (March 1951): 7–30.

Poole, Ernest. "Why I Am No Longer a Pacifist." *McClure's* 49 (August 1917): 19, 67.

Quinlan, Patrick L. "The Paterson Strike and After." *New Review* 2 (January 1914): 26–33.

Reed, John. "The Rights of Small Nations." *New Republic* 5 (27 November 1915): 94–96.

Repplier, Agnes. "The Repeal of Reticence." *Atlantic Monthly* 113 (March 1914): 297–304.

Resek, Carl. "The New Radicalism." *Studies on the Left* 6 (January-February 1966): 64–69. Review of Christopher Lasch, *The New Radicalism in America 1889–1963: The Intellectual as a Social Type*.

Riegel, Robert E. "Changing American Attitudes toward Prostitution, 1800–1920." *Journal of the History of Ideas* 29 (July-September 1968): 437–52.

Robinson, William J., M.D. "The Prevention of Conception." *New Review* 3 (April 1915): 196–99.

Roosevelt, Theodore. "A Premium on Race Suicide." *Outlook* 105 (27 September 1913): 163–64.

Rosenberg, Charles E. "Sexuality, Class, and Role in Nineteenth-Century America." *American Quarterly* (May 1973): 131–53.

Rosenfeld, Paul. "Randolph Bourne." *Dial* 75 (December 1923): 545–60.

Scott, Alexander. "What the Reds are Doing in Paterson." *International Socialist Review* 13 (June 1913): 852–56.

"Sedition Laws and Juries." *Nation* 106 (11 May 1918): 562–63.

"The Seven Arts." *Seven Arts* 1 (November 1916): 52–56.

"Sex O'Clock in America." *Current Opinion* 55 (August 1913): 113–14.

Shannon, David A. "The Socialist Party before the First World War: An Analysis." *Mississippi Valley Historical Review* [later *Journal of American History*] 38 (September 1951): 279–88.

Sherwood Anderson Memorial Number. Newberry Library Bulletin, 2d ser. 2 (December 1948): 1–82.

Simonson, Lee. "The Painters' Ark." *Seven Arts* 2 (June 1917): 202–13.

Sinclair, Upton. "What Life Means to Me." *Cosmopolitan Magazine* 41 (October 1906): 591–95.

Smith, Daniel Scott. "Family Limitation, Sexual Control, and Domestic Feminism in Victorian America." *Feminist Studies* 1 (Winter-Spring 1973): 40–57.

Smith-Rosenberg, Carroll. "Puberty to Menopause: The Cycle of Femininity in Nineteenth-Century America." *Feminist Studies* 1 (Winter-Spring 1973): 58–72.

Sonnenberg, Martha. "Left Literary Notes: Masses Old and New." *Radical America* 3 (November 1969): 67–75.

Spargo, John. "Literature and Art." *International Socialist Review* 9 (April 1909): 814–18.

Stearns, Harold. "A Poor Thing, But Our Own." *Seven Arts* 1 (March 1917): 515–21.

Steffens, Lincoln. "Eugene V. Debs on What the Matter Is in America and What to Do About It."
   Everybody's Magazine 19 (October 1908): 455–69.
Taggard, Genevieve. " 'May Days.' " *Nation* 121 (30 September 1925): 353–56.
Untermeyer, Louis. "The Dance." *Seven Arts* 1 (November 1916): 79–82.
_____. "Growth and Decay in Recent Verse." *Seven Arts* 1 (April 1917): 668–71.
U[ntermeyer], L[ouis]. "Including Clement Wood." *Seven Arts* 2 (May 1917): 120.
_____. "Out of the Storm." *Seven Arts* 2 (July 1917): 278–79.
_____. "A Side Street." *Seven Arts* 1 (December 1916): 130–31.
_____. "The Wave." *Seven Arts* 1 (February 1917): 342–44.
Van Vechten, Carl. "Music and the Electrical Theatre." *Seven Arts* 2 (May 1917): 97–102.
Vorse, Mary Heaton. "An Adventure in Respectability." *Harper's Magazine* 135 (July 1917):
   210–20.
_____. "The Sinistrées of France." *Century Magazine* n.s. 71 (January 1917): 445–50.
"Votes for Women." *Crisis* 8 (August 1914): 179–80.
Wallace, M. G. "Constitutionality of Sedition Laws." *Virginia Law Review* 6 (March 1920):
   385–99.
Walling, William English. "Industrialism or Revolutionary Unionism." *New Review* 1 (11
   January 1913): 45–51.
_____. "Industrialism vs. Syndicalism." *International Socialist Review* 13 (March 1913):
   666–67.
_____. "The Race War in the North." *Independent* 65 (3 September 1908): 529–34.
"What Haywood Says on Political Action." *International Socialist Review* 13 (February 1913):
   622.
Wood, Clement. "Prelude." *Seven Arts* 1 (December 1916): 132.
Wyman, Margaret. "The Rise of the Fallen Woman." *American Quarterly* 3 (Summer 1951):
   167–77.
Yeats, John Butler. "John Sloan's Exhibition." *Seven Arts* 2 (June 1917): 257–59.
"The Younger Generation." *Dial* 57 (1 November 1914): 323–24.
Zaretsky, Eli. "Capitalism, the Family, and Personal Life: Part 1." *Socialist Revolution* 3
   (January-April 1973): 69–125.
_____. "Capitalism, the Family, and Personal Life: Part 2." *Socialist Revolution* 3 (May-June
   1973): 19–70.

Index

Aaron, Daniel, 183
Abbott, Leonard, 107
Alienation, 66–70, 74
American Federation of Labor, 100, 161, 167, 207
Anarchism, 64, 82, 101, 102, 108, 120, 190
Anarchists, 4, 18, 22, 26, 30, 63, 69, 74, 76, 82, 99, 124, 190, 194, 205
Anderson, Cornelia, 16
Anderson, Margaret, 16, 190; *The Little Review*, 16
Anderson, Sherwood, 16, 32, 36–37, 40, 82, 196, 207; on need for vulgarity in art, 53; on alienation, 71–72; on new sexual frankness, 74–75; on failure of church to make Christianity meaningful, 117; on art and family responsibilities, 196–97; works: *Marching Men*, 53, 71; *Windy McPherson's Son*, 53, 117, 193
Antiwar activities, 24, 26, 31, 206
Antiwar propaganda, 16, 24, 28, 186
Armory Show of 1913, 31
Art, 4, 16, 17, 18, 22, 30, 34, 35, 54, 55, 58, 60, 62, 129, 130, 134, 163, 165, 182–92, 193, 194, 195, 196, 197, 199, 202, 204, 205–6, 207; impact of new American culture, 51–53
Art for art's sake, 52, 66, 182, 187, 191
Artists, 3, 4, 13, 15, 16, 17, 18, 31, 36, 52, 53, 55, 58, 60, 65, 84, 129, 164, 165, 168, 184, 185, 187, 188, 193, 195, 196, 198, 206; Freudian view of, 5–6; *Masses'* artists' revolt of 1916, 21–22, 24; artistic legacy of *The Masses*, 29
Ash Can School, 31

Ashley, Jessie: role in birth control campaign, 107–8
Associated Press: lawsuit against *The Masses*, 20–21
Associated Press vs. *Max Eastman and Art Young* (1913–14), 20–21
Atlantic Monthly, 137

Bachofen, Johann Jakob: *Mutterrecht*, 94
Baker, Ray Stannard, 182; exposé of Trinity Church, 114; on growth of religion while church decays, 114, 116
Balzac, Honoré: *Un Prince de Bohème*, 59
Banks, Charles Eugene: *In Hampton Roads*, 128
Barber, John, 24
Barnes, Earl, 26, 28
Beard, Charles, 167
Bebel, August, 38
Becker, Maurice, 168; role in 1916 *Masses'* artists' revolt, 22, 24; "Their Last Supper," 114
Bell, Josephine, 25–26
Bellamy, Edward, 9; *Looking Backward*, 9
Bellows, George, 187; "This Man Subjected Himself to Imprisonment . . . ," 187
Beresford, J. D., 196; *These Riese Lynnekers*, 103
Berger, Victor, 15
Bergson, Henri, 36, 58; influence on new radicals, 38–39
Berkman, Alexander, 26, 137, 194; on criminals, 176; on revolutionary poetry, 190
Birth control, 5, 7, 8, 12, 18, 34, 35, 39, 60, 63, 64, 78, 87, 102, 103–4, 106–11, 126,

140, 157, 206. *See also* Contraception;
Family limitation
Bisexuality, 40
Blacks, 48, 160–67, 174, 176, 178, 191, 199;
Claude McKay, 13, 199; visit to Mabel
Dodge's salon, 45, 163
Blatch, Harriot Stanton, 168
Bligh, S. M., 92
Bohemia, 4, 5, 6, 12, 42, 50, 70, 133, 215,
226 (n. 61); Greenwich Village as, 59–66
Bohemianism, 6, 12, 18, 22, 59, 60, 66, 98,
185, 187, 193, 195, 196, 199, 202, 204,
206, 207; Max Eastman's response to com-
munist charges of, 62–63; Joseph Freeman
on, 63
Bohemians, 3, 4, 54, 60, 74, 75, 112, 168,
183, 187, 191, 202, 204
Bohn, Frank, 158
Bolshevik Revolution, 161, 183, 186,
193–94, 203, 204, 205, 206, 207
Bolsheviks, 111, 206
Bolshevism, 28, 196, 204, 206
Boulton, Agnes, 37, 130
Bourne, Randolph, 6, 32, 36, 40, 65, 87, 97,
140, 147, 186, 189, 202; father, 9; family
life, 9, 13; on puritanism, 35–36; on cultural nationalism, 48, 50; on transnational
culture, 51; on American art, 51–52; apostle
of cult of youth, 55, 57; experience with
psychoanalysis, 91–92; on Freudianism, 93;
on religion, 121; on Christianity and
socialism, 123–24; on feminism, 137–38;
on immigrant families, 170; on immigrants
and transnational culture, 173; on radical
art, 188; works: "The War and the Intellectuals," 16; "Our Cultural Humility," 50
Boyce, Neith, 48 (wife of Hutchins Hapgood),
79, 97, 129, 131, 137; works: *Constancy*,
64; *Enemies* (with Hutchins Hapgood), 92
Brady, Edward, 194
Brill, Abraham A., 84, 85, 90
Brisbane, Arthur, 20
Brook Farm, 71, 216 (n. 65)
Brooks, Van Wyck, 38, 39–40, 44, 51, 60, 66;
America's Coming-of-Age, 39
Brown, Robert Carlton: role in 1916 *Masses'*
artists' revolt, 22, 24
Bruere, Robert, 167
Bryant, Louise, 79; *The Game*, 78

Bullard, Arthur, 60; *A Man's World*, 73; on
social work in slums, 73
Burleson, Albert, 28
Burns, John, 195
Butler, Samuel, 126

Cahan, Abraham: works: *The Rise of David
Levinsky*, 128, 171; *Yekl*, 172
Calhoun, Arthur W., 55
Capitalism, 32, 41, 63, 69, 100, 110, 113,
157, 158
Carpenter, Edward: on free love and feminism,
94–95; *Love's Coming-of-Age*, 132
Carson, William E.: *The Marriage Revolt*, 35,
100, 132
Cary, Lucian, 88
Catholicism, 60; Margaret Sanger's father's
opposition to, 8; Elizabeth Gurley Flynn
baptized a Catholic, 13; Elizabeth Gurley
Flynn's father a Catholic, 14; Catholic
church denounced as foe of socialism, 114
Chamberlain, K. R.: "Afterwards," 143
Chapin, Anna Alice, 66; on morality of
Greenwich Village inhabitants, 59–60
Chaplin, Ralph, 198
Cheney, E. Ralph, 187
Chicago Evening Post, 54
Chicago Renaissance, 50
Christ, Jesus, 37, 41, 42, 114, 116, 119, 121,
122–26, 178
Christianity, 37, 38, 41, 45, 113, 114,
116–26, 178
Church, 7, 13, 14, 87, 113, 114, 116–19,
121, 123–26
Churchill, Winston, 182
Claflin, Tennessee, 94, 152
Clark University Conference of 1909, 83–84,
199
Cleghorn, Sarah N., 140
Cocaine, 45, 48
Coleman, Glenn: role in 1916 *Masses'* artists'
revolt, 22, 24
Columbia University, 18, 45, 51
Commercial Advertiser, 172
Communism, 42, 62, 63, 67, 100, 158, 196,
199, 201, 202, 203, 204, 205, 207
Communist party, 64, 87, 165, 188, 204, 205,
206, 207
Communists, 29, 62, 207

Comrade, The, 16–17

Comstock, Anthony, 32, 34, 107, 124; "MORALS, Not Art or Literature," 32

Conlin, Joseph R., 198

Contraception, 34, 104, 106, 108, 109, 110, 141. *See also* Birth control; Family limitation

Cook, George Cram, 6, 37, 44, 61, 66, 72, 79, 203, 216 (n. 59); founder of Provincetown Players, 54; on bucolic ideal, 71; use of theater as "a laboratory of human emotions," 92; on Christianity, 121; on Yiddish theater, 172; works: *Suppressed Desires* (with Susan Glaspell), 64, 92; *In Hampton Roads*, 128

Cooperative-store movement, 17

Cowley, Malcolm, 70, 204; *Exile's Return*, 65

Craftsman, The, 52

Craftsmanship, 66, 67

Craig, Gordon, 97

Creel, George, 24

Crime, 174–76, 179–80

Criminals, 125, 126, 174–81

Crisis, The, 162

Croly, Herbert, 67

Cult of youth, 55, 57–58, 126

Current Literature, 120, 165

Currey, Margery, 16, 98

Daily Worker, 204

Dance, 30, 37, 40, 44–45, 54, 55, 121, 194

Darrow, Clarence, 16, 118, 153; on criminals and jail, 175–76

Darwin, Charles, 117

Davis, Stuart, 187; role in 1916 *Masses'* artists' revolt, 22, 24; cartoons of blacks, 165

Debs, Eugene V., 16, 100, 101; influence of mother, 11; on women's suffrage, 11; Christianized socialist movement, 122; on Christ, 124; on Socialist party and black question, 160–61; on criminals, 174, 176

Deland, Margaret: on new woman, 137

Dell, Floyd, 6, 16, 17, 18, 21, 31, 34, 35, 40, 54, 61, 67, 78, 79, 84, 87, 129, 135, 136, 166, 182, 183, 184, 185, 186, 197, 202, 203, 205, 216 (n. 59), 217 (n. 40), 218 (n. 75), 219 (n. 82); use of psychoanalysis, 5; father, 10–11; family life, 10–11, 13; move to Greenwich Village, 12; role in 1916

Masses' artists' revolt, 22; role in *Masses'* Espionage Act cases, 25–26, 28; on paganism, 42, 44; on Greenwich Villagers, 60; on Village sanctions on free-love alliances, 64; on demise of old Greenwich Village, 65; on alienation, 68; on bucolic ideal, 70–71; on legitimacy of female sexual drive, 81; popularization of Freudian doctrine, 85–86; on psychoanalysis and Freudianism, 88–89, 92; on Freudianism and free love, 96–97; on free love, 97, 98–99; on artist's need to be free of family responsibilities, 102–3; religious background, 118; religiosity, 120; on Christ as radical, 126; on women as maternal creatures, 127; on dream-girl, 130; celebration of motherhood, 133–34; on feminism, 138–39, 144–46; on prostitution, 158; review of James Weldon Johnson's poetry, 164; on criminality, 179, 180; on need for radicals to control mass media, 189–90; on life-style and radicalism, 195–96, 199, 201; refusal to join a communist party, 205; retreat from radicalism, 206; works: *Homecoming: An Autobiography*, 10, 86; *Women as World Builders*, 31, 138–39, 144, 146; *Runaway*, 42; "A Psycho-Analytic Confession," 42, 44, 201; *The Briary-Bush*, 42, 97, 145, 196; *This Mad Ideal*, 62; *Love in the Machine Age*, 68, 89, 133–34, 145–46, 201; *The Angel Intrudes*, 92; *King Arthur's Socks*, 92; "Babes in the Wood," 98; "The Perfect Husband," 98; *Janet March*, 98–99, 145; *Souvenir*, 130, 145; "St. George of the Minute: A Comedy of Feminism," 141; "Cynthia," 144; *Love Without Money*, 145; *The Golden Spike*, 179; "Keep Your Eyes on the Sidewalk," 179

Deutsch, Helen, 92

Dewey, John: on alienation, 67; influence on sexual stereotyping of work, 128, 135; works: "In a Time of National Hesitation," 50; *Democracy and Education*, 67

Divorce, 101–2

Dodge, Edwin, 83

Dodge, Mabel, 6, 31, 37, 61, 64, 65, 78, 84, 88, 120, 129, 133, 134, 202; blacks' visit to her salon, 45, 163; peyote party at her salon,

48; salon at 23 Fifth Avenue, 63; on own homosexual tendencies, 82–83; *Intimate Memories*, 83, 131; introduction of Freudianism to Greenwich Village, 85; as exemplar of feminine cult of love, 131; retreat from radicalism, 205–6. *See also* Luhan, Mabel Dodge

Dorr, Rheta Childe, 140, 142, 146

Dos Passos, John, 204

Dostoevski, Feodor, 38

Drama, 163; Harold Stearns on drama as cultural agent, 53; little theater movement, 54. *See also* Little theater; Theater

Dreiser, Theodore, 30, 60, 192, 196; on puritanism, 34–35; *Sister Carrie*, 152

Drinnon, Richard, 183

Drugs: Carl Van Vechten's experimentation with, 45, 48

Du Bois, W. E. B., 21, 161; on blacks and socialism, 161; on racism in American military, 162; on black desire not to be written about by whites, 164

Du Maurier, George: *Trilby*, 59

Dunbar, Paul Laurence, 164

Duncan, Isadora, 6, 37, 40, 55, 82, 89, 97–98, 117, 129, 131; as pagan symbol, 44–45; on religiosity, 120–21; on art and sublimation, 194

Dutch Treat Club, 202

Eastman, Annis Ford, 9; influence on Max Eastman's feminism, 12–13; religious doubts, 13, 117

Eastman, Crystal, 229 (n. 182); on women's suffrage and pacifism, 156–58

Eastman, Max, 6, 17, 18, 21, 31, 36, 60, 71, 78, 79, 82, 86, 87, 102, 107, 114, 116, 125, 180, 183, 184, 185, 186, 191, 197, 205, 206, 210 (n. 23), 216 (n. 59), 235 (n. 13); use of psychoanalysis, 5, 84; mother, 9; family life, 9, 13; maternal influence on his feminism, 12–13; role in Associated Press lawsuit, 20; role in 1916 *Masses'* artists' revolt, 21–22; role in *Masses'* Espionage Act trials, 25–26, 28; *Liberator* editorship, 29; on Isadora Duncan, 44; response to charges of bohemianism by communists, 62; on bucolic ideal, 70–71; popularizer of Freudianism, 85; on psychoanalysis, 90; Freudian interpretation of war, 90–91; on free love, 97–99; religious background, 117; on socialism and religion, 122; on prostitution, 154; on Stuart Davis's cartoons of blacks, 165; call for black power, 166; on criminality, 181; on "mere Bohemianism," 187; on John Reed, 202–3; works: *Enjoyment of Living*, 18; "The Worst Trust," 20; *Journalism versus Art*, 21, 170; *Venture*, 38, 70, 120; *Understanding Germany*, 90; "War Psychology and International Socialism," 90; *Great Companions*, 91; "Child of the Amazons," 137; "Confession of a Suffrage Orator," 141

Edwards, Bobby, 85

Eliot, Charles W., 76

Eliot, T. S., 31

Ellis, Edith, 101

Ellis, Fred, 192

Ellis, Havelock, 38, 101, 106; influence on new radicals, 39; *The Psychology of Sex*, 39; on sexual liberation, 77–78; influence on Margaret Sanger, 78

Emerson, Ralph Waldo, 48, 51, 190

Engels, Friedrich, 111, 187; on alienation, 66–67; works: *Anti-Dühring*, 66, 86; *The Origin of the Family, Private Property, and the State*, 94, 100

Espionage Act of 1917, 24, 28–29

Eugenics, 35

Everybody's Magazine, 85

Fagnan, Charles P., 125

Family, 39, 68, 74, 78, 79, 82, 87, 99–100, 101, 102, 103, 104, 108, 110, 131, 132, 133, 137, 144, 145, 146–48, 152, 195, 206; Freud's support for traditional family, 5; family life of *The Masses'* radicals, 7–14

Family limitation, 104, 106–7, 109, 111. *See also* Birth control; Contraception

Fangel, Henry, 164

Faulkner, Harold U., 142

Fawcett, Edgar: *The Evil That Men Do*, 152

Federal Writers' Project, 206

Feldman, Egal, 150

Feminism, 11, 12, 16, 64, 79, 81, 94, 95, 102, 103, 104, 127–59 passim, 229 (n. 182)

Feminists, 3, 4, 5, 30, 31, 39, 40, 75, 77, 94, 101, 102, 104, 107, 136, 138–40, 146–48, 149, 150, 152, 229 (n. 182)

Fineshriber, William, 120, 199, 201

Fitzgerald, Richard, 205
Flynn, Elizabeth Gurley, 129, 137, 158; family life, 9; mother, 11; on vitality of immigrant cultures, 172–73
Forward (*Jewish Daily Forward*), 172
Frank, Waldo, 50, 188
Free love, 5, 18, 31, 69, 78, 81, 94–99, 100, 101, 104, 111, 113, 124, 131–32, 145, 206
Freeman, Joseph, 79, 89, 182, 189–90, 206, 207; family life, 8; father, 8; on Greenwich Village cult of youth, 62; on bohemianism, 63; on immigrant families, 170–71; on bohemianism and radicalism, 202, 204
Free thought, 13, 117, 124
Freud, Sigmund, 3, 5, 10, 31, 38, 63, 79, 83, 87, 88, 90, 91, 94, 96, 106, 111, 113, 127, 155, 195; at Clark University Conference of 1909, 83–84; dialogue with Max Eastman on causes of World War I, 90–91; on art and neurosis, 199; works: *Leonardo da Vinci*, 41; "Thoughts for the Times on War and Death," 90; *The Interpretation of Dreams*, 91; *Civilization and Its Discontents*, 199
Freudianism, 5, 7, 62, 63, 64, 65, 68, 79, 83–93, 94, 97, 111, 113, 127, 149, 151, 153, 185, 190, 196, 199, 201, 206, 218 (n. 75), 218 (n. 77)
Freudians, 3, 5, 30, 31, 77, 88, 90, 181, 185, 193, 218 (n. 77)
Frick, Henry Clay, 176
Friedan, Betty: *The Feminine Mystique*, 132

Gage, B. Marie, 44, 97, 130
Gellert, Hugo, 192
Genteel tradition, 15, 30, 31, 32, 39, 45, 51, 52, 53, 173
George, Henry, 8
Ghent, William J., 15, 183
Gilman, Charlotte Perkins, 20, 149, 157; *Women and Economics*, 142–43, 147–48
Gilmore, Inez Haynes, 60
Giovannitti, Arturo, 21, 182; "The Bum," 180
Glaspell, Susan, 60, 61, 66, 69, 79, 129, 137, 148, 172, 207; works: *Suppressed Desires* (with George Cram Cook), 64, 92; *The Visioning*, 75; *The Glory of the Conquered*, 129–30, 147; *Fidelity*, 147
Glintenkamp, Henry J.: role in 1916 *Masses*' artists' revolt, 22
Gogol, Nikolai, 38

Gold, Mike, 29, 63, 182, 191, 192, 207; criticism of Carl Van Vechten's patronage of black intellectuals. *See also* Granich, Irwin
Goldman, Emma, 6, 26, 37, 40, 63, 67, 68, 75, 102, 111, 129, 131, 137, 141; on sex education, 77; on homosexuality, 82; "Love and Marriage," 109; role in birth control campaign, 109; attack on Christianity, 119–20; on new woman, 139–40; on feminism, 149–50; on prostitution, 155; on criminals, 174; on prisons, 175; on revolutionary poetry, 190–91; on life-style and radicalism, 194, 204
Gompers, Samuel, 100
Good Housekeeping, 164
Gorky, Maxim, 16
Grand Street Players, 172
Granich, Irwin, 63. *See also* Gold, Mike
Greenwich House, 60
Greenwich Village, 4, 6, 7, 12, 14, 45, 46, 84, 85, 89, 108, 120, 128, 136, 137, 139, 140, 145, 148–49, 156, 159, 162, 168, 170, 172, 187, 189, 193, 204, 205, 216 (n. 59), 226 (n. 61); as bohemian community, 59–66; as locus for study of problems of urbanization and industrialization, 66–70; anti-urban tone of, 70–71. *See also* Villagers
Griffith, D. W.: *Birth of a Nation*, 166
Gropper, William, 192
Gurdjieff, George Ivanovich, 65

Hahn, Emily, 98
Hale, Jr., Nathan, 88
Hall, Bolton, 108
Hall, G. Stanley, 84
Hanau, Stella, 92
Hand, Augustus, 25–26
Hapgood, Emilie, 163
Hapgood, Hutchins, 6, 30, 48, 78, 79, 183, 199; family life, 8–9; father, 8–9; on puritanism, 34; influence of Walt Whitman on, 40–41; on work alienation, 67–69; on free love, 97, 99; religious background, 117–18; on religious temperament of anarchists, 120; on Christ's charity to criminals, 126; on prostitution, 154–55; failure to persuade W. E. B. Du Bois to introduce him to blacks, 164; celebration of lower classes, 168, 170; on criminals, 177–78; on life-

style and radicalism, 197–98; works: *Enemies* (with Neith Boyce), 92; *Types from City Streets*, 168–69; *The Spirit of the Ghetto*, 172; *An Anarchist Woman*, 177; *The Spirit of Labor*, 180; *A Victorian in the Modern World*, 197
Harlem, 45, 161, 162, 163, 178
Harlem Renaissance, 162, 166–67
Harriman, Job, 123
Harrington, Raymond, 48
Harvard University, 76
Havel, Hippolyte, 22
Haywood, William D. (Big Bill), 64, 107, 158, 161, 180, 189; religious background, 118–19; family life and radicalism, 198
Hearst, William Randolph, 15
Heine, Heinrich, 16
Henle, James: on prostitution, 153–54; "Nobody's Sister," 153–54
Henri, Robert, 52, 55
Heroin, 45
Herron, George D., 15
Hicks, Granville, 202, 204
Hill, Joe, 189
Hillquit, Morris, 15, 25, 100, 101, 121, 167
Hinkle, Beatrice, 90
Hoffman, Frederick, 92, 219 (n. 82)
Holmes, John Haynes, 20, 162; future of Christianity, 123; on criminals, 174
Homosexuality, 82–83, 88, 145, 217 (n. 40)
Howells, William Dean: *The Coast of Bohemia*, 59
Humphrey, Robert E.: *Children of Fantasy*, 6
Hunter, Robert, 15

Ibsen, Henrik, 126
Imagists, 190
Imago, 91
Immigrants, 167, 168, 170, 172–73, 174, 176
Independent movement, 30
Industrial Workers of the World (IWW), 18, 31, 64, 69–70, 89, 106, 113, 158, 161, 187, 189, 197, 206. See also Wobblies
Ingersoll, Robert, 8, 117, 124, 126, 178
International Socialist Review, 17

James, Henry, 51
James, William, 36, 51
Jazz, 45
Jelliffe, Smith Ely, 84, 88, 90

Jewish Daily Forward, 172
Jewish heritage, 8
Jews, 122, 163, 168, 171, 172
Johnson, James Weldon: on black poetry, 164
Jones, Ernest, 91
Jones, Mary (Mother Jones), 16, 20
Jones, Robert Edmond, 163
Journal of Abnormal Psychology, 84
Judaism, 120, 122
Jung, Carl, 84, 88; *Psychology of the Unconscious*, 86

Kallen, Horace, 173
Kanter, Rosabeth Moss: *Commitment and Community*, 64, 215 (n. 13)
Karsner, David, 138
Kautsky, Karl, 187
Kazin, Alfred: *On Native Grounds*, 50
Keller, Helen, 15, 140
Kelley, Florence, 161
Kemp, Harry, 40, 99, 102, 120, 180; on Christ as "divine hobo," 125–26; on prostitution, 153; on criminals, 178; on life-style and radicalism, 201–2; works: *More Miles*, 62, 97; "Impenitence," 126; "The Painted Lady," 153; *Tramping on Life: An Autobiographical Narrative*, 178
Kent, Rockwell, 192
Kerr, Charles H., 17; *International Socialist Review*, 17
Key, Ellen, 101, 103; on free love and the cult of motherhood, 94–95; *Love and Marriage*, 132–33
Kimbrough, Mary Craig, 195
Kindergarten movement, 7
Kipnis, Ira, 158, 160
Knights of Labor, 8
Knopf, Alfred A., 195
Kropotkin, Pyotr Alekseyevich, 71, 92
Kuttner, Alfred Booth: debate over art and neurosis, 5–6; popularization of Freudian theory, 91

Labor Herald, The, 207
Labor movement, 51, 161, 197, 203, 207
Lasch, Christopher, 3, 146, 176
Lawrence, D. H., 196
Lawrence strike, 189, 203
Lee, Algernon, 15
Lenin, Vladimir Ilyich, 207

Lesbianism, 82
Lewis, Lena Morrow, 146, 147
Lewis, Sinclair: "Hobohemia," 64–65
Liberal Club, 63, 88, 168
Liberator, The, 25, 29, 42, 186, 187, 191, 205, 207
Life, 16, 74
Lindsey, Ben, 76
Lippmann, Walter, 21, 37, 64, 85, 118, 138, 188, 206; on syndicalism, 69; on Freudianism, 91, 93; on women's suffrage, 140–41; on prostitution, 155; works: *A Preface to Politics*, 34, 69, 91, 155; *Drift and Mastery*, 51, 135
Little magazines, 15, 16, 50, 53, 183
Little Red Song Book, The, 189
Little Renaissance, 30, 31, 205
Little Review, The, 16
Little theater, 30, 37, 163, 189
Lombroso, Caesare, 174
London, Jack, 16, 38, 180, 182
Los Angeles Times building, 123
Lowell, Carlotta Russell, 165
Lower East Side, 106, 167, 168, 171, 172, 197
Luhan, Mabel Dodge, 34. *See also* Dodge, Mabel

McKay, Claude, 118, 165, 180; youthful free thinking, 13; on paganism of Isadora Duncan, 44–45; friendship with criminal, 178; on proletarian art, 191; on Bolshevik Revolution and his poetry, 199
McNamara, J. B., 123–24
McNamara, J. J., 123–24
Magazine Distributing Company, 21
Malone, Dudley Field, 25
Mann Act of 1910, 151
Markham, Edward, 16
Marx, Karl, 3, 10, 31, 58, 87, 88, 111, 113, 144, 155, 187, 195; on alienation, 66–67; on family life, 100–101; works: 1844 Manuscripts, 66; *The Communist Manifesto*, 100
Marxism, 11, 28, 66–67, 68, 86, 87, 88, 89, 90, 93, 100–101, 113, 167, 182, 184, 188, 196, 198, 201, 204, 207, 218 (n. 75), 218 (n. 77)
Marxists, 5, 53, 106, 154, 158, 183, 185, 193, 202, 206, 207, 218 (n. 77)

Masses, The, 3, 4, 5, 7, 11, 12, 13, 14, 15, 16, 41, 50, 62, 63, 65, 69, 70, 79, 81, 82, 85, 87, 90, 95, 96, 103, 107, 110, 111, 114, 119, 120, 122, 123, 125, 130, 135, 136, 143, 153, 154, 157, 158, 165, 166, 167, 168, 170, 182, 183, 184, 187, 203, 204, 206, 207, 210 (n. 23), 216 (n. 59); history of the magazine, 17–29; 1916 *Masses*' artists' revolt, 21–22, 24; antiwar activities and propaganda, 24–26, 28–29; *Masses*' Espionage Act trials, 24–26, 28–29
Masses Book Shop, *The*, 38, 81
Masses' radicals, *The*, 5, 38, 52, 61–62, 63, 78, 87, 88, 95, 96, 97, 99, 103, 111, 114, 117, 125, 128, 133, 143, 144, 178, 181, 183, 184, 187, 193, 202, 204, 206, 207, 208; family life of, 7–14; antiwar activities of, 24–26, 28–29
Masses Review, The, 21
Matthews, F. H., 185
Meisel-Hess, Grete: *The Sexual Crisis*, 96
Mencken, H. L., 30, 36, 212 (n. 11); *A Book of Prefaces*, 32
Messenger, The, 161
Metropolitan, The, 16
Mexican Revolution, 16, 177–78
Milholland, Inez, 20
Millay, Edna St. Vincent, 98
Minor, Robert, 24, 63, 183, 187; family life, 8, 12, 16; religious background, 14; on criminals, 174–75; abandonment of art to become Communist party functionary and political agitator, 188, 204, 207; on art as a weapon in the class struggle, 191–92; works: "PUGILISM IN EXCELSIS: The Grinning Negro as He Appears to Robert Minor," 165; "The Sifter," 174–75; "No Individual Criminal Has Ever Equaled the Crime Committed on Men by Prisons Themselves," 175
Modern Monthly, The, 29
Morgan, Lewis H.: *Ancient Society*, 94
Morris, William, 66
Mother Earth, 119
Muckraking, 8, 17, 182
Munsterberg, Hugo, 85
Murger, Henry: *Scènes de la vie de Bohème*, 59
Murray, Gilbert, 42

Nast, Thomas, 16
National Association for the Advancement of
  Colored People (NAACP), 161–62, 166
National Socialist Association, 146
New Masses, The, 29, 192, 207
New Republic, The, 21, 51, 107
New Review, The, 21
New woman, 95, 132, 137–39, 143, 144,
  147, 171, 194
New York Call, The, 106, 175, 188
New Yorker, The, 29
New York Evening Journal, The, 20
New York Evening Post, The, 15, 172
New York Exhibition of Independent Artists,
  52
New York Journal, The, 15
New York Times, The, 15, 107
New York World, The, 188
Nietzsche, Friedrich, 31, 48, 58, 118, 188;
  influence on new radicals, 36–39; works:
  The Birth of Tragedy, 36; *Thus Spake
  Zarathustra*, 36, 37; *Anti-Christ*, 38
Norris, Frank, 182, 196
North, Joseph, 191

O'Brien, Joe, 197, 203
O'Carroll, Wild Joe, 180
O'Hare, Kate Richards, 158
Older, Fremont, 203
O'Neill, Eugene, 37, 51, 207; on dream-girl,
  130; *Emperor Jones*, 163
O'Neill, William L., 30, 101; *Divorce in the
  Progressive Era*, 79
Onslow, Genevieve, 48
Oppenheim, James, 55, 88, 185; use of
  psychoanalysis, 5; debate over art and
  neurosis, 5–6; on need for vulgarity in art,
  52–53; on need for sex education, 76; on
  popular art, 188–89; works: "America,"
  50–51; *The Nine-Tenths*, 53; *Wild Oats*, 76;
  The Pioneers, 137; "Bread and Roses," 189
Others Group, 30
Ovington, Mary White: on de facto segregation of NAACP executive board, 161–62

Paganism, 32, 35, 36, 40, 58, 65, 96, 117,
  145, 162; influence on new radicals, 41–42,
  44–45, 48
Pankhurst, Sylvia, 40

Parsons, Elsie Clews, 107; "Privacy in Love
  Affairs," 79, 81
Partisan Review, The, 192
Paterson Pageant, 31, 187, 202
Paterson strike, 186
Patterson, Joseph Medill, 15
Peyote: use by Carl Van Vechten, 48; peyote
  party at Mabel Dodge's salon, 48
Phillips, David Graham, 182; *Susan Lenox:
  Her Fall and Rise*, 152
Phrenology, 84
Pinchot, Amos, 20
Poe, Edgar Allan, 59, 84
Poole, Ernest, 87; mother, 11; family life,
  11–12, 13; *The Harbor*, 38
Populism, 8
Post, Robert, 186
Pound, Ezra, 31
Proletarian literature, 29
Proletarian realism, 62
Prostitution, 72, 74, 96, 100, 101, 140, 142,
  144, 145, 150–55, 177
Protestant ethic, 9
Protestantism, 41
Provincetown, 61, 69, 71, 92, 108, 128, 130,
  131, 135
Provincetown Players, 37, 54, 55, 92, 163,
  172
Psychoanalysis, 5, 44, 62, 63, 65, 66, 78,
  83–93 passim, 94, 111, 127, 183, 186, 195,
  199, 201, 217 (n. 40), 219 (n. 82)
Psycho-Analytic Review, The, 85
Puritanism, 5, 31–32, 34–36, 40, 41, 42, 44,
  50, 51, 58, 64–66, 87, 93, 104, 118, 120,
  121, 137, 162, 168, 171, 202, 206

Quill, The, 85

Race suicide, 104
Racism, 160–62, 163, 165
Radicalism, 13, 31, 52, 65, 93, 94, 113, 167,
  182, 184, 188, 190, 193, 194, 195, 198,
  201, 202, 203; Randolph Bourne on
  radicalism of youth, 55, 57
Radicals, 3, 5, 6, 7, 11, 12, 13, 14, 15, 17,
  24, 28, 30, 31, 32, 35, 38, 39, 40, 41, 42,
  48, 55, 58, 62, 63, 65, 66, 67, 68, 70, 73,
  77, 79, 84, 87, 90, 91, 92, 93, 94, 95, 96,
  97, 99, 101, 102, 103, 106, 107, 108, 111,

112, 113, 114, 116, 117, 124, 126, 127, 128, 134, 135, 137, 139, 144, 146, 150, 151, 153, 154, 155, 156, 157, 160, 162, 163, 164, 165, 166, 168, 171, 173, 174, 175, 176, 177, 178, 179, 180, 182, 183, 184, 185, 186, 187, 188, 189, 190, 191, 192, 193, 194, 195, 199, 202, 203, 204, 205, 206, 207

Randolph, A. Philip, 161

Rand School of Social Science, 17, 167

Rankin, Jeanette, 134

Rauh, Ida, 73, 79; role in birth control campaign, 107–8

Rauschenbusch, Walter: on Social Gospel, 113–14

Reed, John, 6, 16, 31, 63, 64, 70, 78, 79, 87, 97, 107, 120, 131, 180, 182–83, 186, 187, 192, 204, 235 (n. 13); role in second *Masses'* Espionage Act trial, 26, 28; resignation from *The Liberator*, 29, 207; on alienation and worker control, 70; on prostitution, 154; on ex-outlaws in Mexican Revolution, 177–78; urged Hutchins Hapgood to go to Russia, 197–98; on art and radicalism, 202–3; as revolutionary, 205–6; inability to succumb to Bolshevik political discipline, 206–7; works: *The Day in Bohemia, or Life Among the Artists*, 60, 64; "The Rights of Small Nations," 138; "A Daughter of the Revolution," 154; "Where the Heart Is," 154

Reedy, William Marion, 74, 216 (n. 5)

Religion, 14, 36, 39, 91, 113–14, 116–26; parental encouragement of free thinking, 13

Republicanism, 8, 117

Republican party, 8

Resek, Carl, 9, 188

Revolutionary Age, The, 70

Rideout, Walter B., 117

Robinson, Boardman, 16, 24, 192, 205, 206; mother, 11

Robinson, William J.: role in birth control campaign, 109–11

Rockefeller Vice Investigation, 197

Rodman, Henrietta, 148–49, 157, 229 (n. 182)

Roe, Gilbert, 20, 107

Rogers, Merrill, 24, 25, 28

Roosevelt, Theodore, 106

Royce, Josiah, 51

Ruskin, John, 66

Russell, Charles Edward, 15, 161; family life, 8; father, 8

Russian Revolution. *See* Bolshevik Revolution

Sabotage, 184

St. Louis Declaration of 1917 of Socialist party, 28

St. Louis *Mirror*, 216 (n. 5)

St. Louis Post-Dispatch, 191

Sandburg, Carl, 66, 207; "To Billy Sunday," 116

Sanger, Margaret, 6, 12, 37, 126, 129, 216 (n. 59); father, 7; family life, 13; influence of Havelock Ellis, 39, 78; on adolescent girls' love for one another, 82; birth control campaign, 106–11; *Woman Rebel*, 106, 107

Sanger, William, 12

Santayana, George, 39, 51

Saturday Evening Post, The, 64

Schoonmaker, Edwin Davies, 116

Schreiner, Olive, 103, 134; *Women and Labour*, 77

Schroeder, Theodore, 107

Seltzer, Thomas, 187

Seroff, Victor, 97

Seven Arts, The, 52; debate over art and neurosis, 5–6; editorial intention, 16; cultural nationalist mission, 50–51

Sex education, 76–77, 151

Sexual freedom, 35, 39, 95, 159. *See also* Free love; Sexual liberation; Sexual revolution

Sexuality, 32, 35, 39, 40, 78, 95, 106

Sexual liberation, 40, 94, 156. *See also* Free love; Sexual freedom; Sexual revolution

Sexual revolution, 74–79, 81–83, 87, 111, 195. *See also* Free love; Sexual freedom; Sexual liberation

Shaw, George Bernard, 35, 38, 39, 120, 196; *Getting Married*, 82, 146

Sidis, Boris: "The Psychopathology of Everyday Life," 84

Simkhovitch, Mary, 60

Sinclair, Upton, 15, 16, 20–21, 36, 89–90, 98, 107, 134, 182, 196, 197; alcoholism of father, 7; family poverty, 7; hatred of urban vice, 72; need for artist to be free of family

responsibility, 102; religious background, 118; on women's economic liberation, 142; on crime, 174, 180–81; on life-style and radicalism, 194–95, 198–99; works: *The Brass Check*, 20–21; *The Jungle*, 68, 180–81; *The Metropolis*, 72; *Love's Pilgrimage*, 102, 194–95; *The Cry for Justice*, 116; *The Journal of Arthur Stirling*, 198
Sloan, John, 6, 18, 52, 60, 87, 165, 203; father, 7; family life, 7–8, 13; role in 1916 *Masses'* artists' revolt, 22, 24; "Piddlin' Roun' 1904," 164
Smart Set, The, 30
Smith, Daniel Scott, 103–4
Sochen, June, 135, 146, 226 (n. 61), 229 (n. 182)
Social Gospel, 113, 114, 124
Socialism, 7, 8, 11, 15, 16, 17, 18, 21, 22, 36, 38, 39, 41, 42, 44, 62, 70, 86, 87, 88, 89, 93, 94, 95, 99, 100, 101, 107, 109, 110, 111, 112, 113, 114, 121, 122, 124, 125, 128, 133, 134, 148, 155, 156, 157, 158, 160, 161, 167, 168, 171, 173, 176, 179, 182, 183, 184, 186, 187, 192, 195, 196, 197, 198, 199, 201, 202, 204, 206, 207
Socialist party, 8, 15, 18, 22, 25, 28, 100, 113, 121, 122, 123, 157, 158, 160–62, 167, 168, 197, 198–99; pre-World War I electoral gains, 3
Socialist press, 7, 15, 16, 18, 21, 96, 182, 188
Socialists, 4, 8, 15, 18, 22, 25, 31, 32, 36, 41, 44, 69, 76–77, 85, 92, 99, 100, 106, 107, 113, 121, 122, 124, 134, 144, 145, 149, 156, 157, 158, 161, 167, 177, 179, 181, 183, 184, 185, 187, 190, 193, 196, 197, 201, 202
Socialists, utopian, 4
Sonnenberg, Martha, 184
Spargo, John, 133, 167; on socialism and family life, 100–101; on women and socialism, 128; works: *The Spiritual Significance of Modern Socialism*, 121–22; *Socialism and Motherhood*, 144
Sparks, G. S., 24
Stearns, Harold, 53
Steffens, Lincoln, 20, 64, 168, 170, 172, 178, 182–83, 203, 216 (n. 59); *Upbuilders*, 76; application of Christianity to McNamara Brothers case, 123–25

Sterne, Maurice, 163
Stieglitz Group, 30
Stokes, J. G. Phelps, 15
Stokes, Rose Pastor, 82, 107, 137, 158; *The Woman Who Wouldn't*, 96; on free motherhood, 96
Strindberg, August, 38
Stuttgart International Socialist Congress of 1907, 167
Success, 7, 11
Suffragettes, 140, 168
Sullivan, Mark, 84, 151
Sumner, William Graham: on socialist attack on marriage and family, 99–100
Sunday, Billy, 116, 119, 178, 189
Syndicalism, 69, 113
Syndicalists, 4

Taggard, Genevieve: on failure of *The Masses* to reach proletariat, 183–84
Tanenbaum, Frank, 116
Tannenbaum, Samuel, 84, 88
Tarbell, Ida, 182
Tarkington, Booth, 182
Thackeray, William Makepeace: *Vanity Fair*, 59
Theater, 30, 44, 53, 55, 92, 163. *See also* Drama; Little theater
Thoreau, Henry David, 40, 51
Tolstoi, Leo, 35, 37, 71
Torrence, Ridgely: contribution to black drama, 163; works: *Granny Maumee*, 163; *The Rider of Dreams*, 163; *Simon the Cyrenian*, 163
Traubel, Horace, 40, 118, 126, 138; *Chants Communal*, 122–23, 180
Tresca, Carlo, 137
Trial marriage, 101
Tri-City Workers Magazine, The, 34, 68
Trinity Church, 114, 116
Trotsky, Leon, 28
Twain, Mark, 40, 124

Unionization, 3, 7, 69, 198
United News Company, 21
United States Department of Justice, 29
United States Post Office: suppression of *The Masses*, 24–25, 28–29
Untermeyer, Louis, 18, 28, 31, 44, 87, 168, 184, 206, 207, 211 (n. 55)

Untermeyer, Sam, 20

Vanity Fair, 85
Van Vechten, Carl, 186; mother advocate of women's suffrage, 11; experimentation with drugs, 45, 48; liaison between Harlem blacks and Greenwich Village radicals, 45, 162–63; review of Ridgely Torrence's *Granny Maumee*, 163; works: *Nigger Heaven*, 45, 162; *Peter Whiffle*, 48, 162
Varietism, 96
Villa, Pancho, 180
Villagers, 4, 5, 7, 63, 64, 65, 66, 69, 70, 73, 78, 79, 85, 94, 98, 162, 163, 168, 170, 171, 172, 186, 206, 216 (n. 59); Anna Alice Chapin on morality of, 59–60; Floyd Dell on respectability of, 60; Mary Simkhovitch on relationship between Village intellectuals and older residents, 60
Villard, Oswald Garrison, 162
Vlag, Piet, 17, 180; on radical artist, 186–87
Vorse, Mary Heaton, 60, 61, 63, 135, 137, 147, 197; *The Heart's Country*, 75, 130–31; on feminine opposition to war, 134; on radicalizing effect of Lawrence strike, 203

Waite, John, 136
Walling, Anna Strunsky, 143
Walling, William English, 15, 20, 21, 37–38, 41, 111, 114, 133, 143, 161; on sex education, 77; opposition to religion, 122; on new woman, 135–36
Wanhope, Joshua, 167
War, 25, 66, 69, 116, 117, 134, 135, 140, 194, 205, 206; Max Eastman's Freudian interpretation of war, 90–91. *See also* World War I
Ward and Gow, 21
Wedekind, Frank: *The Awakening of Spring*, 77
Weeks, Rufus, 17
Wells, H. G., 103, 196
Wertheim, Arthur Frank: *The New York Little Renaissance*, 30–31
West Virginia labor war of 1913, 20
White, Bouck: celebration of Christian paganism, 41–42; *The Call of the Carpenter*, 42, 125; on antagonism toward church but esteem for Jesus, 114
White, William Allen, 136, 203

White slavery, 151
Whitlock, Brand, 151
Whitman, Walt, 16, 45, 51, 54, 82, 84, 180; influence on new radicals, 39–41; bisexuality, 40; works: *Democratic Vistas*, 39; "I Hear America Singing," 40; *Leaves of Grass*, 40
Wilcox, Ella Wheeler, 16
Wilde, Oscar, 190
Williams, William: "A Ballad," 119
Williams, William Carlos, 31
Wilson, Woodrow, 25, 29, 91, 207
Wobblies, 30, 180, 189, 198. *See also* Industrial Workers of the World
Woman Rebel, The, 106, 107
Woman's Peace Party, 156–58
Women's International League for Peace and Freedom, 158
Women's movement, 138, 139
Women's suffrage, 7, 25, 81, 104, 107, 114, 139, 140–41, 145, 150, 153, 156–58, 167; advocacy by Max Eastman, 9; advocacy by Eugene Debs, 11; support from families of *The Masses'* radicals, 11–12
Wood, Charles Erskine Scott, 123, 127; *Heavenly Discourse*, 124, 178–79; on criminals, 178–79
Wood, Charles W., 82, 146
Wood, Clement, 119; on bucolic ideal, 71; flirtation with socialism, 197; retreat from radicalism, 203–4; works: "The Return," 71; "The Withholder," 96; "Comradeship," 203
Wood, Eugene: "Foolish Female Fashions," 135
Woodhull, Victoria, 94; on prostitution, 152–53, 155
Woodhull and Claflin's Weekly, 94, 152
Workers' Monthly, The, 207
World War I, 24, 37, 50, 51, 65, 69, 90, 116, 134, 183, 194, 205, 206. *See also* War
Writers, 15, 17, 65, 198; role in 1916 *Masses'* artists' revolt, 22, 24
Wyman, Margaret, 152

Yiddish theater, 172–73
Young, Art, 6, 16, 18, 60, 125, 134, 184, 192, 202, 203, 206, 216 (n. 59); family life, 13; role in Associated Press lawsuit, 20–21; role in *Masses'* Espionage Act trials,

25–26, 28; on bucolic ideal, 73; depiction of blacks in his art, 164–65; on life-style and radicalism, 202; works: "Having Their Fling," 26; "Nearer My God to Thee," 114

Zangwill, Israel: *The Melting Pot,* 173
Zinoviev, Grigory Yevseyevich, 199
Zola, Emile, 38